ORATIONS

GENERAL SHERMAN

Orations—Volume eighteen

ORATIONS

FROM HOMER TO
WILLIAM McKINLEY

EDITED BY

MAYO W. HAZELTINE, A.M.

ILLUSTRATED
IN TWENTY-FIVE VOLUMES
VOL. XVIII

NEW YORK
P. F. COLLIER AND SON
MCMII

CONTENTS

VOLUME EIGHTEEN

CONTENTS

ii

ORATIONS

BELLOWS

WILLIAM HENRY BELLOWS, an eminent American pulpit orator and philanthropist, was born in 1814, and graduated at Harvard in 1832. He studied at the Harvard Divinity School, and, having been called to the Unitarian Church on Fourth Avenue, New York city, he soon became a distinct power in the religious and social life of the metropolis. He was an eloquent speaker and took an active part in all patriotic and philanthropic enterprises, especially in the formation and conduct of the Sanitary Commission at the time of the Civil War. He published a book entitled "On the Treatment of Social Diseases." He died January 30, 1882.

ORATION AT THE FUNERAL OF WILLIAM CULLEN BRYANT

DELIVERED IN ALL SOULS' CHURCH, NEW YORK, JUNE 14, 1878

THE whole country is bending with us, their favored representatives, over the bier that holds the dust of Bryant! Private as the simple service is that consigns the ashes of our illustrious poet and journalist to the grave, there is public mourning in all hearts and homes, making these funeral rites solemn and universal by the sympathy that from every quarter flows toward them, and swells the current of grateful and reverent emotion.

Much as the modest, unworldly spirit of the man we mourn shrunk from the parade of public rites, leaving to his heirs the duty of a rigid simplicity in his funeral, neither his wishes nor theirs could render his death and burial less than an event of general significance and national concern. It is not for his glory that we honor and commemorate him. Public fame, for more than half a century, has made it needless, or impossible, to add one laurel to his crown. So long ago he took the place he has since kept in public admiration, respect, and reverence, that no living tongue could now dislodge or add to the security and mild splendor of his reputation.

For three generations he has been a fixed star in our firmament, and no eulogy could be so complete as that which by accumulation of meaning dwells in the simple mention of his name.

Few lives have been as fortunate and complete as his. Born in 1794, when this young nation was in its teens, he has been contemporary with nearly the whole first century of its life. If no country ever experienced in the same period such a miracle of growth, if none ever profited so much by discoveries and inventions — never before so wonderful as those made in the half century which gave us steam navigation, the railroad, and the telegraph — he saw the birth, he antedates the existence of every one of the characteristic triumphs of modern civilization, and yet he has not died until they became wholly familiar and nearly universal in their fruitful influence!

Born and bred in New England, and on the summits of the Green Mountains, he inherited the severe and simple tastes and habits of that rugged region, and having sprung from a vigorous and intellectual parentage, and in contact with a few persons with whom nature and books took the place of social pleasures and the excitements of town and cities, his native genius made him, from a tender age, the thoughtful and intimate companion of woods and streams, and constituted him nature's own darling child. It was a friendship so unfeigned, so deep, so much in accordance with his temperament and mental constitution that it grew into a determining passion and shaped his whole life, while in the poetry to which it gave birth it laid the foundations and erected the structure of his poetic fame.

What Wordsworth did for English poetry, in bringing back the taste for nature, as the counterpart of humanity — a world to be interpreted not by the outward eyes, but by the soul — Bryant did for America. One who knew them both, as I did, could not fail to observe the strong resemblance in character and feeling, with the marked difference between them on which I will not dwell. Both were reserved, unsmiling, austere, or irresponsive men in aspect; not at home in cities or in crowds, not easy of access, or dependent on companionship; never fully themselves except when alone with nature. They coveted solitude, for it gave them uninterrupted intercourse with that beautiful, companionable, tender, unintrusive world, which is to ordinary souls, dull, common, familiar, but to them was ever new, ever mysterious, ever delightful and instructive.

Few know how small a part intercourse with nature, for itself alone,— not for what it teaches, but for what it is, a revelation of divine beauty and wisdom and goodness,— had even a half century ago for the common mind. Wordsworth in England, Bryant in America, awoke this sleeping capacity, and by their tender and awed sense of the spiritual meaning conveyed in nature's consummate beauties and harmonies, gave almost a new sense to our generation.

Before their day we had praises of the seasons and passages of poetry in which cataracts, sunsets, rainbows and garden flowers were faithfully described; but nature as a whole, as a presence, the very garment of God, was almost unheeded and unknown. When we consider what Bryant's poems — read in the public schools in happy selection — have done to form the taste and feed the sentiment of two generations, we shall begin to estimate the value of his influence.

And when we recall in all his writings not a thought or

feeling that is not pure, uplifting, and reverent, we can partly measure the gratitude we owe to a benefactor whose genius has consecrated the woods, and fields, and brooks and wayside flowers, in a way intelligible to plainer minds, and yet above the criticism of the most fastidious and cultivated.

But if fortunate in passing his early life in the country and forming his taste and his style in communion with nature, and with a few good books and a few earnest and sincere people, he was equally fortunate in being driven by a love of independence into the study of the law and a ten years' practice in a considerable town in western Massachusetts, and then drawn to this city where he drifted into the only form of public life wholly suited to his capacities — the editorial profession.

It was no accident that made Bryant a politician and an editor. Sympathy with individual men and women was not his strong point; but sympathy with our common humanity was in him a religious passion. He had a constitutional love of freedom and an intense sentiment of justice, and they constituted together his political creed and policy. He believed in freedom; and this made him a friend of the oppressed, an enemy of slavery, a foe to special and class legislation, an advocate of free trade, a natural Democrat, though born and reared in a federal community that looked with suspicion upon extensions of the suffrage and upon the growth of local and State rights.

But his love of freedom was too genuine to allow him to condone the faults even of his own party, when freedom's friends were found on the other side. He could bear, he did bear the odium of his unpopular conviction, when what was called the best society in New York was of another opinion and belonged to another party — and he could bear with equal fortitude the ignominy of lacking party fidelity, when his patriotic spirit felt that his old political friends were less faithful than they should be to freedom and union.

The editorial profession enabled his shy and somewhat unsocial nature to work at arm's length for the good of humanity and the country; and I can conceive of no other calling in life that would have economized his temperament and faculties so fully in the public service. His literary skill, his industry, his humane philosophy, his sentiments of justice, his patriotism, his love of freedom, here found full scope without straining and tasking his personal sympathies, which lacked the readiness, the tact, and the geniality that in some men make direct contact with their fellow creatures an increase of power and of influence.

What an editor he made you all know. None could long doubt the honesty, the conscientiousness, the elevation and purity of his convictions or his utterances. Who believes he ever swerved a line, for the sake of popularity or pelf, from what he felt to be right and true? That he escaped all prostitution of his pen, or his conscience, in his exposed and tempted calling, we all admiringly confess. And what moderation, candor, and courage he carried into his editorial work. Purity of thought, elegance and simplicity of style, exquisite taste and high morality characterized all he wrote. He rebuked the headlong spirit of party, sensational extravagances of expression, even the use of new-fangled phrases and un-English words. He could see and acknowledge the merits of those from whom he widely differed, while unbecoming personalities found no harbor in his columns. Young men and women never found anything to corrupt their taste or their morals in his paper, and families could safely lay the

"Evening Post" upon the table where their children and their guests might take it up.

Uncompromising in what his convictions commanded, and never evading the frankest expression of his real opinion, however unpopular, he was felt to be above mere partisanship, and so had a decided influence with men of all political preferences. His prose was in its way as good as his poetry, and has aided greatly to correct the taste for swollen, gaudy and pretentious writing in the public press. He was not alone in this respect, for none can fail to recall the services in this direction of Charles King and Horace Greeley, not to name less conspicuous instances. But Bryant's poetic fame gave peculiar authority to his editorial example, and made his style specially helpful and instructive.

That he should have succeeded in keeping the poetic temperament and the tastes and pursuits of a poet fully alive under the active and incessant pressure of his journalistic labors,— making his bread and his immediate influence as a citizen and a leader of public sentiment by editorial work while he "built the lofty rhyme" for the gratification of his genius and for the sake of beauty and art, without one glance at immediate suffrages or rewards,— if not a solitary, is at least a perfect example of the union in one man of the power to work with nearly equal success in two planes where what he did in one did not contradict or conflict with what he did in the other, while they were not mingled or confounded. Nobody detects the editor, the politician, the man of business, in Bryant's poetry, and few feel the poet in his editorial writings; but the man of conscience, of humanity, of justice and truth, of purity and honor, appears equally in both.

This is somewhat the more remarkable, because affluence,

versatility, and humor are not characteristic of his genius. It is staid, earnest, profoundly truthful and pure, lofty and perfectly genuine; but not mercurial, vivacious, protean and brilliant. Like the Jordan that leaps into being full, strong, crystal-pure, but swells little in its deep bed all its course to its sea, admitting few tributaries and putting out no branches, Bryant's genius sprang complete into public notice when he was still in his teens; it retained its character for sixty years almost unchanged, and its latest products are marked with the essential qualities that gave him his first success. Never, perhaps, was there an instance of such precocity in point of wisdom and maturity as that which marked "Thanatopsis," written at eighteen, or of such persistency in judgment, force, and melody as that exhibited in his last public ode, written at 83, on occasion of Washington's last birthday. Between these two bounds lies one even path, high, finished, faultless, in which comes a succession of poems always meditative, always steeped in love and knowledge of nature, always pure and melodious, always stamped with his sign-manual, a flawless taste and gem-like purity — but never much aside from the line and direction that marked the first outburst and last flow of his genius.

Happy the man that knows his own powers — their limits and their aptitudes — and who confines himself rigidly within the banks of his own peculiar inspiration. Bryant was too genuine, too real a lover of nature, too legitimate a child of the muse, ever to strain his own gift. He never made verses, but allowed his verse to flow, inspired by keen observation and hearty enjoyment of nature, watching only that it flowed smoothly and without turbulence or turbidity, which his consummate art enabled him perfectly to accomplish.

Never, perhaps, was a natural gift more successfully

trained and cultured, without losing its original raciness and simplicity. Nothing less than the widest and deepest study of poetry, in all literatures, young and old, in all languages and schools, could have enabled him to keep his verse in such perfect finish for sixty successive years. He knew all the wiles of the poet, some of which he disdained to practise — but of no man in his time was it less safe to assume ignorance or neglect of anything that belonged to the poet's art. His knowledge of poetry was prodigious, his memory of it precise and inexhaustible. He had considered all the masters, and knew their quality and characteristics.

But marked as his own style is, it is marked only with its native hues. There is no trick in his adroitness, no artifice in his art; nothing that tires, except it be the uniformity of its excellence. Considering how long his genius has been known and acknowledged, and how thoroughly he represents the old school of Dryden in his purity and fastidiousness of language, it is, perhaps, not to be wondered at that his popularity, as a citizen and a man, has even somewhat eclipsed his immediate popularity as a poet. I think him fortunate in not having the popularity of novelty, of fashion, of sing-song verse, of morbid sentiment, of mere ingenious thinking, or some temporary adaptation to passing moods of popular feeling, whether in universities or in social circles.

He curiously escaped, if indeed his truthful genuineness of nature did not give him an original defence against it, from the introversive, self-considering, and individualistic temper which has characterized much of the poetry of the highest academic culture in our time. Either he was born too early, or he emigrated from New England too early, to fall under the influence of this morbid subjectiveness; or his active and practical pursuits kept him in the current of real life, and near to the universal feeling of men. At any rate,— free, rational, as his genius ever was,— there is not a suspicion of the sceptical or denying element in his works. He is not sick or morbid, or melancholy, or discouraged.

Sentiment enough he has, but no sentimentality; awe of the Infinite, but no agnosticism; a recognition of all human sorrows and sins, but no querulousness, much less any despair. He loved and honored human nature; he feared and reverenced his Maker; he accepted Christianity in its historic character; he believed in American institutions; he believed in the Church and its permanency, in its ordinances and its ministry; and he was no backward-looking praiser of the times that had been and a mere accuser and defamer of the times that are.

This made his poetry, as it made his prose and his whole influence, wholesome, hopeful, nutritious; young, without being inexperienced; ripe, without tending to decay. The very absence of those false colors which give immediate attractiveness to the clothing of some contemporary poetry, gives his undyed and natural robes a fadeless charm which future generations will not forget to honor. Every one must notice that great immediate popularity is not a good augury for enduring fame; and further, that poetry, like all the products of the fine arts, must have not only positive quality, power and harmony, but must add to these freedom from defects.

It is strange what an embalming power lies in purity of style to preserve thoughts that would perish, even though greater and more original if wrapped in a less perfect vesture. What element of decay is there in Bryant's verse? How universal his themes; how intelligible and level to the common heart; how little ingenious, vague or technical; how free from what is provincial, temporary, capricious; how unflawed with doubtful figures or strained comparisons or new and strange words; how unmarred by a forced order or weary mannerisms!

He is a rigid Puritan, alike in his morals and his vocabulary; there is scarcely a false foot, a doubtful rhyme, a luckless epithet, a dubious sentiment anywhere to be found in his works. And, perhaps nature withheld from him what is called an ear for music only to emphasize his ear for rhythm and save him from the danger of a clogging sweetness and a fatiguing sing-song.

It is the glory of this man that his character outshone even his great talent and his large fame. Distinguished equally for his native gifts and consummate culture, his poetic inspiration and his exquisite art, he is honored and loved to-day, even more for his stainless purity of life, his unswerving rectitude of will, his devotion to the higher interests of humanity, his unfeigned patriotism and his broad humanity. It is remarkable that with none of the arts of popularity a man so little dependent on others' appreciation, so self-subsistent and so retiring, who never sought or accepted office, who had little taste for co-operation, and no bustling zeal in ordinary philanthropy, should have drawn to himself the confidence, the honor and reverence of a great metropolis, and become, perhaps, it is not too much to say, our first citizen.

It was, in spite of a constitutional reserve, a natural distaste for crowds and public occasions, and a somewhat chilled bearing toward his kind, that he achieved, by the force of his great merit and solid worth, this triumph over the heart of his generation. The purity of the snow that enveloped him was more observed than its coldness, and his fellow citizens believed that a fire of zeal for truth, justice, and human rights burned steadily at the heart of this lofty personality, though it never flamed or smoked.

And they were right! Beyond all thirst for fame or poetic honor lay in Bryant the ambition of virtue. Reputation he did not despise, but virtue he revered and sought with all his heart. He had an intense self-reverence, that made his own good opinion of his own motives and actions absolutely essential. And though little tempted by covetousness, envy, worldliness or love of power, he had his own conscious difficulties to contend with, a temper not without turbulence, a susceptibility to injuries, a contempt for the moral weaknesses of others.

But he labored incessantly at self-knowledge and self-control, and attained equanimity and gentleness to a marked degree. Let none suppose that the persistent force of his will, his incessant industry, his perfect consistency and coherency of life and character, were not backed by strong passions. With a less consecrated purpose, a less reverent love of truth and goodness, he might easily have become acrid, vindictive, or selfishly ambitious. But he kept his body under, and, a far more difficult task for him, his spirit in subjection.

God had given him a wonderful balance of faculties in a marvellously harmonious frame. His spirit wore a light and lithe vesture of clay — that never burdened him. His senses were perfect at fourscore. His eyes needed no glasses; his hearing was exquisitely fine. His alertness was the wonder of his contemporaries. He outwalked men of middle age. His tastes were so simple as to be almost ascetic. Milk and cereals and fruits were his chosen diet. He had no vices, and no approach to them, and he avoided any and everything that could ever threaten him with the tyranny of the senses or of habit.

Regular in all his habits, he retained his youth almost to the last. His power of work never abated, and the herculean translation of Homer, which was the amusement of the last lustre of his long and busy life, showed not only no senility or decline in artistic skill, but no decrease of intellectual or physical endurance.

Perhaps the last ten years of his life have made him nearer and dearer to his fellow citizens than any previous decade; for he had become at last not only resigned to public honors, but had even acquired a late and tardy taste for social and public gatherings. Who so often called to preside in your public meetings or to speak at your literary or social festivals? who has pronounced as many hearty welcomes to honored strangers, unveiled as many statues, graced as many occasions of public sympathy? who so ready to appear at the call of your public charities, or more affectionately welcomed and honored on your platforms? All this, coming late in life, was a grateful, I might almost say a fond surprise.

He had wrapped himself in his cloak to contend with the winter wind of his earlier fortunes, and the harder it blew (and it was very rough in his middle life) the closer he drew it about him. But the sun of prosperity and honor and confidence that warmed and brightened the two closing decades of his life fairly melted away his proud reserve toward the public, and he lay himself open to the warm and fragrant breeze of universal favor. He was careful, however, to say that he did not hold himself at the public's high estimate.

In a long conversation I had with him at Roslyn, two years ago, he showed such a surprising self-knowledge and such a just appreciation of popular suffrages, that it was impossible to doubt his genuine humility, or jealous determination not to be deceived by any contagious sentiment of personal reverence or honor springing up in a generation that was largely ignorant of his writings. Yet he fully and greatly enjoyed these tributes — and more and more, the longer he lived.

Of Mr. Bryant's life-long interest in the fine arts; his large acquaintance with our older artists and close friendship with some of them; of his place in the Century Club, of which he was perhaps the chief founder, and of which he died the honored president, I could speak with full knowledge; but artists and centurions both are sure to speak better for themselves in due time, as the city and the nation surely will.

I must reserve the few moments still left me to bear the testimony which no one has a better right to offer to Mr. Bryant's strictly religious character. A devoted lover of religious liberty, he was an equal lover of religion itself; not in any precise dogmatic form, but in its righteousness, reverence, and charity. What his theology was you may safely infer from his regular and long attendance in this place of Christian worship.

Still he was not a dogmatist, but preferred practical piety and working virtue to all modes of faith. What was obvious in him for twenty years past was an increasing respect and devotion to religious institutions and a more decided Christian quality in his faith. I think he had never been a communicant in any church until he joined ours, fifteen years ago. From that time, nobody so regular in his attendance on public worship, in wet and dry, cold and heat, morning and evening, until the very last month of his life. The increasing sweetness and beneficence of his character, meanwhile, must have struck his familiar friends. His last years were his devoutest and most humane years. He became beneficent as he grew able to be so, and his hand was open to all just need, and to many unreasonable claimants.

The first half or even two thirds of his life had been a hard struggle with fortune. And he had acquired saving habits, thanks chiefly to the prudence of his honored and ever-lamented wife. But the moment he became successful and acquired the means of beneficence, he practised it bountifully, indeed, perhaps often credulously. For he was simple-hearted and unsuspecting, easily misled by women's tears and entreaties, and not always with the fortitude to say No — when only his money was at stake. Indeed he had few defensive weapons either against intrusion or supplication, and could with difficulty withstand the approaches of those that fawned upon him, or those that asked his countenance for selfish purposes. Perhaps he understood their weaknesses, but he had not the heart to medicine them with brave refusal.

He endowed a public library in Cummington, his birthplace, at a cost of many thousands. He built and gave a public hall to the village of Roslyn, L. I., the chosen and beloved summer home of his declining years. When, at his request, I went to dedicate it to public use, and at a proper moment asked, "What shall we call this building?" The audience shouted "Bryant Hall." "No," said the modest benefactor, "let it be known and called simply 'The Hall,'" and The Hall it was baptized.

I shall have spoken in vain if I have not left upon your hearts the image of an upright, sincere, humane and simple yet venerable manhood — a life full of outward honors and inward worth. When I consider that I have been speaking of one whose fame fills the world, I feel how vain is public report compared with the honor of God and the gratitude and love of humanity! It is the private character of this unaffected, Christian man that it most concerns us to consider and to imitate. He was great as the world counts greatness, he was greater as God counts it.

He is gone! and the city and the country is immeasurably poorer that his venerable and exalted presence no more adorns and crowns our assemblies. But heaven is richer! The Church of Christ adds one unaffected, unsanctimonious saint to its calendar. The patriarch of American literature is dead. The faithful Christian lives evermore:

> " Thou'rt gone, the abyss of heaven
> Hath swallowed up thy form; yet on my very heart
> Deeply hath sunk the lesson thou hast given
> And shall not soon depart."
> —Bryant's lines " To a Waterfowl."

We are about to bear his remains to their quiet and green resting-place, by the side of his beloved wife — the good angel of his life — in Roslyn, L. I. Let me read in conclusion the warrant for this step in his own poem called " June," which I am persuaded you will feel to be the only fit conclusion of these memorial words:

> " I gazed upon the glorious sky,
>   And the green mountains round,
> And thought that when I came to lie
>   At rest within the ground,
> 'Twere pleasant that in flowery June,
> When brooks send up a cheerful tune,
>   And groves a cheerful sound,
> The sexton's hand, my grave to make,
> The rich, green mountain-turf should break.

> " A cell within the frozen mold,
>   A coffin borne through sleet,
> And icy clods above it rolled,
>   While fierce the tempests beat—
> Away!—I will not think of these,
> Blue be the sky and soft the breeze,
>   Earth green beneath the feet,
> And be the damp mold gently pressed
> Into my narrow place of rest.

" There, through the long, long summer hours,
    The golden light should lie,
And thick young herbs and groups of flowers,
    Stand in their beauty by,
The oriole should build and tell
His love-tale close beside my cell;
    The idle butterfly
Should rest him there, and there be heard
The housewife bee and humming-bird.

" And what if cheerful shouts at noon
    Come from the village sent,
Or song of maids beneath the moon
    With fairy laughter blent?
And what if, in the evening light,
Betrothed lovers walk in sight
    Of my low monument?
I would the lovely scene around
Might know no sadder sight nor sound.

" I know that I no more should see
    The season's glorious show,
Nor would its brightness shine for me,
    Nor its wild music flow;
But if, around my place of sleep,
The friends I love should come to weep,
    They might not haste to go.
Soft airs, and song, and light and bloom
Should keep them lingering by my tomb.

" These to their softened hearts should bear
    The thought of what has been,
And speak of one who cannot share
    The gladness of the scene;
Whose part, in all the pomp that fills
The circuit of the summer hills,
    Is that his grave is green;
And deeply would their hearts rejoice
To hear again his living voice."

COLENSO

JOHN WILLIAM COLENSO, a distinguished English theologian, was born at St. Austell, Cornwall, January 24, 1814, and educated at St. John's College, Cambridge University. After taking orders in the Established Church he was tutor at Cambridge for several years prior to becoming rector of Forncett Saint Mary, Norfolk, in 1846. He was by this time well known as a mathematician, and had published treatises on algebra and arithmetic which have been adopted as college text-books. In 1853 he was consecrated bishop of Natal in South Africa. In 1861 he published a "Commentary on St. Paul's Epistle to the Romans," which speedily aroused the heresy-hunters of the day, and when, the next year, he put forth the first volume of "The Pentateuch and Book of Joshua Critically Examined," an almost universal storm of theological abuse was at once directed against him. The subsequent controversy arising from this event proved most disastrous to the welfare of the South African Church and shook the Church of England to its centre. Colenso was thereupon deposed by the Bishop of Cape Town, but the English Privy Council overruled his action and decided that Bishop Colenso should receive the income of his see. The Bishop was inhibited from preaching in several English dioceses and continued for many years to be the target of theological hostility. He kept on, however, with his critical labors, completing the work on the Pentateuch in 1879. He was greatly beloved by the Zulus, and labored for years to secure just treatment for them. He died at Durban, Natal, June 20, 1883, and since his death much of the bitter feeling against his biblical studies has passed away. Beside a series of twelve mathematical works and a long list of books in the Zulu tongue for the instruction of the natives, Bishop Colenso was the author of "Village Sermons" (1854); "Ten Weeks in Natal" (1855); "Lectures on the Pentateuch and Moabite Stone;" "The Worship of Baalim in Israel," from the Dutch of R. Dozy; "First Lessons in Science;" and two series of "Natal Sermons."

THE EXAMPLE OF OUR LORD

[From "Natal Sermons."]

WE often say that our Lord's example is to be the guide to us in all our duties of life. And so, indeed, it should be,—yet not in the way that many seem to suppose, by his having actually shared in the performance of those duties and resisted the temptations more especially connected with them. . . .

(7451)

Of his childhood and boyhood we know scarcely anything: of his youth we know nothing. We have very little to show us how he acted as a son or a brother; we have no example in his life of a husband or a parent; no exact pattern for students or men of business, for artisans, domestic servants, village laborers, for professional men, soldiers, or statesmen. The duties of later middle life and of old age were not discharged by him; the lot of the noble, wealthy, and powerful was not experienced by him, nor that of the pauper in the poorhouse, of the prisoner immured for years in the dungeon of the oppressor, of the patient racked with pain, or worn with lingering disease in the wards of the hospital. The example which he has actually given us in the Bible is chiefly that of an active ministry of almost three years in the prime of life, under circumstances which can never happen again in the history of the world. . . .

How is it, then, that we are able at once to appeal to Christ's example as the perfect model of what human beings ought to be, or ought to do, under all circumstances? It is because we appeal to the spirit of his life, to the principle which ruled it; to that conformity to the perfect will of God, that desire to please his heavenly Father, that surrender of his own will to God's will, which he manifested on all occasions. And taught as we are ourselves by the divine Word, enlightened by the Light which is the life of men, we are able in our own minds to fill up that which is wanting for our actual guidance amid the duties of life,— to say to ourselves, in different situations, "In this way Christ would act or would have acted."

We are able to set before us an ideal Christ, a perfect image of the divine Man. That image of perfect beauty and holiness — of the perfect Man — which we thus by divine grace behold, each in our own mind, is not set before us at full length in the gospels, nor could it possibly be; no record of his life could have supplied minutely all the details needed for this purpose — for setting a mere copy of which we are closely to follow in all our different relations of life, even if our Lord had actually entered into human relationship more fully than he has done. It is, I repeat, to the spirit of his life — to the principle which ruled it — that we must be appealing continually, day by day and hour by hour, if we would " put on Christ," put on the Christian spirit. . . .

The example, then, of Christ is not less valuable to us because the details of his life are few and leave many and most important points of our lives without models of conduct. Our following of any model, to be true, to be of any worth, must not be an imitation of certain acts, of certain demeanor, appropriate to this or that situation or relation, in which as human beings we may be placed. . . .

Christ is our great Example, because he came not to do his own will, but the will of the Father who sent him — because he sought not his own glory, but in all that concerned him was simply obedient, leaving his cause in God's hands; because he bore witness for the truth on all occasions, regardless of consequences.

TILDEN

SAMUEL JONES TILDEN, a noted American statesman, was born in Lebanon, New York, February 9, 1814, and was educated at Yale University and the University of the City of New York. During his college course he wrote an able series of papers in defence of Van Buren's United States Bank policy, and in 1840 delivered a speech on currency and the history of the United States Bank which was greatly admired. He was at this time studying law, and in 1841 was admitted to the bar and began practice in New York city, where ere long he attained a high place in the profession and was employed in the management of many noted cases. From the first he had taken a keen interest in politics and in 1848 joined the Free-Soil wing of the Democratic party. During the Civil War period he contended that the struggle with the Confederacy could be conducted without resort to extra-constitutional methods, and after 1868 he was the acknowledged leader of the New York Democracy. In the proceedings against the Tweed " ring " in New York, a few years later, Tilden took an active part. In 1874 he was elected governor of New York, and in 1876 was the Democratic candidate for the presidency, receiving a popular majority of 250,000. The votes, however, of Louisiana, South Carolina, and Florida were claimed by both parties, and after much controversy the decision was left to an electoral commission of fifteen members, which by a vote of eight to seven accepted the returns of the three States and on March 2, 1877, reported a single vote in favor of the Republican candidate, Mr. Hayes. This decision was acquiesced in by the country, though not without more or less remonstrance. After this period Tilden declined all further nominations and resumed his professional practice, dying at his country seat of Greystone, near Yonkers, New York, August 4, 1886. His fortune of nearly $5,000,000 was bequeathed to found a free library for New York city, but the will was broken by his heirs, who gave a much smaller sum. Tilden's " Writings and Speeches " were issued in 1885.

ADDRESS ON ADMINISTRATIVE REFORM

DELIVERED AT SYRACUSE ON HIS NOMINATION FOR GOVERNOR,
SEPTEMBER 17, 1874

FELLOW CITIZENS,— I thank you for the honor you do me. I know it is the cause, more than its representative, that in such a storm calls out this manifestation of interest and enthusiasm. And well it may!

A peaceful revolution in all government within the United

(7454)

States is going on to a sure consummation. Ideas of change pervade the political atmosphere. They spring up from the convictions of the people. The supporters of the administration have lost confidence in it and themselves. The Opposition become more intense in their convictions and in their action. Multitudes pass over from support to opposition, or sink into silent discontent.

Are we asked the causes? The answer is found in the condition of our country. The fruits of a false and delusive system of government finances are everywhere around us. All business is in a dry-rot. In every industry it is hard to make the two ends meet. Incomes are shrinking away, and many men hitherto affluent are becoming anxious about their means of livelihood. Workingmen are out of employment. The poor cannot look out upon the light or air of heaven but they see the wolf at the door.

Inflation no longer inflates. Even while paper money is swelling out a new emission, values sink. Bankers' balances in the monetary centres are increased, and call loans are cheaper; but those who need more capital can neither buy nor borrow any of the forty-four millions of new greenbacks. The truth is that our body politic has been over-drugged with stimulants. New stimulants no longer lift up the languid parts to a healthy activity, they merely carry more blood to the congested centres.

Only one thing remains in its integrity,— that is our taxes. Amid general decay, taxation puts out new sprouts and grows luxuriantly. If I may borrow a figure from the greatest of our American poets,—

> " It seats itself upon the sepulchre,
> And of the triumphs of its ghastly foe
> Makes its own nourishment."

national taxes, State taxes, county taxes, town taxes, municipal taxes! The collector is as inevitable as the grim messenger of death. Incomes, profits, wages, all these fall; but taxes rise.

Six years ago I had occasion to say that while values were ascending, and for some time after, it might be easy to pay these taxes out of the froth of our apparent wealth; but that when the reaction of an unsound system of government finance should set in, the enormous taxation which that system had created would not only consume our incomes and profits, but trench upon our capital. What was then prediction is now experience. Retrenchment in public expenditure; reform in public administration; simplification and reduction of tariffs and taxes; accountability of public officers, enforced by better civil and criminal remedies,— the people must have these measures of present relief, measures of security for the future.

The federal government is drifting into greater dangers and greater evils. It is rushing onward in a career of centralism, absorbing all governmental powers and assuming to manage all the affairs of human society. It undertakes to direct the business of individuals by tariffs not intended for legitimate taxation, by granting special privileges, and by fostering monopolies at the expense of the people. It has acquired control of all banks. It has threatened to seize on all the telegraphs. It is claiming jurisdiction of all railroad corporations chartered by the States, and amenable to the just authority of the States. It is going on to usurp control of all our schools and colleges. Stretching its dragnet over the whole country, and forcing editors and publishers away from their distant homes into the courts of the District of Columbia, it is subjecting the free press of the whole United States, for criticism of the administration, to trial by creatures of the administration, acting under the eye of the administration. It has dared to enforce this tyranny against a freeman of the metropolis of our State.

These tendencies must be stopped, or before we know it the whole character of our government will be changed; the simple and free institutions of our fathers will not only have become the worst government that has ever ruled over a civilized people, but it will also be the most ignorant. A distinguished Republican statesman — I mean Senator Conkling — lately told me that more than five thousand bills were before Congress at its last session. In a little time, as we are now going on, there will be twenty thousand. Nobody can know what is in them.

We have a country eighteen times as large as France, with a population of forty-three millions, doubling every thirty years, and full of activities and interests. A centralized government, meddling with everything and attempting to manage everything, could not know the wants or wishes of the people of the localities; it would be felt only in its blunders and its wrongs. It would be the most irresponsible, and therefore not only the most oppressive, but also the most corrupt, with which any people have been cursed.

To-day the advances which we have made toward this system are maturing their fatal fruits. The federal administration is tainted with abuses, with jobbery, and with corruption. In the dominion which it maintains over the reconstructed southern States, organized pillage, on a scale tenfold greater than that of the Tweed ring, is the scandal and shame of the country.

Civil liberty is endangered. It is now certain that President Grant nourishes the bad ambition of a third term. If the sacred tradition established by Washington, Jefferson,

Madison, and Jackson can be broken, the President may be re-elected indefinitely; and wielding from the centre the immense patronage which will grow out of such vast usurpation of authorities by the federal government, he will grasp the means of corrupt influence by which to carry the elections. There will be no organized thing in the country of sufficient power to compete with him or to resist him. The forms of free government may remain, but the spirit and substance will be changed; an elective personal despotism will have been established; Roman history, in the person of Augustus Cæsar, will be repeated.

Thoughtful men are turning their minds to the means of escape from these overshadowing evils. The Republican party cannot save the country. Ideas of governmental meddling and centralism dominate it; class interests hold it firmly to evil courses. Throngs of office-holders, contractors, and jobbers, who have grown up in fourteen years of administration, in four years of war, and during an era of paper money, are too strong in the machinery of the party for the honest and well-intending masses of the Republicans. The Republican party could contribute largely to maintain the Union during the Civil War; it cannot reconstruct civil liberty and free institutions after the peace.

A change of men is necessary to secure a change of measures. The Opposition is being matured and educated to take the administration. The Democracy, with the traditions of its best days, will form the nucleus of the opposition. It embraces vastly the larger body of men of sound ideas and sound practices in political life. It must remove every taint which has touched it in evil times. It must become a compact and homogeneous mass. It must gather to its alliance all who think the same things concerning the interests of our

Republic. It is becoming an adequate and effective instrument to reform administration and to save the country. It reformed itself in order that it might reform the country.

And now in your name and in the name of five hundred thousand voters we represent, we declare that in this great work we will tread no step backward. Come weal or come woe, we will not lower our flag. We will go forward until a political revolution shall be worked out, and the principles of Jefferson and Jackson shall rule in the administration of the federal government.

Let us never despair of our country. Actual evils can be mitigated; bad tendencies can be turned aside; the burdens of government can be diminished; productive industry will be renewed; and frugality will repair the waste of our resources. Then shall the golden days of the Republic once more return, and the people become prosperous and happy.

CHAPIN

EDWIN HUBBELL CHAPIN, a noted American preacher and lecturer, was born at Union Village, New York, December 29, 1814. He was educated at a seminary in Bennington, Vermont, and after studying law for a short time relinquished it for theology and was ordained in the Universalist ministry in 1837. For the next two years he was pastor of a church in Richmond, Virginia, and from 1840 to 1846 of a church in Charlestown, Massachusetts. After two years more as pastor of a Boston church he was called to the Fourth Universalist Church in New York city. In 1866 his congregation built the Church of the Divine Paternity in Fifth Avenue, of which he was pastor at the time of his death in New York, December 26, 1880. He was one of the most popular of the New York preachers of his time and was an equal favorite on the lecture platform. In 1850 he delivered a fine address before the Peace Convention at Frankfort-on-the-Main, to which he had been sent as a delegate. Among the opponents of slavery he was long conspicuous, and during the Civil War he made many patriotic addresses which were very effective in forming and directing public sentiment. For many years Chapin was the foremost man in his denomination, but his sympathies were not confined to those within the Universalist fold. His writings include "Duties of Young Men" (1840); "Hours of Communion" (1844); "Duties of Young Women" (1849); "Discourses on the Lord's Prayer" (1850); "Moral Aspects of City Life" (1853); "Characters in the Gospels" (1852); "Discourses on the Beatitudes" (1853); "True Manliness" (1854); "Humanity in the City" (1854); "Select Sermons Preached in the Broadway Church" (1859); "The Crown of Thorns, a Token for the Suffering," his best-known book (1860); "Living Words" (1861); "Lessons of Faith" (1871); "Discourses on the Book of Proverbs" (1881); "Church of the Living God, and Other Sermons" (1881), and "God's Requirements" (1881).

NICODEMUS: THE SEEKER AFTER RELIGION

"There was a man of the Pharisees, named Nicodemus, a ruler of the Jews: The same came to Jesus by night."—John iii, 1, 2.

ALTHOUGH we have but few glimpes of Nicodemus in the Gospels, he is a personage of peculiar interest. A Pharisee, and a member of the great Jewish senate, or Sanhedrin, he shows us that the influence of Christ was not limited to the poor and the obscure; but that, while his words and works awoke enmity and fear among the higher classes, they struck in the breasts of some of these a holier chord.

It may not be certain that Nicodemus ever openly confessed Christ; yet, in this chapter, he appears in the attitude of a disciple, and we find him defending Jesus before the Sanhedrin, and assisting at his burial.   Still, unless the last-mentioned act be considered as such, we do not discover in his conduct that public and decisive acknowledgment which the Saviour required; we do not behold the frank avowal of Peter, or the intrepidity of Paul.   There is an air of caution and of timidity about him.   He carefully feels the ground of innovation, before he lets go the establishment; and, indeed, he appears to have taken no step by which he forfeited his caste or his office.

It is difficult, too, to discover the precise purpose of this visit to Jesus.   Perhaps he sought the interview from mixed motives.   A religious earnestness kindled by the teachings and the character of Christ may have blended with speculative curiosity, and even with the throbbings of political ambition.   His coming by night, too, may have indicated timidity, or he may have chosen that season as the best time for quiet and uninterrupted discourse.   But, whatever may have been his motives, the position in which we find him shows, I repeat, that the power of Christ's ministry was felt, not only by the excitable multitude, but by the more thoughtful and devout of the Jewish people.

Nicodemus, however, presents a peculiar interest, not only because he exhibits the influence of Jesus upon the higher orders of his nation, but because he appears as a seeker after religion, and as one personally interested in its vital truths.   His interview with the Saviour gives occasion for one of the most important passages in the New Testament.

The conversation of Christ, in this instance, is not uttered in general principles and accommodated to the multitude, but it is directed to an intelligent and inquiring spirit, in the calm privacy of the night-time, laying bare its very depths, and craving the application of religion to its own peculiar wants.

To be sure, Nicodemus did not profess this want, but commenced the conversation with the language of respect, and with suggestion of more general inquiry. But he who "knew what was in man," had already penetrated the folds of the Ruler's breast, and saw the real need that had sent him; so, putting by all compliments, and all secondary issues, he struck at once the conscious chord that throbbed there, and exclaimed:

"Verily, verily, I say unto thee, except a man be born again, he cannot see the Kingdom of God!" These words must have filled Nicodemus with surprise, both from their sudden heart-searchingness, and as addressing to him a term which was usually applied to men of very different condition. For the phrase, "new birth," was a customary one to express the change through which the Gentile passed in becoming a Jew.

But it was, indeed, a strange doctrine that he, a son of Abraham, a Pharisee, a Ruler, must be born again before he could be fit for the Messiah's kingdom. Therefore, really or affectedly, he misunderstood the Saviour's words, and gave to a phrase, plain enough when applied to a heathen, the most gross and literal interpretation.

But Christ reiterated the solemn truth, assuring him that an inward change, and an outward profession, a regeneration of the affections and the will, and a renunciation of pride and fear, by the symbol of baptism — a new birth of water

B and of the Spirit — was essential to true discipleship. And thus, stripping away all the reliances of formal righteousness, and all the supports of birth and position, in reply to the earnest question of Nicodemus: "How can these things be?" the great Teacher proceeded to utter some of the sublimest doctrines of the Gospel.

As I have already said, whether Nicodemus became an avowed follower of Jesus, or not, is uncertain; but we know that the truths which he then heard are of everlasting importance, have a personal application to every man, and appeal to wants in our own souls, which are as real and as deep as those of the Ruler of old.

But while thus Nicodemus exhibits a need of our common humanity, he especially represents a class who may be called "Seekers after Religion," either as being unsettled and inquiring in their spirits, or as resting upon something which is not religion, but only, perhaps, a tendency toward it — they are seekers after it, as not having actually found it. In other words, for this class, religion has its meaning and its pressure; they think about it, and they feel its claims, yet they do not thoroughly and mentally know it; or, like Nicodemus, they rest upon some substitute. Some of these positions I propose now to illustrate.

I observe, then, in the first place, that some seek religion in rituals and sacraments. The tendency of the human mind, as to matters of faith and devotion, has always been to complicate rather than to simplify, and to associate these with set forms and symbols. In all ages, men have shrunk from naked communion with God, from the solitude of an intense spirituality, and have conducted transactions with the Invisible, through the mediation of ceremony.

But that which, at first, was an expression of the individual soul, has grown into a fixed and consecrated rite. Gestures and modes of worship, suggested by the occasion, have been repeated in usage, and grown venerable with age, until they have become identified with religion itself. They have been exalted into mystic vehicles of grace, have been considered as possessing virtue in themselves, and as constituting an awful paraphernalia, through which, alone, God will deign to communicate with man, and through which man may even propitiate and move God. Christianity has not escaped this tendency; and, even now, there are many with whom the sacraments are something more than expressive signs and holy suggestions, and with whom the position of an altar, the shape of a vestment, and the form of a church are among the essentials of religion.

With such, baptism speaks, not merely to the eye of an inward washing, but it is of itself a regenerative process. In their view the communion bread is not simply a representation of the broken body of the Redeemer; but is itself so sacred, so identical with that body, that they must receive it by a special posture, and upon a particular part of the hand. As a matter of course, to such, religion must appear eminently conservative and retrospective; the genius of the established and the past, rather than of the reformatory and the future. Cherishing the minutest fibres of these ancient rites, they chiefly venerate the men who authenticate them, and the soil out of which they grow. With them, the fluent spirit of religion became organized and fixed into a form, with fast-days and feast-days, with mitre and cassock, and a lineal priesthood, ages ago.

It cannot be said that this method is entirely unfounded. It has its justification in human nature, if not elsewhere. There are those who can find peace only in the arms of an hereditary faith: who can feel the inspiration of worship, only among forms that have kindled worship in others for a thousand years: with whose earliest thoughts and dearest memories is entwined a ritual and an established church, so that personal affection and household sanctity, as well as religious feeling, demand that every great act of life—of joy or sorrow—should be consecrated by the familiar sacrament.

For that church, too, their fathers have died in darker times, and beneath its chancels sainted mothers molder into dust. All, too, that can exalt the ideal, or wake the pulses of eloquent emotion, is connected with such a church. To them it opens a traditional perspective, the grandest in all history. Behind its altars, sweep the vestments of centuries of priests, and rises the incense of centuries of prayer. In its stony niches, stand rows of saints, who have made human life sublime, and who, through all the passing ages, look down upon the turmoil of that life with the calm beatitude of heaven; while its flushed windows still keep the blood-stain of its own martyrs, plashed against it ere yet it had become an anchored fact, and while it tossed upon the stormy waves of persecution. I can understand, then, how an imaginative and reverential mind can find the truest religious life only in connection with ritual and sacrament.

I can understand, moreover, the reaction in this direction, which is taking place at the present day. It is the retreat of the religious sentiments from the despotism of an imperious reason. It is the counter-protest of loyal affections against what is deemed an anarchical tendency. It is the clinging of men's sympathies to the concrete, alarmed by the irreverent and analytic methods of science. It is the retirement of faith and devotion to those cloistered sanctities that shut out the noise of the populace, and the diversions of the street. It is the reluctance of taste and imagination at our new and varnished Protestantism, with its bare walls, its cold services, and its angular churches, of which one wing, perchance, rests upon a market, and the other upon a dram-shop. Especially would I not deny the profound spiritual life, the self-sacrifice, and the beautiful charities which have consisted at all times, and which consist in the present time, with this ritual and sacramental form of religion.

But when men claim that this alone is the genuine form — that these are essentials of the only true church — then I deny that claim. If it fills some wants of our nature, it repudiates others equally authentic. If one class of minds find peace only under its consecrated shadows, others find no satisfaction but in the discipline of a spontaneous devotion, and the exercise of an individual reason. If it suffices for men like Borromeo or Newman, it does not suffice for men like George Fox or Channing; and the religion of these is as evident, in their simple spirituality, as of those in their mystic symbolism.

When it sneers at the Puritan, then I must vindicate that rugged independence of soul, that faithfulness to the individual conscience, that sense of the divine sovereignty, which could kneel at no man's altar, and to God alone; which sacrificed all things for the right, but yielded not a hair to the wrong; which could find no medicine for the spirit in sacraments, but only in the solitude of the inner life; and which has, under God, wrought out this noble consummation of modern times, whereby others may plant their vine of ritual under the broad heaven of toleration, and have liberty to sneer. When the ritualist deprecates the ultraism and irreverence of the anti-formalist, I must urge the tendency of his own principles to mummery and absolutism.

And, finally, when he falls back upon Tradition, I must fall back upon the Bible. The spirit of the New Testament is not that of rituals or sacraments; and the universal sentiments of the Old are not. The prophet Isaiah, who exclaims: "Bring no more vain oblations; incense is an abomination unto me; your new moons, and your appointed feasts, my soul hateth . . . Wash you, make you clean . . . cease to do evil, learn to do well!" joins with the Apostle, who says that Christ "blotted out the handwriting of ordinances . . . nailing it to his cross," and that no man should judge us in meat or drink, or times, or seasons. And, surely, there is no argument for forms or places in those divine words, which declare that "God is a spirit, and they who worship him, must worship him in spirit and in truth."

We cannot deny, then, that pure religion may consist with rituals and sacraments; we cannot deny that it may exist without these. But I insist upon this point: that the sacrament, the ritual, is not, itself, religion. It may be a beautiful sign — it may be a quick suggestion — it may be a medium of spiritual influence; but, alone, it cannot take the place of inward, personal piety, of right affections, and an obedient will. No punctilious form can stand substitute for a vigilant conscience; no posture of devotion can supply the place of living deeds; no ascetic mortification can atone for guilt; no auricular confession can speak, instead of the breathings of repentance, in the ear of God, and out from the depths of the solitary soul. He who relies upon these forms, and finds sanctity only in them, may be sincere, may be serious about religion, but as yet he is only a seeker; and, speaking to his heart with all-penetrating meaning, comes to him the decree: "Ye must be born again."

Again; there is a class who seek religion in philosophy. They believe in God by a course of reasoning. They believe in immortality, because it is a conclusion riveted in their minds by the iron links of induction. They pray, or not, according as it seems logical to do so. They would be good, because goodness is useful. But every proposition upon which they act must first be strained through the alembic of the intellect, and must stand out in the clear definition of science. They verify and build up their religion with callipers and dissecting knife. It is a system of digestion and pneumatology. They find an organ for veneration, and another for conscientiousness, and therefore conclude that religion has a legitimate place in the harmony of human character.

But all must be calm and balanced. They dare not trust the feelings, and give but little scope to enthusiasm. Sometimes, indeed, they rise to eloquence in expatiating upon the truths of natural theology, and of "the elder scripture;" though they believe in Christ also, because he seems well authenticated as an historical fact. In short, such men are religious like Cicero, or Seneca, with some modification from modern science, and from the Sermon on the Mount.

Now, there is a close alliance between true philosophy and true religion. That the New Testament is eminently free from fanaticism, and makes no appeal to mere credulity, any one will see who examines. That it is rational and sober, constitutes one of its great internal evidences. A Christian philosopher is no anomaly, but a beautiful expression of the essential harmony of all truth. Knowledge and piety burn and brighten with an undivided flame. Revelation and science are continually interpreting one another, while every day the material universe is unfolding a more spiritual significance, and indicating its subservience to a spiritual end. But, after all, in order to be religious, it is not necessary that a man should be a philosopher, and it is certain that often he is a philosopher without being religious. Religion and philosophy may coalesce, but they are two different spheres. Philosophy is out-looking and speculative; religion is inner and vital. In the scheme of philosophy, religion is reasoned out as a consequence, and adopted as an appendage to character. In the true scheme, it is the central germ of our being, the controlling force of life. The religion of philosophy consists of right views of things, and a prudential schooling of the passions. True religion consists in a right state of the affections, and a renunciation of self. In the one case religion may "play round the head, but come not near the heart;" in the other it breaks up the great deep of conscience, and pours an intense light upon the springs of motive. Philosophy contains the idea of intellectual rectitude; religion, of moral obedience. Philosophy speaks of virtue; religion, of holiness. Philosophy rests upon development; religion requires regeneration. In short, we make an every-day distinction between the two, which is far more significant than any verbal contrast. It is the one, rather than the other, that we apply, in the profounder experiences of our moral nature, in the consciousness of sin, and in the overwhelming calamities of life. The one pours a purifying, healing, uplifting power into the homes of human suffering, and into the hearts of the ignorant and the poor, that the other has not to bestow. Philosophy is well, under all circumstances; but it is not the most inner element of our humanity. Religion, in its humility, penitence, and faith — at the foot of the cross, and by the open sepulchre — rejoices in a direct and practical vision, to which philosophy, with its encyclopædia and telescope, cannot attain.

Under this head, too, may be ranked a class of men who, though they may not be exactly philosophers, fall into the same conception of religion, as a matter of the intellect — as the possession of correct views — rather than a profound moral life. They estimate men according to what they believe, and attribute the same sanctity to the creed that others attribute to the ritual. And as religion, in their conception of it, consists in a series of correct opinions, the great work should be an endeavor to make men think right. So the pulpit should be an arsenal of controversial forces, incessantly playing upon the ramparts of dogmatic error, with the artillery of dogmatic truth, and forever hammering the same doctrinal monotony upon the anvils of logic and of textual interpretation. They are satisfied if some favorite tenet is proved to a demonstration, and go forth rejoicing in the superiority of their "views," without asking if saving love has melted and transfigured their own hearts or whether personal sin may not canker in their souls, if hereditary guilt is not there. Now, it is true that great principles lie at the foundation of all practical life, and the more elevated and clear our views, the more effectual are the motives to holiness and love. But it matters little to what pole of doctrine the intellect swings, if the heart hangs unpenetrated and untouched. It matters little to what opinions in theology the pulpit has made converts, if all its mighty truths have not heaved the moral nature of the hearer — if it has not shot into the individual soul, like an arrow, the keen conviction: "I must be born again!"

Once more: there are those who seek religion in a routine of outward and commendable deeds — in mere morality.

With such, the great sum of life is to be sober, chaste, humane; laying particular stress upon the business-virtues, honesty, industry, and prudence. In their idea, that man is a religious man who is an upright dealer, an orderly citizen, a good neighbor, and a charitable giver. To be religious, means to do good, to keep your promises, and mind your own business. They tell us that benevolence is the richest offering, and that the truest worship is in the workshop and the field — that a man prays when he drives a nail or ploughs a furrow, and that he expresses the best thanksgiving when he enjoys what he has got, and is content if he gets no more.

Now, the world is not so bad that there is not a good deal of this kind of religion in it. It would be unjust to deny that many golden threads of integrity wind through the fabric of labor; that there is a strong nerve of rectitude holding together the transactions of daily life, and a wealth of spontaneous kindness enriching its darker and more terrible scenes.

But, after all, these easy sympathies, and these prudential virtues, lack the radicalness of true religion. Religion cannot exist without morality; but there is a formal morality which exists without religion. I say, a formal morality; for essential morality and essential religion are as inseparable as the sap and the fruit. Nor is morality a mere segment of religion. It is one half of it. Nay, when we get at absolute definitions, the two terms may be used interchangeably; for then we consider religion presenting its earthly and social phase, and we consider morality with its axis turned heavenward.

But, in the case of these outside virtues, which are so common, we behold only one half of religion, and that is its earthly and social form; and even this lacks the root and sanction of true morality. For the difference between the morality of a religious man and that of another consists in this: with the one, morality bears the sanctions of an absolute law, and God is at its centre. It is wrought out by discipline, and maintained at all cost.

With the other, it is an affair of temperament, and education, and social position. He has received it as a custom, and adopted it as a policy; or he acts upon it as an impulse. With the one, it is a matter of profit and loss, or a fitful whim of sentiment. With the other, it is the voice of a divine oracle within, that must be obeyed; it is the consecrated method of duty, and the inspiration of prayer. Now, to say that it makes no difference about the motive of an act, so long as the act itself is good, indicates that very lack of right feeling, and right perception, which confounds the formal morality of the world with religion.

For, in the distinctions of the Christian system, the motive makes the deed good or bad; makes the two mites richer than all the rest of the money in the treasury; makes the man who hates his brother a murderer. The good action may bless others, but if I do not perform it from a right motive, it does not bless me; and the essential peculiarity of religion is, that it regards inward development, individual purity, personal holiness — so that one essential excellence of the good deed consists in its effect upon the agent — consists in the sinews which it lends to his moral power, and the quantity it adds to his spiritual life. When, from a right motive, with effort and sacrifice, I help a weak and poor man, I enrich my individual and spiritual being. If I bestow from a mere gush of feeling, I receive no permanent spiritual benefit; if from a bad motive, I impoverish my own heart.

Acts, then, which appear the same thing in form, differ

widely, considered in their religious bearings. There is the morality of impulse, the morality of selfishness, and the morality of principle, or religious morality. The motive of the first-named, we obey instantaneously, and it may do good, just as we draw our hands from the flame, and thereby obey a law of our physical nature, though we act without any consideration of that law. A great deal of the morality in the world is of this kind. It may do good, but has no reference to the law of rectitude. It is impulsive, and therefore does not indicate a steadfast virtue, or a deep religious life.

For the very impulsiveness that leads to the gratification of the sympathies leads to the gratification of the appetites, and thus we often find generous and benevolent characteristics mixed with vicious conduct. Then, as I have said, there is the morality of selfishness. In this instance, I may perform many good actions from sheer calculation of material profit. I may be benevolent, because it will increase my reputation for philanthropy. I may be honest, because "honesty is the best policy." But is this the highest, the religious sanction of morality? No: the morality of the religious man is the morality of principle. The motive in his case is not "I will," or "I had better," but "I ought."

He recognizes morality as a law, impersonal, over-mastering the dictates of mere self, and holding all impulses in subservience to the highest good. The morality of impulse is uncertain. The morality of policy is mean and selfish. The morality of religion is loyal, disinterested, self-sacrificing. It acts from faith in God, and with reference to God.

But another trait separates the religious from the merely formal moralist. It consists in the fact that with him, "morality," as we commonly employ the term, is not all. Piety has its place. His affections not only flow earthward.

but turn heavenward. He not only loves his neighbor as himself, but he loves the Lord his God. He not only visits the widows and the fatherless in their affliction, but he keeps himself unspotted from the world. With him, toil is prayer, and contentment is thanksgiving, but because he infuses into them a spirit of devotion, which he has cultivated by more solitary and special acts. With him it is a good thing to live honestly, industriously, soberly; but all life is not outward, is not in traffic and labor, and meat and drink. There is an inward world, to which his eyes are often introverted — a world of spiritual experience, of great realities, and everlasting sanctions — a world behind the veil — a holy of holies in his soul, where rests the Shechinah of God's more immediate presence; yea, where he meets God face to face. And it is this that directs his public conduct. The orderly and beautiful method of his life is not the huddled chancework of good impulses, is not the arithmetic of selfishness; but it is a serene and steady plan of being projected from the communion of the oratory, and the meditation of the closet.

Again, I say, let us not depreciate morality. Let us condemn that ostentatious piety which lifts up holy hands to God, but never stretches them out to help man — which anoints its head with the oil of sanctity, but will not defile its robes with the blood of the abused, or the contact of the guilty — which is loud in profession and poor in performance — which makes long prayers, but devours widows' houses. Let us condemn this, but remember that this is not real religion, only its form; as often, the kind deed, the honest method, is not true morality, only its form. Of both these departments of action, let it be said: that these we have done, and not left the other undone. Let us recognize the perfect harmony, nay, the identity of religion and morality, in that one who came from the solitary conflict of the desert, to go about doing good, and who descended, from the night-prayer on the mountain, to walk and calm the troubled waves of the sea.

But those who rest in a mere routine of kind and prudential deeds, need the deeper life and the inner perception which detects the meaning and gives the sanction to those deeds. Such need the vital germ of morality — the changed heart, the new birth.

And, as I have spoken of a subordinate yet somewhat distinct class who may be ranked under the general head of seekers after religion in philosophy, let me here briefly allude to some with whom religion is a matter of mere sentiment and good feeling. Such are easily moved by the great doctrines of the New Testament. They are affected by the sermon; they have gushes of devout emotion during the prayer. But with them, religion is not a deep and steady pulse of divine life. Prayer is not a protracted aspiration — is not a habit. They feel well towards God, because they consider him a good-natured, complacent Being; but they do not meditate upon the majesty of his nature, upon his justice and his holiness. From the doctrine of immortality they draw consolation, but not sanctity. They regard it as a good time coming, but it furnishes them with no personal and stringent applications for the present. They need a more solemn and penetrating vision; a profounder experience in the soul. They need to be born again.

Then, again, there are those who may be called amateurs in religion. That is, they are curious about religious things. They like to speculate about it, to argue upon its doctrines, and to broach or examine new theories. They go about from sect to sect, and from church to church, tasting what is novel in the reasoning, or pleasing in the manner of the preacher; in one place to-day to hear an orator; in another to-morrow to hear a latter-day saint; it is all the same thing to them. All they want with religion is entertainment and excitement. They are Athenians, ever seeking some new thing. They smack at a fresh heresy as if they were opening a box of figs, and are as delighted with a controversy, as a boy with a sham-fight. They have no fixed place in the Church universal. They are liberalists, without any serious convictions and cosmopolites without any home affections.

In fact, to them religion is a sham-fight — a matter of spectacle and zest — not a personal interest, or an inward life. They would seek Jesus by night, because they hope to learn something wonderful or new, and would be startled to hear his solemn words tingling in their hearts: " Ye must be born again! "

Nay, my friends, would not these solemn words startle many of us? It may be, we have never made any inquiry concerning religion — have never even come to Jesus, as it were, by night. Such, with their barks of being drifting down the stream of time, have never asked the meaning of their voyage, or reckoned their course; nay, perhaps they live as though religion were a fable, as though earth were our permanent abiding-place, and heaven a dream. If such there are, they have not even listened to the Saviour's words. But there are others among us, perhaps, who are interested in the subject of religion, who are in some way or another engaged in it; but who are restless seekers after it, rather than actual possessors of it; who are resting upon insufficient substitutes for it. And I ask, would not these words, breaking forth from the lips of Jesus, startle us in our ritualism, our philosophy, our outside morality, our sentimentalism, or our mere curiosity? And do they not speak to us? Are they not as true now as when they struck upon the shivering ear of Nicodemus? Do they not make us feel as intensely our obligation and our religious want, as he might have felt there, with the wind flitting by him as though the Holy Spirit were touching him with its appeal, and with the calm gaze of the Saviour looking into his heart? Do they not demand of us, resting here awhile from the cares and labors of the world, something more than mere conformity, or intellectual belief, or formal deeds? Do they not demand a new and better spirit, a personal apprehension of the religious life, a breaking up and regeneration of our moral nature, a change of heart?

EULOGY OF HORACE GREELEY

DELIVERED AT THE FUNERAL CEREMONIES, DECEMBER 4, 1872

ONE month ago, many of us now present met in this place to express our sympathy with one who sat with pallid face and quivering lips, a heart-stricken mourner for his wife. To-day, as in the freshness of his great sorrow himself wished, he is to be by her side. The shadow of death, through which he was then passing, has enfolded him utterly. Such is the providence that checks all human purposes and makes life a continual surprise! And now, as I stand here to discharge no mere professional function, to do that which I feel is no more imperative for me as a pastor than as a personal friend, I still must beg leave to limit myself quite closely to the offices of the hour. I cannot attempt here and now to unfold the life or estimate the worth of Horace Greeley. Such an attempt would, on one hand, be premature, and on the other hand, be unnecessary. Premature, because the traits and lessons of a great life can best be summed up and fixed in history in calmer moments, when the first vibrations of grief and excitement have ceased. This work ought to be done, and, I trust, will be done, in the utterances of public memorial service, which will deserve and receive a much wider hearing than I can claim. On the other hand, this work of appreciation is unnecessary; it has already been done. There have been but few instances in our history when the salient points of a man's character have been so instinctively apprehended; but very few instances when the expressions of regret and regard have been so spontaneous, so widespread and so similar.

The record of Mr. Greeley's life, like his person, was known everywhere. These eulogies that pour in so thick and fast from every quarter of the land are not made up with artificial rhetoric. They are genuine. Those tears, as freely shed to-day by country fireside, and in distant States as under the shadowing drapery of these walls, are not conventional tears. They are no official symbols of mourning that hang around us; they represent the people's thought, and are twined about the people's heart. A career of honest purpose and beneficent tendencies vindicates itself under all transient misconception. Where to-day are our party badges and political distinctions? They coil to ashes! Where in the reverent sadness of this hour are differences of creed? They melt away in the broad light of Christian recognition that testifies to a true man's life and arches over a good man's grave. All this, then, I say, indicates an instructive appreciation of character that could not be made more distinct by any labored analysis.

And, now, my friends, as one lesson adapted to this place

and this hour, I ask you before the face of the dead to consider for a moment or two what it was to which this affectionate remembrance attaches, and which draws this spontaneous regard. It was not mere intellectual ability, large and undeniable as it was in the present instance. It was not official station. Mr. Greeley held no official station. The will of the people, expressed through its Electoral College, to-day decreed that he should hold no such station. To-day the will of God elects him to a place from which all human honors look small and dim. No, my friends, the attraction in this instance is the magnetism of simple goodness. I need not say that Mr. Greeley's heart was as large as his brain — that love for humanity was an inwrought element of his nature. This was so complete, so broad in him, that it touched all sides of humanity, so to speak. It was manifest in a kindness and regard that keep their silent record in many private hearts; in a hand ever open and ready to help; in one of the kindest faces ever worn by man, the expression of which was

"A meeting of gentle lights without a name."

The hundreds of poor, toil-worn men who yesterday passed through the crowd to take a last look at that worn countenance were moved by no idle curiosity. They went there, not merely to gaze at the face of a great journalist and a famous politician; they were drawn by the conviction that he was the poor man's friend, the sympathetic champion of workingmen, who had struggled through their experiences and never forgotten their claims. Mr. Greeley's public action was directed by the same impulse. It was the motive power of his entire efforts, his almost unprecedented work for so many years and in so many ways. It enlisted him in the

service of every humane cause. Not only did it inspire his
life-long war with oppression, and evil, and meanness of
every sort — it made him exceptionally generous and tolerant. Some may think that he erred on the side of mercy
against justice. Perhaps so; but if we must err at all, that
is a good side to err on. A sweet disposition may hold even
an error in harmless solution, while there is a precision that
is as sour as it is sound. But let it be remembered that often
mercy is the synonym of justice. Another danger attendant
upon such a spirit is credulity — too much readiness to
believe the most and to believe the best. But this human
nature of ours, which, discipline it as we may, will still be
fallible, is full as likely to be wise at this extreme as at the
other. Truth is better than fiction. Nevertheless, if the
disparaging estimate of humanity is the true one, then fiction
is better than fact. The doctrine of a trust in man, however qualified by painful experiences, is necessary as the
inspiration to all noble effort, and for any content of mind,
for the working machinery of life, and for every fibre of the
social organism. Do you tell us that there is no substance
in human virtue? — that all honesty is marketable, and all
love a selfish mask? — that in this world there are no loyal
friendships, no unpurchased benefits, no faithful hearts, no
incorruptible souls? Is all that sentimental illusion?
Then, I say, let us be cheated by that illusion, always shutting out minor truths, and deceiving us even to the grave.

Whatever may have been the mistakes of him who lies
dead before us, there was no mistake in the main current
of that principle which inspired his labors and characterized
his life. And here, I repeat, is a lesson for us all. In trying to do the work of life, one may be discouraged by
instances of conspicuous greatness,— at least greatness that

expresses intellectual power and achieves splendid success. It may seem to us that because we cannot do great things, we can do nothing that is of worth, and that it matters little what we do. But goodness is richer than greatness. It lifts us nearer to God than any intellectual elevation, and, moreover, it is accessible for the humblest life. I do not say that all duty, that all religion is expressed in love for man — though we have ample warrant for belief that all the law is fulfilled in this one word, " Thou shalt love thy neighbor as thyself." The love of God, however, is the spring of, and kindles and nourishes love to man. But how is the love of God to be manifested? It is to be manifested according to our abilities, within our sphere, whether broad or narrow, and every day I bless God that the great necessary work of the world is so faithfully carried on by humble men in narrow spaces and by faithful women in narrow circles, true to the impulse of the divine love within them, performing works of simple goodness. And so we are encouraged, not discouraged, when the greatness which the world confesses is the greatness of goodness, because that, unlike intellectual power, is a communicable power for the goodness of the community. Therefore, from the cup of our sorrow here to-day we may drink inspiration for our best endeavors, while we are thankful for the achievement that in this instance was so large and so effective.

To men of different power different kinds of work are assigned. Some are discoverers of truth; some are vehicles of inspiration; some are inventors of instruments; some are builders of states. But truly has it been said that the philanthropists, in the measure of their wisdom and their purity of zeal, are the real " fellow workmen of the Most High." Other agents explore God's works and illustrate this truth.

But this is of little value save as it diffuses his blessedness and confesses his help. Therefore, they who by earnest effort against evil, by indignant rebuke of wrong, by steadfast advocacy of truth, justice and freedom, work beneficently for man, most truly work for God and work with God. How faithfully, how effectively he, for whom we hold these solemnities to-day, wrought his work to those ends it is superfluous for me to show. He enlisted in that war from which there is no discharge. He contended against what he believed to be wrong — inspired not less by the goodness of his heart than by the strength of his mind. He struck for what he believed to be right until mind and heart gave way, and, marked by scars and honors, he lies dead upon the field.

Permit me still further to say — as unfolding, also, in this hour, its practical lesson for ourselves — that Mr. Greeley's work in life was eminently practical work; his goodness was no mere sentiment; for him it was an organic force. There are those, also, who regarded him as what they call a " visionary man." For my part, I am thankful for all such visions as rest upon such solid ground of usefulness and precipitate such concrete results. No man, it seems to me, was less given to mere idle speculation by speech or pen, or used more telling words to tangible effects. How wide, how manifold was the circle of interests which he touched! How close to men's homes and bosoms the convictions which he wrought! How many, many minds has he instructed with practical wisdom! How many lives had he stimulated to wholesome energy! How many young men gratefully acknowledge him as their teacher and guide! What various interests of arts and labor, of education and temperance, of domestic purity, and of freedom miss him, mourn for him to-day. Wielding with so much power the mightiest engine of the times — placed in the editorial chair, which in our day, whether for good or evil, exercises an influence greater than any official seat or throne on earth — it is no light thing to say that, however strenuously, and some may think severely, he used it as the instrument of his own thoughts and purposes — he never debased it as a stimulant of impurity, or made it a vehicle of a single social wrong.

His work was wide and various — how wide and how various this spectacle here to-day bears witness. The associations represented here are of all opinions, all differences of pursuit. They are composed of men who disagreed with Mr. Greeley upon many points, yet who truthfully claim fellowship with him upon some one point, and spontaneously honor his memory. All these testify how closely his life was incorporated with the practical interests of men. At least they testify that while Horace Greeley had many antagonists, he had few, if any, enemies. May I not, without violating any of the proprieties of this occasion, express my satisfaction that while all political issues, as it were, lie sealed within those inclosing lids in demonstration of the truth that peace has victories more renowned than war, the highest representative of the nation joins with this national testimony in honor of the thinker, the worker, the patriot, and the man.

Let me refer to one more lesson of the hour, and I will relieve your patience. It is the lesson of Horace Greeley's life, it is the lesson of his death; would that in life and death it might be the lesson illustrated by us all — the lesson of the power, sufficiency of the Christian faith! Far be it from me to take advantage of this occasion, which has assembled men of different creeds and different forms of worship, to urge the point of Mr. Greeley's sympathy with those interpretations of Christianity which usually find expression here. Only suffer me to say, however, that he found at least, whatever errors may be mixed with his view — he found in it strength to live and strength to die by. But it is a grander fact than this that upon the essential truth of Christianity, the truth which all believers trust in, Horace Greeley leaned his weary head and weary heart and died. Now, my friends, not because it is my office, not because it is a professional duty that I should speak so, do I say that the more I see, the longer I live, the more I believe in every fibre of my heart that in Christian faith alone is true peace and quiet in our life and in our death. The mere intellect may find satisfaction in speculation concerning God, or whether there be any God at all, or in scientific excursions through the universe. In the seeming remote prospects of our own dissolution we may raise curious queries about a future life; whether this still old form which lies before us is itself the compact substance, the finality of our being, or whether from this motionless frame there has not vanished something that thought, and knew, and spoke, and lived, and evidently is not here.

In the assumptions of our modern wisdom, knowing so many things, and as we think impartially, we may criticise the claims of the ancient Bible, and of the historical Christ; but when the forces of nature press upon the life-springs of our own being, and we want to know something of the power that bears us up and carries us along — when the lamp of our conscious being flickers in the advancing darkness of the grave, and the question rises straight before us — " Is this the end of all, or is there something more? " Oh! when our evil habits accuse us, and our false lives rebuke us, and we feel our moral weakness, and know we cannot erect ourselves, then, indeed, does it come to us as a joy and as a victory — the truth that was uttered by Horace Greeley —" I know that my Redeemer liveth."

Job was a great sufferer. Affliction after affliction came upon him with whirlwind blast and lightning stroke. He mourned and wept, and looked through a tumultuous struggle that came upon him; he ended with the peace of the grave, where the wicked cease from troubling and the weary are at rest; but still, through and beyond all, he recognized this truth, that there was to him a Helper, a Vindicator, a Redeemer, and that was his strength and his victory. Our friend and brother had his hour of desolation and darkness. Affliction after affliction fell upon him, and he longed for rest. No doubt he breathed the spirit of the simple verse:

—— " Life is the torrid day
Burned by the wind and sun;
And death the calm, cool, evening hour
When the weary day is done."

But he looked through and beyond this. Those were the transient shadows, and I thank God from my heart and from my soul, not only for myself, but for all, that, when all earthly good was crumbling like scaffolding, this dying man was so strong and triumphant as to utter from his soul this simple sentence that is written over me.

My friends, that was the victory of Horace Greeley's life, as well as the lesson of his death. It is the consolation of the hour. I dare not trust myself to speak to those smitten hearts. I dare not trust words to convey even one atom of human sympathy, for they would fail me before those who have thus repeatedly been smitten. There, there is your consolation! " I know that my Redeemer liveth." And now, as we take the body of our friend and brother, and bear it to its final rest, from these walls that have known him so often, but shall know him no more — now, as we bend over him with these tears that will not be restrained, God grant that this may be our consolation.

"Farewell, dear friend! farewell, honored associate! farewell, noble champion!" each may say, speaking for some great interest and affection of his life. Farewell! We know that our Redeemer liveth! and God grant that we may know it in that final hour, when, like him, there is nothing for us but to turn to God.

MACDONALD

SIR JOHN ALEXANDER MACDONALD, a distinguished Canadian statesman, was born at Glasgow, Scotland, January 11, 1815. He removed
to Canada with his parents in 1820 and was educated at the Royal Grammar School, Kingston. He then studied law, was admitted to the bar
of Upper Canada in 1836, and soon attained a high place in his profession,
his command of criminal and commercial law being especially noteworthy,
while his abilities as a pleader were of no ordinary character. In 1844
he entered the Canada Assembly as member for Kingston, his position
being that of a progressive Conservative as distinguished from a purely
Tory attitude, and from 1856 until his death he was the leader of the
Canadian Conservatives. He entered the cabinet as receiver-general in
1847, and was attorney-general 1854-62, resigning in the latter year only
to resume the position in 1864. Macdonald, more than any other person,
was instrumental in bringing about the union of the Provinces in 1867,
in which year he received the honor of knighthood. He was the first
minister of public affairs and attorney-general of the Dominion, and in
1869 became prime minister, his ministry remaining in power until November, 1873, when it fell on the question of the Pacific Railroad charges.
For the next six years Macdonald led the Conservative Opposition, but
in 1878 came once more into power as prime minister, retaining this office
continuously until his death at Ottawa, June 6, 1891. In 1880 he signed
the contract for constructing the Canadian Pacific Railway, the most important act of his administration, the railway being completed in June,
1886. As a public speaker Macdonald displayed signal ability, and while
frequently visiting England and other countries on diplomatic errands
performed his various missions with skill and diplomatic finesse. He was
sometimes styled " the Canadian Disraeli," in allusion to his personal
likeness to the English statesman, whom he resembled to some extent
in the character of his statesmanship. Among the many measures of
importance successfully carried out by him were the improvement of the
Canadian criminal laws, the extension of the municipal system, military
organization, extension of the franchise, ratification of the Washington
treaty, and the extension and consolidation of the Dominion. He had a
profound knowledge of human nature and was often able to carry his
point without antagonizing his opponents.

SPEECH ON CONFEDERATION

DELIVERED IN THE HOUSE OF COMMONS, FEBRUARY, 1865

[The Dominion of Canada was born July 1, 1867. In February, 1865,
the proposed union was discussed in the Parliament of Canada. Sir E. P.
Taché moved a series of resolutions in the Legislative Council, while
Attorney-General Macdonald (afterward Sir John) moved a resolution in

the Legislative Assembly to the effect that the colonies of Canada, Nova Scotia, New Brunswick, Newfoundland, and Prince Edward Island should be united in one government, with provisions based on certain resolutions which were adopted at a conference of delegates from the said colonies, held at the city of Quebec on the 10th of October, 1864. In moving this resolution Mr. Macdonald made what is possibly his most famous speech.]

MR. SPEAKER,—In fulfilment of the promise made by the government to Parliament at its last session, I have moved this resolution. I have had the honor of being charged, on behalf of the government, to submit a scheme for the confederation of all the British North American Provinces,— a scheme which has been received, I am glad to say, with general if not universal approbation in Canada. The scheme, as propounded through the press, has received almost no opposition. While there may be occasionally, here and there, expressions of dissent from some of the details, yet the scheme as a whole has met with almost universal approval, and the government has the greatest satisfaction in presenting it to this House.

This subject, which now absorbs the attention of the people of Canada and of the whole of British North America, is not a new one. For years it has more or less attracted the attention of every statesman and politician in these provinces, and has been looked upon by many far-seeing politicians as being eventually the means of deciding and settling very many of the vexed questions which have retarded the prosperity of the colonies as a whole, and particularly the prosperity of Canada. The subject was pressed upon the public attention by a great many writers and politicians; but I believe the attention of the legislature was first formally called to it by my honorable friend the Minister of Finance. Some years ago, in an elaborate speech, my honorable friend, while an independent member of Parliament, before being connected with any government, pressed his views on the legislature at great length and with his usual force. But the subject was not taken up by any party as a branch of their policy until the formation of the Cartier-Macdonald administration in 1858, when the confederation of the colonies was announced as one of the measures which they pledged themselves to attempt, if possible, to bring to a satisfactory conclusion. In pursuance of that promise the letter or despatch which has been so much and so freely commented upon in the press and in this House was addressed by three of the members of that administration to the Colonial Office.

The subject, however, though looked upon with favor by the country, and though there were no distinct expressions of opposition to it from any party, did not begin to assume its present proportions until last session. Then men of all parties and all shades of politics became alarmed at the aspect of affairs. They found that such was the opposition between the two sections of the Province, such was the danger of impending anarchy in consequence of the irreconcilable differences of opinion with respect to representation by population between Upper and Lower Canada, that unless some solution of the difficulty was arrived at we would suffer under a succession of weak governments,— weak in numerical support, weak in force, and weak in power of doing good. All were alarmed at this state of affairs. We had election after election, we had ministry after ministry, with the same result. Parties were so equally balanced that the vote of one member might decide the fate of the administration and the course of legislation for a year or a series of years.

This condition of things was well calculated to arouse the earnest consideration of every lover of his country, and I am happy to say it had that effect. None were more impressed by this momentous state of affairs, and the grave apprehensions that existed of a state of anarchy destroying our credit, destroying our prosperity, destroying our progress, than were the members of this present House; and the leading statesmen on both sides seemed to have come to the common conclusion that some step must be taken to relieve the country from the deadlock and impending anarchy that hung over us. With that view my colleague, the President of the Council, made a motion founded on the despatch addressed to the Colonial Minister, to which I have referred, and a committee was struck, composed of gentlemen of both sides of the House, of all shades of political opinion, without any reference to whether they were supporters of the Administration of the day or belonged to the Opposition, for the purpose of taking into calm and full deliberation the evils which threatened the future of Canada.

That motion of my honorable friend resulted most happily. The committee, by a wise provision — and in order that each member of the committee might have an opportunity of expressing his opinions without being in any way compromised before the public or with his party in regard either to his political friends or to his political foes — agreed that the discussion should be freely entered upon without reference to the political antecedents of any of them, and that they should sit with closed doors, so that they might be able to approach the subject frankly and in a spirit of compromise. The committee included most of the leading members of the House,— I had the honor myself to be one of the number; and the result was that there was found an ardent desire — a creditable desire I must say — displayed by all the members of the committee to approach the subject honestly, and to attempt to work out some solution which might relieve Canada from the evils under which she labored. The report of that committee was laid before the House, and then came the political action of the leading men of the two parties in this House, which ended in the formation of the present government. The principle upon which that government was formed has been announced and is known to all. It was formed for the very purpose of carrying out the object which has now received to a certain degree its completion, by the resolutions I have had the honor to place in your hands.

As has been stated, it was not without a great deal of difficulty and reluctance that that government was formed. The gentlemen who compose this government had for many years been engaged in political hostilities to such an extent that it affected even their social relations. But the crisis was great, the danger was imminent, and the gentlemen who now form the present administration found it to be their duty to lay aside all personal feelings, to sacrifice in some degree their position, and even to run the risk of having their motives impugned, for the sake of arriving at some conclusion that would be satisfactory to the country in general. The present resolutions were the result. And, as I said before, I am proud to believe that the country has sanctioned, as I trust that the representatives of the people in this House will sanction, the scheme which is now submitted for the future government of British North America.

Everything seemed to favor the project, and everything seemed to show that the present was the time, if ever, when this great union between all her Majesty's subjects dwelling in British North America should be carried out. When the government was formed it was felt that the difficulties in the way of effecting a union between all the British North American colonies were great,— so great as almost, in the opinion of many, to make it hopeless. And with that view it was the policy of the government, if they could not succeed in procuring a union between all the British North American colonies, to attempt to free the country from the deadlock in which we were placed in Upper and Lower Canada, in consequence of the difference of opinion between the two sections, by having a severance, to a certain extent, of the present union between the two Provinces of Upper and Lower Canada, and the substitution of a federal union between them. Most of us, however,— I may say, all of us,— were agreed,— and I believe every thinking man will agree,— as to the expediency of effecting a union between all the Provinces, and the superiority of such a design, if it were only practicable, over the smaller scheme of having a federal union between Upper and Lower Canada alone.

By a happy concurrence of events the time came when that proposition could be made with a hope of success. By a fortunate coincidence the desire for union existed in the Lower Provinces, and a feeling of the necessity of strengthening themselves by collecting together the scattered colonies on the seaboard had induced them to form a convention of their own for the purpose of effecting a union of the Maritime Provinces of Nova Scotia, New Brunswick, and Prince Edward Island, the legislatures of those colonies having formally authorized their respective governments to send a delegation to Prince Edward Island for the purpose of attempting to form a union of some kind. Whether the union should be federal or legislative was not then indicated, but a union of some kind was sought for the purpose of making of themselves one people instead of three.

We, ascertaining that they were about to take such a step, and knowing that if we allowed the occasion to pass, if they did indeed break up all their present political organizations and form a new one, it could not be expected that they would again readily destroy the new organization which they had formed,—the union of the three Provinces on the seaboard,—and form another with Canada,— knowing this, we availed ourselves of the opportunity and asked if they would receive a deputation from Canada who would go to meet them at Charlottetown for the purpose of laying before them the advantages of a larger and more extensive union by the junction of all the Provinces in one great government under our common sovereign. They at once kindly consented to receive and hear us. They did receive us cordially and generously and asked us to lay our views before them. We did so at some length, and so satisfactory to them were the reasons we gave; so clearly, in their opinion, did we show the advantages of the greater union over the lesser, that they at once set aside their own project, and joined heart and hand with us in entering into the larger scheme, and trying to form, as far as they and we could, a great nation and a strong government.

Encouraged by this arrangement, which, however, was altogether unofficial and unauthorized, we returned to Quebec, and then the government of Canada invited the several governments of the sister colonies to send a deputation here from each of them for the purpose of considering the question with something like authority from their respective governments.

The result was that when we met here on the tenth of October, on the first day on which we assembled, after the full and free discussions which had taken place at Charlottetown, the first resolution now before this House was passed unanimously, being received with acclamation as, in the opinion of every one who heard it, a proposition which ought to receive

the sanction of each government and each people. The resolution is:

" That the best interests and present and future prosperity
of British North America will be promoted by a federal union
under the Crown of Great Britain, provided such union can
be effected on principles just to the several Provinces."

It seemed to all the statesmen assembled,— and there are
great statesmen in the Lower Provinces, men who would do
honor to any government and to any legislature of any free
country enjoying representative institutions,— it was clear to
them all that the best interest and present and future prosperity of British North America would be promoted by a federal
union under the Crown of Great Britain. And it seems to me,
as to them, and I think it will so appear to the people of this
country, that if we wish to form — using the expression which
was sneered at the other evening — a great nationality, commanding the respect of the world, able to hold our own against
all opponents, and to defend those institutions we prize; if we
wish to have one system of government and to establish a
commercial union with unrestricted free trade between people
of the five Provinces, belonging, as they do, to the same
nation, obeying the same sovereign, owning the same allegiance, and being, for the most part, of the same blood and
lineage; if we wish to be able to afford to each other the means
of mutual defence and support against aggression and attack,
— this can only be obtained by a union of some kind between
the scattered and weak boundaries composing the British
North American Provinces.

The very mention of the scheme is fitted to bring with it its
own approbation. Supposing that in the spring of the year
1865 half a million of people were coming from the United
Kingdom to make Canada their home; although they brought

C only their strong arms and willing hearts; though they brought neither skill nor experience, nor wealth,— would we not receive them with open arms and hail their presence in Canada as an important addition to our strength? But when, by the proposed union, we not only get nearly a million of people to join us; when they contribute not only their numbers, their physical strength, and their desire to benefit their position; but when we know that they consist of old-established communities, having a large amount of realized wealth — composed of people possessed of skill, education, and experience in the ways of the New World — people who are as much Canadians, I may say, as we are — people who are imbued with the same feelings of loyalty to the queen and the same desire for the continuance of the connection with the mother country as we are, and at the same time having a like feeling of ardent attachment for this our common country, for which they and we would alike fight and shed our blood, if necessary,— when all this is considered, argument is needless to prove the advantage of such a union.

There were only three modes — if I may return for a moment to the difficulties with which Canada was surrounded — only three modes that were at all suggested by which the deadlock in our affairs, the anarchy we dreaded, and the evils which retarded our prosperity, could be met or averted. One was the dissolution of the union between Upper and Lower Canada, leaving them as they were before the union of 1841. I believe that that proposition, by itself, had no supporters. It was felt by everyone that, although it was a course that would do away with the sectional difficulties which existed; though it would remove the pressure on the part of the people of Upper Canada for the representation based upon population, and the jealousy of the people of Lower Canada lest their institutions should be attacked and prejudiced by that principle in our representation; yet it was felt by every thinking man in the Province that it would be a retrograde step which would throw back the country to nearly the same position as it occupied before the union; that it would lower the credit enjoyed by United Canada; that it would be the breaking up of the connection which had existed for nearly a quarter of a century, and, under which, although it had not been completely successful, and had not allayed altogether the local jealousies that had their root in circumstances which arose before the union, our Province, as a whole, had nevertheless prospered and increased. It was felt that a dissolution of the union would have destroyed all the credit that we had gained by being a united Province, and would have left us two weak and ineffective governments instead of one powerful and united people.

The next mode suggested was the granting of representation by population. Now, we all know the manner in which that question was and is regarded by Lower Canada; that, while in Upper Canada the desire and cry for it was daily augmenting, the resistance to it in Lower Canada was proportionably increasing in strength. Still, if some such means of relieving us from the sectional jealousies which existed between the two Canadas, if some such solution of the difficulties as confederation had not been found, the representation by population must eventually have been carried, no matter though it might have been felt in Lower Canada as being a breach of the treaty of union, no matter how much it might have been felt by the Lower Canadians that it would sacrifice their local interests, it is certain that in the progress of events representation by population would have been carried; and, had it been carried — I speak here my own individual sentiments — I do not think it would have been for the interests of Upper Canada. For although Upper Canada would have felt that it had received what it claimed as a right, and had succeeded in establishing its right, yet it would have left the Lower Province with a sullen feeling of injury and injustice. The Lower Canadians would not have worked cheerfully under such a change of system, but would have ceased to be what they are now — a nationality, with representatives in Parliament, governed by general principles, and dividing according to their political opinions, and would have been in great danger of becoming a faction, forgetful of national obligations, and actuated only by a desire to defend their own sectional interests, their own laws, and their own institutions.

The third and only means of solution for our difficulties was the junction of the Provinces either in a federal or a legislative union. Now, as regards the comparative advantages of a legislative and a federal union, I have never hesitated to state my own opinions. I have again and again stated in the House that, if practicable, I thought a legislative union would be preferable. I have always contended that if we could agree to have one government and one Parliament legislating for the whole of these peoples it would be the best, the cheapest, the most vigorous, and the strongest system of government we could adopt.

But on looking at the subject in the conference, and discussing the matter as we did, most unreservedly and with a desire to arrive at a satisfactory conclusion, we found that such a system was impracticable. In the first place it would not meet the assent of the people of Lower Canada, because they felt that in their peculiar position — being in a minority, with a different language, nationality, and religion from the majority — in case of a junction with the other Provinces, their

institutions and their laws might be assailed, and their ancestral associations, on which they prided themselves, attacked
and prejudiced; it was found that any proposition which
involved the absorption of the individuality of Lower Canada
— if I may use the expression — would not be received with
favor by her people.

We found, too, that though their people speak the same
language and enjoy the same system of law as the people of
Upper Canada, a system founded on the common law of England, there was as great a disinclination on the part of the various Maritime Provinces to lose their individuality as separate
political organizations as we observed in the case of Lower
Canada herself. Therefore we were forced to the conclusion
that we must either abandon the idea of union altogether, or
devise a system of union in which the separate provincial
organizations would be in some degree preserved so that those
who were, like myself, in favor of a legislative union, were
obliged to modify their views and accept the project of a federal union as the only scheme practicable, even for the Maritime Provinces. Because, although the law of those Provinces is founded on the common law of England, yet every one
of them has a large amount of law of its own,— colonial law
framed by itself, and affecting every relation of life, such as
the laws of property; municipal and assessment laws; laws
relating to the liberty of the subject and to all the great interests contemplated in legislation; we found, in short, that the
statutory law of the different Provinces was so varied and
diversified that it was almost impossible to weld them into a
legislative union at once.

Why, sir, if you only consider the innumerable subjects of
legislation peculiar to new countries, and that every one of
those five colonies had particular laws of its own, to which its

people had been accustomed and are attached, you will see the difficulty of effecting and working a legislative union and bringing about an assimilation of the local as well as general laws of the whole of the Provinces. We in Upper Canada understand, from the nature and operation of our peculiar municipal law, of which we know the value, the difficulty of framing a general system of legislation on local matters which would meet the wishes and fulfil the requirements of the several Provinces. Even the laws considered the least important — respecting private rights in timber, roads, fencing, and innumerable other matters, small in themselves, but in the aggregate of great interest to the agricultural class, who form the great body of the people — are regarded as of great value by the portion of the community affected by them. And when we consider that every one of the colonies is a body of law of this kind, and that it will take years before those laws can be assimilated, it was felt that at first, at all events, any united legislation would be almost impossible. I am happy to state — and indeed it appears on the face of the resolutions themselves — that as regards the Lower Provinces a great desire was evinced for the final assimilation of our laws. One of the resolutions provides that an attempt shall be made to assimilate the laws of the Maritime Provinces and those of Upper Canada, for the purpose of eventually establishing one body of statutory law founded on the common law of England, the parent of the laws of all those Provinces.

One great objection made to a federal union was the expense of an increased number of legislatures. I will not enter at any length into that subject, because my honorable friends, the Finance Minister and the President of the Council, who are infinitely more competent than myself to deal with matters of this kind — matters of account — will, I think, be able to

show that the expenses under a federal union will not be
greater than those under the existing system of separate governments and legislatures.   Here, where we have a joint legislature for Upper and Lower Canada, which deals not only with
subjects of a general interest common to all Canada, but with
all matters of private right and of sectional interest, and with
that class of measures known as " private bills," we find that
one of the greatest sources of expense to the country is the
cost of legislation.   We find, from the admixture of subjects
of a general with those of a private character in legislation,
that they mutually interfere with each other; whereas, if the
attention of the legislature was confined to measures of one
kind or the other alone, the session of Parliament would not
be so protracted and therefore not so expensive as at present.

In the proposed constitution all matters of general interest
are to be dealt with by the general legislature; while the local
legislatures will deal with matters of local interest which do
not affect the confederation as a whole, but are of the greatest
importance to their particular sections.   By such a division of
labor the sittings of the general legislature would not be so
protracted as even those of Canada alone.   And so with the
local legislatures : their attention being confined to subjects
pertaining to their own sections, their sessions would be shorter
and less expensive.

Then, when we consider the enormous saving that will be
effected in the administration of affairs by one general government; when we reflect that each of the five colonies has a
government of its own with a complete establishment of public
departments and all the machinery required for the transaction of the business of the country; that each has a separate
executive, judicial, and militia system; that each Province has
a separate ministry, including a minister of militia, with a

complete adjutant-general's department; that each has a finance minister, with a full customs and excise staff; that each colony has as large and complete an administrative organization with as many executive officers as the general government will have,— we can well understand the enormous saving that will result from a union of all the colonies, from their having but one head and one central system. We in Canada already know something of the advantages and disadvantages of a federal union.

Although we have nominally a legislative union in Canada; although we sit in one Parliament, supposed constitutionally to represent the people without regard to sections or localities, — yet we know, as a matter of fact, that since the union in 1841 we have had a federal union, that, in matters affecting Upper Canada solely, members from that section claimed and generally exercised the right of exclusive legislation, while members from Lower Canada legislated in matters affecting only their own section. We have had a federal union in fact, though a legislative union in name; and in the hot contests of late years, if on any occasion a measure affecting any one section were interfered with by the members from the other,— if, for instance, a measure locally affecting Upper Canada were carried or defeated, against the wishes of its majority, by one from Lower Canada,—my honorable friend, the President of the Council, and his friends denounced with all their energy and ability such legislation as an infringement of the rights of the Upper Province. Just in the same way, if any act concerning Lower Canada were pressed into law, against the wishes of the majority of her representatives, by those from Upper Canada, the Lower Canadians would rise as one man and protest against such a violation of their peculiar rights.

The relations between England and Scotland are very similar to that which obtains between the Canadas. The union between them in matters of legislation is of a federal character, because the Act of Union between the two countries provides that the Scottish law cannot be altered except for the manifest advantage of the people of Scotland. This stipulation has been held to be so obligatory on the legislature of Great Britain that no measure affecting the law of Scotland is passed unless it receives the sanction of a majority of the Scottish members in Parliament. No matter how important it may be for the interests of the empire as a whole to alter the laws of Scotland, no matter how much it may interfere with the symmetry of the general law of the United Kingdom, that law is not altered except with the consent of the Scottish people as expressed by their representatives in Parliament. Thus we have in Great Britain to a limited extent, an example of the working and effects of a federal union as we might expect to witness them in our own confederation.

The whole scheme of confederation as propounded by the conference as agreed to and sanctioned by the Canadian government, and as now presented for the consideration of the people and the legislature, bears upon its face the marks of compromise. Of necessity there must have been a great deal of mutual discussion. When we think of the representatives of five colonies, all supposed to have different interests, meeting together, charged with the duty of protecting those interests and of pressing the views of their own localities and sections, it must be admitted that had we not met in a spirit of conciliation and with an anxious desire to promote this union; if we had not been impressed with the idea contained in the words of the resolution,—" that the best interests and present and future prosperity of British North America would be promoted by a federal union under the Crown of Great

Britain,"—all our efforts might have proved to be of no avail.
If we had not felt that, after coming to this conclusion, we
were bound to set aside our private opinions on matters of
detail; if we had not felt ourselves bound to look at what was
practicable,—not obstinately rejecting the opinions of others
nor adhering to our own; if we had not met, I say, in a spirit
of conciliation, and with an anxious, overruling desire to
form one people under one government, we never would have
succeeded.

With these views we press the question on this House and
the country. I say to this House, if you do not believe that
the union of the colonies is for the advantage of the country,
that the joining of these five peoples into one nation under one
sovereign is for the benefit of all, then reject the scheme.
Reject if you do not believe it to be for the present advantage
and future prosperity of yourselves and your children. But
if, after a calm and full consideration of this scheme, it is
believed, as a whole, to be for the advantage of this Province,
—if the House and country believe this union to be one which
will ensure for us British laws, British connection, and British
freedom, and increase and develop the social, political, and
material prosperity of the country,— then I implore this
House and the country to lay aside all prejudices and accept
the scheme which we offer. I ask this House to meet the
question in the same spirit in which the delegates met it. I
ask each member of this House to lay aside his own opinions as
to particular details and to accept the scheme as a whole if he
think it beneficial as a whole.

As I stated in the preliminary discussion, we must consider
this scheme in the light of a treaty. By a happy coincidence
of circumstances, just when an administration had been
formed in Canada for the purpose of attempting a solution

of the difficulties under which we labored, at the same time the Lower Provinces, actuated by a similar feeling, appointed a conference with a view to a union among themselves, without being cognizant of the position the government was taking in Canada. If it had not been for this fortunate coincidence of events, never, perhaps, for a long series of years would we have been able to bring this scheme to a practical conclusion. But we did succeed. We made the arrangement, agreed upon the scheme, and the deputations from the several governments represented at the Conference went back pledged to lay it before their governments, and to ask the legislatures and people of their respective Provinces to assent to it. I trust the scheme will be assented to as a whole. I am sure this House will not seek to alter it in its unimportant details; and if altered in any important provisions the result must be that the whole will be set aside and we must begin *de novo*. If any important changes are made, every one of the colonies will feel itself absolved from the implied obligation to deal with it as a treaty, each Province will feel itself at liberty to amend it *ad libitum* so as to suit its own views and interests; in fact, the whole of our labors will have been for naught, and we will have to renew our negotiations with all the colonies for the purpose of establishing some new scheme.

I hope the House will not adopt any such course as will postpone, perhaps forever, or at all events for a long period, all chances of union. All the statesmen and public men who have written or spoken on the subject admit the advantages of a union if it were practicable; and now, when it is proved to be practicable, if we do not embrace this opportunity, the present favorable time will pass away, and we may never have it again. Because, just so surely as this scheme is defeated, will be revived the original proposition for a union of the

Maritime Provinces irrespective of Canada; they will not remain as they are now, powerless, scattered, helpless communities; they will form themselves into a power which, though not so strong as if united with Canada, will nevertheless be a powerful and considerable community, and it will be then too late for us to attempt to strengthen ourselves by this scheme, which, in the words of the resolution, " is for the best interests and present and future prosperity of British North America."

If we are not blind to our present position we must see the hazardous situation in which all the great interests of Canada stand in respect to the United States. I am no alarmist, I do not believe in the prospect of immediate war. I believe that the common sense of the two nations will prevent a war; still we cannot trust to probabilities. The government and legislature would be wanting in their duty to the people if they ran any risk. We know that the United States at this moment are engaged in a war of enormous dimensions, that the occasion of a war with Great Britain has again and again arisen and may at any time in the future again arise. We cannot foresee what may be the result; we cannot say but that the two nations may drift into a war as other nations have done before. It would then be too late, when war had commenced, to think of measures for strengthening ourselves or to begin negotiations for a union with the sister Provinces.

At this moment, in consequence of the ill feeling which has arisen between England and the United States,— a feeling of which Canada was not the cause,— in consequence of the irritation which now exists owing to the unhappy state of affairs on this continent, the reciprocity treaty, it seems probable, is about to be brought to an end; our trade is hampered by the passport system, and at any moment we may be de-

prived of permission to carry our goods through United States
channels; the bonded goods system may be done away with,
and the winter trade through the United States put an end to.
Our merchants may be obliged to return to the old system of
bringing in, during the summer months, the supplies for the
whole year. Ourselves already threatened, our trade interrupted, our intercourse, political and commercial, destroyed,
if we do not take warning now when we have the opportunity,
and, while one avenue is threatened to be closed, open another
by taking advantage of the present arrangement and the desire
of the Lower Provinces to draw closer the alliance between
us, we may suffer commercial and political disadvantages it
may take long for us to overcome.

The conference having come to the conclusion that a legislative union, pure and simple, was impracticable, our next
attempt was to form a government upon federal principles
which would give to the general government the strength
of a legislative and administrative union while at the same
time it preserved that liberty of action for the different sections which is allowed by a federal union. And I am strong
in the belief that we have hit upon the happy medium in those
resolutions, and that we have formed a scheme of government
which unites the advantages of both, giving us the strength
of a legislative union and the sectional freedom of a federal
union, with protection to local interests.

In doing so we had the advantage of the experience of the
United States. It is the fashion now to enlarge on the defects
of the constitution of the United States, but I am not one of
those who look upon it as a failure. I think and believe that
it is one of the most skilful works which human intelligence
ever created; is one of the most perfect organizations that
ever governed a free people. To say that it has some defects

is but to say that it is not the work of Omniscience, but of human intellects. We are happily situated in having had the opportunity of watching its operation, seeing its working from its infancy till now. It was in the main formed on the model of the constitution of Great Britain, adapted to the circumstances of a new country, and was perhaps the only practicable system that could have been adopted under the circumstances existing at the time of its formation. We can now take advantage of the experience of the last seventy-eight years during which that constitution has existed, and I am strongly in the belief that we have in a great measure avoided in this system which we propose for the adoption of the people of Canada the defects which time and events have shown to exist in the American constitution.

In the first place, by a resolution which meets with the universal approval of the people of this country, we have provided that for all time to come, so far as we can legislate for the future, we shall have as the head of the executive power the sovereign of Great Britain. No one can look into futurity and say what will be the destiny of this country. Changes come over nations and peoples in the course of ages. But so far as we can legislate we provide that for all time to come the sovereign of Great Britain shall be the sovereign of British North America. By adhering to the monarchical principle we avoid one defect inherent in the constitution of the United States. By the election of the President by a majority and for a short period, he never is the sovereign and chief of the nation. He is never looked up to by the whole people as the head and front of the nation. He is at best but the successful leader of a party. This defect is all the greater on account of the practice of re-election. During his first term of office he is employed in taking steps to secure his own re-election, and for his party a continuance of power. We avoid this by adhering to the monarchical principle — the sovereign whom you respect and love. I believe that it is of the utmost import-ance to have that principle recognized so that we shall have a sovereign who is placed above the region of party — to whom all parties look up — who is not elevated by the action of one party nor depressed by the action of another, who is the common head and sovereign of all.

In the constitution we propose to continue the system of responsible government which has existed in this Province since 1841, and which has long obtained in the mother coun-try. This is a feature of our constitution as we have it now, and as we shall have it in the federation in which, I think, we avoid one of the great defects in the constitution of the United States. There the President, during his term of office, is in a great measure a despot, a one-man power, with the command of the naval and military forces; with an immense amount of patronage as head of the executive, and with the veto power as a branch of the legislature; perfectly uncontrolled by responsible advisers, his Cabinet being departmental officers merely, whom he is not obliged by the constitution to consult with unless he chooses to do so.

With us the sovereign, or in this country the representa-tive of the sovereign, can act only on the advice of his min-isters, those ministers being responsible to the people through Parliament. Prior to the formation of the American Union, as we all know, the different States which entered into it were separate colonies. They had no connection with each other further than that of having a common sovereign, just as with us at present. Their constitutions and their laws were different. They might and did legislate against each other, and when they revolted against the mother country they acted as separate sovereignties and carried on the war by a kind of treaty of alliance against the common enemy. Ever since the Union was formed, the difficulty of what is called " State rights " has existed, and this had much to do in bringing on the present unhappy war in the United States. They commenced, in fact, at the wrong end. They declared by their constitution that each State was a sovereignty in itself, and that all the powers incident to a sovereignty belonged to each State, except those powers which by the constitution were conferred upon the general government and Congress.

Here we have adopted a different system. We have strengthened the general government. We have given the general legislature all the great subjects of legislation. We have conferred on them, not only specifically and in detail, all the powers which are incident to sovereignty, but we have expressly declared that all subjects of general interest not distinctly and exclusively conferred upon the local governments and local legislatures shall be conferred upon the general government and legislature. We have thus avoided that great source of weakness which has been the cause of the disruption of the United States. We have avoided all conflict of jurisdiction and authority, and if this constitution is carried out, as it will be in full detail in the imperial act to be passed if the colonies adopt the scheme, we will have in fact, as I said before, all the advantages of a legislative union under one administration, with at the same time the guaranties for local institutions and for local laws which are insisted upon by so many in the Provinces now, I hope, to be united.

I think it is well that in framing our constitution our first act should have been to recognize the sovereignty of her

Majesty. I believe that while England has no desire to lose her colonies, but wishes to retain them; while I am satisfied that the public mind of England would deeply regret the loss of these Provinces — yet, if the people of British North America, after full deliberation, had stated that they considered it was for their interest, for the advantage of the future British North America, to sever the tie, such is the generosity of the people of England that, whatever their desire to keep these colonies, they would not seek to compel us to remain unwilling subjects of the British Crown. If, therefore, at the conference, we had arrived at the conclusion that it was for the interest of these Provinces that a severance should take place, I am sure that her Majesty and the imperial Parliament would have sanctioned that severance. We accordingly felt that there was a propriety in giving a distinct declaration of opinion on that point, and that in framing the constitution its first sentence should declare that "The executive authority or government shall be vested in the sovereign of the United Kingdom of Great Britain and Ireland, and be administered according to the well-understood principles of the British constitution, by the sovereign personally, or by the representative of the sovereign duly authorized."

That resolution met with the unanimous assent of the conference. The desire to remain connected with Great Britain and to retain our allegiance to her Majesty was unanimous. Not a single suggestion was made that it could by any possibility be for the interest of the colonies, or of any section or portion of them, that there should be a severance of our connection. Although we knew it to be possible that Canada, from her position, might be exposed to all the horrors of war by reason of causes of hostility arising

JOHN A. ANDREW

between Great Britain and the United States,— causes over which we had no control and which we had no hand in bringing about,— yet there was a unanimous feeling of willingness to run all the hazards of war, if war must come, rather than lose the connection between the mother country and these colonies.

We provide that " the executive authority shall be administered by the sovereign personally, or by the representative of the sovereign duly authorized." It is too much to expect that the queen should vouchsafe us her personal governance or presence except to pay us — as the heir-apparent to the throne, our future sovereign, has already paid us — the graceful compliment of a visit. The executive authority must therefore be administered by her Majesty's representative. We place no restriction on her Majesty's prerogative in the selection of her representative. As it is now, so it will be if this constitution is adopted. The sovereign has unrestricted freedom of choice. Whether in making her selection, she may send us one of her own family, a royal prince, as a viceroy to rule over us, or one of the great statesmen of England to represent her, we know not. We leave that to her Majesty in all confidence. But we may be permitted to hope that when the union takes place, and we become the great country which British North America is certain to be, it will be an object worthy the ambition of the statesmen of England to be charged with presiding over our destinies.

FROM SPEECH ON CANADIAN FISHERIES

DELIVERED MAY 5, 1872

TO come to the various subjects which interest Canada more particularly. I will address myself to them in detail, and first I will consider the question of most importance to us, the one on which we are now specially asked to legislate, that which interests Canada as a whole most particularly, and which interests the Maritime Provinces especially,— I mean the articles of the treaty with respect to our fishery rights.

I would in the first place say that the protocols which accompany the treaty, and which are in the hands of every member, do not give chronologically an every-day account of the transactions of the conference, although as a general rule I believe, the protocols of such conferences are kept from day to day; but it was thought better to depart from the rule on this occasion, and only to record the conclusions arrived at. Therefore, while the protocols substantially contain the result of the negotiations ended in the treaty, they must not be looked upon as chronological details of facts and incidents as they occurred.

I say so because the protocol which relates more especially to the fisheries would lead one to suppose that at the first meeting and without previous discussion the British commissioners stated " that they were prepared to discuss the question of the fisheries, either in detail or generally, so as either to enter into an examination of the respective rights of the two countries under the treaty of 1818 and the general law of nations, or to approach at once the settlement of the question on a comprehensive basis."

Now the fact is that it was found by the British commissioners, when they arrived at Washington and had an opportunity of ascertaining the feeling that prevailed at that time, not only among the United States commissioners, but among the public men of the United States whom they met there, and from their communications with other sources of information, that the feeling was universal that all questions should be settled beyond the possibility of dispute in the future, and more especially that if, by any possibility, a solution of the difficulty respecting the fisheries could be arrived at, or a satisfactory arrangement made by which the fishery question could be placed in abeyance as in 1854, it would be to the advantage of both nations.

It must be remembered that the commission sat in 1871; that the exclusion of American fishermen from our waters was enforced and kept up during the whole of 1870; and that great and loud, though I believe unfounded, complaints had been made that American fishing-vessels had been illegally seized although they had not trespassed upon our waters. Persons interested had been using every effort to arouse and stimulate the minds of the people of the United States against Canada and the Canadian authorities, and it was felt and expressed that it would be a great bar to the chance of the treaty being accepted by the United States if one of the causes of irritation which had been occurring a few months before should be allowed to remain unsettled; collisions would occur between American fishermen claiming certain rights, and Canadians resisting those claims; that thereby unfriendly feelings would be aroused, and all the good which might be effected by the treaty would be destroyed, by quarrels between man and man engaged on the fishing-grounds. . . .

Under these circumstances, Mr. Speaker, I felt myself powerless; and when the American commissioners made their last offer, which is now in the treaty, offering reciprocity in fisheries: that Canadians should fish in American waters, and that Americans should fish in Canadian waters; that fish and fish oil should be reciprocally free; and that if, on arbitration, it were found that the bargain was an unjust one to Canada, and Canada did not receive sufficient compensation for her fisheries by that arrangement, it was remitted to her Majesty's government to say what should be done; and, as will be seen by the last sentence of the protocol:

" The subject was further discussed in the conferences of April 18 and 19, and, the British commissioners having referred the last proposal to the government, and received instructions to accept it, the treaty articles, 18 to 25, were agreed to at the conference of April 23."

Thus, then, it occurred that these articles from 18 to 25 are portions of the treaty. One of these articles reserves to Canada the right of adoption or rejection, and it is for this Parliament now to say whether, under all the circumstances, it should ratify or reject them.

The papers that have been laid before the House show what was the opinion of the Canadian government. Under the present circumstances of that question the Canadian government believe that it is for the interest of Canada to accept the treaty, to ratify it by legislation. They believe it is for the interest of Canada to accept it, and they are more inclined to believe it from the fact which I must say has surprised me, and surprised my colleagues, and has surprised the country,— that the portion of the treaty which was supposed to be most unpopular and most prejudicial to the interests of the Maritime Provinces, has proved to be the least unpopular.

Sir, I could not have anticipated that the American fishermen, who were offered the advantages of fishing in our waters, would be to a man opposed to the treaty as inflicting upon them a great injury. I could not have anticipated that the fishermen of the Maritime Provinces, who at first expressed hostility, would now, with a few exceptions, be anxious for its adoption.

In viewing these articles of the treaty I would call the consideration of the House to the fact that their scope and aim have been greatly misrepresented by that portion of the Canadian press which is opposed to the present government. It has been alleged to be an ignominious sale of the property of Canada, a bartering away of the territorial rights of this country for money. Sir, no allegation could be more utterly unfounded than this. It is no more a transfer and sale of the territorial rights of Canada than was the treaty of 1854. The very basis of this treaty is reciprocity.

To be sure, it does not go as far and embrace as many articles as the treaty of 1852. I am sorry for it. I fought hard that it should be so, but the terms of this treaty are terms of reciprocity, and the very first clause ought to be sufficient evidence upon that point, for it declares that Canadians shall have the same right to fish in American waters that Americans will have under the treaty to fish in Canadian waters.

True it may be said that our fisheries are more valuable than theirs, but that does not affect the principle. The principle is this: that we were trying to make a reciprocity arrangement and going as far in the direction of reciprocity as possible. The principle is the same in each case, and as regards the treaty that has been negotiated it is not confined to reciprocity in the use of the inshore fisheries of the two countries. It provides that the products of the fisheries of the two nations — fish oil as well as fish — shall be interchanged free.

The only departure from the principle of reciprocity in the present treaty is the provision that if it shall be found that Canada had made a bad bargain and had not received a fair compensation for what she gave; if it shall be found that while there was reciprocity as to the enjoyment of rights and privileges there was not true reciprocity in value, then the difference in value should be ascertained and paid to this country. Now, if there is anything approaching to the dishonorable and the degrading in these proposals, I do not know the meaning of those terms. This provision may not be one that will meet the acceptance of the country, but I say that the manner in which it has been characterized is a wilful and deliberate use of language which the parties employing it did not believe at the time to be accurate, and to which they resorted for political reasons and in order to create misapprehensions in the country. Sir, there was no humiliation. Canada would not tolerate an act of humiliation on the part of its government. England would neither advise nor permit one of her faithful colonies to be degraded and cast down.

But it is said that the American fisheries are of no value to us. They are not as valuable as ours, it is true, but still they have a substantial value for us in this way, — that the exclusion of Canadian fishermen from the American coast fisheries would have been a loss to the fishing interests of the Maritime Provinces, and I will tell you why. It is quite true that the mackerel fishery, which is the most valuable fishery on these coasts, belongs chiefly to Canada, and that the mackerel of the American coast is far inferior in every respect to the Canadian fish; but it is also true that in American waters the favorite bait to catch the mackerel with, known as the menhaden, is found, and it is so much the favorite bait that one fishing-vessel having this bait on board will draw a whole school of mackerel in the very face of vessels having an inferior bait.

Now the value of the privilege of entering American waters for catching that bait is very great. If Canadian fishermen were excluded from American waters by any combination among American fishermen or by any act of Congress, they might be deprived of getting a single ounce of the bait. American fishermen might combine for that object, or a law might be passed by Congress forbidding the exportation of menhaden; but by the provision made in the treaty Canadian fishermen are allowed to enter into American waters to procure the bait, and the consequence of that is that no such combination can exist, and Canadians can purchase the bait and be able to fish on equal terms with the Americans.

It is thus seen, sir, that this reciprocity treaty is not a mere matter of sentiment; it is a most valuable privilege, which is not to be neglected, despised, or sneered at. With respect to the language of these articles some questions have been raised and placed on the paper, and I have asked the honorable gentlemen who were about to put them to postpone doing so; and I now warn honorable members — and I do it with the most sincere desire to protect the interests of Canada — if this treaty becomes a treaty, and we ratify the fishery articles, I warn them not to raise questions which otherwise might not be raised.

I think, Mr. Speaker, there is no greater instance in which

a wise discretion can be used than in not suggesting any doubts. With respect, however, to the question which was put by the honorable member for the county of Charlotte,— and it is a question which might well be put, and which requires some answer,— I would state to that honorable gentleman, and I think he will be satisfied with the answer, that the treaty of 1871, in the matter his questions refer to, is larger and wider in its provisions in favor of Canada than was the treaty of 1854, and that under the treaty of 1854 no question was raised as to the exact locality of the catch, but all fish brought to the United States market by Canadian vessels were free.

I say this advisedly, and I will discuss it with the honorable gentleman whenever he may choose to give me the opportunity. The same practice will, I have no doubt, be continued under the treaty of 1871 unless the people of Canada themselves raise the objection. The warning I have just now expressed I am sure the House will take in the spirit in which it is intended. No honorable member will, of course, be prevented from exercising his own discretion, but I felt it my duty to call the attention of the House to the necessity of great prudence in not raising, needlessly, doubts as to the terms of the treaty.

It will be remembered that we have not given all our fisheries away: the treaty applies only to the fisheries of the old Province of Canada; and in order that the area should not be widened it is provided that it shall apply only to the fisheries of Quebec, Nova Scotia, New Brunswick, and Prince Edward Island, so that the treaty does not allow the Americans to have access to the Pacific coast fisheries, nor yet to the inexhaustible and priceless fisheries of the Hudson Bay. Those are great sources of revenue yet undeveloped, but after the treaty is ratified they will develop rapidly; and in twelve years from now, when the two nations sit down to reconsider the circumstances and readjust the treaty, it will be found that other and great wealth will be at the disposal of the Dominion.

I may be asked, though I have not seen that the point has excited any observation, why were not the products of the lake fisheries laid open to both nations, and in reply I may say that these fisheries were excepted at my instance. The Canadian fisheries on the north shores of the Great Lakes are most valuable. By a judicious system of preservation and protection we have greatly increased that source of wealth. It is also known that from a concurrence of circumstances and from situation the fisheries on the south shores are not nearly so valuable as ours, and it therefore appeared that if we once allowed the American fishermen to have admission to our waters, with their various engines of destruction, all the care taken for many years to cultivate that source of wealth would be disturbed, injured, and prejudiced, and there would be no end of quarrels and dissatisfaction in our narrow waters, and no real reciprocity, and therefore that Canada would be much better off by preserving her own inland lake fisheries to herself, and have no right to enter the American market with the products of those fisheries. This was the reason why the lake fisheries were not included in this arrangement.

Now, sir, under the present circumstances of the case, the Canadian government has decided to press upon this House the policy of accepting this treaty and ratifying the fishery articles. I may be liable to the charge of injuring our case in discussing the advantages of the arrangement, because every word used by me may be quoted and used as evidence against us hereafter. The statement has been so thrown broadcast that the arrangement is a bad one for Canada, that, in order to show to this House and the country that it is one that can be accepted, one is obliged to run the risk of his language being used before the commissioners to settle the amount of compensation as an evidence of the value of the treaty to us.

It seems to me that in looking at the treaty in a commercial point of view, and looking at the question whether it is right to accept the articles, we have to consider that interest which is most peculiarly first affected. Now, unless I am greatly misinformed, the fishing interests, with one or two exceptions for local reasons in Nova Scotia, are altogether in favor of the treaty. They are anxious to get admission of their fish into the American market; they would view with sorrow any action of this House which would exclude them from that market; they look forward with increasing confidence to a large development of their trade and of that great industry; and I say, that being the case, if it be to the interest of the fishermen and for the advantage of that branch of the national industry, setting aside all other considerations, we ought not wilfully to injure that interest. What is the fact of the case as it stands now? The only market in the world for the Canadian number one mackerel is the United States. That is their only market, and they are practically excluded from it by the present duty.

The consequence of that duty is that they are at the mercy of the American fishermen; they are made the hewers of wood and drawers of water for the Americans. They are obliged to sell their fish at the Americans' own price. The American fishermen purchase their fish at a nominal value and control the American market. The great profits of the trade are handed over to the American fishermen, or the American merchants engaged in the trade, and they profit to the loss of our own people. Let any one go down the St. Lawrence on a summer trip, as many of us do, and call from the deck of the steamer to a fisherman in his boat, and see for what a nominal price you can secure the whole of his catch; and that is from the absence of a market and from the fact of the Canadian fishermen being completely under the control of the foreigner.

With the duty off Canadian fish, the Canadian fisherman may send his fish at the right time, when he can obtain the best price, to the American market, and thus be the means of opening a profitable trade with the United States in exchange. If, therefore, it is for the advantage of the Maritime Provinces, including that portion of Quebec which is also largely interested in the fisheries, that this treaty should be ratified and that this great market should be opened to them, on what ground should we deprive them of this right? Is it not a selfish argument that the fisheries can be used as a lever in order to gain reciprocity in flour, wheat, and other cereals? Are you to shut them off from this great market in order that you may coerce the United States into giving you an extension of the reciprocal principle?

Why, Mr. Speaker, if it were a valid argument, it would be a selfish one. What would be said by the people of Ontario if the United States had offered, for their own purposes, to admit Canadian grains free, and Nova Scotia had objected, saying, "No, you shall not have that market; you must be deprived of that market forever unless we can take in our fish also; you must lose all that great advantage until we can get a market for our fish"? Apply the argument in this way and you will see how selfish it is.

But the argument has no foundation, no basis of fact, and
I will show this House how.   In 1854, by a strict and rigid
observance of the principle of exclusion, the American fishermen were driven out of those waters.   At that time the
United States was free from debt and from taxation, and
they had large capital invested in their fisheries.   Our fisheries were then in their infancy.   They were a " feeble "
people, just beginning as fishermen with little capital and little skill and their operations were very restricted.   I do not
speak disparagingly, but in comparison with the fishermen of
the United States there was an absence of capital and skill.
The United States were free from taxation, they had this capital and skill, and all they wanted was our Canadian waters
in which to invest that capital and exercise that skill, but
how is it altered now?

Our fisheries are now no lever by which to obtain reciprocity in grain.   What do the United States care for our
fisheries?   The American fishermen are opposed to the treaty.
Those interested in the fisheries are sending petition after
petition to the United States government and Congress praying that the treaty may be rejected.   They say they do not
want to come into our waters.   The United States government has gone into this treaty with every desire to settle all
possible sources of difficulty; their fishermen complain that
they will suffer by it, but the United States government
desires to meet us face to face, hand to hand, heart to heart,
and to have an amicable settlement of all disputes.   They know
that they are not making political friends or gaining political
strength because nearly the whole of the interest most affected
by the fishery articles is against the treaty.   But they desire
that the ill feelings which arose during the Civil War and from
the " Alabama " case should be forgotten.   A feeling of friend-

ship has grown up between the nations, and it can be no other desire than to foster and encourage that feeling which dictates the agreeing to these particular articles. The United States government will simply say, Well, if you do not like these arrangements, reject them, and the consequence will be on your own head if this friendship so auspiciously commenced is at any time broken by unhappy collisions in your waters.

BISMARCK

OTTO EDWARD LEOPOLD VON BISMARCK was born April 1, 1815. He received the usual education of young men belonging to the class of the country gentry, graduating in due course at a Gymnasium and a university. When he first entered upon a diplomatic career, it was as a type of the Junkers, that is to say, as a representative of the most conservative, not to say reactionary, landed proprietors. He was opposed to the assumption of the imperial crown by the King of Prussia in 1848–49, because the offer of the dignity came from the Frankfort Parliament, and not from the German princes. When he subsequently represented Prussia at Frankfort in the Diet of the German Confederation, he steadily set himself to diminish the preponderant influence of Austria, and to organize a pro-Prussian party among the smaller German States. Having been made head of the Prussian Ministry in 1862, he governed for four years in defiance of the will of the Prussian Legislature, and literally risked his head in order to bring about the evolution of an army which should secure for Prussia the leadership of Germany. His designs were triumphantly carried out in 1866 and 1870–71, and he continued to govern the Fatherland as Chancellor of the German Empire and Prime Minister of Prussia until after the accession of the present Emperor, William II. He died in 1898, ten years after the delivery of his speech on the Army bill, which is here reproduced.

A PLEA FOR IMPERIAL ARMAMENT

IF I rise to speak to-day it is not to urge on your acceptance the measure the President has mentioned (the army appropriation). I do not feel anxious about its adoption, and I do not believe that I can do anything to increase the majority by which it will be adopted—by which it is all-important at home and abroad that it should be adopted. Gentlemen of all parties have made up their minds how they will vote, and I have the fullest confidence

in the German Reichstag that it will restore our armament
to the height from which we reduced it in the period between 1867 and 1882; and this not with respect to the
conditions of the moment, not with regard to the apprehensions which may excite the stock exchanges and the
mind of the public; but with a considerate regard for
the general condition of Europe. In speaking, I will have
more to say of this than of the immediate question.

I do not speak willingly, for under existing conditions
a word unfortunately spoken may be ruinous, and the
multiplication of words can do little to explain the situation, either to our own people or to foreigners. I speak
unwillingly, but I fear that if I kept silent there would
be an increase rather than a diminution of the expectations
which have attached themselves to this debate, of unrest
in the public mind, of the disposition to nervousness at
home and abroad. The public might believe the question
to be so difficult and critical that a minister for foreign
affairs would not dare to touch upon it. I speak, therefore, but I can say truly that I speak with reluctance. I
might limit myself to recalling expressions to which I gave
utterance from this same place a year and a day ago.
Little change has taken place in the situation since then.
I chanced to-day on a clipping from the "Liberal Gazette,"
a paper which I believe stands nearer to my friend, Representative Richter, than it does to me. It pictures one
difficult situation to elucidate another, but I can take only
general notice of the main points there touched on, with
the explanation that if the situation has since altered, it
is for the better rather than for the worse.

We had then our chief apprehension because of a war
which might come to us from France. Since then, one

peace-loving President has retired from administration in France, and another peace-loving President has succeeded him. It is certainly a favorable symptom that in choosing its new chief executive France has not put its hand into Pandora's box, but that we have assurance of a continuation under President Carnot of the peaceful policy represented by President Grévy. We have, moreover, other changes in the French administration whose peaceful significance is even stronger than that of the change in the presidency—an event which involved other causes. Such members of the ministry as were disposed to subordinate the peace of France and of Europe to their personal interests have been shoved out, and others, of whom we have not this to fear, have taken their places. I think I can state, also—and I do it with pleasure, because I do not wish to excite but to calm the public mind—that our relations with France are more peaceful, much less explosive than a year ago.

The fears which have been excited during the year have been occasioned more by Russia than by France, or I may say that the occasion was rather the exchange of mutual threats, excitement, reproaches, and provocations which have taken place during the summer between the Russian and the French press. But I do not believe that the situation in Russia is materially different now from what it was a year ago. The "Liberal Gazette" has printed in display type what I said then—"Our friendship with Russia sustained no interruption during our war, and it is elevated above all doubt to-day. We expect neither assault nor attack nor unfriendliness from Russia." Perhaps this was printed in large letters to make it easier to attack it. Perhaps also with the hope that I had reached a different

D conclusion in the meantime and had become convinced that
my confidence in the Russian policy of last year was erro-
neous. This is not the case. The grounds which gave occasion for it lie partly in the Russian press and partly in
the mobilization of Russian troops. I cannot attach decided importance to the attitude of the press. They say
that it means more in Russia than it does in France. I
am of the contrary opinion. In France the press is a
power which influences the conclusions of the administration. It is not such a power in Russia, nor can it be; but
in both cases the press is only spots of printer's ink on
paper against which we have no war to wage. There can
be no ground of provocation for us in it. Behind each
article is only one man—the man who has guided the pen
to send the article into the world. Even in a Russian
paper, we may say in an independent Russian paper,
secretly supported by French subsidies, the case is not
altered. The pen which has written in such a paper an
article hostile to Germany has no one behind it but the
man whose hand held the pen, the man who in his cabinet
produced the lucubration and the protector which every
Russian newspaper is wont to have—that is to say the
official more or less important in Russian party politics
who gives such a paper his protection. But both of them
do not weigh a feather against the authority of his Majesty,
the Czar of Russia. . . .

Since the great war of 1870 was concluded, has there
been any year, I ask you, without its alarm of war? Just
as we were returning, at the beginning of the seventies,
they said: When will we have the next war? When will
the Revanche be fought? In five years at latest. They
said to us then: "The question of whether we will have

war and of the success with which we shall have it (it was a representative of the Centre who upbraided me with it in the Reichstag) depends to-day only on Russia. Russia alone has the decision in her hands.''

Perhaps I will return to this question later. In the meantime, I will continue the pictures of these forty years and recall that in 1876 a war-cloud gathered in the South; that in 1877, the Balkan War was only prevented by the Berlin Congress from putting the whole of Europe in a blaze, and that quite suddenly after the Congress a new vision of danger was disclosed to us in the East because Russia was offended by our action at the conference. Perhaps, later on, I will recur to this also if my strength will permit.

Then followed a certain reaction in the intimate relations of the three emperors which allowed us to look for some time into the future with more assurance; yet on the first signs of uncertainty in their relations, or because of the lapsing of the agreements they had made with each other, our public opinion showed the same nervous and, I think, exaggerated excitement with which we had to contend last year—which, at the present time, I hold to be specially uncalled for. But because I think this nervousness uncalled for now, I am far from concluding that we do not need an increase of our war-footing. On the contrary! Therefore, I have unrolled before you this tableau of forty years—perhaps not to your amusement! If not, I beg your pardon, but had I omitted a year from that which you yourselves had experienced with shuddering, the impression might have been lost that the state of anxiety before wars, before continually extending complications, the entanglements of which no one can anticipate

—that this condition is permanent with us; that we must reckon upon it as a permanency; and that independently of the circumstances of the moment, with the self-confidence of a great nation which is strong enough under any circumstances to take its fate into its own hands against any coalition; with the confidence in itself and in God which its own power and the righteousness of its cause, a righteousness which the care of the government will always keep with Germany—that we shall be able to foresee every possibility and, doing so, to look forward to peace.

The long and the short of it is that in these days we must be as strong as we can; and if we will, we can be stronger than any other country of equal resources in the world. I will return to that. And it would be a crime not to use our resources. If we do not need an army prepared for war, we do not need to call for it. It depends merely on the not very important question of the cost— and it is not very important, though I mention it incidentally. I have no mind to go into figures, financial or military, but France during the last few years has spent in improving her forces three thousand millions, while we have spent hardly fifteen hundred millions including that we are now asking for. But I leave the ministers of war and of finance to deal with that. When I say that we must strive continually to be ready for all emergencies, I advance the proposition that, on account of our geographical position, we must make greater efforts than other powers would be obliged to make in view of the same ends. We lie in the middle of Europe. We have at least three fronts on which we can be attacked. France has only an eastern boundary; Russia only its western, exposed to assault. We are, moreover, more exposed than any other people to the danger of hostile coalition because of our geographical position, and because, perhaps, of the feeble power of cohesion which, until now, the German people has exhibited when compared with others. At any rate, God has placed us in a position where our neighbors will prevent us from falling into a condition of sloth—of wallowing in the mire of mere existence. On one side of us he has set the French, a most warlike and restless nation; and he has allowed to become exaggerated in the Russians fighting tendencies which had not become apparent in them during the earlier part of the century. So we are spurred forward on both sides to endeavors which perhaps we would not make otherwise. The pikes in the European carp-pond will not allow us to become carp, because they make us feel their stings in both our sides. They force us to an effort which, perhaps, we would not make otherwise, and they force us also to a cohesion among ourselves as Germans which is opposed to our innermost nature; otherwise we would prefer to struggle with each other. But when we are enfiladed by the press of France and Russia, it compels us to stand together, and through such compression it will so increase our fitness for cohesion that we may finally come into the same condition of indivisibility which is natural to other people— which thus far we have lacked. We must respond to this dispensation of Providence, however, by making ourselves so strong that the pike can do nothing more than encourage us to exert ourselves. We had, years ago, in the times of the Holy Alliance (I recall an old American song which I learned from my dead friend, Motley:

> In good old colonial times
> When we lived under a king!)

We had then patriarchal times and with them a multitude of balustrades on which we could support ourselves, and a multitude of dikes to protect us from the wild European floods. That was the German confederation, and the true beginning, and continuance, and conclusion of the German confederation was the Holy Alliance, for whose service it was made. We depended on Russia and Austria, and, above everything, we relied on our own modesty, which did not allow us to speak before the rest of the company had spoken. We have lost all that, and we must help ourselves. The Holy Alliance was shipwrecked in the Crimean War—through no fault of ours! The German confederation has been destroyed by us because our existence under it was neither tolerable for us nor for the German people. Both have ceased to exist. After the dissolution of the German confederation, after the war of 1866, we would have been obliged to reckon on isolation for Prussia or North Germany, had we been obliged to stop at reckoning with the fact that, on no side would they forgive us the new and great successes which we had obtained. Never do other powers look with pleasure on the triumphs of a neighbor.

Our connection with Russia was not disturbed, however, by the events of 1866. In 1866 the memory of the politics of Count von Buol and of Austrian politics during the Crimean War was too fresh in Russia to allow them to think of supporting the Austrian against the Prussian monarchy, or of renewing the campaign which Czar Nicholas had conducted for Austria in 1849. For us, therefore, there remained a natural inclination toward Russia, which, foreseen in the last century, had in this its recognized origin in the politics of Czar Alexander I.

To him Prussia owes thanks indeed. In 1813 he could easily have turned on the Polish frontiers and concluded peace. Later he could have brought about the fall of Prussia. We have then, as a fact, to thank, for the restoration of the old footing, the goodwill of Czar Alexander I.; or, if you are inclined to be sceptical, say to the need felt in Russian politics for Prussia. This feeling of gratitude has controlled the administration of Frederick William the Third.

The balance which Russia had on its account with Prussia was used up through the friendship, I may say through the serviceability of Prussia during the entire reign of Czar Nicholas, and, I may add, settled at Olmutz. At Olmutz, Czar Nicholas did not take the part of Prussia, did not shield us from adverse experience, did not guard us against humiliation; for, on the whole, he leaned toward Austria more than toward Prussia. The idea that during his administration we owed thanks to Russia results from a historical legend. But while Czar Nicholas lived, we, on our side, did not violate the tradition with Russia. During the Crimean War, as I have already told you, we stood by Russia in spite of threats and of some hazard. His Majesty, the late king, had no desire to play a decided part in the war with a strong army, as I think he could easily have done. We had concluded treaties by which we were bound to put a hundred thousand men in the field by a set time. I advised his Majesty that we should put not a hundred thousand but two hundred thousand in the field, and to put them there *à cheval* so that we could use them right and left; so that his Majesty would have been the final arbiter of the fortunes of the Crimean War. But his late Majesty was not inclined to warlike undertakings, and the people ought to be grateful to him for it. I was younger and less experienced then than I am now. We bore no malice for Olmutz, however, during the Crimean War. We came out of the Crimean War as a friend of Russia, and while I was ambassador to Russia I enjoyed the fruit of this friendship in a very favorable reception at court and in Russian society. Our attitude toward Austria in the Italian War was not to the taste of the Russian cabinet, but it had no unfavorable consequences. Our Austrian War of 1866 was looked upon with a certain satisfaction. No one in Russia then grudged Austria what she got. In the year 1870 we had, in taking our stand and making our defence, the satisfaction of coincidently rendering a service to our Russian friends in the Black Sea. The opening of the Black Sea by the contracting powers would never have been probable if the Germans had not been victorious in the neighborhood of Paris. Had we been defeated, for example, I think the conclusion of the London agreement would not have been so easily in Russia's favor. So the war of 1870 left no ill humor between us and Russia. . . .

The bill will bring us an increase of troops capable of bearing arms—a possible increase, which, if we do not need it, we need not call out, but can leave the men at home. But we will have it ready for service if we have arms for it. And that is a matter of primary importance. I remember the carbine which was furnished by England to our Landwehr in 1813, and with which I had some practice as a huntsman—that was no weapon for a soldier! We can get arms suddenly for an emergency, but if we have them ready for it, then this bill will count for a strengthening of our peace forces and a reinforcement of the peace league as great as if a fourth great power had

joined the alliance with an army of seven hundred thousand men—the greatest yet put in the field.

I think, too, that this powerful reinforcement of the
army will have a quieting effect on our own people, and
will in some measure relieve the nervousness of our exchanges, of our press, and of our public opinion. I hope
they all will be comforted if they make it clear to themselves that after this reinforcement and from the moment
of the signature and publication of the bill the soldiers are
there! But arms are necessary, and we must provide better ones if we wish to have an army of triarians—of the
best manhood that we have among our people; of fathers
of family over thirty years old! And we must give them
the best arms that can be had! We must not send them
into battle with what we have not thought good enough
for our young troops of the line. But our steadfast men,
our fathers of family, our Samsons, such as we remember
seeing hold the bridge at Versailles, must have the best
arms on their shoulders, and the best clothing to protect
them against the weather which can be had from anywhere.
We must not be niggardly in this. And I hope it will re-
assure our countrymen if they think now it will be the case
—as I do not believe—that we are likely to be attacked on
both sides at once. There is a possibility of it, for, as I
have explained to you in the history of the Forty Years'
War, all manner of coalitions may occur. But if it should
occur we could hold the defensive on our borders with a
million good soldiers. At the same time, we could hold in
reserve a half million or more, almost a million, indeed;
and send them forward as they were needed. Some one
has said to me: "The only result of that will be that the
others will increase their forces also." But they cannot.

They have long ago reached the maximum. We lowered it in 1867 because we thought that, having the North-German confederation, we could make ourselves easier and exempt men over thirty-two. In consequence our neighbors have adopted a longer term of service—many of them a twenty year term. They have a maximum as high as ours, but they cannot touch us in quality. Courage is equal in all civilized nations. The Russians or the French acquit themselves as bravely as the Germans. But our people, our seven hundred thousand men, are veterans trained in service, tried soldiers who have not yet forgotten their training. And no people in the world can touch us in this, that we have the material for officers and under-officers to command this army. That is what they cannot imitate. The whole tendency of popular education leads to that in Germany as it does in no other country. The measure of education necessary to fit an officer or under-officer to meet the demands which the soldier makes on him, exists with us to a much greater extent than with any other people. We have more material for officers and under-officers than any other country, and we have a corps of officers that no other country can approach. In this and in the excellence of our corps of under-officers, who are really the pupils of our officers' corps, lies our superiority. The course of education which fits an officer to meet the strong demands made on his position for self-denial, for the duty of comradeship, and for fulfilling the extraordinarily difficult social duties whose fulfilment is made necessary among us by the comradeship which, thank God, exists in the highest degree among officers and men without the least detriment to discipline—they cannot imitate us in that—that relationship between officers and men which, with a few unfortunate exceptions, exists in the German army. But the exceptions confirm the rule, and so we can say that no German officer leaves his soldiers under fire, but brings them out even at the risk of his own life; while, on the other hand, no German soldier, as we know by experience, forsakes his officer.

If other armies intend to supply with officers and sub-officers as many troops as we intend to have at once, then they must educate the officers, for no untaught fool is fit to command a company, and much less is he fit to fulfil the difficult duties which an officer owes to his men, if he is to keep their love and respect. The measure of education which is demanded for that, and the qualities which, among us especially, are expressed in comradeship and sympathy by the officer—*that* no rule and no regulation in the world can impress on the officers of other countries. In *that* we are superior to all, and in that they cannot imitate us! On that point I have no fear.

But there is still another advantage to be derived from the adoption of this bill: The very strength for which we strive shows our peaceful disposition. That sounds paradoxical, but still it is true.

No man would attack us when we have such a powerful war-machine as we wish to make the German army. If I were to come before you to-day and say to you—supposing me to be convinced that the conditions are different from what they are—if I were to say to you: "We are strongly threatened by France and Russia; it is evident that we will be attacked; my conviction as a diplomat, considering the military necessities of the case, is that it is expedient for us to take the defensive by striking the first blow, as we are now in a position to do; an aggressive war is to our advantage, and I beg the Reichstag for a milliard or half a milliard to begin it at once against both our neighbors"—indeed, gentlemen, I do not know that you would have sufficient confidence in me to consent! I hope you would not.

But if you were to do it, it would not satisfy me. If we, in Germany, should wish to wage war with the full exertion of our national strength, it must be a war with which all who engage in it, all who offer themselves as sacrifices in it—in short, the whole nation takes part as one man; it must be a people's war; it must be a war carried on with the enthusiasm of 1870, when we were ruthlessly attacked. I well remember the ear-splitting, joyful shouts at the Cologne railway station; it was the same from Berlin to Cologne; and it was the same here in Berlin. The waves of public feeling in favor of war swept us into it whether we wished or not. It must always be so if the power of a people such as ours is to be exerted to the full. It will be very difficult, however, to make it clear to the provinces and states of the confederation and to their peoples that war is now unavoidably necessary. They would ask: "Are you sure of that? Who knows?" In short, when we came to actual hostilities, the weight of such imponderable considerations would be much heavier against us than the material opposition we would meet from our enemies. "Holy Russia" would be irritated; France would bristle with bayonets as far as the Pyrenees. It would be the same everywhere. A war which was not decreed by the popular will could be carried on if once the constituted authorities had finally decided on it as a necessity; it would be carried on vigorously, and perhaps successfully, after the first fire and the sight of blood. But it would not be a finish fight in its spirit with such fire and *élan* behind it as we would have in a war in which we were attacked. Then all Germany from Memel to Lake Constance would flame out like a powder mine; the country would bristle with arms, and no enemy would be rash enough to join issues with the *furor Teutonicus* (Berserker madness) thus roused by attack.

We must not lose sight of such considerations, even if we are now superior to our future opponents, as many military critics besides our own consider us to be. All our own critics are convinced of our superiority. Naturally every soldier believes it. He would come very near to being a failure as a soldier if he did not wish for war and feel full assurance of victory. If our rivals sometimes suspect that it is fear of the result which makes us peaceful, they are grievously in error. We believe as thoroughly in the certainty of our victory in a righteous cause as any lieutenant in a foreign garrison can believe in his third glass of champagne—and perhaps we have more ground for our assurance! It is not fear which makes us peaceable, but the consciousness of our strength—the consciousness that if we were attacked at the most unfavorable time, we are strong enough for defence and for keeping in view the possibility of leaving it to the providence of God to remove in the meantime the necessity for war.

I am never for an offensive war, and if war can come only through our initiative, it will not begin. Fire must be kindled by some one before it can burn, and we will not kindle it. Neither the consciousness of our strength, as I have just represented it, nor the trust in our alliances will prevent us from continuing with our accustomed zeal our accustomed efforts to keep the peace. We will not allow ourselves to be led by bad temper; we will not yield to prejudice. It is undoubtedly true that the threats, the insults, the provocations which have been directed against us, have aroused great and natural animosities on our side. And it is hard to rouse such feelings in the Germans, for they are less sensitive to the dislike of others toward them than any other nation. We are taking pains, however, to soften these animosities, and in the future as in the past we will strive to keep the peace with our neighbors—especially with Russia. When I say "especially with Russia," I mean that France offers us no security for the success of our efforts, though I will not say that it does not help. We will never seek occasion to quarrel. We will never attack France. In the many small occasions for trouble which the disposition of our neighbors to spy and to bribe has given us, we have made pleasant and amicable settlements. I would hold it grossly criminal to allow such trifles either to occasion a great national war or to make it probable. There are occasions when it is true that the "more reasonable gives way." I name Russia especially, and I have the same confidence in the result I had a year ago when my expression gave this "Liberal" paper here occasion for black type. But I have it without running after—or, as a German paper expressed it, "grovelling before Russia." That time has gone by. We no longer sue for favor, either in France or in Russia. The Russian press and Russian public opinion have shown the door to an old, powerful, and attached friend as we were. We will not force ourselves upon them. We have sought to regain the old confidential relationship, but we will run after no one. But that does not prevent us from observing—it rather spurs us on to observe with redoubled care—the treaty rights of Russia. Among these treaty rights are some which are not con-

ceded by all our friends: I mean the rights which at the
Berlin Congress Russia won in the matter of Bulgaria. . . .

In consequence of the resolution of the Congress, Russia,
up to 1885, chose as prince a near relative of the Czar, concerning whom no one asserted or could assert that he was
anything else than a Russian dependant. It appointed the
minister of war and a greater part of the officials. In short,
it governed Bulgaria. There is no possible doubt of it.
The Bulgarians, or a part of them, or their prince—I do
not know which—were not satisfied. There was a *coup
d'état*, and there has been a defection from Russia. This
has created a situation which we have no call to change
by force of arms—though its existence does not change
theoretically the rights which Russia gained from the conference. But if Russia should seek to establish its rights
forcibly I do not know what difficulties might arise, and it
does not concern us to know. We will not support forcible
measures and will not advise them. I do not believe there
is any disposition toward them. I am sure no such inclination exists. But if through diplomatic means, through the
intervention of the Sultan as the suzerain of Bulgaria, Russia seeks its rights, then I assume that it is the province of
loyal German statesmanship to give an unmistakable support to the provisions of the Berlin Treaty, and to stand by
the interpretation which without exception we gave it—an
interpretation on which the voice of the Bulgarians cannot
make me err. Bulgaria, the Statelet between the Danube
and the Balkans, is certainly not of sufficient importance
to justify plunging Europe into war from Moscow to the
Pyrenees, from the North Sea to Palermo—a war the issue
of which no one could foresee, at the end of which no one
could tell what the fighting had been about.

So I can say openly that the position of the Russian press, the unfriendliness we have experienced from Russian public opinion, will not prevent us from supporting Russia in a diplomatic attempt to establish its rights as soon as it makes up its mind to assert them in Bulgaria. I say deliberately—"As soon as Russia expresses the wish." We have put ourselves to some trouble heretofore to meet the views of Russia on the strength of reliable hints, but we have lived to see the Russian press attacking, as hostile to Russia, the very things in German politics which were prompted by a desire to anticipate Russia's wishes. We did that at the Congress, but it will not happen again. If Russia officially asks us to support measures for the restoration in Bulgaria of the situation approved by the Congress with the Sultan as suzerain, I would not hesitate to advise his Majesty, the Emperor, that it should be done. This is the demand which the treaties make on our loyalty to a neighbor, with whom, be the mood what it will, we have to maintain neighborly relations and defend great common interests of monarchy, such as the interests of order against its antagonists in all Europe, with a neighbor, I say, whose sovereign has a perfect understanding in this regard with the allied sovereigns. I do not doubt that when the Czar of Russia finds that the interests of his great empire of a hundred million people requires war, he will make war. But his interests cannot possibly prompt him to make war against us. I do not think it at all probable that such a question of interest is likely to present itself. I do not believe that a disturbance of the peace is imminent—if I may recapitulate—and I beg that you will consider the pending measure without regard to that thought or that apprehension, looking on it rather as a full restoration of the mighty power which God has created in the German people—a power to be used if we need it! If we do not need it, we will not use it and we will seek to avoid the necessity for its use. This attempt is made somewhat more difficult by threatening articles in foreign newspapers, and I may give special admonition to the outside world against the continuance of such articles. They lead to nothing. The threats made against us, not by the government but in the newspapers, are incredibly stupid, when it is remembered that they assume that a great and proud power such as the German Empire is capable of being intimidated by an array of black spots made by a printer on paper, a mere marshalling of words. If they would give up that idea, we could reach a better understanding with both our neighbors. Every country is finally answerable for the wanton mischief done by its newspapers, and the reckoning is liable to be presented some day in the shape of a final decision from some other country. We can be bribed very easily—perhaps too easily —with love and goodwill. But with threats, never!

We Germans fear God, and nothing else in the world!

It is the fear of God which makes us love peace and keep it. He who breaks it against us ruthlessly will learn the meaning of the warlike love of the Fatherland which in 1813 rallied to the standard the entire population of the then small and weak kingdom of Prussia; he will learn, too, that this patriotism is now the common property of the entire German nation, so that whoever attacks Germany will find it unified in arms, every warrior having in his heart the steadfast faith that God will be with us.

AGAINST LIBERALISM: A PRUSSIAN ROYALIST CONFESSION OF FAITH

DELIVERED JUNE 1, 1847

I WILL not take the trouble to examine the solidity of the various grounds of right, on which each of us presumes himself to stand; but, I believe, it has become certain, from the debate and from everything which I have gathered from the discussion of the question, that a different construction and interpretation of the older estates legislation was possible and practically existent — not among laymen only, but also among weighty jurists — and that it would be very doubtful what a court of justice, if such a question were before it, would decree concerning it. Under such circumstances, the declaration would, according to general principles of law, afford a solution.

This declaration has become implicit upon us, implicit by the patent of the third of February of this year; by this the King has declared that the general promises of former laws have been no other than those fulfilled by the present law. It appears that this declaration has been regarded by a portion of this assembly as inaccurate, but such is a fate to which every declaration is equally subject. Every declaration is considered by those whose opinions it does not confirm, to be wrong, or the previous conviction could not have been sincere. The question really is, in whom the right resides to issue an authentic and legally binding declaration. In my opinion, the King alone; and this conviction, I believe, lies in the conscience of the people. For when yesterday an honorable deputy from Königsberg asserted that there was a dull dissatisfaction among the people on the proclamation of the patent of the third of February, I must reply, on the contrary, that I do not find the majority of the Prussian nation represented in the meetings which take place in the Böttchershöfchen. (Murmurs.)

In inarticulate sounds I really cannot discover any refutation of what I have said, nor do I find it in the goose-quills of the newspaper correspondents; no! not even in a fraction of the population of some of the large provincial towns. It is difficult to ascertain public opinion; I think I find it in some of the middle provinces, and it is the old Prussian conviction that a royal word is worth more than all the constructions and quirks applied to the letter of the law.

Yesterday a parallel was drawn between the method employed by the English people in 1688, after the abdication of James II, for the preservation of its rights, and that by which the Prussian nation should now attain a similar end. There is always something suspicious in parallels with foreign countries. Russia had been held up to us as a model of religious toleration; the French and Danish exchequers have been recommended as examples of proper finances.

To return to the year 1688 in England, I must really beg this august assembly, and especially an honorable deputy from Silesia, to pardon me if I again speak of a circumstance which I did not personally perceive. The English people was then in a different position to that of the Prussian people now; a century of revolution and civil war had invested it with the right to dispose of a crown, and bind up with it conditions accepted by William of Orange.

On the other hand, the Prussian sovereigns were in possession of a crown, not by grace of the people, but by God's grace; an actually unconditional crown, some of the rights of which they voluntarily conceded to the people — an example rare in history. I will leave the question of right, and proceed to that concerning the utility and desirability of asking or suggesting any change in the legislation as it actually now exists. I adhere to the conviction, which I assume to be that of the majority of the assembly, that periodicity is necessary to a real vitality of this assembly; but it is another matter whether we should seek this by way of petition. Since the emanation of the patent of the third of February, I do not believe that it would be consonant with the royal pleasure, or that it is inherent with the position of ourselves as estates, to approach his Majesty already with a petition for an amendment of it.

At any rate let us allow the grass of this summer to grow over it. The King has repeatedly said, that he did not wish to be coerced and driven; but I ask the assembly what should we be doing otherwise than coercing and driving him, if we already approached the throne with requests for changes in the legislation?

To the gravity of this view I ask permission of the assembly to add another reason. It is certainly well known how many sad predictions have been made by the opponents of our polity connected with the fact that the government would find itself forced by the estates into a position which it would not have willingly taken up. But although I do not assume the government would allow itself to be coerced, I still think that it is in the interests of the government to avoid the slightest trace of unwillingness as to concessions, and that it is in all our interests not to concede to the enemies of Prussia the delight of witnessing the fact that, by a petition — a vote — presented by us as the representatives of sixteen millions of subjects, we should throw a shade of unwillingness upon such a concession.

It has been said that his Majesty, the King, and the commissioner of the diet have themselves pointed out this path. For myself, I could not otherwise understand this than that, as the King has done, so also the commissioner of the diet indicated this as the legal way we should pursue in case we found ourselves aggrieved; but that it would be acceptable to his Majesty, the King, and the government that we should make use of this right, I have not been able to perceive. If, however, we did so, it would be believed that urgent grounds existed for it — that there was immediate danger in the future; but of this I cannot convince myself. The next session of the assembly is assured; the Crown, also, is thereby in the advantageous position, that within four years, or even a shorter period, it can with perfect voluntariness, and without asking, take the initiative as to that which is now desired.

Now, I ask, is not the edifice of our State firmer toward foreign countries? — will not the feeling of satisfaction be greater at home, if the continuation of our national polity be inaugurated by the initiative of the Crown, than by petition from ourselves? Should the Crown not find it good to take the initiative, no time is lost. The third diet will not follow so rapidly upon the second, that the King would have no time to reply to a petition presented under such circumstances by the second. Yesterday a deputy from Prussia — I think from the circle of Neustadt — uttered a speech which I could only comprehend as meaning that it was our interest to pull up the flower of confidence as a weed preventing us from seeing the bare ground, and cast it out.

I say with pride that I cannot agree with such an opinion.

If I look back for ten years, and compare that which was written and said in the year 1837 with that which is proclaimed from the steps of the throne to the whole nation, I believe we have great reason to have confidence in the intentions of his Majesty. In this confidence I beg to recommend this august assembly to adopt the amendment of the honorable deputy from Westphalia — not that of the honorable deputy from the county of Mark — but that of Herr von Lilien.

THE IDEAL OF A CHRISTIAN STATE

DELIVERED AT "THE JEWS' DEBATE," JUNE 15, 1847

O N ascending this place to-day, it is with greater hesitation than usual, as I am sensible that by what I am about to utter, some few remarks of the speakers of yesterday, of no very flattering tone, will have in a certain sense to be reviewed. I must openly confess that I am attached to a certain tendency, yesterday characterized by the honorable deputy from Crefeld as dark and mediæval; this tendency which again dares to oppose the freer development of Christianity in the way the deputy from Crefeld regards as the only true one.

Nor can I further deny that I belong to that great mass, which, as was remarked by the honorable deputy from Posen, stands in opposition to the more intelligent portion of the nation, and, if my memory do not betray me, was held in considerable scorn by that intelligent section — the great mass that still clings to the convictions imbibed at the breast,— the great mass to which a Christianity superior to the State is too elevated. If I find myself in the line of fire of such sharp sarcasms without a murmur, I believe I may throw myself upon the indulgence of the honorable assembly, if I confess, with the same frankness which distinguished my opponents, that yesterday, at times of inattention, it did not quite appear certain to me whether I was in an assembly for which the law had provided, in reference to its election, the condition of communion with some one of the Christian churches.

I will pass at once to the question itself. Most of the speakers have spoken less upon the bill than upon emancipation in general. I will follow their example. I am no enemy to the Jews, and if they are enemies to me, I forgive them. Under certain circumstances I even love them. I would grant them every right, save that of holding superior official posts in Christian countries.

We have heard from the minister of finance, and from other gentlemen on the ministerial bench, sentiments as to the definition of a Christian state, to which I almost entirely subscribe; but, on the other hand, we were yesterday told that Christian supremacy is an idle fiction, an invention of recent state philosophers. I am of opinion that the idea of Christian supremacy is as ancient as the ci-devant Holy Roman empire — as ancient as the great family of European states; that it is, in fact, the very soil in which these states have taken root, and that every state which wishes to have its existence enduring, if it desires to point to any justification for that existence, when called in question, must be constituted on a religious basis.

For me, the words " by the grace of God," affixed by Christian rulers to their names, form no empty sound; but I see in the phrase the acknowledgment that princes desire to sway the sceptres intrusted to them by the Almighty according to God's will on earth.

I, however, can only recognize as the will of God that which is contained in the Christian Gospels, and I believe I am within my right when I call such a state Christian, whose problem is to realize and verify the doctrine of Christianity. That our state does not in all ways succeed in this, the honorable deputy from the county of Mark yesterday demonstrated in a parallel he drew between the truths of the Gospel and the paragraphs of national jurisprudence, in a way rather clever than consonant with my religious feelings.

But although the solution of the problem is not always successful, I am still convinced that the aim of the state is the realization of Christian doctrine; however, I do not think we shall approach this aim more closely with the aid of the Jews. If the religious basis of the state be acknowledged, I am sure that among ourselves the basis can only be that of Christianity. If we withdraw from the state this religious basis, our state becomes nothing more than a fortuitous aggregation of rights, a sort of bulwark against the universal war of each against all, such as an elder philosophy instituted. Its legislation then would no longer recreate itself from the original fountain of eternal truth, but only from the vague and mutable ideas of humanity taking shape only from the conceptions formed in the brains of those who occupy the apex.

How such states could deny the right of the practical application of such ideas — as, for instance, those of the communists on the immorality of property, the high moral value of theft, as an experiment for the rehabilitation of the native rights of man — is not clear to me; for these very ideas are entertained by their advocates as humane, and, indeed, as constituting the very flower of humanitarianism.

Therefore, gentlemen, let us not diminish the Christianity of the people by showing that it is superfluous to the legisla-

ture; let us not deprive the people of the belief that our legislation is derived from the fountain of Christianity, and that
the state seeks to promote the realization of Christianity,
though that end may not always be attained. . . .

Besides this, several speakers, as in almost every question,
have referred to the examples of England and France as
models worthy of imitation. This question is of much less
consequence there, because the Jews are so much less numerous than here. But I would recommend to the gentlemen
who are so fond of seeking their ideas beyond the Vosges, a
guide-line distinguishing the English and the French. That
consists in the proud feeling of national honor, which does not
so easily and commonly seek for models worthy of imitation
and wonderful patterns, as we do here, in foreign lands.

GERMAN SOLIDARITY

DELIVERED IN HOLSTEIN, DECEMBER 13, 1868

I AM rejoiced that you thus salute me as a fellow countryman,
and I thank you for the honor you do me. I see in it a
proof that the feeling of solidarity has also grown stronger
and stronger with you; and of this I shall joyfully inform the
King. We have always belonged to each other as Germans —
we have ever been brothers — but we were unconscious of it.
In this country, too, there were different races: Schleswigers,
Holsteiners, and Lauenburgers; as also Mecklenburgers,
Hanoverians, Lübeckers, and Hamburgers exist, and they are
all free to remain what they are, in the knowledge that they
are Germans — that they are brothers. And here in the north
we should be doubly aware of it, with our Platt-Deutsch language, which stretches from Holland to the Polish frontier;

we were also conscious of it, but have not proclaimed it until now. But that we have again so joyfully and vividly been able to recognize our German descent and solidarity — for that we must thank the man whose wisdom and energy have rendered this consciousness a truth and a fact, in bringing our King and Lord a hearty cheer. Long live his Majesty, our most gracious King and Sovereign, William the First!"

CURTIN

ANDREW GREGG CURTIN, a noted American statesman, was born at Bellefonte, Pennsylvania, April 22, 1815, and died there, October 7, 1894. After obtaining an education at Milton Academy he studied law at Dickinson College, was admitted to the bar in 1839, and, beginning to practise in his native county, soon attained prominence in his profession. Engaging in politics as a Whig he was an active worker for Harrison in 1840 and canvassed the State for Henry Clay in 1844. Ten years later he was appointed sscretary of the Commonwealth of Pennsylvania and ex-officio superintendent of common schools. While acting in the latter capacity he did much to reform the school system of his State, and his report to the legislature in 1855 led to the establishment of normal schools. In 1860 he was elected governor of Pennsylvania by the Republicans and in his inaugural address he advocated the forcible suppression of secession. When the call for troops was made by the President in April, 1861, Curtin responded instantly, companies of soldiers sent by him reaching Washington April 18; these being the first volunteer troops to reach the national capital. By his direction fifteen thousand extra volunteers were held in readiness at Harrisburg. Their services were shortly after accepted by the government, and Governor Curtin continued this policy throughout the period of the Civil War. After serving as governor a second term he retired for a short time to private life, but from 1868 to 1872 was minister to Russia. After his return to the United States he supported Greeley as presidential candidate, and from that time he allied himself with the Democratic party. In 1881 he entered Congress as Democratic representative and was twice re-elected, retaining his seat until 1887.

THE PEOPLE'S HERITAGE SQUANDERED

[The House having under consideration the bill to repeal section 22 of the act to incorporate the Texas Pacific Railroad Company, approved March 3, 1878, and to declare the forfeiture of the land grant therein made, and for other purposes, Mr. Curtin said, June 26, 1884:]

MR. SPEAKER,—No American citizen can be insensible to the great benefits conferred on the trade, commerce, and advancement of all the material interests of this country by railroads. It would have been better for the railroads and those who invest money in them, infinitely better for the people who travel and transport goods over them, if they had been confined to the common and statute law as common carriers only. I cannot but believe that the immunities and powers given to our railroad system beyond the rights and powers of common carriers, by water and other means of transportation, would have been infinitely better for them and for the country. But the legislation of this country in the States and by the Congress of the United States in its wisdom has conferred upon railroad companies powers far beyond the purposes for which they may be equally useful to the people and at the same time not oppressive in their exactions.

Mr. Speaker, it was generous, nay it was patriotic, in the States owning vast domains in the West to give to·this people lands to which they had a perfect title and which they generously surrendered for the national good. It was an inspiration of American statesmanship that led Jefferson to purchase Louisiana and the vast territories included in the purchase; and in the war with Mexico this great people conquered and gave to the public still more lands. For seventy-five years the lands given to this country were held in sacred trust for the people, to make homes for the homeless and to give lands to the landless.

Fifty-three millions of acres, sir, were given to the States for internal communications, for the advancement of trade and commerce, the settlement of the States, and for the purpose of education. Two hundred millions of acres have been voted to railroad corporations. In 1862 the Congress of the United States passed a law known as the Homestead Law. That, sir, was beneficent and generous legislation. It gave to the overflow of population in the Atlantic States a welcome to a home and a title to land where the American freeman could settle, turn the virgin soil to the light of the sun, and build upon it a home for himself and his family, and in the fulness of time acquire by his residence a fee-simple title. From 1861 until 1874 these unprecedented and munificent gifts were made to railroad corporations. Since 1874, when the change occurred in the majority of the House, not one acre has been given away, and not one land grant has been revived or extended.

Corporations are almost a necessity, and vast benefits have arisen from such grants and the work accomplished through them, but of immeasurably more value are the lands to the people of this Republic. I repeat, sir, that from 1874 to this time not one acre of land has been given to a corporation and not one grant that has lapsed by reason of the failure on the part of the corporations to comply with its conditions has been revived or extended beyond the time of its limitations.

I must not be understood, sir, to intimate for an instant that this great government should not be held to its contracts, bad as they were in the beginning. " Keep thy covenant proclaimed upon the plains of Mesopotamia so long since in the dark past " applies to individuals as well as to governments and people, and is a safe rule of conduct for all humanity; and where our government has made a contract let us fulfil it to the letter, but do not let the gift of this great government and people be revived into life by management or artifice.

There runs through this entire bill the clearest evidence of management by individuals to take a million of acres of land which should have been dedicated to the people as their homes when they acquire title under the Homestead Law.

This government can be strong and the Republic maintained in its strength only by the occupancy of land by the holders of small property. History is philosophy teaching by example; and tell me in all the line of history where a government republican in form has existed where a few people owned the land and the masses were serfs or peons or small tenants. All the roads of the empire lead to Rome is the boast of history. Armies marched from Rome to conquer and pillage foreign countries. They brought to Rome wealth and power, producing centralization, and too much of the immorality they found in Asiatic countries. Such was the centralization in that great republic that at last a few people, rich and powerful, owned all the lands of the country.

A distinguished citizen of Rome returning from foreign service found upon the slopes of the Alps, in Tuscany and Lombardy, where the Roman law should have given the soldiers one fourth of the lands, one fourth reserved to the state to be sold and the money returned to its treasury, one half to be given to the Roman freemen for homes. Tiberius Gracchus found in all the provinces on the slopes of the Alps scarcely one Roman freeman who owned an acre of land. Returning to Rome, as the tribune of the people, he introduced a law, and in it was generous to the rich patricians.

There were political rings at that time in Rome as there are unfortunately in this country at the present day. The rich and the powerful had their following of henchmen and servitors, and when the law was proposed by Gracchus he made it generous to the patricians, as it provided that they should be paid for the homes by the freemen who had been deprived of them. It was a just, a generous, and a liberal offer. It was just to the patricians; it was equally just to the people; but the rich and the powerful would not accept his generous offer. From the tribune they followed him through the streets of Rome, clubbed and stoned him to death, and threw his body into the Tiber.

Then, sir, equality and liberty commenced to decay and darkness fell upon the civilized world; learning fled to the cloisters; in their ignorance rulers could not even sign their names to their decrees. There was anarchy and pillage and wrong and oppression throughout the civilized world.

I say, Mr. Speaker, that history teaches by example. We can look back and gather wisdom from the events of the past, but who will claim power to look forward and anticipate what is in the future? That condition of the Roman republic has not failed to interest friends of humanity from that time to this.

At the beginning of the French revolution, when France was entering upon revolution and the people struggling for the right to be relieved from oppression, when the exactions of tyrannical landlords had robbed them of all their just rights, reduced to poverty and frenzied by oppression the French people rose in their majesty, and in their struggle for their just rights convulsed the commerce and trade and civilization of the world for fifteen years. But in the end the domain was taken from the church and state and France was divided into small estates by purchase.

There are 10,000,000 property-owners in France to-day, with a population of 37,000,000. There are less than 4,500,000 in this land of liberty with its population of 55,000,000. At that fearful era in the history of the world, Mirabeau, who was a real friend of humanity, uttered from the tribune in the States-General words of wisdom and eloquence: —

"Thus," said he, "perished the last of the Gracchi by the hands of the patricians, who, having received the mortal blow, flung a handful of dust toward heaven attesting the avenging gods, and from this dust rose Marius — Marius less great in having exterminated the Cimbri than in having quelled in Rome the aristocracy of the nobility."

There were never words more sublime in sentiment or more beautiful in rhetoric uttered in the classic age. Burke was never grander in the British Commons or our own Webster in the Senate. And, sir, mark the conclusion — the beauty of the prophecy and the purity of the philosophy: "Privileges," said Mirabeau, "must have an end — the people is eternal." The wisdom of that prophecy and philosophy is not unprofitable in this discussion.

And now, Mr. Speaker, without proposing to speak of the details of this bill, I must refer to it in general terms, as gentlemen on both sides have given all the data necessary for a proper conclusion. I have, sir, the most profound respect for the chairman of the committee on the judiciary for his learning, his integrity, and his patriotism, and yet I find in his bill, as expounded upon the one side and the other, that this land is to be taken from the people by artifice and not by fair dealing. Old charters are revived, life is given worn-out and fanciful grants, and with apparent attempt by indirection to revive a munificent grant of this government. There is running through the entire bill evidences of the want of title and covenant, surely things of interest to this people.

It was the intention of the American people to enjoy this rich heritage given to them by the States and held in trust by the federal government for so many years. If there be no doubt on this subject, the covenant of the government binds it. Let this question go to the courts, where my learned friend, the chairman of the judiciary committee, can be heard and the legal and just rights of the parties can be fairly adjudged.

This is scarcely a question for a popular assembly. This is not the place to decide a question serious as the one under consideration. We perform our duty by maintaining that the grant has lapsed by the failure of the corporations to perform the covenant they made. This question can be settled by the calm deliberation of the courts provided by the constitution. When the court sits upon the question involving the rights of American freemen I trust, sir, the judges will put on ermine that will be spotless. And if the courts decide that the contract with the companies is of such character and requires this means for its fulfilment, I say the American people will bow in submission to the decision. I repeat, " Keep thy covenant; " but if the court should find that there is management and artifice and indirection in the attempt to acquire title to this land, then decree back to the people of this country the lands that belong to them.

Mr. Speaker, the amount of money invested in railroad corporations in the United States is upward of $7,000,000,000 and that does not include the land granted by Congress. In contrast to that the taxable property in the United States is something more than $17,000,000,000, not including the property free from taxation by this government and many of the States. Of the 200,000 miles of railroad in the world we have 120,000 in the United States; we are grid-ironed with railroads.

Who is sensible to the fact that they have advanced the national power and consequence and contributed to the ease and comfort and happiness of our people, united jarring interests, afforded facilities for the interchange of commodi-

E ties, promoted trade and commerce and the social intercourse of our people?

If the railroad system of the United States prior to 1860 had extended their lines to the south, instead of the west, on the isothermal lines, I doubt if we would ever have had that terrible and unhappy war in which so many of our people perished and which left so large a part of our rich country in poverty.

It is fortunate for this country that the vast amount of capital invested in railroads and the enormous wealth of the few men who own most of the capital stock cannot combine together and make common cause in the government of this country. The citizens who control the railroads of this country are generally enlightened men. They know too well the value of this government in the protection of their interests to attempt such a thing. If they should combine they could control this government and mold its destinies for the future. They could say who should sit in this chamber and in the august body at the other end of the Capitol, and what citizen should occupy the palatial residence at the other end of the avenue; and who should be upon the benches of the courts; and, if united, with their vast power they could say who should compose the court of last resort of the American citizen, a court that has power to interpret laws, a tribunal that in power and influence is to the individual American citizen next to his God.

Who would be the keeper of an insane asylum if the inmates could combine; who would undertake the task? But, sir, they cannot combine because reason is dethroned and the inmates madmen; nor can the railroad companies combine to dominate this country by their wealth, the number of people connected with them, or their power. Ambition, rivalry stands in the way of their combination, and as yet there is a degree of patriotism which to an extent controls those in the management of the railroads and the vast capital invested in them.

But, sir, it might come in the future; and while it is scarcely proper to expect such a calamity, there is a time when it is fair to object to a combination such as is presented in this bill enriching railroads with lands which should be taken back and given to actual settlers under the beneficent legislation of our country to soldiers who so gallantly served it in its great peril.

Why, Mr. Speaker, the 200,000,000 acres given to corporations would make seven States like Pennsylvania, and the gift of this vast domain to railroads can scarcely be said to make your country strong. I read in a newspaper that a syndicate of a railroad corporation had in the West 10,000 acres of wheat. I presume that two hundred men could put the seed in the ground and reap and garner it with the modern machinery used in husbandry. Ten or fifteen men could watch and care for this great farm during the winter; but what becomes of those not so employed? Where do they go? Their homes are not there, nor can they settle upon lands. Thrown out of employment they must become what are known in this country as "tramps," and the man who would work for a living if he could get employment is remitted to the highway and to want. Under the ragged clothes of a man called a tramp there may beat a heart as faithful to the government as yours, and no man with proper feeling will refuse a crust of bread to hungry humanity thrown out of work and cast upon cold charity, even though he be called by the opprobrious name of tramp. . . .

I cannot but think it will be better for this country to be

in the hands of small land-owners, especially when as at present power is so centralized in this federal city, and when the jurisdiction of the courts of the national government has been so extended that the people scarcely find a settlement of their rights of property and person in the State courts. Why, sir, I can remember when the American citizen no more felt the power of the federal courts than the air he breathed. When money is centralized in the hands of a few, when a few men dominate and control the business of the country, I tremble, sir, for its liberties and wonder if monopolists shall be allowed to shape its future.

The authorized permit of the government, by statute, and arbitrary assumption if enlarged will, in time, absorb the States and their sovereignty, and the pernicious anti-republican and despotic espionage, under which internal revenue is collected, may be extended to all departments of the government.

Twenty-five million acres of land were recently purchased by foreign people in one body, it is said, by some reports, by fraud. I learned last September in California that an English and Scotch company had purchased a vast tract of the red timber land of that State likely to become of great value and not too much of it to monopolize. I know full well, Mr. Speaker, that if you divide the property of this country it could not remain divided. Every one who has a sense of justice in his soul but would look with horror upon the division of property as an act of communism and socialism. To divide would place the idle and the vicious on a level with the intelligent and industrious. From the former it would soon pass away and the balance would be restored. In addition, the absence of all laws of primogeniture is the surest protection against the accumulation of vast landed estates.

To expect that every man should have a home of his own and a part of the land would be Utopian. It would be a dream, and such dreams would be dissipated by the waking senses which come to us in teaching the actual and not the ideal.

But there is a measure of conservatism which should protect the industrious pursuits of the masses of the world. Lands having been given to corporations, if they have not fulfilled their contracts, it is the highest duty of this Congress to forfeit their contracts and take the lands back and fulfil their pledges with the people, made long before the legislation which gave them these vast properties. The citizens of the United States should have these lands for homes, and the government should regard these as sacred trusts.

Mr. Speaker, I view the future of this country with hope, and I have never believed the corporations could control its destinies. As I have said, they cannot combine to control it; but no one can be insensible to the vast power in the hands of a privileged class, and of the influence they have in the legislation of Congress and of the States. It is an unfortunate fact that men are willing to do as a corporation what they would scorn to do as individuals, and they too often forget in the parlor of a corporation the code of morality that governs them as individuals.

At the beginning of the French revolution in 1790 there were issued 9,000,000,000 of assignats, founded upon the public domain, from which it may be estimated how much of that country was held by the governing classes.

The issue of the assignats was a financial experiment and failed. Then came the revolution, and from it the restoration of the land of the country from the State and church to the people by purchase, and from that time France has been divided into small properties. But two nations in the world could have paid the exactions which were made on France at the end of the war with Germany. France is one; the United States is the other. England could not have paid it. England is owned by a small portion of her people. I have a sincere belief that France will remain a republic, and chiefly from the number of small proprietors.

Our government made these vast concessions, and has also covenants with the people, as it held these lands in trust for their use and benefit. A code of morality that applies to individuals which cannot be applied equally to the government is a fraud and a delusion.

But, sir, the government should be held strictly to the letter of the law, and the people will sustain any such legislation, but beyond that not one step. No part of the lands granted that have been forfeited by the failure to perform the covenants on the part of the companies should remain in their hands one day. And it must be considered as the settled policy of this government that no more of the public domain will be given to corporations.

My time is nearly exhausted, Mr. Speaker, and perhaps there is little more to say on this question. It cannot fail to be noticed with great satisfaction that at a recent national convention there was a declaration made against the importation of foreign laborers by corporations. How wonderfully elastic political opinion is in this country! Its views are as variable and changing as the colors of the kaleidoscope. Why, here in this book upon my desk is a statute passed in 1864, under which foreign labor could be imported, and which expressly provided that the imported man could be mortgaged and held in bondage for a year, and if he built a house his house and land could be sold by summary process on the contract made with him. At that time the war was raging. To give more accommodation and encouragement to these people, it was declared that they should not be subject to military duty. That statute bears date the 4th of July. It is rather remarkable that the birthday of freedom and liberty and equality should be selected on which to sign such a law. That law was afterward repealed, and did not long disgrace our statute-book.

And now, sir, waking after a long period of inexcusable indifference, the convention at Chicago has declared against any such legislation — in fact for the enactment of such legislation as is necessary to prevent it. During the last Congress the passage of the Chinese bill was steadily resisted upon this floor. The bill first passed was sent back with a veto by the President, and it is a notorious fact that every voice raised on this floor and every vote cast against the bill of this session to make that law effectual was by Republican members, whose convention declares for the policy they have opposed; and who, sir, knows what will be the fate of that bill in the august chamber at the other end of the Capitol, controlled as it is by the political friends of the gentlemen on the other side?

It was my good fortune to be here when the first Chinese bill was passed; and it was my privilege to raise my voice and cast my vote for it; and doubtless the convention soon to meet at Chicago will speak with no uncertain sound on this important question. Too many have already been imported, too many are here now; they interfere with the labor of the American citizen.

Mr. Speaker, what becomes of your tariff and revenue laws? They are questions that can be settled in the future; if they are not correct they can be corrected, and the wisdom is here to do it. They are questions that can be settled in accordance with the constant change of industrial conditions and require legislation adapted to these conditions. There is no man of sufficient wisdom to anticipate what the economical and financial necessities of this great people will require. Congress is here to attend to that; to legislate for their interests and their wants.

But the question of giving away the lands, the inheritance of the people, cannot be decided by the platform of a national convention. We have the right in this country now, or if not now in the near future, to say who shall come to this country and who shall not come, and we will not permit corporate wealth and power, either foreign or domestic, to control this country and dominate its destinies by the importation of such labor as has been imported within the last two or three years. In the district I have the honor to represent large numbers of Italians, Hungarians, and Bulgarians have been imported. They do not assimilate with our people, and never can any more than the Chinese. They interfere with our own citizens who labor, native and naturalized, and take from them their legitimate employment.

There is no question that should appeal more strongly to the statesman, philanthropist, and patriot than the condition of the laborers of this country. The wonderful skill and ingenuity of the American people has wrought such marvellous improvement in labor-saving machinery, that it, in a large measure, does the work of man, until the hand of the skilled mechanic is rarely found, and there is an overproduction, and there can scarcely be said to be employment for the labor of this country; if not now that time can be anticipated in the near future. Now, if there is any power for us to legislate so as to protect American labor, it is a duty we owe to the people to do so. And we can do it on this question, for I cannot but believe that if the public lands had been reserved for the purpose for which they were intended, and that the crowded population of the east could go west and find homes there, great good would be done. We are growing in population, and the lands now illegally held by corporations under grants that have been forfeited or being acquired in vast tracts by foreign capitalists, would afford in the future, homes for millions of American freemen.

Let us return, then, to the original condition of things, before that terrible war separated us, making the South poor, and blistering the morality of the North; let us return to the principles of the founders of this government; let us accept the constitution and laws, and live up to them; let us keep our covenant and require the fulfilment of the covenant with us; let us be faithful to our trust; and above all things let liberty and justice, equality, concord, and fraternity prevail.

BINGHAM

JOHN A. BINGHAM, an American orator and judge, was born January 21, 1815, at Mercer, Pennsylvania, of Scotch-Irish stock. He graduated at Franklin College, and after being admitted to practice at the bar went to Cadiz, Ohio, in 1840. In 1854 he was elected to Congress, where he served with only intermission of one term for eighteen years. In 1864 he was made judge-advocate-general, and before the close of the year was appointed solicitor of the United States court of claims. On the assassination of Lincoln, whose warm personal friend he was, he was summoned to Washington to investigate that crime, and within twenty-four hours after his arrival had opened an office and formulated plans which led to the arrest, trial, and conviction of the conspirators. President Johnson appointed him special judge-advocate, and the work of examining and cross-examining the witnesses fell largely to his share. His argument for the prosecution occupied nine hours in its delivery. He was a member of the committee which drew up articles of impeachment against President Johnson, and, as chairman, made the closing argument before the Senate, which held a vast audience for three successive days. His most important work was the formulation of the fourteenth amendment to the constitution. He won his greatest fame as an orator, and all his most famous speeches advocated national honor and national justice. After more than thirty years of public service he returned to Cadiz, where he died, 1901.

SPEECH ON THE SECTIONAL PARTY

DELIVERED IN THE HOUSE OF REPRESENTATIVES, APRIL 24, 1860

MR. CHAIRMAN,—The annual message of the President of the United States, which has been referred to this committee for its consideration, should not be passed over lightly. It contains much that, in my judgment, is offensive to the people and injurious to their interests, and which should not be allowed to go to the country unchallenged. It is my purpose, sir, to speak of this paper with all the respect that is due to the distinguished position of its author, but with the utmost freedom and candor. I speak to-day as a representative of the people and for the people;

not as the representative of party or for party. I speak to-day as an American citizen, claiming every State and section and rood of the Republic as part of my native country, that country which at last has but one constitution and one destiny. I do not intend, in anything I may this day utter, to do injustice to any section of that country, or to any of its interests.

The President of the United States, in this paper, invokes all good citizens to strive to allay " the demon spirit of sectional hatred and strife now alive in the land." This sectional spirit, to which the President refers, manifested itself upon this floor during the first two months of this session. It found fit, fierce, and expressive utterance on the other side of this chamber amongst the avowed political friends of the President himself, in their attempt to arraign and condemn sixty of their peers here as the aiders and inciters of treason, insurrection, and murder; and this, too, without giving to the accused a hearing, without testimony, in defiance of all law, and without subjecting the conscience of these self-constituted triers to the inconvenient obligation of an official oath. While these gentlemen were thus attempting to enforce mob law on this floor, they were loud in proclaiming that the inauguration of a Republican President, elected by the people in conformity with the constitution and laws, should be resisted to the extremity of disunion and civil war.

These were the enunciations with which our ears were greeted for two months, pending the contest for the organization of this House. If it was fit that the President should rebuke this sectional spirit among the people, it is fit that its manifestations upon this floor should be rebuked as well; and it is eminently fit that the sectional policy of the President and of his party should be rebuked in return by the whole people. There is so much in the tone of this paper that is intensely sectional, that I am constrained to believe that the President's plaintive invocation to allay " the demon spirit " was but smooth dissimulation, the better to disguise the sectional policy of himself and his party.

Sir, to put down forever this sectional party; to put an end forever to this sectional strife, and sectional innovation upon the constitution and the rights of the people, I am ready to join hands with good men in every section of the Union. That is a fell spirit, a demon spirit, which, under any pretence or for any purpose, would strike down all the defences of law; would sweep away all the landmarks of right and justice; would break down the traditional policy of this government, as wise as it is beneficent; which, instead of maintaining and perpetuating peace between every section of this country, would inaugurate and perpetuate discord, which would fill this goodly land with the lurid light of civil war; which would give its peaceful homes to conflagration, and its citizens to the sword; staining the white raiment of its mountains and the green vesture of its plains with the blood of human sacrifice shed in that unnatural and unmatched atrocity, fraternal strife.

Notwithstanding all I have heard, sir, upon this floor, of threats of disunion and civil war, I do not fear it; for there is in this land a power stronger than armies — that new power, born of the enlightened intellect and conscience of the people — the power of public opinion. That power speaks to-day, through the pen and the press, the living voice and the silent ballot. That power is stronger, I repeat, than armies. No, sir; notwithstanding all these threats, there can be no conflict of arms between the great sections of this Union. This land, consecrated to freedom and to man, by the blood of patriots and of martyrs, would refuse to bear up upon its holy ground an army of traitors. Local rebellions there may be; but in the future, as in the past, they will be suppressed by the popular will; by that majestic voice of the nation, at whose lightest word the tumult of the mob is still, and the wild, stormy sea of human passion is calm. God is not in the whirlwind, nor in the earthquake, nor in the storm.

The question to-day is, not how shall civil war between the great sections of this Union be averted — for that is not to be, it is an impossibility — but the question of to-day is, how shall this sectional party and this sectional strife be allayed? I answer, sir, that this sectional strife will never be allayed by imitating the example, or adopting the policy of the President and his party; never, while there is an honest head or an honest heart in this land. Neither will this sectional strife be allayed, but fostered, rather, by the attempt, here or elsewhere, either by national or by State legislation, to enact sedition laws, by which to fetter the conscience, or stifle the convictions of American citizens. This sectional strife will never be allayed by the attempt, here or elsewhere, either by national or by State legislation, to annul the sacred right of domicile, to make it a felony for any freeman, born anywhere within the limits of the Republic, to live unmolested on the spot of his origin, so long as he behaves himself well, and it pleases God to let him live.

This sectional strife never will be allayed by the attempt to nationalize chattel slavery, to place it under the shelter of the federal constitution, and to maintain it in all the national domain, either by force of a congressional slave code, which the President recommends in this message, or by force of Territorial legislation, enacted by virtue of congressional grants of power.

Sir, it is in such legislation as I have named, or in the attempt to inaugurate such legislation, that the President's party, sometimes misnamed the Democratic party, lives, and moves, and has its being. The time was, at the organization of this government, when it was conceded by every State and every great statesman in the land, that it was the right and the duty of the federal government to exclude slave labor and chattel slavery from every rood of the national domain, and to protect the free labor of freemen, not only in the Territories of the United States, but in every State of the Union, north, south, east and west, and wherever the jurisdiction of the government extended, either on the land or the sea.

In that day, sir, the grand words of the constitution, " to establish justice, to promote the general welfare, and secure the blessings of liberty," were not denounced as " glittering generalities," or the utterances of " infant philosophers ; " but were reverently held, believed in, and acted upon, as absolute verities. Then, sir, to promote the general welfare Congress — the First Congress — legislated for the greatest good of the greatest number, by protecting the free labor of the whole country ; and to establish justice and secure the blessings of liberty, that Congress re-enacted the ordinance of 1787 (which had ceased with the confederation to be law), for the government of all the national territory ; declaring thereby that no person therein should ever be enslaved, except for crime ; or be deprived of life or liberty, but by due process of law and the judgment of his peers ; nor of his property the product of his toil, without just compensation. Under the influence of this legislation, enacted in the very spirit of the constitution, and sanctioned by the great name of Washington, the country commenced its sublime march of independence; and was not then, as now, possessed of that devil, that demon spirit, which to-day rends and distracts her.

In that day, sir, it was everywhere declared and admitted that slavery did not exist by virtue of the constitution; that the constitution did not operate on any class of men, black or white, as property, but only and always as persons; that the institution of slavery was purely local, sectional, not national; existing only within the limits of such of the States as tolerated it, and there only by force of local, not national, law; that slavery was a great evil to the master and slave, foreign to the spirit of our laws and institutions, an evil to be softened, not aggravated, to be got rid of and ended, not to be spread into new lands to be perpetuated and eternized. Unhappily, the time came in the history of the Republic when these just sentiments and this wise national legislation to which I have referred, came to be questioned and denounced.

This was the beginning of this sectional strife. When and by whom was this strife inaugurated, by whom has it been continued, and who and what party are responsible for its continuance?

In the year 1803, by a treaty of purchase, the United States acquired from France the Territory of Louisiana. This acquisition was made confessedly without warrant in the constitution, but under a supposed public necessity. In 1804, an organic act was passed for the government of so much of this Territory as lay south of the thirty-third parallel of north latitude. By that act the traffic in foreign and domestic slaves was prohibited in that Territory, under the penalty of fine and the emancipation of the slaves. Jefferson, in his approval of this act, was either ignorant or careless of the alleged duty of this government to protect the slave property of the citizens of the slave States in the national Territories. It was clearly a violation of this alleged duty to provide that the citizen should not traffic in his slave property in that Territory without subjecting himself to fine and forfeiture.

The subsequent organization of Missouri as a slave State within that Territory, and her application for admission as such into the Union, gave rise to the first great sectional conflict, which was finally determined by the admission of that State, and the enactment of the compromise act of 1820, by which chattel slavery was forever excluded from all that territory lying west of Missouri and north of the parallel of thirty-six degrees thirty minutes north latitude.

After this compromise, the nation reposed in peace, and its policy in favor of free territory and the protection of free labor was deemed settled, until about the year 1830, when, under the beneficent effects of this policy, it became apparent that, unless it was abandoned, slavery itself must give way and cease to be in the slave States, by the general consent and in obedience to the ever-increasing demands for free labor. Then, sir, Maryland tolerated open and active efforts among her citizens for the abolition of domestic slavery. Then Kentucky tolerated like efforts for the abolition of slavery among her citizens; and Virginia saw and felt in every fibre of her existence that she must either throw off that giant wrong, or perish in its embrace. Her legislative assembly about that time engaged in a debate on the question of the total abolition of the system; some of her ablest citizens insisting upon it, foremost among whom was a distinguished gentleman who, but the other day, was appointed

our minister plenipotentiary to France [Mr. Faulkner] who
repeated the expressive and prophetic admonition of Jefferson: "You must adopt some plan of emancipation, or worse
will follow." It was then, sir, that in the South this sectional strife was again renewed, by opposing emancipation
and by making war upon the great and beneficent policy of
protection to free labor. That strife was by the South
brought into these halls, and here inaugurated, by demanding that the system of protecting and encouraging the free
labor of the freemen of this country by legislation should be
abandoned. That sectional party in the South, then, as now,
ostracized every open and avowed friend of emancipation
and of protection to free labor. . . .

Whatever pretexts may have been urged, the real purpose
of the South, in assailing this policy of protection, was to
secure an advantage to the slave-owners of the South, at the
expense of the free laborers of the whole country, North and
South. The abandonment of this system for such a purpose
involved the practical application, in the legislation of the
country, of the specious dogma that the constitution was
made for the minority; it involved the specific disavowal of
the expressed intent and purpose of the constitution, "the
promotion of the general welfare," of the greatest good of
the greatest number; it involved the sacrifice of the interests
of the many for the benefit of the few. What was this,
sir, but a demand that Congress should so legislate as to
make slave labor more profitable, and free labor less profitable?

That has been the demand, the end, and aim, of this sectional party, from that day to this. The watchword of this
party then was, and still is, the expansion and protection
of slavery and slave labor, at the sacrifice of free labor, by

the withdrawal of legislative protection from it. To accomplish the repeal of the laws which protected free labor, then,
as now, the South blustered, and threatened secession and
treason. South Carolina passed her ordinance and test act,
so offensive and treasonable in terms, as to wring from the
gentle spirit of her Grimké, in her Senate Chamber, the
burning invective:

" Your ordinance . . . is the grave of liberty. Before
I will pollute my lips or perjure my soul with your test oath,
you may cut off my right hand and nail it up as a finger-
board to point my way to the gibbet."

That State became a military encampment; the cry to
arms was everywhere heard within her borders, and the
treasonable purpose of armed resistance to the laws everywhere proclaimed.

Strange, sir, that armed resistance in South Carolina
to the national laws for the protection of free labor should
be hailed as patriotism, and those who advised or attempted
it crowned with honors, while an old man, into whose soul
the iron of oppression has entered, who, in his wild dream
of duty, lifts his hand against the slave laws of Virginia,
hoping thereby to shiver the fetters which bind four million
of men, and lift them from the darkness of their prison-house
into the sunlight of liberty, is denounced as a traitor, and
strangled as a felon. What part, sir, did the President, who
now complains of sectional strife, play in this sectional raid
upon the laws and the interests of free labor, in this attempt
to paralyze the mighty arm of intelligent industry, in which
is the nation's strength, in order to secure increased profits
to the few, who produce by proxy, and live upon the unpaid
toil of slaves ?

Go read the record of his shameless surrender of the interests and rights of free labor to the rebels against the law, the conspirators against the national prosperity. I commend that page which records his conflict with honest John Davis, of Massachusetts. Hear this, our present complacent counsellor and adviser against " sectional hatred and strife," and urge the sectional demands of South Carolina, in words that should be remembered only to blast him: " Reduce," said he, " the standard of prices in this country, to the standard of prices in Europe, and you cover our country with blessings and benefits." That is, make your sons of honest toil, in your fields, and shops, and mines, work for the pittance of sixpence a day, as in plundered, oppressed, and fettered Spain, and France, and Austria, and you cover our country — that is, the non-laboring, non-producing few of the South — " with blessings and benefits." To allay this sectional strife, this demand was, to a great extent, complied with.

Notwithstanding this suicidal change of the national policy, avowedly, to enable the slaveholder to buy cheaper, and sell at an increased profit by obtaining a reciprocal reduction of duties upon his slave products in the foreign market; notwithstanding this blow dealt by the government upon the mighty brotherhood of free, intelligent industry in the North, the free States, though inferior in fertility and in climate and territorial extent and geographical position to the slave States, maintained the ascendency in wealth, population, intelligence; and, unless further interfered with by additional sectional legislation, would inevitably soon assert such an influence in the administration of the government as would permanently restore the time-honored policy of protection to free labor, North and South. That fact was made apparent by the great political revolution of 1840, and the protective enactment of 1842. To check this ever-increasing political influence of free labor — this triumph of freedom over slavery, of light over darkness, of right over wrong — these same pro-slavery sectionalists insisted upon the repeal of the protective act of 1842, and the maintenance by legislation of the political equilibrium of the slave with the free States. That was the proposition of Mr. Calhoun. I regret that an intellect so strong, and once so national as was his, could be cribbed and fettered by this sectional spirit which demanded legislation for the few, to the lasting injury of the many. He yielded to the demands of this sectional spirit, this slave interest, and, as its champion, insisted that the advancing column of free labor should be checked, and made to halt in its rapid and sublime march to await the lagging step of the fettered bondman.

To maintain this political equilibrium, having converted all the territory south of the thirty-sixth parallel into slave States, including Florida, all North was to be declared a trust held in common for the slave and free States, into which slavery was to go with the citizen of the slave States, and to be acknowledged and protected there under the constitution. This proposition involved the avoidance or repeal of all that legislation which had, by the consent of Monroe and Jackson, and Van Buren and Polk, forever excluded slavery from the national Territories between the compromise line of 1820 and the Pacific Ocean. It was but the announcement of that political blasphemy and atheism which declares that it is right to enslave labor, to take away by law from honest toil, and honest endeavor, and honest purpose its just reward — proclaiming that a man shall not reap where he has sown; that he shall not enjoy the fruit of his own toil; that the roof-tree which his own hands have reared shall not be for shelter or defence to him or his children.

To maintain the equilibrium of the slave with the free States, the federal government must, by legislation, counteract the laws of population and growth; must essay to annul the great law of human progress, the law of civilization, that they who cultivate the land shall possess it. Intelligence, the central orb in our industrial, political, and social system, must pale its splendors in the darkening shadows of a perpetual and ever-increasing despotism, that the political equilibrium of the slave States may be maintained. To accomplish this end, this sectional party further demanded that a foreign slave State, as large in territorial extent as New York, Pennsylvania, and Ohio, should be annexed as a slave State to the Union, for the twofold purpose of furnishing to Virginia a new market in which to make merchandise of her children, and securing to a sparse slave population of two hundred thousand a senatorial representation equal to that of the Empire State with her three million freemen.

The proposition shocked right-minded citizens and patriots of all parties and of all sections. The great commoner of Kentucky opposed it as a violation of the nation's plighted faith, and, with the prescience of a seer, proclaimed that its accomplishment would involve the country in the two greatest of all national calamities — national dishonor and national war. That pure and noble man, Mr. J. Q. Adams, who for fifty years had stood a warder of civilization and liberty, denounced it as treason to the rights of man. The once chosen of the Democracy to the chief magistracy, Mr. Van Buren, also denounced it as dangerous to the peace and honor of the country. This proposition, sir, was the very incarnation of that demon spirit of sectional strife. This sectional party banded together and trampled down the good men and true, who rejected, with honest scorn, the monstrous purpose. They hunted the noble and lion-hearted Kentuckian to his grave, and, aided by such traitors to the right in the North as the present chief magistrate, they hunted down the noble and patriotic Silas Wright.

In accomplishing this infamy, this party committed a wanton, deliberate violation of that constitution which the immediate actors in this wrong were sworn to support, that constitution which these same gentlemen have now the audacity to say is with them sacred as life itself! Where, sirs, was your reverence for the constitution when the treaty-making power — the only power under the constitution which can contract with foreign states — was struck down; its solemn rejection of the proposed contract of Texan annexation treated with contempt and set aside by the wicked and flagitious joint resolutions, sustained by a majority of one in the Senate, and by which Texas came into the Union? This perfidious act of aggression was no sooner done, your banner of liberty was no sooner advanced to wave in solemn mockery over a land of slaves in this newly-acquired domain, than this party took another step forward in this war of aggression, and asserted that the left bank of the Rio Grande was the western boundary of this new slave State, and, to establish it, sent the army of the United States forward, under the lead, but against the protest, of that brave man, Zachary Taylor. You did establish and mark that line, not only by the waters of that river, rolling in silent majesty from the mountains to the sea, but you marked it as well by an ineffaceable, crimson line of blood.

Having thus fixed the Texan boundary, this sectional

party demanded indemnity for the past and security for the future. Indemnity, sir, for what? Not for what we lost, but for what we took and held by force, and without color of right. Security for what? Not security for a violated constitution; not security for the rights of freemen and free labor, which had been cloven down; but security for the "great humanitarian fact," as the gentleman from Alabama [Mr. Curry] called the institution of slavery. To this end, this sectional party, by the national arm, conquered large portions of Mexico, and annexed them, softening the venality of the act by the formula of a constrained treaty of peace at Guadalupe Hidalgo. That these acquisitions were made for this purpose, let the subsequent conduct of this sectional party bear witness.

California, a portion of this Mexican acquisition, was rich in gold, in a genial climate, in a fruitful soil, and commanding in geographical and commercial position. Such a country was not without strong attractions to an ardent, energetic, and adventurous people. They forsook all the endearments, and burst away from all the ties of home and kindred, and took possession of the land of gold. A nation was born in a day. A new State was thus created as by magic, washed by the quiet waves and guarded by the Golden Gates of the great Pacific. The people of California, and also of New Mexico, formed each a free constitution, and hand in hand they came, in the white robes of freedom, asking for admission as free States into the Union. This constitutional exercise of the right of petition was made the occasion for a wild storm of sectional agitation.

In the midst of the tumult, the brave patriot, President Taylor, the chosen of the people, resident in the South, but not of this sectional party; full of years and full of honors; calm and collected, just and honest, with a patriarchal simplicity, said, let these new free States come in; there is room for them in the paternal mansion — in that great Union built for freedom by those mighty men of old, whom God taught to build for glory and for beauty. No, cried this sectional party, we insist that the proposed constitutions embrace too much territory for perpetual freedom; those Territories must be divided; a part of these great regions at least must be kept in reserve for slavery; they, together with Utah, must be divided by the thirty-sixth parallel. That was the ultimatum; it must be acceded to, or the Union should perish.

These sectional partisans hissed like so many serpents upon the path of the brave old man, President Taylor, whose whole life had been spent in the camp or on the battle-field. He was denounced as a traitor — not to his country, but to the slave interest — and was hunted, with a relentless persecution, to his grave. He adhered, thank God — he adhered with more than an eastern devotion, to the right of the people and the highest interests of the country. Thus steadfast in his great purpose, the last summons came, not too soon for him, but too soon for us. Death laid his hand upon that manly form, and at its touch his great and noble spirit departed, articulating those grand words, noble as ever fell from hero's or patriot's lips before, "I have tried to do my duty." Sir, it was not in the field of poised battle; it was not when the earthquake and the fire led the charge; it was not when victory, with its lance-light and triumph singing, threw its splendors around the person of that heroic man, that his great character so fully revealed itself, as in that dread hour, and the near coming of the shadow of death, when he said, "I have tried to do my duty."

When all was over, when the strong arm which had conquered, and the clarion voice which had commanded in the storm of battle, were powerless and hushed, those who had assailed his motives — who had resisted his purposes of justice and fair dealing with the young Pacific States — those sectional agitators and aggressors took fresh courage, whispering, like gibbering ghosts, above his perished dust, "after life's fitful fever he sleeps well." The agitation, the aggression, the conspiracy against free principles, free labor, and equal rights, went on. California was admitted; but New Mexico was rejected, and remanded to the condition of a territorial organization, with the concession to the slave interest that Congress should not then exercise its admitted power of legislation for the protection of liberty and right, either in that Territory or in Utah.

Yes, sir; the free North, with her twenty million of freemen, for the sake of peace, submitted to the humiliation of the demand of this sectional party, that in those vast Territories the law of God should not be re-enacted, as Mr. Webster called the law of liberty. That great man, now sleeping in his tomb by the great sea, at the demand of this power, yielded up his own convictions, and not only consented to this, but joined with others in yielding a reluctant assent to the enactment of the Fugitive Slave Law of 1850 — a law which, in direct violation of the constitution, transfers the judicial power from judges duly appointed by the President, with the consent of the Senate, to irresponsible commissioners appointed by the circuit courts, tendering them a bribe of five dollars, if, upon *ex parte* evidence — the affidavit of some unknown man, taken in the rice swamps of Florida, it may be, before some justice of the peace — he shall adjudge a man brought before him on his warrant, a fugitive slave, guilty of the crime of preferring liberty to bondage.

That flagitious law insults the conscience of the people, by declaring it a crime to exercise that highest duty enjoined by God upon man — charity. That law also discriminates most offensively in favor of slave property over all other movable property, by providing that the slave-owner or claimant may, on his affidavit, have his property restored to him at the national expense; while, if the cattle of a Northern farmer escape into another State, he must reclaim them at his own expense.

I should like to be informed of the constitutional provision for this discrimination. Can it be accounted for upon any other hypothesis than that this government is made exclusively to expand, maintain, and protect, the slave institution, and to legislate exclusively for the pecuniary and political benefit of three hundred and fifty thousand slaveholders? The people are told that they shall not repeal this act of 1850, or the Union will fall. How comes it that the Union lasted for sixty years without this enactment? Having thus saved the Union by enacting the fugitive law of 1850, and by refusing, in the territorial acts for Utah and New Mexico, to re-enact the law of God, these sectional disturbers and aggressors, in Democratic convention at Baltimore, in 1852, resolved to suppress all agitation of this question, either in or out of Congress.

Thus, to maintain as a finality this legislation for slavery, this sectional party attempted to muzzle the press, and stifle the lowest whisper of the national conscience, even in humble protest against this infamous enactment. These gentlemen did not themselves obey their own officious and insulting order of silence. The whole country knows who opened anew this angry controversy in 1854, and filled the whole land with the agitation of this question, by the repeal of the eighth section of the act of 1820, known as the Missouri Compromise, under the false pretence of giving to the people of the great Territories north of that line the right of self-government, under the title of popular sovereignty. The demagogue cry was: the people of a Territory, like the people of a State, are perfectly free to establish slavery, black or white. True, the federal government appoints for all the Territories their governors, judges, and marshals; prescribes the qualifications of their electors; limits, as well as confers, their legislative powers; and approves or annuls, at pleasure, all their legislative enactments; but the people have the right to enslave and sell one another. "This," said the President, "is a right as old as the right of self-government"—the right to do wrong, and to be supported in that wrong by the nation. This right of popular sovereignty not only includes the right to convert a man into property, but, for reasons of State necessity, to roast and eat him, if they see fit.

The President, as the chief of this sectional party, in one year after his inauguration, announced, as another principle of this sectional party, that slavery exists in all the Territories, not by virtue of this ancient right of self-government, but by virtue of the constitution of the United States. To make good this proposition, this party, aided by the President, attempted to fasten the Lecompton slave constitution upon the people of Kansas, against their protest — that constitution which declared that it should never be so altered or amended as to affect the ownership of property in slaves, and that this property was higher than all constitutions. This sectional party, foiled in this attempt to legalize this atrocity only by the united action of the Republican party on this floor, next enacted that other statute, the English bill, for the double purpose of restricting the exercise of the right of petition, and of fettering the progress of free labor by the formation of a free State. The population, all-sufficient for a slave State, was held not sufficient for a free State. The demon spirit of this enactment can be seen in the declaration of the President, that slavery exists in Kansas by virtue of the constitution of the United States, and therefore Kansas is as much a slave State as Georgia or South Carolina.

This dogma is the burden of the message now before us. The President has not more than concluded his invocation "to allay the demon spirit," than he informs us that the supreme court has finally determined the question of slavery in the Territories, and established the right of every citizen to take his slave property into the Territories and "have it protected there under the constitution;" and that "neither Congress, nor a territorial legislature, nor any human power, has any authority to annul or impair this vested right." Yes, sir, we are gravely told that a mere stump speech, made in the supreme court in the Dred Scott case, on this territorial question, whereof the court had confessedly no jurisdiction, is a final judicial decision which has "irrevocably fixed the status of a Territory" as a slave Territory. "Had it been decided," says the President, "that either Congress or the territorial legislature possess the power to impair the right of property in slaves, the evil would be intolerable." It is settled that the judiciary must relieve against such territorial legislation as impairs this right, and that Congress "must strengthen their hands by further legislation." I submit that it was bad enough for this party to declare, as it did, from 1854 to 1856, that the scattered settlers of a Territory were perfectly free to enslave their fellow men in the Territories; but who can fathom that lower deep of infamy to which it descends when it avers that property in slaves within the

Territories is a vested right, to be protected by a congressional slave code?

The President seems to think, and so to instruct us, that we are to be bound by the decisions of the supreme court in the discharge of our duties here. The time was, sir, when the President thought and spoke differently. In the Senate, in 1841, when the fiscal bank bill was under consideration, this same person, now President, then a senator, on being told that the constitutionality of the question had been settled by the supreme court, said:

" If the judiciary had settled the question I should never hold myself bound by their decision. . . . If they failed to convince me that the law was constitutional, I should be guilty of perjury before high heaven if I voted in its favor."—Congressional Globe, vol. 10, page 163.

If the supreme court is to decide all constitutional questions for us, why not refer every question of constitutional power to that body, not already decided, before acting upon it. I recognize the decisions of that tribunal as of binding force only as to the parties and privies to the suit, and the rights particularly involved and passed upon. The court has no power, in deciding the right of Dred Scott and of his children to their liberty, to decide, so as to bind this body, that neither Congress, nor a territorial legislature, nor any human power, has authority to prohibit slavery in the Territories; neither has that tribunal the power to decide that five million persons, born and domiciled in this land, "have no rights which we are bound to respect." The judiciary are entitled to respect; but if they arrogate powers not conferred upon them, and attempt by such arrogation of power to take away the legislative power of the whole people, and to deprive large numbers of them of their natural rights, I claim, as a representative, the right to disregard such assumed authority, and as a citizen and a man, to appeal from such decision to that final arbiter, the public opinion of the country.

With Jefferson, I deny that the supreme court is the final arbiter on all questions of political power, and assert that the final arbiter on all such questions is the people — that people which ordained the constitution. While I would condemn armed resistance to any decision of the supreme court, or to the execution of any statute of the United States, I would claim for myself, in common with all my fellow citizens, the right to question their propriety, to denounce their injustice, and to insist that whatever is wrong therein shall be corrected. This is one of "the powers reserved to the people." While the people should habitually revere the judiciary as the ministers of justice, they should not forget that the judge is fallible, and sometimes stains his ermine with that darkest of all crimes that ever blackened the sunny page of human life — the crime of judicial murder! That people which are jealous of all delegated power, whether judicial, legislative, or executive, and ready to avenge the wanton and oppressive abuse of it, are most likely to maintain their liberties.

England had her judicial monster, Jeffreys, who could hang his court in scarlet, fit emblem of cruelty and injustice; who could condemn, without a hearing, innocent men and women to a speedy and violent death, mocking at their fear and laughing at their calamity. That was a just retribution which overtook him when he was made to skulk and hide from the wrath of an outraged people; to disfigure his face and disguise his person in filthy apparel, in hope to elude their stern, searching gaze. Vain hope! no disguise could hide the features of that terrible face, which had glared upon the people from the high places of power with a ferocity that filled them with horror. He who had been chief justice of the king's bench, and lord high chancellor of England; who could boast a judicial massacre of three hundred and twenty victims; this man, unapproached in infamy, in order to be saved from the fury of the people, was trundled by the train-bands through the streets of London, pallid with fear and begrimed with dust, at his own request was committed to the Tower; and accepted with thankfulness the protection of those dark walls, made famous by so many crimes and sorrows, there to remain, amid gloom and solitude, friendless and alone, until remorse should gnaw away his heartstrings, and send him to his last account. With such an example before us, we, the lineal descendants of those who witnessed and avenged Jeffreys's judicial crimes, are not to be told that the judiciary are, at pleasure, and by the assumption of power, to bind the conscience and dispose of the liberties and lives of the people!

But, sir, the President respects the decisions of the supreme court only when it suits his purpose, and accords with the interests of slavery and the demands of the sectional slave party. In this message, in which the President claims that the supreme court has finally settled the vested right of property in slaves beyond the power of Congress or a Territorial legislature, or any human authority, to affect it, he tells us that the Spanish claimants in the " Amistad case " are clearly entitled to compensation under the Spanish treaty of 1795, and recommends that an appropriation be made for that purpose out of the national treasury.

What is this "Amistad" case? Who are these Spanish claimants? On the 28th day of June, 1839, a Spanish schooner, named "Amistad," sailed from the port of Havana, in Cuba, bound to Puerto Principe, in the same island, having on board Captain Ferrer, and two Spanish gentlemen named Ruiz and Montez; also fifty-three Africans, claimed and held by these Spaniards as their slaves. These fifty-three persons were natives of Africa, speaking an African dialect. Ignorant and uninstructed as they were, they had the natural love of liberty, and the natural affections of humanity for home and kindred, sweet visions of which soothed their troubled rest amid the horrors of that second death, the Middle Passage.

The felon-ship, with its cargo of human souls, moved out, like a thing of life, over the calm, blue waters of that western sea, on which was seen, sinking beneath its waves, the lifeless body of one of those captive children of sorrow. The felonship floats on. The day is gone; the mists of night gather, "low and cold, like the shadow of death, upon the doomed and guilty vessel, as it labors in darkness amid the lightnings of the sea, its thin masts written upon the sky in lines of blood, and girded with condemnation." The uplifted arm of one of those sons of wrong and oppression, made strong by the mighty arm of the God of the oppressed, comes down in terrible retribution upon the master at the helm, and he falls a lifeless corpse upon the deck. His body is consigned, with that of his captive who had gone before, to the same silent burial in the deep waters, there to rest until the sea gives up its dead!

On the 27th of August, 1839, the United States brig "Washington" captured the vessel and crew, off the coast of the United States, and brought her into the port of New London, Connecticut. The officers of the brig filed a libel in the District Court of the United States for the district of Connecticut, against the vessel, cargo, and slaves, for salvage.

On the 29th of August, 1839, Ruiz and Montez filed in that court claims to the negroes as their slaves, and claimed the right to hold them under the treaty of 1795. The United States attorney for the district of Connecticut filed an information, stating that the minister of Spain had claimed of the government of the United States, that the vessel, cargo, and slaves should be restored under the provisions of the treaty of 1795, between Spain and the United States. On the 23d of January, 1840, the district judge made a decree in the case, wherein is recited the decree of the government of Spain, made December, 1817, prohibiting the slave-trade, and declaring all negroes brought into the dominions of Spain by slave-traders free, and enjoining the execution of the decree on all officers of Spain in all her dominions.

The court decided that these Africans were kidnapped, and could not be held or claimed under the treaty of 1795. From this decree the United States, in pursuance of the demand of the Minister of Spain, duly accredited to the United States, appealed to the circuit court of the United States for the district of Connecticut. The circuit court affirmed the decree of the district court in the premises; and from this decree of the circuit court, the United States appealed to the supreme court. At the January term, 1841, of the supreme court of the United States, this great cause came on to be heard upon the claim of Ruiz and Montez to these Africans as their slaves, and the answer of the kidnapped Africans, that they were natives of Africa, born free, and of right ought to be free, and not slaves; that in the land of their nativity they were unlawfully kidnapped, and forcibly, and against their will, and under circumstances of great cruelty, carried to Cuba. Spain, and the "Spanish claimants," Ruiz and Montez, were ably represented on the trial of the cause

F by the attorney-general of the United States, Mr. Gilpin. These Africans, captives in a strange land, awaited with fear the issue, in the prisons of Connecticut. To the honor of our country and of our common humanity, these captives found an advocate in one of the most remarkable men of his time, or any time, now gone, the profound and illustrious John Quincy Adams — that venerable man, who had filled the highest and most responsible trusts of his country, and had conferred honor upon each. After an absence of a third of a century from the presence of that great tribunal, Mr. Adams appeared to plead the cause of the poor, the oppressed, and defenceless. He said:

"I appear to plead the cause of justice, . . . of liberty, and life, in behalf of many of my fellow men, before that same court which, in a former age, I had addressed in support of the rights of property."

Touching was his allusion to the fact, that he stood before the same court, but not before the same judges — Marshall and his great associates were gone to join the illustrious dead — stronger than any formal argument was his statement:

"This court is a court of justice; and justice demands that the rights of each party should be allowed to himself."

It was in vain that the treaty of 1795 was set up by the attorney-general as securing to Ruiz and Montez the right to hold these men, women, and children, as their chattels, against their paramount right to themselves, by the law of nature and of nature's God. The court decided the case; and, by their solemn judgment, declared that the kidnapped Africans were free, and should be dismissed from custody, and go hence without day. They did go hence. They went back to their own country, under the protection of our flag, singing their simple songs of thanksgiving to him and his servants who had delivered them from the hand of the spoiler.

How comes it, sir, that the President has so high a regard for the decision of the Supreme Court in the Dred Scott case, and so profound a contempt for its decision in the "Amistad" case? Is it because the Dred Scott case is a decision against liberty and life, and the "Amistad" case a decision in favor of liberty and life? By what logic does the President hold the one binding upon us, and the other not binding upon us? He recommends an appropriation to be made by us, to be paid to Spain, to be distributed among these Spanish claimants, "because," he says, "they are clearly entitled to restitution under the treaty of 1795." Appropriate out of your treasury money to be paid to Ruiz and Montez to the amount of the value of fifty-three human souls. Have you that amount in your treasury? What is the value of a human soul? The question, "What will a man give in exchange for his soul?" has been asked, but never answered. In keeping with this recommendation of the President, to pay those Spanish claimants for their kidnapped Africans, is that other recommendation for the purchase of Cuba and her six hundred thousand slaves, at a price. As a representative and citizen of the United States, I beg leave to protest against this attempt to convert this government into a mere pirate and slave-trader.

This traffic in slaves is condemned and outlawed by all civilized nations. By statute we have declared this traffic on the high seas piracy, and punishable with death. By our treaty at Ghent, with Great Britain, we have solemnly declared, without respect to time or place, that "the traffic in slaves is irreconcilable with the principles of humanity and justice," and that both Great Britain and the United States "are desirous of continuing their efforts to promote its entire abolition;" and it is thereby agreed "that both the contracting parties shall use their best endeavors to accomplish so desirable an object." (U. S. Statutes at Large, vol. 8, p. 223.)

The President gravely says that we should annex Cuba in order to put an end to the African slave-trade, and that until this is done there is no hope for benighted Africa. The sincerity of the President's professions of sympathy for "benighted Africa" might not tax our credulity quite so much, if the President had executed our laws against this traffic at home, and if he had not asked us to pay these Spaniards for kidnapping Africa's children.

This Cuban annexation is only another attempt by legislation to maintain the political equilibrium of the slave with the free States, by the increase of slave representation in Congress. While this sectional party thus press these sectional measures upon us and upon the country, with equal zeal they resist all attempts to enact into a law that much-needed and beneficent national measure, the Homestead Bill, which has thrice passed this House, and has been as often defeated by this sectional party in the Senate. That measure, sir, which would give free homes to the homeless families of all our citizens, North and South (and in the latter section they are legion) finds no favor in this message, and was but the other day resisted and attempted to be defeated by the vote of every representative of the slave interest, save one, on this floor. This measure would fill our vast Territories with a free and industrious population; would greatly increase the number of landed proprietors, and the measure of our wealth; it would secure to every family the means of acquiring that competence which, politically speaking, is the very rock of life, on which the citizen may stand erect, unawed by power, unbribed by gain, ready to return the supercilious sneer, to smile at the haughty frown, to give to truth its due force, and scorn "the embroidered lie."

This measure, so just, so national, and beneficent, is resisted by this sectional party. There stands the long list of aggressions of this sectional. Democratic party, to which, in the brief time allowed me, I have but referred:

The repeal of the laws for the protection of free labor; the repeal of the laws for the protection of freedom and free labor in the Territories; the conquest of foreign territory for slavery; the admission into the Union of a foreign slave State; the rejection by this sectional party of the Homestead Bill; the restriction of the right of petition; the restoration of fugitive slaves at the national expense; the attempt to reward slave pirates for kidnapping Africans; the attempt to acquire Cuba, with her six hundred thousand slaves; the attempt to fasten upon an unwilling people a slave constitution; the attempt to enact a sedition law, thereby restricting the freedom of the press and the freedom of speech, in direct violation of the constitution, which declares that Congress shall make no law abridging either; and the attempt, by extra-judicial interference, to take away from the people and their representatives the power to legislate for freedom and free labor in the Territories.

MITCHEL

JOHN MITCHEL, an Irish patriot and journalist, was born November 3, 1815, near Dungiven, County Derry, Ireland. His father was a Presbyterian clergyman. He studied at Trinity College, Dublin, and after practising as an attorney became assistant editor of the "Nation," the organ of the Young Ireland party. In 1848 he withdrew from the Association and issued a new journal called the "United Irishman," in which he boldly threw down the gauntlet to Lord Clarendon, the Lord-Lieutenant of Ireland, whom he termed "Her Majesty's Executioner-General and General Butcher of Ireland." He was arrested, March 21, 1848, on the charge of publishing three seditious articles, and just after his release on bail was rearrested on a charge of treason-felony. He was convicted and sentenced to transportation for fourteen years. In 1853 he escaped from Van Diemen's Land to the United States, when he published his "Jail Notes." He established the "Citizen" in New York and subsequently the "Southern Citizen" in Knoxville, Tennessee. During the Civil War he was editor of the "Richmond Examiner" and supported the cause of slavery and the South. At the close of the war he suffered imprisonment, but on his release by order of President Johnson he started the "Irish Citizen" in New York. Returning to Ireland in 1874, he was elected to Parliament from Tipperary; but when declared ineligible he was re-elected. He died in 1875. He published "A Life of Hugh O'Neill" (1845) for the "Library of Ireland," and a "History of Ireland from the Treaty of Limerick" (1868).

THE LAW IN IRELAND

SPEECH DELIVERED FROM THE DOCK AT DUBLIN, MAY 26, 1848

I HAVE to say that I have been found guilty by a packed jury—by the jury of a partisan sheriff—by a jury not impanelled even according to the law of England. I have been found guilty by a packed jury obtained by a juggle—a jury not impanelled by a sheriff, but a juggler.

[The high sheriff hereupon called for the protection of the court, upon which Baron Lefroy interposed and declared that the imputation was unwarranted and unfounded, and then proceeded to pass sentence of transportation beyond the seas for a term of fourteen years. John Mitchel broke the silence that followed the realization of the severity of this sentence thus:]

The law has done its part, and the Queen of England, her Crown and government in Ireland, are now secure, pursuant to act of Parliament. I have done my part also. Three months ago I promised Lord Clarendon, and his government in this country, that I would provoke him into his courts of justice, as places of this kind are called, and that I would force him publicly and notoriously to pack a jury against me to convict me, or else that I would walk a free man out of this court and provoke him to a contest in another field. My lord, I know I was setting my life on that cast, but I knew that in either event the victory should be with me, and it is with me. Neither the jury, nor the judges, nor any other man in this court presumes to imagine that it is a criminal who stands in this dock.

I have shown what the law is made of in Ireland. I have shown that her Majesty's government sustains itself in Ireland by packed juries, by partisan judges, by perjured sheriffs.

I have acted all through this business, from the first, under a strong sense of duty. I do not repent anything that I have done, and I believe that the course which I have opened is only commenced. The Roman who saw his hand burning to ashes before the tyrant promised that three hundred should follow out his enterprise. Can I not promise for one, for two, for three, aye for hundreds?

[These words were responded to by an outburst of voices exclaiming—"For me! for me! promise for me, Mitchel! and for me!" together with applause, during which the prisoner was removed.]

ON THE IRISH CAUSE

[On the 12th of October, 1853, Mr. Mitchel landed at San Francisco after his escape from penal exile in Van Diemen's Land. He received an enthusiastic welcome and on the 25th of the same month attended a grand banquet held in his honor at which the governor of California presided. To the toast, "John Mitchel and the Independence of Ireland." Mr. Mitchel replied in part as follows:]

GOVERNOR BIGLER, AND CITIZENS OF SAN FRANCISCO,—You will not wonder—you will indulge me a little, me a captive of five years, after five weary years of living death, immured in dungeons by land and sea, or eating the bitter bread of penal exile in the depths of the forests of a convict colony—if my senses are somewhat overpowered by the thunders of your welcome to a free land. I seem like one slowly opening his eyes to the light of the outer world after a long and painful trance, and the splendor of this republican festival dazzles me.

Perhaps, if I had obeyed the dictates of that humility which becomes a defeated man and a hunted fugitive—if I had taken counsel of my own quiet disposition, naturally averse to display and ostentation, I should have asked permission respectfully to decline the honor you do me this day. God knows it is in no triumph we Irish rebels set foot upon your shores, Americans!

With the load of our chains only just shaken off, and the load of our inglorious defeat—which is bitterer than chains and cannot be shaken off—still heavy on our souls—with some of our dear comrades still pining in bondage—with the bloodhounds of the enemy still questing on our track behind, and a wide world before us, where we have no home, no country—it might be thought happiness enough for us to

fling ourselves, exhausted at last, safe under the hospitable
shadow of your Eagle's wings.

But the terms in which I have been invited to this board
leave me no room for such feelings. I must not think of
myself when you offer me sympathy with my cause. And
Americans, I have heard, are observant of what passes in the
world. You know well what that cause is and what that
sympathy implies.

Here is much more than personal compliment; here is
something that supersedes and would make ridiculous the
affectation of personal diffidence. I, indeed, am nothing; but
liberty is sacred, and Ireland is dear, and justice is eternal;
and my cause was, and is, and while I live shall be, the cause
of Irish freedom against English tyranny—Irish rights
against English bayonets—it is the cause of independent industry for our own living, against base pauperism for England's gain—it is that same old and dear cause of Irish re-
publicanism to which our fathers were sworn in '98, and for
which Tone labored and lived, and for which Emmet could
but die.

Knowing all this, you tender, not to me, but to my country,
on this first point of American land I touch, your frank and
manly indorsement of that righteous cause. And could I
presume to decline this? Could I, with an impudent
modesty, deprecate your sympathy with Ireland's wrongs,
your honest indignation against Ireland's enemies and op-
pressors? No, no; I exult in this hearty welcome. I thank
you for it from my very soul. I take a grim delight in it;
for well I know the warm words of cheer you give me to-
night will reach the poor hearths of some of my broken and
desponding countrymen, and kindle in their hearts again
some sparks of the fire of manhood—the loud echo of free-

men's scorn will ring in the ears of our tyrants in their high places, and bid them beware of the next earthquake of the nations.

Who will dare talk to me of despair? Who is abject enough to despair of the cause of right, and truth, and freedom? In Ireland, indeed, truth has long been called a lie by act of Parliament, and that ancient passion for liberty has been well-nigh, as the enemy hopes, crushed and trampled out of her; but, after all, Irishmen are not negroes—they still belong to that family of the human race whence sprung the heroes and the demi-gods. High hearts and strong hands are bred there still, and the cup of slavery is still a bitter draught, as of old, and the sting of universal contempt is maddening, and time and chance wait on all men, and steel still cuts, and fire still burns—and heaven is above us all.

The graves, indeed, of two millions of our famished, murdered nation will not give up their dead, though the graves are shallow and the dead coffinless. The seven years of Ireland's sore agony in the talons of British civilization have been endured—they cannot be erased from the calendar—they cannot be forgotten—they shall not be forgiven. Nations have no future state, and therefore national punishments and compensations come in this world; and as surely as " sorrow tracketh crime " that foul British Empire will be brought to a strict accounting—Ireland will yet have her victory and her revenge.

High words these, some men will say. The unhappy being forgets, they will say, that he has been five years brooding in solitary cells, or buried in the forests of the antipodes; he forgets human progress, and electric telegraphs, and how far the species has been striding ahead while he has been gnawing his own heart in a jail; he forgets that the Irish he once knew are mostly dead or fled, and the remnant contented, or cowed, or bought,—and bought cheap enough; and so, they will say, he begins to rave about the cruel Saxon and the rights of Irish nationhood, that empty sound the very echoes of which have died out in the wailings of famine, or been wafted over the Atlantic, or drowned in the pæans of peace and joy that hailed a Queen's visit and a Crystal Palace.

I know what the slaves and cowards will say. I know their cruel cant. And I say to them again that I had considered all that. Too well and keenly I feel what a gulf yawns between the to-day of Ireland and the day when I was carried from my home with chains upon my limbs; a gulf deep as the grave, black as the smoke of Tophet. I have heard of the idotic pretence of loyalty that the Irish were once more deluded by British falsehood to make before their tyrant. I have read of their puny and false mimicry of that English humbug of all nations.

Oh! I have heard how Ireland is at last going to begin to be ameliorated, for that two millions and a half of her lawless Celts are famished to death or driven to seek a livelihood in foreign lands—and how the survivors begin to live better —and how a lord-lieutenant continues to encourage the manufacture of tabinet for the viceregal waistcoat, and how a Crystal Palace stands in Dublin to display the productions of Ireland. Oh, mockery! the productions of Ireland! But the committee have not exhibited, as I hear, the real staple and characteristic productions of that country—model paupers in squalid rows—ranks of humble tenants-at-will with their hats in their hands—pyramids of ejectment decrees—basins of transparent poorhouse gruel (a great work of art)—cases of famished corpses, to show how lean an Irishman can walk before he dies, while an Englishman eats his bread—dead children, half-gnawed by wolfish mothers— there were an exposition of Irish industry for a queen of England to open in state—there were the true mirror of the country's condition. But because this ghastly picture is true, it will be carefully turned with its face to the wall, and all manner of glittering, flattering lies will take its place.

Let that palace of falsehood stand while it may—it is but glass. Let the poor worshippers of that obscene golden image which Prince Albert has set up wallow and grovel, eat dirt there, and crave the crumbs that fall from their masters' tables. I tell them that I was a freer man in the Bermuda hulk than the unhappy Irishmen who saunter and simper in the Dublin Crystal Palace and make believe that they are loyal citizens and members of society. Their souls dwell in a hulk. From the brown shades of Tasmanian woods I had a clearer view of the great transactions and destinies of mankind than they in the centre of their vicious civilization and amid the crushing race of hungry candidates for ten thousand offices—which are England's bribes and the Devil's.

Therefore you will see it is not in ignorance or forgetfulness of what has been passing these late years that I dare again to utter the creed of Irish nationality—that I hail your sympathy with Irish rebellion. There are Irishmen here to-night—do you, my countrymen, tell me that our cause is lost forever? Is the history of Ireland over? Do you tell me to go back to my island dungeon, and disturb no more the march of Anglo-Saxon civilization and the Crystal Palace progress of the species? Forgive me the question, my countrymen! Do not our hearts leap out at the very thought of the next European convulsion? Do they not burn within us when we think of all that " peace and order," as tyrants call the chained quiescence of slaves, how it will be shivered to atoms on some early day—a day to be called a white day forever—with a crash which shall shake the pillars of the globe; and how thrones and principalities will totter and rush down into chaos before the stormy wrath and execration of gods and men.

Bear with me. I have plunged at once into the very heart and centre of my absorbing subject. It has been the passion of my life; it has been the dream of my prison hours by day and night. No wonder that I rush so eagerly to meet your offered sympathy, my brother republicans. And let me remind you that I am not a republican because I was transported, but that I was transported because I was a republican. No wonder I gladly hasten to realize to myself the full meaning of that sympathy, and to let all the world, friends and enemies, know the same.

STANLEY

ARTHUR PENRHYN STANLEY, an English clergyman of distinction, was the son of the bishop of Norwich and was born at Alderley, Cheshire, December 13, 1815. He was educated at Rugby under Dr. Arnold, and at Balliol College, Oxford University. He gained a fellowship at University College, Oxford, in 1838, and the next year was admitted to deacon's orders in the Established Church; he was advanced to the priesthood in 1843 and in the same year received an appointment as college tutor. From 1845 to 1847 Stanley was select preacher to the university, his discourses in this capacity being issued in 1847 as "Sermons on the Apostolical Age," and exhibiting very clearly his divergence from High Church and evangelical points of view. He resigned his fellowship in 1851 in order to accept a canonry at Canterbury, but returned to Oxford in 1858 as canon of Christ Church and regius professor of ecclesiastical history. He had already been appointed to such posts of honor as that of chaplain to Prince Albert, in 1854, and chaplain to the Queen and the Prince of Wales in 1862. During these years he came into much prominence as a Broad Church leader, his tolerant mind being opposed in equal measure to severe judgments against the ritualists, or against Bishop Colenso, whose work on the Pentateuch was then convulsing the church. The basis of his theology was insistence upon Christian character rather than dogma as the essential thing in Christianity. In 1863 he declined the archbishopric of Dublin, but accepted in the year following the deanery of Westminster. He had for some years enjoyed the cordial esteem and friendship of the Queen and at the close of 1863 was married to Lady Augusta Bruce, an intimate friend of the Queen. As Dean of Westminster he endeavored to make the services at the Abbey attractive to men of all communions. In 1878 he visited the United States, publishing on his return "Addresses and Sermons Delivered in the United States and Canada." He died at the deanery, July 18, 1881, and was buried in the Chapel of Henry VII. Stanley was a sympathetic rather than a profound scholar, and his writings, while interesting and valuable, can hardly be said to possess enduring excellence. His "Life of Thomas Arnold" (1844) is doubtless his best and most widely known work. Among others are "Lectures on the History of the Eastern Church" (1861); "Lectures on the History of the Jewish Church" (1862-72); "Addresses and Sermons Delivered at St. Andrews" (1877); "Essays, Chiefly on Questions of Church and State from 1850 to 1870" (1870).

SERMON: JESUS OF NAZARETH

" Pilate wrote a title, and put it on the cross. And the writing was,
' Jesus of Nazareth, King of the Jews.' "—John xix, 19.

WHAT are the lessons of Good Friday? especially of Good Friday in Palestine and in this place? In the words of the text, in the title written on the cross, the name of Jesus Christ is at that supreme moment of his Last Passion brought together with the recollection of his early years at Nazareth. What are the lessons which they both teach in common?

Everywhere the event of Good Friday speaks to us of the universal love of God to his creatures. That is why it is so truly called Good Friday. It has its good news as much as Christmas Day or Easter Day. It tells us not only that God is Love, but that he bears love to every one on earth, however far they may seem to be removed from him. It was for this that he sent his Son into the world,— it was for this that Christ died. It was by his death, more even than by his life, that he showed how his sympathy extended far beyond his own nation, his own friends, his own family.

" I, if I be lifted up " on the cross, " will draw all men unto me."

It is this which the Collects of this day bring before us. They speak, in fact, of hardly anything else. They tell us how he died that " all estates," not one estate only, but " all estates in his Holy Church," — that " every member of the Church " in its widest sense, not the clergy or the religious only, but every one, in his " several vocation and ministry," might " truly and godly serve him."

They pray for God's mercy to visit not Christians merely, but all religions, however separate from ours,—" Jews, Turks, Heretics and Infidels,"—in the hope that they may all at last, here or hereafter, be "one fold under one shepherd," the One Good Shepherd who laid down his life not for the flock of one single fold only, but for the countless sheep scattered on the hills, not of the fold of the Jewish people, or of the Christian Church only, but of all mankind.

This is a truth which comes home to us with peculiar force in Palestine. What is it that has made this small country so famous? What is it that has carried the names of Jerusalem and of Nazareth to the uttermost parts of the earth? It is in one word, " the death of Christ." Had he not died as he did, his religion,— his name,— his country,— the places of his birth and education and life,— would never have broken through all the bonds of time and place as they have. That we are here at all on this day, is a proof of the effect which his death has had even on the outward fortunes of the world.

This universal love of God in Christ's death is specially impressed upon us in Nazareth. What Christ was in his death, he was in his life. What he was in his life, he was in his death. And if we wish to know the spirit which pervades both, we cannot do so better than by seeing what we may call the text of his first sermon at Nazareth. He was in the synagogue. The roll of the Hebrew Scriptures was handed to him. He unrolled it. His former friends and acquaintances fixed their eyes upon him to see what he would say.

And what were the words which he chose? They were these: " The Spirit of the Lord is upon me, because he hath anointed me to preach the Gospel to the poor; he hath sent me to heal the broken-hearted, to preach deliverance to the captives, and recovering of sight to the blind, to set at liberty them that are bruised, to preach the acceptable year of the Lord." What he said on this text is not described; we are only told that they "marvelled at the gracious words that proceeded out of his mouth."

But what those gracious words were we can well see from the words of the passage itself.

"The Spirit of the Lord was upon him," first, "to preach the Gospel to the poor," the glad tidings of God's love to the poor, the humble classes, the neglected classes, the dangerous classes, the friendless, the oppressed, the unthought-for, the uncared-for.

The Spirit of God was upon him, secondly, "to heal the broken-hearted:" — to heal, as a good physician heals, not with one medicine, but with all the various medicines and remedies which Infinite Wisdom possesses, all the fractures and diseases and infirmities of our poor human hearts.

There is not a weakness, there is not a sorrow, there is not a grievance, for which the love of God, as seen in the life and death of Christ, does not offer some remedy. He has not overlooked us. He is with us. He remembers us. The Spirit of God was upon him, thirdly, "to preach deliverance to the captive."

Whatever be the evil habit, or the inveterate prejudice, or the master passion, or the long indulgence, which weighs upon us like a bondage, he feels for us, and will do his utmost to set us free,— to set at liberty those that are cramped and bruised and confined by the chain of their sins, their weakness, their misfortunes, their condition in life, their difficulties, their responsibilities, their want of responsibilities, their employments, their want of employments.

And, fourthly, "The Spirit of God was upon him," to

JAMES RUSSELL LOWELL

Orations—Volume eighteen

" give sight to the blind." How few of us there are who know our own failings, who see into our own hearts, who know what is really good for us! That is the knowledge which the thought of Christ's death is likely to give us. That is the truth, which, above all other truths, is likely to set us free. " Lord, that I may receive my sight," is the prayer which each of us may offer up for our spiritual state, as the poor man whom he met at Jericho did for his bodily eyesight.

For every one of these conditions he died. Not for those only who are professedly religious, but for those who are the least so,— to them the message of Good Friday and of Nazareth is especially addressed. Christianity is, one may almost say, the only religion, of which the Teacher addressed himself, not to the religious, not to the ecclesiastical, not to the learned world, but to the irreligious, or the non-religious, to those who thought little of themselves and were thought little of by others, to the careless, to the thoughtless, to the rough publican, to the wild prodigal, to the heretical Samaritan, to the heathen soldier, to the thankless peasants of Nazareth, to the swarming populations of Galilee. He addresses himself now, to each of us, however lowly we may be in our own eyes, however little we think that we have a religious call, however encompassed we are with infirmities; his love is ready to receive, to encourage, to cherish, to save us.

I pass to the other lesson which Good Friday teaches us here. It is that, whatever good is to be done in the world, even though it is God himself who does it, cannot be done without an effort,— a preparation,— a Sacrifice. So it was especially in the death of Christ,— so it was in his whole life. His whole life from the time when he grew up, " as a tender plant " in the seclusion of this valley, to the hour when he died at Jerusalem, was one long effort,— one long struggle.

against misunderstanding, opposition, scorn, hatred, hardship, pain.

He had doubtless his happier and gentler hours, we must not forget them: his friends at Bethany, his apostles who hung upon his lips, his mother who followed him in thought and mind wherever he went. But here, amongst his own people, he met with angry opposition and jealousy. He had to bear the hardships of toil and labor, like any other Nazarene artisan. He had here, by a silent preparation of thirty years, to make himself ready for the work which lay before him. He had to endure the heat and the cold, the burning sun and the stormy rain, of these hills and valleys. " The foxes " of the plain of Esdraelon " have holes," " the birds " of the Galilean forests " have their nests," but " he had " often " not where to lay his head."

And in Jerusalem, though there were momentary bursts of enthusiasm in his behalf, yet he came so directly across the interests, the fears, the pleasures, and the prejudices of those who there ruled and taught, that at last it cost him his life. By no less a sacrifice could the world be redeemed, by no less a struggle could his work be finished.

In that work, in one sense, none but he can take part. " He trod the winepress alone." But in another sense, often urged upon us in the Bible, we must all take part in it, if we would wish to do good to ourselves or to others. We cannot improve ourselves, we cannot assist others, we cannot do our duty in the world, except by exertion, except by unpopularity, except with annoyance, except with care and difficulty. We must, each of us, bear our cross with him. When we bear it, it is lightened by thinking of him. When we bear it, each day makes it easier to us. Once the name of " Christian," of " Nazarene," was an offence in the eyes of the world; now, it is a glory. But we cannot have the glory without the labor which it involves. To "hear his words, and to do them," to hear of his death, and to follow in the path of his sufferings, this, and this only, as he himself has told us, is to build our house, the house of our life; of our faith, of our happiness, upon a rock; a rock which will grow firmer and stronger the more we build upon it, and the more we have to bear.

"The rains may descend, and the floods may come, and the winds may blow and may beat upon that house;" but the house will not fall, "for it will have been founded upon the rock."

OUR COMMON CHRISTIANITY

LECTURE DELIVERED MARCH 22, 1877

THERE is such a thing as Christianity common to all the various churches of Christendom. There are common elements in our faith which may be found, if not in the actual practices and doctrines of the several churches, at any rate in the original documents to which they all appeal.

We are wandering to and fro in the labyrinths of our various churches and sects. What I propose to do is not to compare doctrine with doctrine, or institution with institution, although that might be a very interesting and instructive task, and might, perhaps, lead to the same result. But what I propose to do is to endeavor to penetrate, if possible, behind the forms and doctrines of the outward ordinances of Christendom, and to ask what are the inward principles which give them paramount value; what are the essential supernatural elements of Christianity which are above the assaults of criticism, above the turmoil of the world, because above the level of our ordinary carnal, earthly nature. If we can arrive, in ever so rough and imperfect a measure, at those fundamental principles, we shall then be in a better position to understand what it is that gives a peculiar glory to our common faith.

We will endeavor, then, to answer this question as briefly and as plainly as we can. Let us only observe, first of all, that there are many principles in Christianity which it shares with other religions, and which, therefore, we cannot truly enumerate among its direct results. The unity of God, for example, which is one of the most important of all religious principles, was known to the Jewish people long before the Christian era. It assumed a new form of life; but it was still from Abraham, or at least from Moses, that we first received it. Again, the immortality of the soul was and is a truth which the psalmists in their highest moods had reached, which the Egyptian and Grecian priests and philosophers had accepted. He who was the Light of the world turned, indeed, the full rays of his lamp upon it, and revealed, as you see, its inner meaning; but the principle had already been received, and he illuminated and explained rather than expressly discovered it. But there are some principles which were so little known, or which existed in such feeble rudiments, before Christianity, that practically they were not known at all. Let us, in plain words, try to state what those principles are. Some of them, through the influence of Christianity, have become so familiar to us that we shall, perhaps, be startled to hear them named as among its peculiar products. Some are even now so strange, so little recognized, that it may be almost difficult for us to acknowledge that they are Christian at all.

First, there is the principle of the universal benevolence of the Supreme Ruler of the universe, which is expressed in the words " Father," " Our Father," to believe that the relation of the Supreme Mind to man is that of a father. No doubt the word in relation to the Deity was known before, both in Jewish and heathen times; but it was not manifest, it was not brought to the front of religion as it was by Christianity. In the Old Testament it is used two or three times; but in the New Testament it is used two hundred times. It is the mode in which the Supreme Ruler is expressed throughout the Gospels. It is the name by which he is called in the form of devotion furnished in the New Testament. The Lord's Prayer, or, as it is called in Latin, the " Pater Noster," teaches us these two things: That the Supreme Governor of the world, like a father, is careful of his earthly children; and,

Secondly, that there is not only a universal Deity, but a common humanity; in other words, there is something in every race of man which attracts the divine good will towards them. In the old heathen religions, each country had its own deity, each deity had his own country,— gods of Troy, gods of Greece, gods of Rome; and in the Jewish religion God for a long time was regarded only as the God of the people of Israel: but with Christianity all this was changed. The truth of the universality of God's care for man, and of the universality of a capacity for true religion in man, was known in some degree to some of the Jewish prophets; and it was expressed in one striking sentence by Alexander the Great, when he said, " God is the common father of all men, especially of the best men." But it was placed in the forefront of the Jewish doctrine only when Christianity was revealed. Read the description of the Judgment in the twenty-fifth chapter of St. Matthew, and also the second chapter of the Epistle to the Romans. The supreme object of our worship was now known as the God, not of Judaism only, not of Christianity only, but of all good men,— and, as far as there is any goodness in them, of all men throughout the world.

Thirdly, it is a truth running parallel with this, that in the Christian dispensation morality is religion, and religion, morality; or that religion is the sanctification of morality, and morality is the action of religion. This great principle had, no doubt, been foreshadowed by the warning of the Jewish prophets, and by Grecian philosophers and poets; but it was through the first teaching of Christianity that it assumed paramount importance. However much in the various churches correct opinion, or correct ceremonial, or decoration of churches, or venerations of priesthood and ecclesiastical independence, have taken the place of morality, and however enormous the crimes which have been perpetrated in the name of religion have been, still the better and wiser spirits of every age of Christendom have recognized the fact that the original principles of our faith teach exactly the reverse. Read the description in the beatitudes of those that are truly happy, read the two great commandments, read the twelfth and thirteenth chapters of the Epistle to the Romans, read the thirteenth chapter of the First Epistle to the Corinthians,— and you will see how, in each original conception of Christianity, the moral elements of religion outweigh all others.

Fourthly, it is the goodness thus made most essential in the religious man, and in man altogether, which gives us the best conception of God. This principle no doubt existed in some degree in heathen religion, and to a large degree in the Jewish; but in the former it was liable to constant obscuration. The Homeric divinities, as a general rule, were not better, but worse, than the Homeric heroes; the description of God in the Old Testament, again, was often too far removed from human thought, represented to us in the form of human goodness; but the Christian idea of God was that it is the perfection of virtue and wisdom. God is love; God is light; and when to this we add that the Founder of our religion is set before us, not only as an example of humanity, but as the representation and personification of divinity, this truth concerning the moral nature of the divine essence attains that vividness and power which has never been reached in any other faith. In all these theories, if not equal, at any rate in a predominant and impressive form, the chief, Supreme Ruler is set before us as a mirror in which we see the perfection of the Deity. The more human the representation of his virtues, the more we feel him to be divine. The more attractive and persuasive to all our moral convictions, so much the more we feel that he has disclosed to us the secret of him whom no man hath seen or can see.

But, fifthly, it is not enough that there should be this general identification of morality with religion, or of this perfect human goodness with the divine nature. We have to ask, What are the special points of goodness on which Christianity lays the chief stress? The chief virtues of Greek morality were fortitude, wisdom, self-control, and justice; of the ancient Roman religion, patriotism and imperial courage; of the Hebrew religion, resignation, reverence, and faith. All these several virtues have their places in Christianity; but there are other moral gifts which shine with the most transcendent glory in the New Testament. The main char-

acteristics of the Founder of our religion and of his disciples
are kindness, universal kindness and beneficence, to which
is given the new name of grace, love, or charity; purity in
word and deed, to which is given the new name of holiness,
or consecration to God; truthfulness and absolute sincerity, to
which the very word became a synonym of the Founder's
life; humility and lowliness, for which neither Greek nor
Latin had any adequate expression; — these were the principles which, in the Epistles, were deemed to be essentially
Christian, and which were called divine.

Sixthly, there is the method by which these qualities,
whether in God or man, were to be propagated and extended
in the world.   One is the process which regards the individual
himself: it is self-abnegation; that is, the constant sacrifice
of the lower part of his nature to the highest and best.   In
every one of us there is this higher and this lower nature.
It is for the disciples of Christianity to find out, to endeavor
to find out, what is the better part that is the one thing needful; and for this a transformation, a transfiguration, and a
regeneration of the soul, is necessary; the constant renunciation of that which is behind; the perpetual reaching forward
to that which is before; the noble ambition which is satisfied
with nothing less than the highest ideal.   This sense of the
need of an endless moral renovation and progress, this dissatisfaction with the littleness and meanness of things earthly
and commonplace, and striving after things above us,— that
is what is called in the New Testament by many names, all
meaning the same thing,— conversion, repentance, the second
birth, the cross, the grave, the resurrection, the new life, a
spiritual mind.   Of this, heathen moralists speak but little,—
even the Jewish psalmists and prophets only in their loftiest
flights.   But of this the New Testament is full.   It is the

forgiveness of sins, of which the most consummate picture is given in the story of the Prodigal Son; it is that which is described with a peculiar metaphor throughout the Epistles by the word edification, which means building up one story above another; and that is the new heaven and the new earth which in figure and imagery fills the visions of the Apocalypse.

This leads us, seventhly, to the mode of looking at our fellow men, and the judgment we are to pronounce upon them. It may be called the method, the judgment, of surprises. The principle of the New Testament is that the characters of those of whom we should least expect a great future are those in whom we shall sometimes most surely find it. The irregular and despised publican often comes before the correct Pharisee; the generous prodigal, before the complacent elder brother; the repentant Magdalene, before the supercilious host; the outcast heathen and heretical Samaritan, before the orthodox Jew: the first last, and the last first. On this widely ramifying experience, which cuts across the grain of so many common-place prejudices, both of the ancient and modern world, is built the whole life of the friend of sinners, the shepherd of the lost sheep, the leader of the Christian chivalry, the champion of the weak, the defender of the oppressed, the refuge of the helpless. In it is contained, so to speak, the romance, the poetry, of the gospel. This it is which makes it especially a gospel to the poor even more than the rich, the gospel to the Gentile even more than to the Jew, the gospel to little children even more than to theologians. The gospel may sometimes say to the heathen and misbeliever even more than to the Christian. This is not the way of other religions; this has often not been the way of the Christian religion; but it was in the beginning, and may yet in the end, be the way of the religion of Jesus Christ.

Eighthly, this leads us to yet another kindred principle. It is that which is held with such amazing tenacity by the gifted person lately withdrawn from among us,— Charles Kingsley; the doctrine, namely, that the whole world is God's world, and not the Devil's. There were moments when this was taught both by Hebrew and by Greek; but it was held by Christians, for the gospel set it forth in its most commanding and persuasive form. Alone of the founders of religions, our Founder was no hermit, no ascetic, no visionary, no armed soldier. He lived a social, happy life with the sons and daughters of men: eating and drinking, delighting in the merry faces of little children, considering the lilies of the field and the birds of the air; making no distinction, except for the sake of tender scruples, between Christian and heathen, between the world and the Church; and as he was in his life, so were his first followers in their teaching,— that of all created things, which God had cleansed, there was not one that Peter was allowed to call common or unclean. Among all the institutions of the earth, there is none which Paul regards with so much reverential awe as the laws of the ancient Roman empire. Among all the predictions of St. John, none is more majestic than that which declares that the kingdoms of this world shall become the kingdom of the Lord and of his Christ. The identification of things secular with things sacred, the refusal to acknowledge anything as supremely sacred except what is good, or profane except what is sinful,— this is the wide-reaching principle of the gospel which strikes at the root of a thousand superstitions, and is the fruitful source of a thousand truths. It carries with it the hope of the final triumph of good over evil. It carries with it the germ of all modern philosophy, modern art and statesmanship. This is the element which liberates, redeems, and purifies both the Church and the world.

Along with this there is, ninthly, the principle that the darkest and dreariest side of human life has also a glorious and divine aspect: sorrow, suffering, pain, and death,— all those evils of which the existence and the very thought shake the faith and try the patience, and overcloud the serenity, even of the best, and which in Jewish and in Pagan religions were for the most part regarded as curses and penalties, as signs of wrath, as works of the Devil,— all these are in the gospel transformed and transfigured so as to be represented, if not as blessings, yet at least as the channels of blessings, if not as direct gifts of divine love, yet as opportunities for working out the purposes of that divine love to the human race. The rude manger of Bethlehem, the reproaches of Nazareth, the hardships of Capernaum, the tears of Bethany, the cross of Calvary, all concentrate in one focus what the great German poet Goethe called the divine depth of sorrow,— out of which, as out of all sorrow and pain, is to be wrought the improvement, the redemption, the regeneration, the purification, of mankind. Contrast the Prometheus of Æschylus, contrast the riddle of the book of Job, with the unhesitating, unswerving termination of the gospel story,— the glorified humiliation of bereavement and grief. This is the peculiarity of Christianity, which was but seen afar off by Hebrew prophet or Grecian seer; but which, even in the worst corruptions of Christian faith, has retained its hold on the human spirit.

This leads me, tenthly, to this principle, that religion, as viewed by Christianity, is spiritual; that it depends not on

material or formal or technical questions of any kind, but on
its connection with the invisible spirit of man, with the
invisible spirit of God. Hence the definition that God is a
spirit, and that his true worship is in the spirit; hence the constant use of parables in our Saviour's teaching, that we might
always be taught to turn from the letter to the spirit,— to
remember that the spirit, even in all sacred writings, is greater
than the letter; hence the absence of any form of ritual, or
any form of government, prescribed in the New Testament;
hence the persistent command to look from the outward to
the inward, from the outside to the inside, from the act to
the motive, from external, particular words and deeds to the
character as a whole, from the things which are seen to the
things which are unseen, from the sufferings which are but
for the moment to the eternal which belongs to all time and all
space. It is not that the acts and graces and courtesies of
life are of no value. Yes, they are of value; but their value
is as nothing compared with a high, honorable, upright course
of life. It is not that the splendor of worship or the simplicity of worship, the excellence of music or the beauty of
architecture, have no attraction for the truly Christian mind.
Yes, they have much attraction; but compared with matters
of duty,— compared with charity, forbearance, humility, and
truth,— they have in the judgment of the supreme God very
slight attraction, indeed. Hence, again, the new light thrown
by Christianity, as I said at the outset, on the doctrine of
immortality, the new solution of the perplexing difficulties
concerning a future state,—the principle, namely, that it
rests on spiritual communion with the Eternal. The silence
concerning all details, combined with the clearness of conviction which pervades the New Testament on the divine
existence of the spirit after death, is the crowning consolation

that we have won from the evangelic and apostolic account of the resurrection and of heaven.

These, then, are the ten chief inward principles which lie behind all the facts, institutions, and history of Christianity; which would not, so far as we know, have struck root in the world at all but for the coming of Christianity; and which, wherever they are found bearing fruit, constitute a Christian, whatever be the outward profession; which, wherever they are not found, cause a failure, a falling short of the privileges and the hope, the consolations, of Christianity. These ten principles, let me, for the sake of clearness, briefly repeat. They are,— firstly, the universal benevolence of God as our Father; secondly, the universal capacity for religion in mankind as his children; thirdly, religion is the sanctification of morality, and morality is the action of religion; fourthly, the identification of moral goodness with the divine nature; fifthly, the supreme importance of charity, purity, truth, and humility; sixthly, the necessity and the possibility of continued progress, both in the individual and in the race; seventhly, the reversal of the superficial judgments of the world; eighthly, the identification of things secular and things sacred; ninthly, the divinity of sorrow and suffering; and, tenthly, the spiritual character of real religion, both in worship and in doctrine.

There are three observations which I have to make on the enumeration of these principles, before I conclude.

First, I would wish to impress upon you that the enforcement of these principles does not supersede or conflict with any of the various doctrines or institutions which any of us, in our several sects or churches, may have learned in childhood, manhood, or old age. No. What I wish you to understand is, that these principles lie behind and above those mere technical and outward manifestations of religion. Turn them, if you like, into other phrases. Clothe them, if you will, in more ordinary forms of speech. The words I have used to express them are perhaps not better — perhaps are worse — than those which others may choose for themselves. At any rate, they may serve as touchstones to enable us to know whether we have really grasped the faith which we all believe that we have in common; or whether we are merely repeating words by rote, and contenting ourselves with the husks and shells, with the beggarly elements of Judaism and heathenism. Somewhere or other, in our conception of Christianity, we must find room for these fundamental principles; or else we shall have missed some of the main purposes for which Christianity was given to us.

Secondly, perchance to some of us the thought that these ten principles, or something like these ten principles, are among the chief products of our religion, may give us a new ground for the hope that is in us,— a pledge that the Christian religion is not dead or dying, but is still instinct with immortal life. No doubt, the human intellect and the human conscience do themselves occasionally suffer relapses. The supply of lofty souls and great intelligences may sometimes dwindle, peak, and pine. And, with that decay, those privileges which we have enumerated may for a time decay also. But there is an inextinguishable source of life in the very width and depth of their nature; and that, even if they should for a time be forced out of and beyond the Christian pale, they will strike root elsewhere, and that as they were the Alpha, or beginning, of the education of Christendom, so also they will be the Omega, its end. They form, indeed, the tissue of the common Christianity of which we speak. And this common Christianity, so viewed, is certainly, at least as definite, precise, and intelligible as any of the special forms in which it has been clothed: for it is the Christianity of little children, and of the very poor; it is the Christianity of the greatest philosophers; it is the Christianity of States and statesmen.

There is, finally, thus a supreme stimulus to our hope, that these principles, of which I have been speaking to you, incontestably made their way, not by being enunciated as dry and formal statements, nor by outward authority, nor by the sword of conquerors, but by being personified, exemplified, made flesh and blood in him who was manifested on earth in these very things; that it is this living, personal interest which gave them their first chance, and which has ever since maintained their universal capability of application. You may remember, some of you, those fine lines of the poet laureate, in his "In Memoriam": —

> " We yield all blessing to the name
>   Of him that made them current coin:
>
> " For Wisdom dealt with mortal powers,
>   Where truth in closest words shall fail,
>   When truth embodied in a tale
> Shall enter in at lowly doors.
>
> " And so the Word had breath; and wrought
>   With human hands the creed of creeds
>   In loveliness of perfect deeds,
> More strong than all poetic thought."

Yes; and the poet might have added, more strong than all philosophic or theologic thought. Christianity is what it is by the fact that there once lived upon earth a sacred and divine life,— sacred and divine because it was supremely, superhumanly, and transcendently good; because it was above the limitations of time, country, and party; because it revealed to mankind the fullest insight ever given into the heart of the Eternal and Supreme: and Christianity shall be what it may yet become, in proportion as that life, or anything like it, is lived over again in personal example and influence of any human spirit that aspires toward that perfect ideal.

I was much struck this afternoon by an extract which Mr. Oakley read from one of the earliest inspectors of schools in England. " As I go," he says, " from school to school, I perceive in each a distinctive character, which is that of the master. I look at the school and I look at the master, and there is no mistaking the resemblance: his idiosyncrasy has passed upon the school. I seem to see him reflected in the children as in so many fragments of a broken mirror." Yes, it is perfectly true with regard to masters in schools. I know it myself. I remember, when engaged in education at Oxford, we tutors of the different colleges used to look with the utmost interest at the different types of character and intelligence impressed upon the scholars who came from our different public schools. I remember how this type penetrated even into details; how the sagacious observer of character at one of the colleges said, on seeing the original hand-writing of the greatest public teacher in this century, " That is the handwriting which I have seen in a hundred different forms in the handwriting of all the scholars that came from Rugby."

Now it is this power of impressing our own characters on others which is especially given to school-masters and school-mistresses of any institution; it is the power which is their greatest privilege and their greatest responsibility. It is also the best illustration,— with all reverence be it spoken,— the best of the illustrations and the effect produced on the world by the Founder of our common Christianity, and also

G of our relations toward him. Whenever any trait of justice, or generosity, or far-sighted wisdom, or wide tolerance, or compassion, or purity, is seen in any man or woman throughout the whole human race, there, as in the fragments of a broken mirror, we see the reflection of the divine image. There we see, as in the various characters of a manifold handwriting, the letters, the turns, the spirit of the character of his hand. If, in the effect produced among us on any single human will, we see any one of the principles which I have endeavored to describe; if we see truthfulness, if we see graciousness, if we see perception, the keen perception of the true needs of his or her time or situation; if in the effect on the world, if even in a few instances, some such boy or girl, some such man or woman, were planted in any neighborhood, in any nation, in any church,— would not definite, precise, unmistakable evidence be seen of the principles of our common Christianity, because it would express the incontestable features, the unquestionable characteristics, of our common Master?

ROBERTSON

REDERICK WILLIAM ROBERTSON, a distinguished English clergy-man, was the son of an army officer, and was born in London, February 3, 1816. His early wish was to enter the army, but relinquishing this desire he matriculated at Brasenose College, Oxford University, and took orders in the Anglican Church in 1840. For the next two years he was curate of the church of St. Mary Kalendar at Winchester, and for four years more curate of Christ Church, Cheltenham. On August 15, 1847, he became incumbent of Trinity Chapel in Brighton, where he immediately became a living force in the community. As an eminent English critic has remarked, " There is perhaps no parallel in English church history to the influence of Robertson's ministry at a small proprietary chapel." The six years of his ministry at Brighton marked an important epoch, not only in the history of Brighton, but in that of English religious thought, his liberalizing influence being felt in constantly widening circles in the Established Church and in the Nonconformist bodies also, and before long extending to America. Robertson displayed a singular apti-tude in reaching the working classes, and his founding of a workingmen's institute in 1849 was one of the important incidents in his career. No English preacher of his time was more untrammelled than he, and per-haps none more original. His fearless course subjected him to more or less detraction and misrepresentation, and being a man of extreme sensi-tiveness and no sense of humor he felt very keenly the attacks that from his position he could hardly hope to escape. His sensitiveness to adverse criticism and the intense earnestness with which he threw himself into his work wore him out long before his time, and on August 15, 1853, he died at Brighton of inflammation of the brain. At his funeral two thou-sand persons followed him to the grave. His reputation as a preacher is firmly established upon five series of " Sermons Preached at Trinity Chapel " (1855-90). Other works which he left are " Lectures and Ad-dresses on Literary and Social Topics " (1858); " Expository Lectures on St. Paul's Epistles to the Corinthians " (1859); " Notes on Genesis " (1877).

SERMON: THE LONELINESS OF CHRIST

" Jesus answered them, Do ye now believe? Behold, the hour cometh, yea, is now come, that ye shall be scattered every man to his own, and shall leave me alone; and yet I am not alone, because the Father is with me."—John xvi, 31, 32.

(7624)

THERE are two kinds of solitude: the first consisting of insulation in space; the other, of isolation of the spirit. The first is simply separation by distance. When we are seen, touched, heard by none, we are said to be alone. And all hearts respond to the truth of that saying, This is not solitude; for sympathy can people our solitude with a crowd. The fisherman on the ocean alone at night is not alone, when he remembers the earnest longings which are arising up to heaven at home for his safety. The traveller is not alone, when the faces which will greet him on his arrival seem to beam upon him as he trudges on. The solitary student is not alone, when he feels that human hearts will respond to the truths which he is preparing to address to them.

The other is loneliness of soul. There are times when hands touch ours, but only send an icy chill of unsympathizing indifference to the heart; when eyes gaze into ours, but with a glazed look which cannot read into the bottom of our souls; when words pass from our lips, but only come back as an echo reverberated without reply through a dreary solitude; when the multitude throng and press us, and we cannot say, as Christ said, " Somebody hath touched me: " for the contact has been not between soul and soul, but only between form and form.

And there are two kinds of men, who feel this last solitude in different ways. The first are the men of self-reliance,— self-dependent: who ask no counsel, and crave no sympathy; who act and resolve alone,— who can go sternly through duty, and scarcely shrink, let what will be crushed in them. Such men command respect: for whoever respects himself constrains the respect of others. They are invaluable in all those professions of life in which sensitive feeling

would be a superfluity: they make iron commanders, sur-
geons who do not shrink, and statesmen who do not flinch
from their purpose for the dread of unpopularity. But mere
self-dependence is weakness; and the conflict is terrible when
a human sense of weakness is felt by such men.

Jacob was alone when he slept in his way to Padan Aram,
the first night that he was away from his father's roof, with
the world before him, and all the old broken up; and Elijah
was alone in the wilderness when the court had deserted him,
and he said, " They have digged down thine altars, and slain
thy prophets with the sword: and I, even I, only am left, and
they seek my life to take it away." But the loneliness of the
tender Jacob was very different from that of the stern
Elijah. To Jacob the sympathy he yearned for was realized
in the form of a gentle dream. A ladder raised from earth
to heaven figured the possibility of communion between the
spirit of man and the Spirit of God. In Elijah's case, the
storm, and the earthquake, and the fire, did their convulsing
work in the soul, before a still, small voice told him that he
was not alone. In such a spirit the sense of weakness comes
with a burst of agony, and the dreadful conviction of being
alone manifests itself with a rending of the heart of rock.
It is only so that such souls can be taught that the Father is
with them, and that they are not alone.

There is another class of men, who live in sympathy.
These are affectionate minds, which tremble at the thought
of being alone: not from want of courage nor from weakness
of intellect comes their dependence upon others, but from
the intensity of their affections. It is the trembling spirit
of humanity in them. They want not aid, nor even countenance, but only sympathy. And the trial comes to them not
in the shape of fierce struggle, but of chill and utter loneli-

ness, when they are called upon to perform a duty on which the world looks coldly, or to embrace a truth which has not found lodgment yet in the breasts of others.

It is to this latter and not to the former class that we must look, if we would understand the spirit in which the words of the text were pronounced. The deep humanity of the Soul of Christ was gifted with those finer sensibilities of affectionate nature which stand in need of sympathy. He not only gave sympathy, but wanted it, too, from others. He who selected the gentle John to be his friend,— who found solace in female sympathy, attended by the women who ministered to him out of their substance,— who in the Trial hour could not bear even to pray without the human presence, which is the pledge and reminder of God's presence, had nothing in him of the hard, merely self-dependent character. Even this verse testifies to the same fact. A stern spirit never could have said, "I am not alone: the Father is with me;" never would have felt the loneliness which needed the balancing truth. These words tell of a struggle, an inward reasoning, a difficulty and a reply, a sense of solitude,— "I shall be alone;" and an immediate correction of that: "Not alone: the Father is with me."

There is no thought connected with the life of Christ more touching, none that seems so peculiarly to characterize his Spirit, as the solitariness in which he lived. Those who understood him best only understood him half. Those who knew him best scarcely could be said to know him. On this occasion the disciples thought, Now we do understand, now we do believe. The lonely Spirit answered, "Do ye now believe? Behold the hour cometh that ye shall be scattered, every man to his own, and shall leave me alone."

Very impressive is that trait in his history. He was in

First, then, we meditate on the loneliness of Christ; Secondly, on the temper of his solitude.

The loneliness of Christ was caused by the divine elevation of his character. His infinite superiority severed him from sympathy; his exquisite affectionateness made that want of sympathy a keen trial.

There is a second-rate greatness which the world can comprehend. If we take two who are brought into direct contrast by Christ himself, the one the type of human, the other that of divine excellence, the Son of Man and John the Baptist, this becomes clearly manifest. John's life had a certain rude, rugged goodness, on which was written, in characters which required no magnifying glass to read, spiritual excellence. The world, on the whole, accepted him. Pharisees and Sadducees went to his baptism. The people idolized him as a prophet; and, if he had not chanced to cross the path of a weak prince and a revengeful woman, we can see no reason why John might not have finished his course with joy, recognized as irreproachable. If we inquire why it was that the world accepted John and rejected Christ, one reply appears to be, that the life of the one was finitely simple and one-sided, that of the other divinely complex. In physical nature, the naturalist finds no difficulty in comprehending the simple structure of the lowest organizations of animal life, where one uniform texture, and one organ performing the office of brain and heart and lungs, at once, leave little to perplex.

But when he comes to study the complex anatomy of man, he has the labor of a lifetime before him. It is not difficult to master the constitution of a single country; but when you try to understand the universe, you find infinite appearances of contradiction: law opposed by law; motion balanced by motion; happiness blended with misery; and the power to elicit a divine order and unity out of this complex variety is given to only a few of the gifted of the race. That which the structure of man is to the structure of the limpet, that which the universe is to a single country, the complex and boundless soul of Christ was to the souls of other men.

Therefore, to the superficial observer, his life was a mass of inconsistencies and contradictions. All thought themselves qualified to point out the discrepancies. The Pharisees could not comprehend how a holy Teacher could eat with publicans and sinners. His own brethren could not reconcile his assumption of a public office with the privacy which he aimed at keeping. " If thou doest these things, show thyself to the world." Some thought he was " a good man; " others said, " Nay, but he deceiveth the people."

And hence it was that he lived to see all that acceptance which had marked the earlier stage of his career — as, for instance, at Capernaum — melt away. First, the Pharisees took the alarm; then the Sadducees; then the political party of the Herodians; then the people. That was the most terrible of all, for the enmity of the upper classes is impotent; but when that cry of brute force is stirred from the deeps of society, as deaf to the voice of reason as the ocean in its strength churned into raving foam by the winds, the heart of mere earthly oak quails before that. The apostles, at all events, did quail. One denied; another betrayed; all deserted. They " were scattered, each to his own: " and the Truth himself was left alone in Pilate's judgment-hall.

Now learn from this a very important distinction. To feel solitary is no uncommon thing. To complain of being alone, without sympathy, and misunderstood, is general enough. In every place, in many a family, these victims of diseased sensibility are to be found, and they might find a weakening satisfaction in observing a parallel between their own feelings and those of Jesus. But before that parallel is assumed be very sure that it is, as in his case, the elevation of your character which severs you from your species. The world has small sympathy for divine goodness; but it also has little for a great many other qualities which are disagreeable to it. You meet with no response; you are passed by; find yourself unpopular; meet with little communion.

Well! Is that because you are above the world,— nobler, devising and executing grand plans, which they cannot comprehend; vindicating the wronged; proclaiming and living on great principles; offending it by the saintliness of your purity, and the unworldliness of your aspirations?

Then yours is the loneliness of Christ. Or is it that you are wrapped up in self,— cold, disobliging, sentimental, indifferent about the welfare of others, and very much astonished that they are not deeply interested in you? You must not use these words of Christ. They have nothing to do with you.

Let us look at one or two of the occasions on which this loneliness was felt.

The first time was when he was but twelve years old, when his parents found him in the Temple, hearing the doctors and asking them questions. High thoughts were in the Child's soul: expanding views of life; larger views of duty, and his own destiny.

There is a moment in every true life — to some it comes very early — when the old routine of duty is not large enough; when the parental roof seems too low, because the Infinite above is arching over the soul; when the old formulas, in creeds, catechisms, and articles, seem to be narrow, and they must either be thrown aside, or else transformed into living and breathing realities; when the earthly father's authority is being superseded by the claims of a Father in heaven.

That is a lonely, lonely moment, when the young soul first feels God — when this earth is recognized as an " awful place, yea, the very gate of heaven; " when the dream-ladder is seen planted against the skies, and we wake, and the dream haunts us as a sublime reality.

You may detect the approach of that moment in the young man or the young woman by the awakened spirit of inquiry; by a certain restlessness of look, and an eager earnestness of tone; by the devouring study of all kinds of books; by the waning of your own influence, while the inquirer is asking the truth of the doctors and teachers in the vast Temple of the world; by a certain opinionativeness, which is austere and disagreeable enough; but the austerest moment of the fruit's taste is that in which it is passing from greenness into ripe-ness. If you wait in patience, the sour will become sweet Rightly looked at, that opinionativeness is more truly anguish; the fearful solitude of feeling the insecurity of all that is human; the discovery that life is real, and forms of social and religious existence hollow. The old moorings are torn away, and the soul is drifting, drifting, drifting, very often without compass, except the guidance of an unseen hand, into the vast infinite of God. Then come the lonely words, and no wonder, "How is it that ye sought me? Wist ye not that I must be about my Father's business? "

That solitude was felt by Christ in trial. In the desert, in Pilate's judgment-hall, in the garden, he was alone; and alone must every son of man meet his trial-hour. The individuality of the soul necessitates that. Each man is a new soul in this world untried, with a boundless Possible before him. No one can predict what he may become, prescribe his duties, or mark out his obligations. Each man's own nature has its own peculiar rules; and he must take up his life-plan alone, and persevere in it in a perfect privacy with which no stranger intermeddleth. Each man's temptations are made up of a host of peculiarities, internal and external, which no other mind can measure.

You are tried alone; alone you pass into the desert; alone you must bear and conquer in the Agony; alone you must be sifted by the world. There are moments known only to a man's own self, when he sits by the poisoned springs of existence, " yearning for a morrow which shall free him from the strife." And there are trials more terrible than that. Not when vicious inclinations are opposed to holy, but when virtue conflicts with virtue, is the real rending of the soul in twain. A temptation, in which the lower nature struggles for mastery, can be met by the whole united force of the spirit.

But it is when obedience to a heavenly Father can be only paid by disobedience to an earthly one; or fidelity to duty can be only kept by infidelity to some entangling engagement; or the straight path must be taken over the misery of others; or the counsel of the affectionate friend must be met with a " Get thee behind me, Satan: " — O! it is then, when human advice is unavailable, that the soul feels what it is to be alone.

Once more: — the Redeemer's soul was alone in dying. The hour had come, — they were all gone, and he was, as he predicted, left alone. All that is human drops from us in that hour. Human faces flit and fade, and the sounds of the world become confused. "I shall die alone,"—yes, and alone you live. The philosopher tells us that no atom in creation touches another atom,— they only approach within a certain distance; then the attraction ceases, and an invisible something repels,— they only seem to touch.

No soul touches another soul except at one or two points, and those chiefly external,— a fearful and a lonely thought, but one of the truest of life. Death only realizes that which has been fact all along. In the central deeps of our being we are alone.

The spirit or temper of that solitude.

Observe its grandeur. I am alone, yet not alone. There is a feeble and sentimental way in which we speak of the Man of Sorrows. We turn to the Cross, and the Agony, and the Loneliness, to touch the softer feelings — to arouse compassion. You degrade that loneliness by your compassion. Compassion! compassion for him! Adore if you will,— respect and reverence that sublime solitariness with which none but the Father was,— but no pity; let it draw out the firmer and manlier graces of the soul. Even tender sympathy seems out of place.

For even in human things, the strength that is in a man can be only learnt when he is thrown upon his own resources and left alone. What a man can do in conjunction with others does not test the man. Tell us what he can do alone. It is one thing to defend the truth when you know that your audience are already prepossessed, and that every argument will meet a willing response; and it is another thing to hold the truth when truth must be supported, if at all alone,— met by cold looks and unsympathizing suspicion. It is one thing to rush on to danger with the shouts and the sympathy of numbers; it is another thing when the lonely chieftain of the sinking ship sees the last boat-full disengage itself, and folds his arms to go down into the majesty of darkness, crushed, but not subdued.

Such and greater far was the strength and majesty of the Saviour's solitariness. It was not the trial of the lonely hermit. There is a certain gentle and pleasing melancholy in the life which is lived alone. But there are the forms of nature to speak to him; and he has not the positive opposition of mankind, if he has the absence of actual sympathy. It is a solemn thing, doubtless, to be apart from men, and to feel eternity rushing by like an arrowy river. But the solitude of Christ was the solitude of a crowd. In that single human bosom dwelt the Thought which was to be the germ of the world's life — a thought unshared, misunderstood, or rejected. Can you not feel the grandeur of those words, when the Man, reposing on his solitary strength, felt the last shadow of perfect isolation pass across his soul: — "My God, my God, why hast thou forsaken me?"

Next, learn from these words self-reliance. "Ye shall leave me alone." Alone, then, the Son of Man was content to be. He threw himself on his own solitary thought: did not go down to meet the world; but waited, though it might be for ages, till the world should come round to him. He appealed to the future, did not aim at seeming consistent, left his contradictions unexplained: — I came from the Father, — I leave the world, and go to the Father.

"Now," said they, "thou speakest no proverb:" that is, enigma. But many a hard and enigmatical saying before he had spoken, and he left them all. A thread runs through all true acts, stringing them together into one harmonious chain: but it is not for the Son of God to be anxious to prove their consistency with each other.

This is self-reliance — to repose calmly on the thought which is deepest in our bosoms, and be unmoved if the world will not accept it yet. To live on your own convictions against the world, is to overcome the world — to believe that what is truest in you is true for all: to abide by that, and not be over-anxious to be heard or understood, or sympathized with, certain that at last all must acknowledge the same, and that, while you stand firm, the world will come round to you — that is independence. It is not difficult to get away into retirement, and there live upon your own convictions; nor is it difficult to mix with men, and follow their convictions; but to enter into the world, and there live out firmly and fearlessly according to your own conscience — that is Christian greatness.

There is a cowardice in this age which is not Christian. We shrink from the consequences of truth. We look round and cling dependently. We ask what men will think; what others will say; whether they will not stare in astonishment. Perhaps they will; but he who is calculating that will accomplish nothing in this life. The Father — the Father which is with us and in us — what does he think? God's work cannot be done without a spirit of independence. A man is got some way in the Christian life when he has learned to say humbly, and yet majestically, "I dare to be alone."

Lastly, remark the humility of this loneliness. Had the Son of Man simply said, I can be alone, he would have said no more than any proud, self-relying man can say; but when he added, "because the Father is with me," that independence assumed another character, and self-reliance became only another form of reliance upon God. Distinguish between genuine and spurious humility. There is a false humility which says, "It is my own poor thought, and I must not trust it. I must distrust my own reason and judgment, because they are my own. I must not accept the dictates of my own conscience; for is it not my own, and is not trust in self the great fault of our fallen nature?"

Very well. Now, remember something else. There is a

Spirit which beareth witness with our spirits; there is a God who "is not far from any one of us;" there is a "Light which lighteth every man which cometh into the world." Do not be unnaturally humble. The thought of your own mind perchance is the Thought of God. To refuse to follow that may be to disown God. To take the judgment and conscience of other men to live by, where is the humility of that? From whence did their conscience and judgment come? Was the fountain from which they drew exhausted for you? If they refused like you to rely on their own conscience, and you rely upon it, how are you sure that it is more the Mind of God than your own which you have refused to hear?

Look at it in another way. The charm of the words of great men — those grand sayings which are recognized as true as soon as heard — is this, that you recognize them as wisdom which passed across your own mind. You feel that they are your own thoughts come back to you, else you would not at once admit them: " All that floated across me before, only I could not say it, and did not feel confident enough to assert it, or had not conviction enough to put into words." Yes, God spoke to you what he did to them: only they believed it, said it, trusted the Word within them, and you did not. Be sure that often when you say, " It is only my own poor thought, and I am alone," the real correcting thought is this, " Alone, but the Father is with me," — therefore I can live by that lonely conviction.

There is no danger in this, whatever timid minds may think — no danger of mistake, if the character be a true one. For we are not in uncertainty in this matter. It has been given us to know our base from our noble hours: to distinguish between the voice which is from above, and that which speaks from below, out of the abyss of our animal and selfish nature. Samuel could distinguish between the impulse — quite a human one — which would have made him select Eliab out of Jesse's sons, and the deeper judgment by which "the Lord said, Look not on his countenance, nor on the height of his stature, for I have refused him."

Doubtless deep truth of character is required for this: for the whispering voices get mixed together, and we dare not abide by our own thoughts, because we think them our own, and not God's: and this because we only now and then endeavor to know in earnest. It is only given to the habitually true to know the difference. He knew it, because all his blessed life long he could say, "My judgment is just, because I seek not my own will, but the will of him which sent me."

The practical result and inference of all this is a very simple, but a very deep one: the deepest of existence. Let life be a life of faith. Do not go timorously about, inquiring what others think, and what others believe, and what others say. It seems the easiest, it is the most difficult thing in life to do this — believe in God. God is near you. Throw yourself fearlessly upon him. Trembling mortal, there is an unknown might within your soul, which will wake when you command it. The day may come when all that is human — man and woman — will fall off from you, as they did from him. Let his strength be yours. Be independent of them all now. The Father is with you. Look to him, and he will save you.

HALL

CHRISTOPHER NEWMAN HALL, a noted English Nonconformist divine, was born at Maidstone, Kent, May 22, 1816, and was educated at Highbury College and London University. Entering the Congregational ministry he was from 1842 to 1854 the pastor of a Congregational church in Hull, and in the latter year was called to the Surrey Chapel in London. His London congregation subsequently built a great church in Westminster Bridge Road, in Early English Gothic style, its tower, two hundred feet high, being erected in memory of Abraham Lincoln with funds collected in England and the United States. At the opening of the Civil War in America, Newman Hall warmly advocated the cause of the North and subsequently made two extended tours in the United States, lecturing in many places, in the endeavor to bring about international good feeling. Since 1893 he has been paster emeritus of the Westminster Bridge Road congregation. He is not only widely known as an eloquent preacher, but has had an extended influence as a religious and devotional writer as well, his famous tract, " Come to Jesus " (1846), having been translated into more than twenty languages. Other works by him are " The Land of the Forum and the Vatican " (1855); " The Christian Philosopher Triumphant Over Death;" " Garlands for a Mother's Grave;" " It Is I;" " Antidote to Fear; " " Memoir of Rowland Hill; " " Sermons " (1868); " From Liverpool to St. Louis " (1870); " Mountain Musings;" Pilgrim Songs in Cloud and Sunshine " (1871); Gethsemane;" " Prayer: Its Reasonableness and Efficacy " (1875).

SERMON: CHRISTIAN VICTORY

" To him that overcometh will I give to eat of the hidden manna, and will give him a white stone, and in the stone a new name written, which no man knoweth saving he that receiveth it."—Rev. ii, 17.

THE Christian life is often compared in Scripture to a warfare. Followers of Jesus are " soldiers." They are exhorted to put on " the whole armor of God." They " fight the good fight of faith." Some of you have long been engaged in the conflict: others have more recently entered upon it. But, whether young or old in the Christian career, all find it necessary to be constantly stirred up to watchfulness against the never-ceasing assaults of the foe. It is not enough to put on the armor and to commence the battle. He that overcometh, and he alone, will receive the salutation, " Well done, good and faithful servant,"—he alone shall " lay hold upon eternal life."

But we are not left to fight without encouragement. As generals before a battle go in front of their troops to stimulate them to valor, so Christ, the Captain of our Salvation, leads on the consecrated hosts of his elect; and having himself set us a glorious example of valor and victory, animates us to follow in his footsteps by the " exceeding great and precious promises" of his Word. Christian warrior! — let your eye be lifted up to him. Behold him beckoning you onward. Listen to him, as from his throne of glory he exhorts you to persevering valor against the foe; and pray earnestly that his promise may be fulfilled in your case: " To him that overcometh will I give to eat of the hidden manna, and will give him a white stone, and in the stone a new name written, which no man knoweth saving he that receiveth it."

Let us consider first, the promise; then, the condition attached to it.

I. The Promise.

This is twofold,— the Hidden Manna and the White Stone.

1. The Hidden Manna.— God fed the Israelites in the wilderness with manna. A portion of this was laid by in the ark, and thus was hidden from public view. It is here referred to as a figurative representation of the spiritual blessings bestowed upon the victor in the heavenly fight. Christ, speaking of the manna as a type of himself, said, "I am the bread which came down from heaven." The manna in the wilderness sustained the life of the Israelites. But there is another life more important than that of the

body. By sin the soul is dead, dead toward God. By the Holy Spirit, the "dead in trespasses and sins" are "quickened," or made alive. As the life of the new-born infant cannot be preserved without food, so the new spiritual life, which God imparts, needs continual support. Both the life, and the nourishing of it, come from Christ, and Christ alone. By his sacrifice that life becomes possible; and by his Spirit working within our hearts that life becomes actual. He sustains as well as imparts spiritual vitality. He is the food of our faith: "believe in the Lord Jesus Christ, and thou shalt be saved." He is the food of our love: "we love him because he first loved us." He is the food of our obedience: "the love of Christ constraineth us." He is the food of our peace: for when "justified by faith, we have peace with God through Jesus Christ our Lord." He is the food of our joy: for if "we joy in God" it is "through Jesus Christ our Lord."

The manna which sustained the Israelites was evidently the gift of God. And so this "hidden manna" is from heaven. It is no contrivance of man—no philosophy of human invention. It is a divine plan for the salvation of our ruined race. "God so loved the world that he gave his only begotten Son, that whosoever believeth in him should not perish but should have everlasting life." That manna in the wilderness was sweet to the taste; yet they who fed on it grew weary of it. But the more we eat of the bread of life, the more we relish it—the greater is our appetite for it. That manna in the wilderness was needed daily. And so with this heavenly bread. Yesterday's supply will not suffice for to-day. The prayer is as needful for the soul as for the body: "Give us this day our daily bread." But if that manna was needed daily, so it was supplied; none went in vain at the appointed season—and no soul that "hungers and thirsts after righteousness" is sent empty away. The manna was supplied to the Israelites till they came to the promised land—so God has promised that his grace shall not fail his people through all their wanderings.

It is spoken of as the "hidden manna." Such is the Christian's life. "Our life is hid with Christ in God." The outward effects of it may be seen, but the inner life is invisible. So is the nourishing of the life. You may see the Christian on his knees, you may hear the words which he utters, but you cannot see the streams of divine influence which are poured into his spirit; nor hear the sweet whispers of divine love which fill him with joy; nor comprehend the peace passing all understanding which he is permitted to experience. Unbelievers are often amazed at what they see in the Christian. He is troubled on every side, yet not in despair. Waves of sorrow beat upon his frail vessel, yet it does not sink. Men now threaten, now allure, but he holds on his way. What to others is an irresistible charm, is no attraction to him. What is a terror to others, deters not him. Why does he not faint beneath the burden? why does he not sink in the storm? Because he eats of the "hidden manna." "The secret of the Lord is with them that fear him." "He hath taken him into his banqueting-room, and the banner over him is love."

Were this promise merely the reward of final victory, that victory itself would never be gained. We need to eat this manna during our pilgrimage. We cannot live without it. Every act of overcoming will be followed by a verification of the promise, "I will give him to eat of the hidden manna." Yet we must look beyond the present life for its full accomplishment. "To him that overcometh" at the last, "shall be

given the hidden manna," in a sense of which at present we
have but a very faint conception.

As the manna was hidden in the ark, and that ark was
hidden behind the curtain of the Holy of Holies, so the
Christian's hope, "as an anchor of the soul, sure and steadfast, enters into that which is within the veil." Those joys
we cannot yet conjecture; their splendor is too intense; we
should be blinded by excessive light; we should be overpowered by the excellent glory.

One look of heaven would unfit us for earth. It is wisely
appointed that at present this manna should in one sense be
hidden, even from ourselves. We are as yet but babes —
such strong meat would not suit us now; we must be content
with simpler fare. But Oh! if the manna, though at present
so partially and imperfectly appreciated, can produce such
peace and joy, what must be the bliss of entering into the
holiest of all, and there, in the presence of God himself, feast-
ing on it eternally! Unceasing, unlimited reception of
divine influences into the soul!

Uninterrupted fellowship with him who is the only fountain of life, and purity, and happiness! Perfect love! But
at present, such full fruition is "hidden." "Now we see
through a glass darkly;" "now we know but in part;" "it
doth not yet appear what we shall be." But how unspeaka-
bly blessed are they to whom, partially in this world and perfectly in the next, the promise shall be verified: "To him that
overcometh will I give to eat of the hidden manna!"

The White Stone.— Reference is made to the *tessera hos-*
pitalis, the tally or token of hospitality employed by the
ancients. At a time when houses of public entertainment
were less common, private hospitality was the more necessary. When one person was received kindly by another, or

a contract of friendship was entered into, the *tessera* was given. It was so named from its shape, being four-sided; it was sometimes of wood, sometimes of stone; it was divided into two by the contracting parties; each wrote his own name on half of the *tessera;* then they exchanged pieces, and therefore the name or device on the piece of the *tessera* which each received, was the name the other person had written upon it, and which no one else knew but him who received it. It was carefully prized, and entitled the bearer to protection and hospitality.

Plautus, in one of his plays, refers to this custom. Hanno inquires of a stranger where he may find Agorastocles, and discovers to his surprise, that he is addressing the object of his search.

"If so," he says, "compare, if you please, this hospitable *tessera;* here it is; I have it with me."

Agorastocles replies, "It is the exact counterpart; I have the other part at home."

Hanno responds, "O, my friend! I rejoice to meet thee; thy father was my friend, my guest; I divided with him this hospitable *tessera.*" "Therefore," said Agorastocles, "thou shalt have a home with me, for I reverence hospitality."

Beautiful illustration of gospel truth! The Saviour visits the sinner's heart, and being received as a guest, bestows the white stone, the token of his unchanging love. It is not we who, in the first instance, desire this compact. Far from it.

But Jesus, anxious to bless us, kindly forces himself on our regard. By his Spirit, he persuades us to give him admission to our hearts. "Behold, I stand at the door and knock; if any man hear my voice and open the door, I will come in to him, and will sup with him, and he with me." We often disregarded his appeal. Yet, with what condescending kindness did he persevere! And when at length we opened the door, we saw him laden with blessings which he had been long waiting to bestow. The feast which was then spread was all of his providing. He who went to be "the guest of one that was a sinner," inverts the usual course. He invites himself and brings the feast. What have we fit to set before so august and holy a visitant? But he who chooses the sinner's heart as his banqueting-chamber, spreads there his choicest gifts, his exceeding great and precious promises, his finished sacrifice, his human sympathy, his perfect example, his pure precepts, his all-prevailing intercession, the various developments of his infinite love.

He "sups with us," and makes us "sup with him." He enrolls our name among his friends. "He makes an everlasting covenant with us, ordered in all things and sure." He promises never to leave nor forsake us. He tells us we "shall never perish." He gives us the *tessera*, the White Stone!

Is not this "the witness of the Spirit," the "earnest of the promised possession?" Does not "the Spirit witness with our spirit that we are born of God?" Does not our experience of the friendship of Jesus correspond with what we are taught of it in the Scriptures? "I know in whom I have believed, and am persuaded that he is able to keep that which I have committed unto him, against that day." The "love of God is shed abroad" in the heart of the believer. He says, with humble confidence, "My Lord, and my God!"

On this white stone is inscribed a "new name." The part of the *tessera* which each of the contracting parties received contained the name of the other. And, therefore, "the new name" on the "white stone," which he that overcometh receives, is that of him who gives it. By the unbeliever, God is known as Power, as Majesty, as Justice. He is dreaded.

"The carnal mind is enmity against God." The Christian alone knows him as "Love!" Jehovah has now "a new name." He was once Ruler—now he is Friend; he was once Judge—now he is Father.

Reader! do you know God by his "new name?" Do you so know him as to wish no longer to hide from him, but to hide in him, as the only home the universe can furnish in which you can be safe and happy? Have you learned to say, "Our Father which art in heaven?" If we have indeed received this "white stone," let us continually be reading the "new name" engraven on it. Here I am assured that the Holy Ghost is my Teacher, my Guide, my Comforter; that the Eternal Word, the only begotten Son, is my Saviour, my Friend, my Brother; that the infinite Jehovah is my Father, and that "like as a father pitieth his children, so the Lord pitieth them that fear him."

We are told that no man knoweth this new name, "saving he that receiveth it." He knows it for himself, but no one else can read it for him. Thus it resembles the "hidden manna." The frivolous may deride, fools may mock, the unbeliever may deny, the sceptic may bring forth his objections in all the pride of a false philosophy; but the Christian, even if unable to reply to the caviller, or to make intelligible to any other mind his own strong assurance, has an evidence within him which nothing can shake, for God has written on his heart, "his new best name of Love."

Fellow pilgrims to the heavenly Canaan, how precious is this token! We are travellers through the desert; for though the enjoyments of earth are many, yet this life, compared with what is to come, is a wilderness. We are away from home; we are exposed to privations, tempests, foes; we constantly need a refuge. But we are never far from the house of a friend. Everywhere, in every city and every village, on the desert and on the ocean, in the solitude of secrecy, and in the solitude of a crowd, in the bustle of business, and in the sick chamber, a Friend is at hand, who will always recognize the white stone he gave us a token of his love. We have only to present it to claim the fulfilment of his promise.

How wide will the door be thrown open for our reception! What divine entertainment we shall receive! What safety from peril! what succor in difficulty! what comfort in trouble! what white raiment! what heavenly food! O, that we valued the *tessera* more, that we sought more frequent interviews with our heavenly Friend, that we more habitually resorted as invited guests to Jesus, and dwelt in him as the home of our souls! We shall never find the door closed against us; we shall never be received reluctantly; he will never allow us to think that we are intruders. Jesus is never ashamed of his poor relations, nor treats them coldly because they need his help. The greater our distress, the more shall we prove his liberality and tender sympathy.

And as regards this stone, as well as the hidden manna, we can look beyond the present life. A day is coming when we shall be compelled to leave the homes of earth, however endeared. We must embrace for the last time the friends united to us as our own souls. Though we have travelled along the road many a year together, we must now separate, and go on alone. They may accompany us to the river side, but we must cross it by ourselves. What cheering voice will greet us then? What kind roof will receive us then? What loving friend will welcome us then?

But we shall not have left our best treasure behind us! No! we shall carry the white stone with us; and with this we shall look for no inferior abode, but with unhesitating step shall advance at once right up to the palace of the Great King. We present the *tessera;* the "new name" is legible upon it; the angelic guards recognize the symbol; the everlasting gates lift up their heads; and the voice of Jesus himself invites us to enter, saying, "Come, ye blessed of my Father, inherit the kingdom!"

Such is the welcome that every soul shall experience to whom the promise is fulfilled: "I will give him a white stone, and in the stone a new name written, which no man knoweth, saving he that receiveth it."

II. The Condition annexed to the Promise, "To him that Overcometh!"

A great war is going on between the Church and the powers of darkness. It is not an affair of strategy between two vast armies, wherein skilful manœuvres determine the issue, many on either side never coming into actual combat; but every Christian has to fight hand to hand with the enemy. We cannot be lost in the crowd. We may not stand in the middle of the hollow square, without sharing the perils of the outer rank. Every Christian must not only occupy his post in the grand army, but must personally grapple with the foe.

Before conversion there was no fighting. The devil's suggestions and the heart's inclinations were allied. Then we did the enemy's bidding, or were lulled to sleep by his intoxicating cup. But when light shone into the soul, and we strove to escape, the struggle began. God, as our Creator and Redeemer, justly demands our obedience and love. Whatever interferes with these claims, is an enemy summoning us to battle. The world of frivolity is our foe. How numerous and insinuating are its temptations — the more perilous because of the difficulty of defining them!

Moreover, lawful pleasures and necessary cares become dangerous when they cease to be subordinate to the love of God. The enjoyments he bestows and the labors he appoints, are calculated to minister to godliness,— and yet they may be perverted to idolatry, by our forgetting him on whom our highest thoughts should be fixed. What danger is there that things in themselves holy and beautiful may thus become pernicious and destructive!

The flesh, too, furnishes its contingent to the army of our foes. Not that any of our natural appetites, being divinely bestowed, can have in them the nature of sin. No! the flesh, as God made it, is pure and holy. But those instincts, which, regulated by the revealed will of their Author, are "holiness to the Lord," may, by unhallowed gratification, become those "fleshly lusts which war against the soul." As we carry about with us these animal propensities, there is necessity for constant vigilance lest our own nature, being abused, should become our destroyer.

Inbred depravity lurks in the heart of even the true believer. Though dethroned, it is not completely expelled. With what selfishness, covetousness, vanity, hastiness of temper, uncharitableness, have we not to contend! Who has not some sin which most easily besets him? How varied are the forms of unbelief! Spiritual pride, too, corrupts our very graces, piety itself furnishing an occasion of evil, so that when we have conquered some temptation or performed some duty, our victory is often tarnished, our holy things corrupted, by our falling into the snare of self-complacency.

Above all, there is that great adversary who "goeth about as a roaring lion, seeking whom he may devour." He avails himself of the world, and the flesh, and the infirmities of the spirit, to tempt the soul to sin. This is no fable, although one of Satan's most skilful stratagems is to make men disbelieve in his existence. Overlooked or despised, a foe is already half victorious. But the Captain of our Salvation, in his word, often warns us both of the craft and of the violence of our adversary. We sometimes read of "the wiles of the devil;" and sometimes of "the fiery darts of the wicked one." They who fail to watch and pray, are sure to be vanquished by such a foe.

These are our enemies! And if we would possess the promise we must "overcome." A mere profession of religion is of no avail. It is not enough for our name to appear on the muster-roll of the camp. Many wear the soldier's dress who know nothing of the soldier's heart. Many are glad to glitter on the grand parade who fall off from the hard-fought, blood-stained battle-field. It is not enough to buckle on our armor; many do this, and lay it aside again. We must devote ourselves entirely and unreservedly to this great daily battle of life.

There is no exemption of persons. Women must fight, as well as men; the tender and the timid must be as Amazons in the conflict. Children must carry the shield, and wield the sword. The aged and infirm must keep the ranks. The sick and wounded must not be carried to the rear. No substitute can be provided, and there is no discharge in this war.

There is no exemption on account of circumstances. The rich and poor, the learned and the unlearned, the cheerful and the sad, all must fight. No accumulation of trouble, no unexpected death of friends, can be an excuse for laying down our arms. We must go to the marriage feast, and we must attend the funeral procession, as warriors, wearing our armor and grasping our weapons. We must be like those spoken of by Nehemiah, "every man with one hand wrought in the work, and with the other hand held a weapon."

There is no exemption of place. Foes lie in wait for the Christian wherever he goes — in the mart of commerce, in the busy workshop, when he returns to his home, when he rests on his bed, in the bustle of the day, in the silence of the night, in the circle of his friends, in the bosom of his family, in society, alone, in the city, in the fields, in his walks of benevolence, in his private meditations, in the church, in his secret retirement, when he worships with the great congregation, and when he enters his closet and shuts the door. He can never elude the enemy; he carries the foe in his own breast; the conflict ceases not!

There is no exemption of time, no season of rest. No truce is sounded. Satan never beats a retreat, except to lead us into an ambuscade. No white flag comes out that can be trusted. If we parley, it is at our peril; if we pause, we are wounded or taken captive. Wars on earth may often terminate by mutual agreement. It is a war of extermination; no quarter is given; either we must trample Satan under foot, or Satan will drag us down to hell!

It is a warfare until death. While we are in the body it will be always true — "We wrestle." The oldest Christian cannot lay aside his weapons. "Having done all, stand." A great word that! "Having done all!" "What!" you may say, "after a long life of conflict, surely I may put aside my armor, and sheathe my sword, and recline on some sunny bank, and enjoy myself after my victory!"

No; you must not expect it; "having done all" it is enough if you stand at bay on the battle-ground; all you can hope for in this world is to maintain your post, still defying the foe, who will be still meditating fresh attacks. You will never be able to say with St. Paul, "I have fought a good fight," until you can also say, "I have finished my course."

It is not the appearance of fighting. It is not a few faint, irresolute strokes. "So fight I," said the Apostle, "not as one that beateth the air." We must be resolute, determined, in earnest, giving our enemy no advantage. We must "not give place to the devil." We must watch against the smallest beginnings of sin. By "keeping the heart with all diligence," by putting on "the whole armor of God," by having faith as our shield, righteousness as our breastplate, the hope of salvation as our helmet, by keeping "the sword of the Spirit" bright with exercise, "praying with all prayer," standing near our Captain, looking to him, relying upon him, knowing that "without him we can do nothing,"—so must we fight! All this is necessary, if we would overcome.

It is not so easy to fight this fight as some suppose. It is not a true faith merely, an evangelical creed, a scriptural church, a comfortable sermon once or twice a week, a little Sabbath-keeping, an agreeable pause in your pleasures, giving to them a new relish — it is not this which constitutes Christianity. You that think religion so very easy a thing, have a care lest, when too late, you find that you knew not what true religion meant.

Easy? A depraved being to trample upon his lusts — a proud being to lie prostrate with humility and self-reproach — they that are "slow of heart to believe," to receive the Gospel as little children?

Easy? To "crucify the flesh," "to deny ungodliness," "to cut off a right hand, and to pluck out a right eye?"

Easy? To be in the world, and yet not of the world — to come out from it, not by the seclusion of the cloister, but by holiness of life — to be diligent in its duties, yet not absorbed by them; appreciating its innocent delights, and yet not ensnared by them; beholding its attractions, and yet rising superior to them?

Easy? To live surrounded by objects which appeal to the sight, and yet to endure as seeing what is invisible?

Easy? To pray and see no answer to prayer, and still pray on — to fight this battle, and find fresh foes ever rising up, yet still to fight on — to be harassed with doubts and fears, and yet walk on in darkness, though we see no light, staying ourselves upon God?

Easy? To be preparing for a world we have never visited, in opposition to so much that is captivating in a world where we have always dwelt, whose beauties we have seen, whose music we have heard, whose pleasures we have experienced?

Easy? To resist that subtle foe who has cast down so many of the wise and the mighty?

Easy? When Jesus says it is a "strait gate," and that if we would enter we must "strive," bidding us "take up our cross daily, deny ourselves and follow him?" Ah! it is no soft flowery meadow, along which we may languidly stroll, but a rough, craggy cliff that we must climb. "To him that overcometh!" It is no smooth, placid stream, along which we may dreamily float, but a tempestuous ocean we must stem. "To him that overcometh!" It is no easy lolling in a cushioned chariot, that bears us on without fatigue and peril. The trumpet has sounded to arms; it is not peace, but war, war for liberty, war for life, on the issue of which our everlasting destiny depends! If we are to be saved, we must "overcome."

But though the conflict is arduous, the encouragements are great. We have armor of proof. We have a mighty Champion. Victory is ensured to the brave. Others who stood on the same battle-field and fought with the same enemies, are now enjoying an eternal triumph. Not one faithful warrior ever perished. Their foes were not fewer than ours, their strength was not greater. They overcame by the same "blood of the Lamb" on which we rely.

> " Once they were mourning here below,
>   And wet their couch with tears;
> They wrestled hard, as we do now,
>   With sins, and doubts, and fears."

But they are wearing their crowns, they are enjoying their rest; and the feeblest and most unworthy of our own day, trusting in the same Saviour, shall inherit the same promise. Then let us overcome. Sheathe not the sword, and it shall never be wrested from you; lay not down the shield, and no fiery dart shall ever penetrate it; face the foe, and he shall never trample you down, never drive you back.

Listen to your Captain; how he animates you onward! Look to the crown he is ready to bestow upon you; eat of the hidden manna which he gives; read the name in the "white stone,"—the name of God,—his name of love, recorded for your encouragement; and thus be animated to walk worthy of this holy alliance, and not to allow the foe to wrench from you such an assurance of divine favor, such a passport to heavenly bliss.

A little more conflict, and that "white stone" shall introduce you to the inheritance above, where, in the everlasting repose of the inner sanctuary, you shall without intermission eat of the hidden manna.

> " Then let my soul march boldly on,
>   Press forward to the heavenly gate;
> There peace and joy eternal reign,
>   And glittering robes for conquerors wait."

Some of you may consider this subject visionary and unreal. You say, "I know nothing of this warfare. I know what the conflict of business is, the race of fashion, the bustle of toil or pleasure; but to anxiety about spiritual things I am a stranger."

You are enjoying peace — but — what peace? There is a captive in a dungeon — his limbs are fast chained to the walls — yet he is singing songs. How is it? Satan has given him to drink of his drugged cup, and he does not know where he is. Look at that other. He says, "it is peace." There is truly no fighting, but he is grovelling in the dust, and the heel of his foe is upon his neck. Such is the peace of every one going on in his wickedness, unpardoned and unsaved. "Taken captive by the devil at his will."

Chained in Satan's boat, you are swiftly gliding down the stream to ruin, and because it is smooth, you dream that it is safe! What is the difference between the saint and the sinner? Not that in the saint there is no sin. Not that in the sinner there is never a thought about God. The difference is this — that the saint is overcoming his sin; but the sin is overcoming the sinner. O, what a terrible thing if sin have the upper hand! No "hidden manna" is yours. The symbols of religion you may look at, but real religion must be a stranger to you. You know not its enjoyment. You do not taste it. It is a hidden thing. Heaven too will be hidden. You hear of its gates of pearl — but they will never open to you. You may catch the distant accents of its songs — but in those songs you will never join. And that "white stone" cannot be yours. You have no joyful anticipation of heaven—but a fearful looking-for of fiery indignation— or else the insensate resolve not to think at all. And the "new name"—no! you cannot read it! You know God by

H no such name as makes you seek his company. The thought of him renders you unhappy, and therefore you banish it from your mind. You are not now alarmed, but soon the spell may be broken, and you may find the chains riveted upon your soul forever.

I fancy I hear you say, "I wish that before it is too late, I could escape! But mine is a hopeless case. My heart is hardened against the Gospel, and evil habit has so got the mastery over me, that I have no power to begin this conflict!"

No, you have no power; but One has visited this world, and taken our nature, who can help you. The mighty Son of God became the suffering Son of Man, that he might be the Liberator of our enslaved race. He burst open the prison doors, that captive souls might escape. He stands near you, ready to break off your fetters and strengthen you to fight the enemy who has so long oppressed you. Tell him your simple but sad tale; how helpless, how miserable, how ruined you are! Tell him you want to be saved, but know not how to begin the work, and ask him both to begin and complete it for you! Let your prayer be this: "Be merciful to me a sinner;" and he who "came to destroy the works of the devil," he "whose nature and property is ever to have mercy and to forgive," will receive your "humble petitions; and though you be tied and bound with the chain of your sins, he, in the pitifulness of his great mercy, will loose you."

He will pardon your past shameful concessions to the foe, and, arraying you in "the whole armor of God," and animating you with his Holy Spirit, he will enable you so to fight against the world, the flesh, and the devil, that you also shall share in the prize of them that overcome; you also shall eat of the "hidden manna," and receive the "white stone."

DAWES

HENRY LAURENS DAWES, an American congressman, was born in Cummington, Massachusetts, October 30, 1816, and was educated at Yale University. He studied law and, after admittance to the bar in 1842, at once began to practise in North Adams, in his native State, removing to Pittsfield, in the same county, in 1864. He served in the State legislature, 1848-52, and, entering Congress as representative in 1857, was soon active in anti-slavery legislation. In 1875 he succeeded Sumner in the United States Senate and was re-elected in 1881 and 1887. During his congressional career he served on innumerable committees and was conspicuous in legislative action on the tariff and other topics of importance. To him is due the establishment in 1869 of the "Weather Bulletin" and the origin of the severalty law dividing the Indian lands, and he was the creator of the system of Indian education as far as it is due to legislation. Many of his speeches have been issued singly, but no collection has yet been made.

ON THE INDIAN POLICY

DELIVERED IN THE SENATE OF THE UNITED STATES, APRIL 5, 1880

NO tribe of Indians ever entered into a treaty with the United States that did not result in putting fetters upon them. They have been lassoed into imprisonment and confinement within limits that the necessities of growth in this government required, and no sooner have we made treaties than we have gone to work deliberately to violate them.

But it is not treaty obligations alone of which the Indian has to complain. Why, sir, the treatment of the Indian agents, and the army, and the whole department, with the Indian for long back is covered with blots, and stains, and bad faith, and aggravations to the Indian, and provocation to violence on his part.

While we have been deliberating over this very measure

in our committee on Indian affairs, a peaceable Indian chief who never raised his hand in violence upon a white man, whose home had been ceded to him by words of grant on the part of the United States as solemn and effective as a warranty deed, in consideration of his good behavior and peaceable deportment toward the United States — this is the language of the grant — who had been driven at the point of the bayonet from that home into the malaria of the Indian Territory, has there been enticed by false pretences into the Indian agent's own house, an agent of this modern civilization, and there shot down upon the floor in cold and cowardly murder by the soldiers of the United States under the direction of an Indian agent.

Sir, the Northern Cheyennes, taken by the army from their home and the graves of their fathers among the cool mountain streams of the Northwest, down to the torrid jungles and malaria of the Indian Territory, there to fall before the ravages of disease, when they broke away and wandered through the wilds of western Kansas seeking their old home, were taken by the armed soldiers of the United States and shut up in midwinter, in January, in a guard-house, when the thermometer was ten degrees below zero, without clothing to protect them from the inclemency of the weather. They were told by the officer whose official report I have here, " You shall have neither food nor drink nor fuel till you consent to go back to your doom in the Indian Territory," and there they were kept without either food or fuel or drink four or five days — the officer reports four, the Indians say it was seven — in what the officer calls " the freezing-out process." And then, when the chief was called out of the guard-room under pretence of a conference, armed soldiers were placed in siderooms, out of sight, and when he and his fellows came into a room for a peaceable conference they were seized and put in irons, and those in the guard-house breaking out with the resolution to die in flight for their homes rather than to die in the Indian Territory the victims of disease, were fired upon with shot and shell and every male member of the band but those in irons and two others, with thirty women and children, were laid corpses in the process.

Sir, I have before me the process pursued toward men supposed to be guilty of the murder of a young man from Massachusetts upon a stage route in Arizona. When an officer of the army called the Indians into council, having previously arranged with a half-breed that like Judas he should go among his brethren and betray the men he was willing to say were guilty, and when that process was gone through with, under the pretence of a council with friendly Indians, soldiers at a given signal shot them all dead.

Does anybody wonder, when these instances multiply around us every day, when flags of truce, like that under which General Canby fell at the hands of the Modocs, are violated by our own soldiers when they treat with the Indians; when the whole history of the dispensing of the Indian annuities and of the Indian appropriations is one long history of plunder; when we make our promises with no apparent intention of keeping them,—is it to be wondered at that the Indian question has come upon us with difficulties almost passing solution?

Sir, before we can do anything toward making something out of the Indian we must do justice to him. The process of extermination, I think, is substantially abandoned by our people. It has proved a failure, at least, with all the advantages under which it has been tried and the fidelity with which it has been pursued: sparing no expense of Indian warfare or cruel treatment, transferring the Indian from place to place, taking him from the cold regions of the north to the almost inhospitable and uninhabitable regions of the Indian Territory, there to die by hundreds; still the truth stares us in the face that there are more of them to-day than there were yesterday.

Take the Poncas, who lived upon a reservation the title to which was a grant, in so many words, from the United States, in which it was recited that it was in consideration of two things: first, of a like grant on the part of the Poncas to the United States, and next, of their long, peaceable, and quiet life and demeanor towards the United States. Take them and follow their band of eight hundred men, driven by soldiers into the Indian Territory, and falling down in the process and in the acclimation to four hundred and eighty-four, or about that number; yet it is true that within the last year, since they have come to be acclimated and taken care of, there are more of them than there were when the year began. So it is true of them all. And, sir, that policy pursued so faithfully has got to be abandoned, and I thank God that it has.

Then we have to deal with these Indians by some other process. Another process is like that shadowed forth in the argument of the senator from Alabama, that we shall violently break up their tribal relations and scatter them, wild and savage and uneducated, abroad in the community; subject to the laws and enjoying all the rights and privileges of citizens of the United States, having no other restraint upon them than the feeble and ineffectual restraint that comes from bringing them into a court of justice to plead to an indictment they cannot understand for the violation of a law they do not know the meaning of.

Sir, the senator from Colorado [Mr. Teller] well described the strength of the cords which bind the Indians to their bands. I venture to say there is not power enough in the United States to violently and against their will rend those cords. They are the ties of family, and kindred, and blood, as strong in the savage as in the civilized man, and stronger, perhaps, in some respects. If there were no question of humanity in it, it is an impossibility. You cannot with an army larger in number than all the bands themselves rend asunder by violence those cords and attachments which bind them one to another in families, any more than you could invade the homes of the civilized, scatter them and think vainly that thereby you had broken asunder all the ties that bind man to his family and to his kindred.

You may give up, then, Mr. President, all attempts thus to disintegrate and separate from their clans and their tribes the two hundred and fifty thousand Indians you have upon your hands and are obliged to feed by daily rations and clothe as you do your soldiers. You can neither exterminate them, nor can you violently separate and scatter them in the community and expect that you can make citizens of them. If you did it you would have two hundred and fifty thousand people gathering in the western States more than in the eastern, for they would not trouble us, but you might just as well turn loose the inmates of an insane asylum and impose upon them the restraints of law and require at their hands obedience to the obligations of citizenship as to undertake by this process to make citizens,— self-supporting, obedient to the law of the land,— of these Indians.

Then, sir, if you can neither exterminate them nor by the puny, ineffectual attempt at an enactment here at your desk, disintegrate and scatter them around through the forty-five millions of people we have here in this land, what next? Sir, you ought to improve them, make something of them, undertake to relieve yourselves of this burden which comes upon you as a just retribution for the long line of treatment in the past which finds no justification in any standard of justice, or of the right between the powerful and the weak. No one expects that you can make much out of the adult Indians. You cannot teach them much how to work and support themselves. Industrious habits do not come by the force of enactments. Industrious habits are the result of long years of training, beginning with early life.

You have, them, too, without the ability to speak our language, to understand those with whom they are obliged to treat daily in order to obtain the merest necessities of life. Take one of them, allot him in severalty, which seems now to be the panacea for all evils, one hundred and sixty acres of land, and surround him, as this bill and the other proposes, with the enterprising western pioneer who purchases the real estate, the one hundred and sixty acres on each side of him, and what then? He goes out to support himself. He cannot understand his neighbor. He only knows from sad experience, because he cannot forget that he never treats with that color without having the worst of it. How long would he live and support himself?

I had an interesting conversation a few days since with a chief of one of these tribes, as intellectual a man, as clear-headed, and as honest and truthful a man, according to the department and everybody else, as any one could be; a man who realized the condition of the Indians, a man who made it a study as well as he could, of what, so far as his tribe was concerned, was the best solution of this question. I asked him if he could have for each male member of his tribe one hundred and sixty acres of land allotted in severalty with the condition that it could not be alienated for twenty-five years, what he would say to that. It was a great while before he could be made to comprehend what I meant, with an earnest desire to understand the full meaning of these words; and when at last he seemed fully to comprehend them, shaking his head, he said, "It would not do us any good; it might our children; but we do not understand your language; we do not know how to treat with white men; they always get the better of us; they would pluck us as you do a bird."

Then I put the question in another form: "Suppose you were so allotted, and a good, honest Indian agent"— my friend from Illinois [Mr. Davis] almost laughs when I say that —" a good, honest Indian agent were put over you to keep off the white people and let you develop yourselves?"

"We don't know how to work very well; we were never taught to work; if our children could be brought up to understand your language and to understand what comes of work, to understand that what they earned to-day is theirs, and they can hold it against the world, they could take these lands and they could take care of themselves and of us, but we cannot do it."

There is more philosophy in that Indian's statement of the question than all that has been developed in the Indian policy of the government for the last quarter of a century. Take their children; above all take their girls into schools in which they may be taught the English language and English ways and English habits and ideas. They bring up the families; they take care of the children; from them the children learn to talk and learn to think and learn to act; and yet, in all the schools established in Indian agencies for the education of the Indians, the Indian girl is hardly thought of. Take the boy and make something of him; not keep him till he forgets his race and his parentage, but keep him until there shall be inspired in him a missionary spirit to go forth among those of his blood and attempt to make something of them.

Appropriate this $125,000 which in this bill you pledge yourselves to distribute every year *per capita* around among these people, to the education each year of these four thousand Ute Indians, and by the time this experiment shall have failed and the Indian question, so far as Colorado is concerned, shall have come back upon us with increased force, you will have raised up among those Indians a restraining and at the same time an elevating influence that shall quicken in the whole tribe a desire to acquire, and with it shall come also the desire to protect and keep their daily earnings; and with that comes the necessity and the desire for peace, and with peace comes respect for law, and that is the simple natural process and the only one, it seems to me, Mr. President, which opens up to us with any hope of success.

It is a long and tedious process out of this difficulty; it is beset with embarrassments and discouragements on every side; but those who understand best and appreciate more fully than I do all these difficulties have themselves the strongest confidence in its ultimate success. Certainly, sir, these puny efforts on the part of the government to deal with the Indian question, these homeopathic doses, are idle and are folly in the extreme. If I could see any good to come from this bill, recognizing as I do the imperative necessity of action in respect to these Utes, recognizing as I am free to do the earnest desire on the part of the Indian department to do the best possible thing, I should like to support it. I know that with great propriety and with necessity the department turns to Congress; for it is Congress, and Congress alone, that can solve this question; but I fear that by no such processes as those we are considering to-day, involving as they do (and which I do not think the Senate quite realize) an enormous expenditure of public moneys with so little in return, can the great result I desire be accomplished.

DOUGLASS

FREDERICK DOUGLASS, a famous American orator, was born a slave, the son of a white father and African mother, in Tuckahoe, Maryland, February, 1817. At ten years of age he was sent to Baltimore to live with one of his master's relatives and after a time found work in a shipyard, having by this time learned to read and write. In 1838 he escaped from slavery and fled to New Bedford, Massachusetts, where he lived for several years, and was aided in his efforts at self-education by William Lloyd Garrison. He now dropped his former master's name of Lloyd and adopted that of Frederick Douglass. At an anti-slavery convention in Nantucket in 1841 he delivered a speech that was so well liked that he was made the agent of the Massachusetts Anti-Slavery Society, and for four years lectured to large audiences throughout New England. He then went to Europe for two years in behalf of the anti-slavery cause, and during this time his freedom was purchased by his English friends. For several years following his return he edited at Rochester, New York, the "North Star," a weekly paper, and in 1870 became editor of the "New National Era" at Washington. He was appointed assistant secretary of the Santo Domingo commission in 1871 and the next year was presidential elector at large for New York State. He held the post of United States marshal of the District of Columbia, 1876-81, and recorder of deeds for the District for the five years following. In 1888-89 he was United States minister resident and consulgeneral to Hayti. He died near Washington, February 20, 1895. Douglass was a man of commanding appearance, fine manners, and a very noble style of delivery. His orations exhibited great refinement of language and grace of expression. Beside his orations and addresses he was the author of "Narrative of My Experiences in Slavery" (1844); "My Bondage and My Freedom" (1855); "Life and Times of Frederick Douglass" (1881).

WHAT THE BLACK MAN WANTS

DELIVERED AT THE ANNUAL MEETING OF THE MASSACHUSETTS
ANTI-SLAVERY SOCIETY AT BOSTON, 1865

MR. PRESIDENT,— I came here, as I come always to the meetings in New England, as a listener, and not as a speaker; and one of the reasons why I have not been more frequently to the meetings of this society, has been because of the disposition on the part of some of my friends to call me out upon the platform, even when they knew that there was some difference of opinion and of feeling between those who rightfully belong to this platform and myself; and for fear of being misconstrued, as desiring to interrupt or disturb the proceedings of these meetings, I have usually kept away, and have thus been deprived of that educating influence, which I am always free to confess is of the highest order, descending from this platform. I have felt, since I have lived out West, that in going there I parted from a great deal that was valuable; and I feel, every time I come to these meetings, that I have lost a great deal by making my home west of Boston, west of Massachusetts; for, if anywhere in the country there is to be found the highest sense of justice, or the truest demands for my race, I look for it in the East, I look for it here. The ablest discussions of the whole question of our rights occur here, and to be deprived of the privilege of listening to those discussions is a great deprivation.

I do not know, from what has been said, that there is any difference of opinion as to the duty of Abolitionists, at the present moment. How can we get up any difference at this point, or at any point, where we are so united, so agreed? I went, especially, however, with that word of Mr. Phillips, which is the criticism of General Banks and General Banks's policy. I hold that that policy is our chief danger at the present moment; that it practically enslaves the negro, and makes the proclamation of 1863 a mockery and delusion. What is freedom? It is the right to choose one's own employment. Certainly it means that, if it means anything; and when any individual or combination of individuals undertakes to decide for any man when he shall work, where he shall work, at what he shall work, and for what he shall work, he or they practically reduce him to slavery. He is a slave. That I understand General Banks to do — to determine for the so-called freedman, when, and where, and at what, and for how much he shall work, when he shall be punished, and by whom punished. It is absolute slavery. It defeats the beneficent intentions of the government, if it has beneficent intentions, in regard to the freedom of our people.

I have had but one idea for the last three years to present to the American people, and the phraseology in which I clothe it is the old abolition phraseology. I am for the " immediate, unconditional, and universal " enfranchisement of the black man, in every State in the Union. Without this, his liberty is a mockery; without this, you might as well almost retain the old name of slavery for his condition; for, in fact, if he is not the slave of the individual master, he is the slave of society, and holds his liberty as a privilege, not as a right. He is at the mercy of the mob, and has no means of protecting himself.

It may be objected, however, that this pressing of the negro's right to suffrage is premature. Let us have slavery abolished, it may be said, let us have labor organized, and then, in the natural course of events, the right of suffrage will be extended to the negro. I do not agree with this. The constitution of the human mind is such, that if it once disregards the conviction forced upon it by a revelation of truth, it requires the exercise of a higher power to produce the same conviction afterward. The American people are now in tears. The Shenandoah has run blood, the best blood of the North. All around Richmond, the blood of New England and of the North has been shed, of your sons, your brothers, and your fathers. We all feel, in the existence of this rebellion, that judgments terrible, widespread, far-reaching, overwhelming, are abroad in the land; and we feel, in view of these judgments, just now, a disposition to learn righteousness. This is the hour. Our streets are in mourning, tears are falling at every fireside, and under the chastisement of this rebellion we have almost come up to the point of conceding this great, this all-important right of suffrage. I fear that if we fail to do it now, if Abolitionists fail to press it now, we may not see, for centuries to come, the same disposition that exists at this moment. Hence, I say, now is the time to press this right.

It may be asked, "Why do you want it? Some men have got along very well without it. Women have not this right." Shall we justify one wrong by another? That is a sufficient answer. Shall we at this moment justify the deprivation of the negro of the right to vote, because some one else is deprived of that privilege? I hold that women, as well as men, have the right to vote, and my heart and my voice go with the movement to extend suffrage to woman; but that question rests upon another basis than that on which our right rests. We may be asked, I say, why we want it. I will tell you why we want it. We want it because it is our right, first of all. No class of men can, without insulting their own nature, be content with any deprivation of their rights. We want it, again, as a means for educating our race. Men are so constituted that they derive their conviction of their own possibilities largely from the estimate formed of them by others. If nothing is expected of a people, that people will find it difficult to contradict that expectation. By depriving us of suffrage, you affirm our incapacity to form an intelligent judgment respecting public men and public measures; you declare before the world that we are unfit to exercise the elective franchise, and by this means lead us to undervalue ourselves, to put a low estimate upon ourselves, and to feel that we have no possibilities like other men. Again, I want the elective franchise, for one, as a colored man, because ours is a peculiar government, based upon a peculiar idea, and that idea is universal suffrage. If I were in a monarchical government, or an autocratic or aristocratic government, where the few bore rule and the many were subject, there would be no special stigma resting upon me, because I did not exercise the elective franchise. It would do me no great violence. Mingling with the mass, I should partake of the strength of the mass; I should be supported by the mass, and I should have the same incentives to endeavor with the mass of my fellow men; it would be no particular burden, no particular deprivation; but here, where universal suffrage is the rule, where that is the fundamental idea of the government, to rule us out is to make us an exception, to brand us with the stigma of inferiority, and to invite to our heads the missiles of those about us; therefore, I want the franchise for the black man.

There are, however, other reasons, not derived from any consideration merely of our rights, but arising out of the condition of the South, and of the country; considerations which have already been referred to by Mr. Phillips; considerations which must arrest the attention of statesmen. I believe that when the tall heads of this rebellion shall have been swept down, as they will be swept down, when the Davises and Toombses and Stephenses, and others who are leading in this rebellion shall have been blotted out, there will be this rank undergrowth of treason, to which reference has been made, growing up there, and interfering with, and thwarting the quiet operation of the federal government in those States. You will see those traitors handing down, from sire to son, the same malignant spirit which they have manifested, and which they are now exhibiting, with malicious hearts, broad blades, and bloody hands in the field, against our sons and brothers. That spirit will still remain; and whoever sees the federal government extended over those southern States will see that government in a strange land, and not only in a strange land, but in an enemy's land. A postmaster of the United States in the South will find himself surrounded by a hostile spirit; a collector in a southern port will find himself surrounded by a hostile spirit; a United States marshal or United States judge will be surrounded there by a hostile element. That enmity will not die out in a year, will not die out in an age. The federal government will be looked upon in those States precisely as the governments of Austria and France are looked upon in Italy at the present moment. They will endeavor to circumvent, they will endeavor to destroy, the peaceful operation of this government. Now, where will you find the strength to counterbalance this spirit, if you do not find it in the negroes of the South? They are your friends, and have always been your friends. They were your friends even when the government did not regard them as such. They comprehended the genius of this war before you did. It is a significant fact, it is a marvellous fact, it seems almost to imply a direct interposition of Providence, that this war, which began in the interest of slavery on both sides, bid fair to end in the interest of liberty on both sides. It was begun, I say, in the interest of slavery on both sides. The South was fighting to take slavery out of the Union, and the North fighting to keep it in the Union; the South fighting to get it beyond the limits of the United States constitution, and the North fighting to retain it within those limits; the South fighting for new guarantees, and the North fighting for the old guarantees; both despising the negro, both insulting the negro. Yet, the negro, apparently endowed with wisdom from on high, saw more clearly the end from the beginning than we did. When Seward said the status of no man in the country would be changed by the war, the negro did not believe him. When our generals sent their underlings in shoulder-straps to hunt the flying negro back from our lines into the jaws of slavery, from which he had escaped, the negroes thought that a mistake had been made, and that the intentions of the government had not been rightly understood by our officers in shoulder-straps, and they continued to come into our lines, treading their way through bogs and fens, over briers and thorns, fording streams, swimming rivers, bringing us tidings as to the safe path to march, and pointing out the dangers that threatened us. They are our only friends in the South, and we should be true to them in this their trial hour, and see to it that they have the elective franchise.

I know that we are inferior to you in some things, virtually inferior. We walk about among you like dwarfs among giants. Our heads are scarcely seen above the great sea of humanity. The Germans are superior to us; the Irish are superior to us; the Yankees are superior to us; they can do what we cannot, that is, what we have not hitherto been allowed to do. But while I make this admission, I utterly deny that we are originally, or naturally, or practically, or in any way, or in any important sense, inferior to anybody on this globe. This charge of inferiority is an old dodge. It has been made available for oppression on many occasions. It is only about six centuries since the blue-eyed and fair-haired Anglo-Saxons were considered inferior by the haughty Normans, who once trampled upon them. If you read the history of the Norman Conquest, you will find that this proud Anglo-Saxon was once looked upon as of coarser clay than his Norman master, and might be found in the highways and byways of Old England laboring with a brass collar on his neck, and the name of his master marked upon it. You were down then!

You are up now. I am glad you are up, and I want you to be glad to help us up also.

The story of our inferiority is an old dodge, as I have said; for wherever men oppress their fellows, wherever they enslave them, they will endeavor to find the needed apology for such enslavement and oppression in the character of the people oppressed and enslaved. When we wanted, a few years ago, a slice of Mexico, it was hinted that the Mexicans were an inferior race, that the old Castilian blood had become so weak that it would scarcely run down hill, and that Mexico needed the long, strong, and beneficent arm of the Anglo-Saxon care extended over it. We said that it was necessary to its salvation, and a part of the "manifest destiny" of this Republic, to extend our arm over that dilapidated government. So, too, when Russia wanted to take possession of a part of the Ottoman Empire, the Turks were "an inferior race." So, too, when England wants to set the heel of her power more firmly in the quivering heart of Old Ireland, the Celts are an "inferior race." So, too, the negro, when he is to be robbed of any right which is justly his, is an "inferior man." It is said that we are ignorant. I admit it. But if we know enough to be hung, we know enough to vote. If the negro knows enough to pay taxes to support the government, he knows enough to vote; taxation and representation should go together. If he knows enough to shoulder a musket and fight for the flag, fight for the government, he knows enough to vote. If he knows as much when he is sober as an Irishman knows when drunk, he knows enough to vote, on good American principles.

But I was saying that you needed a counterpoise, in the persons of the slaves to the enmity that would exist at the South after the rebellion is put down. I hold that the American people are bound, not only in self-defence, to extend this right to the freedmen of the South, but they are bound by their love of country, and by all their regard for the future safety of those southern States, to do this—to do it as a measure essential to the preservation of peace there. But I will not dwell upon this. I put it to the American sense of honor. The honor of a nation is an important thing. It is said in the Scriptures, " What doth it profit a man if he gain the whole world, and lose his own soul? " It may be said, also, What doth it profit a nation if it gain the whole world, but lose its honor? I hold that the American government has taken upon itself a solemn obligation of honor, to see that this war, let it be long or let it be short, let it cost much or let it cost little, that this war shall not cease until every freedman at the South has the right to vote. It has bound itself to it. What have you asked the black men of the South, the black men of the whole country to do? Why, you have asked them to incur the deadly enmity of their masters, in order to befriend you and to befriend this government. You have asked us to call down, not only upon ourselves, but upon our children's children, the deadly hate of the entire Southern people. You have called upon us to turn our backs upon our masters, to abandon their cause and espouse yours; to turn against the South and in favor of the North; to shoot down the Confederacy and uphold the flag — the American flag. You have called upon us to expose ourselves to all the subtle machinations of their malignity for all time. And now, what do you propose to do when you come to make peace? To reward your enemies, and trample in the dust your friends? Do you intend to sacrifice the very men who have come to the rescue of your banner in the South, and incurred the lasting displeasure of their masters thereby? Do you intend to sacrifice them and reward your enemies? Do you mean to give your enemies the right to vote, and take it away from your friends? Is that wise policy? Is that honorable? Could American honor withstand such a blow? I do not believe you will do it. I think you will see to it that we have the right to vote. There is something too mean in looking upon the negro, when you are in trouble, as a citizen, and when you are free from trouble, as an alien. When this nation was in trouble, in its early struggles, it looked upon the negro as a citizen. In 1776 he was a citizen. At the time of the formation of the constitution the negro had the right to vote in eleven States out of the old thirteen. In your trouble you have made us citizens. In 1812 General Jackson addressed us as citizens — "fellow citizens." He wanted us to fight. We were citizens then! And now, when you come to frame a conscription bill, the negro is a citizen again. He has been a citizen just three times in the history of this government, and it has always been in time of trouble. In time of trouble we are citizens. Shall we be citizens in war, and aliens in peace? Would that be just?

I ask my friends who are apologizing for not insisting upon this right, where can the black man look in this country for the assertion of this right, if he may not look to the Massachusetts Anti-Slavery Society? Where under the whole heavens can he look for sympathy, in asserting this right, if he may not look to this platform? Have you lifted us up to a certain height to see that we are men, and then are any disposed to leave us there, without seeing that we are put in possession of all our rights? We look naturally to this platform for the assertion of all our rights, and for this one especially. I understand the anti-slavery societies of this country to be based on two principles,—first, the freedom of the blacks of this country; and, second, the elevation of them. Let me not be misunderstood here. I am not asking for sympathy at the hands of Abolitionists, sympathy at the hands of any. I think the American people are disposed often to be generous rather than just. I look over this country at the present time, and I see educational societies, sanitary commissions, freedmen's associations and the like,—all very good: but in regard to the colored people there is always more that is benevolent, I perceive, than just, manifested towards us. What I ask for the negro is not benevolence, not pity, not sympathy, but simply justice. The American people have always been anxious to know what they shall do with us. General Banks was distressed with solicitude as to what he should do with the negro. Everybody has asked the question, and they learned to ask it early of the Abolitionists, "What shall we do with the negro?" I have had but one answer from the beginning. Do nothing with us! Your doing with us has already played the mischief with us. Do nothing with us! If the apples will not remain on the tree of their own strength, if they are worm-eaten at the core, if they are early ripe and disposed to fall, let them fall! I am not for tying or fastening them on the tree in any way, except by nature's plan, and if they will not stay there, let them fall. And if the negro cannot stand on his own legs, let him fall also. All I ask is, give him a chance to stand on his own legs! Let him alone! If you see him on his way to school, let him alone,— don't disturb him! If you see him going to the dinner table at a hotel, let him go! If you see him going to the ballot-box, let him alone,— don't disturb him! If you see him going into a workshop, just let him alone,— your interference is doing him a positive injury.

General Banks's " preparation " is of a piece with this attempt to prop up the negro. Let him fall if he cannot stand alone! If the negro cannot live by the line of eternal justice, so beautifully pictured to you in the illustration used by Mr. Phillips, the fault will not be yours, it will be his who made the negro, and established that line for his government. Let him live or die by that. If you will only untie his hands, and give him a chance, I think he will live. He will work as readily for himself as the white man. A great many delusions have been swept away by this war. One was, that the negro would not work; he has proved his ability to work. Another was, that the negro would not fight; that he possessed only the most sheepish attributes of humanity; was a perfect lamb, or an " Uncle Tom;" disposed to take off his coat whenever required, fold his hands, and be whipped by anybody who wanted to whip him. But the war has proved that there is a great deal of human nature in the negro, and that " he will fight," as Mr. Quincy, our President, said, in earlier days than these, " when there is a reasonable probability of his whipping anybody."

INAUGURATION OF THE FREEDMEN'S MEMORIAL MONUMENT TO ABRAHAM LINCOLN

DELIVERED AT WASHINGTON, APRIL 14, 1876

FRIENDS AND FELLOW CITIZENS,— I warmly congratulate you upon the highly interesting object which has caused you to assemble in such numbers and spirit as you have to-day. This occasion is in some respects remarkable. Wise and thoughtful men of our race, who shall come after us, and study the lessons of our history in the

United States, who shall survey the long and dreary space over which we have travelled, who shall count the links in the great chain of events by which we have reached our present position, will make a note of this occasion — they will think of it, and with a sense of manly pride and complacency.

I congratulate you also upon the very favorable circumstances in which we meet to-day. They are high, inspiring and uncommon. They lend grace, glory and significance to the object for which we have met. Nowhere else in this great country, with its uncounted towns and cities, uncounted wealth, and immeasurable territory extending from sea to sea, could conditions be found more favorable to the success of this occasion than here.

We stand to-day at the national centre to perform something like a national act, an act which is to go into history, and we are here where every pulsation of the national heart can be heard, felt, and reciprocated.

A thousand wires, fed with thought and winged with lightning, put us in instantaneous communication with the loyal and true men all over the country.

Few facts could better illustrate the vast and wonderful change which has taken place in our condition as a people than the fact of our assembling here for the purpose we have to-day. Harmless, beautiful, proper, and praiseworthy as this demonstration is, I cannot forget that no such demonstration would have been tolerated here twenty years ago. The spirit of slavery and barbarism, which still lingers to blight and destroy in some dark and distant parts of our country, would have made our assembling here to-day the signal and excuse for opening upon us all the flood-gates of wrath and violence. That we are here in peace to-day is a compliment and credit to American civilization, and a prophecy of still greater national enlightenment and progress in the future.

I refer to the past not in malice, for this is no day for malice, but simply to place more distinctly in front the gratifying and glorious change which has come both to our white fellow citizens and ourselves, and to congratulate all upon the contrast between now and then, the new dispensation of freedom with its thousand blessings to both races, and the old dispensation of slavery with its ten thousand evils to both races — white and black. In view, then, of the past, the present, and the future, with the long and dark history of our bondage behind us, and with liberty, progress and enlightenment before us, I again congratulate you upon this auspicious day and hour.

Friends and fellow citizens: The story of our presence here is soon and easily told. We are here in the District of Columbia; here in the city of Washington, the most luminous point of American territory — a city recently transformed and made beautiful in its body and in its spirit; we are here, in the place where the ablest and best men of the country are sent to devise the policy, enact the laws, and shape the destiny of the republic; we are here, with the stately pillars and majestic dome of the Capitol of the nation looking down upon us; we are here with the broad earth freshly adorned with the foliage and flowers of spring for our church, and all races, colors, and conditions of men for our congregation; in a word, we are here to express, as best we may, by appropriate forms and ceremonies, our grateful sense of the vast, high, and pre-eminent services rendered to ourselves, to our race, to our country, and to the whole world, by Abraham Lincoln.

The sentiment that brings us here to-day is one of the noblest that can stir and thrill the human heart.   It has crowned and made glorious the high places of all civilized nations, with the grandest and most enduring works of art, designed to illustrate characters and perpetuate the memories of great public men. It is a sentiment which from year to year adorns with fragrant and beautiful flowers the graves of our loyal, brave, and patriotic soldiers who fell in defence of the Union and liberty.

It is the sentiment of gratitude and appreciation, which often, in the presence of many who hear me, has filled yonder heights of Arlington with the eloquence of eulogy and the sublime enthusiasm of poetry and song; a sentiment which can never die while the republic lives.

For the first time in the history of our people, and in the history of the whole American people, we join in this high worship and march conspicuously in the line of this time-honored custom. First things are always interesting, and this is one of our first things. It is the first time that, in this form and manner, we have sought to do honor to any American great man, however deserving and illustrious. I commend the fact to notice.

Let it be told in every part of the republic; let men of all parties and opinions hear it; let those who despise us, not less than those who respect us, know that now and here, in the spirit of liberty, loyalty, and gratitude; let it be known everywhere and by everybody who takes an interest in human progress and in the amelioration of the condition of mankind, that in the presence and with the approval of the members of the American House of Representatives, reflecting the general sentiment of the country; that in the presence of that august body, the American Senate, representing the highest intelligence and the calmest judgment of the country; in presence of the supreme court and chief justice of the United States, to whose decisions we all patriotically bow; in the presence and under the steady eye of the honored and trusted President of the United States, we, the colored people, newly emancipated and rejoicing in our blood-bought freedom, near the close of the first century in the life of this republic, have now and here unveiled, set apart, and dedicated a monument of enduring granite and bronze, in every line, feature, and figure of which the men of this generation may read — and those of after-coming generations may read — something of the exalted character and great works of Abraham Lincoln, the first martyr President of the United States.

Fellow citizens, in what we have said and done to-day, and in what we may say and do hereafter, we disclaim everything like arrogance and assumption. We claim for ourselves no superior devotion to the character, history, and memory of the illustrious name whose monument we have here dedicated to-day. We fully comprehend the relation of Abraham Lincoln both to ourselves and to the white people of the United States.

Truth is proper and beautiful at all times and in all places, and it is never more proper and beautiful in any case than when speaking of a great public man whose example is likely to be commended for honor and imitation long after his departure to the solemn shades, the silent continents of eternity. It must be admitted, truth compels me to admit, even here in the presence of the monument we have erected to his memory.

Abraham Lincoln was not, in the fullest sense of the word, either our man or our model. In his interest, in his associations, in his habits of thought, and in his prejudices, he was a white man. He was pre-eminently the white man's President, entirely devoted to the welfare of white men. He was ready and willing at any time during the first years of his administration to deny, postpone, and sacrifice the rights of humanity in the colored people, to promote the welfare of the white people of this country. In all his education of feelings he was an American of the Americans.

He came into the presidential chair upon one principle alone, namely, opposition to the extension of slavery. His arguments in furtherance of this policy had their motive and mainspring in his patriotic devotion to the interests of his own race. To protect, defend, and perpetuate slavery in the States where it existed, Abraham Lincoln was not less ready than any other President to draw the sword of the nation.

He was ready to execute all the supposed constitutional guarantees of the constitution in favor of the slave system anywhere inside the slave States. He was willing to pursue, recapture, and send back the fugitive slave to his master, and to suppress a slave rising for liberty, though his guilty master were already in arms against the government. The race to which we belong were not the special objects of his consideration. Knowing this, I concede to you, my white fellow citizens, a pre-eminence in this worship at once full and supreme. First, midst, and last you and yours were the object of his deepest affection and his most earnest solicitude. You are the children of Abraham Lincoln. We are at best only his stepchildren, children by adoption, children by force of circumstances and necessity. To you it especially belongs to sound his praises, to preserve and perpetuate his memory, to multiply his statues, to hang his pictures on your walls, and commend his example, for to you he was a great and glorious friend and benefactor.

Instead of supplanting you at this altar we would exhort you to build high his monuments; let them be of the most costly material, of the most costly workmanship; let their forms be symmetrical, beautiful, and perfect; let their bases be upon solid rocks, and their summits lean against the unchanging blue overhanging sky, and let them endure forever!

But while in the abundance of your wealth and in the fulness of your just and patriotic devotion you do all this, we entreat you to despise not the humble offering we this day unveil to view; for while Abraham Lincoln saved for you a country, he delivered us from a bondage, according to Jefferson, one hour of which was worse than ages of the oppression your fathers rose in rebellion to oppose.

Fellow citizens, ours is a new-born zeal and devotion, a thing of the hour. The name of Abraham Lincoln was near and dear to our hearts, in the darkest and most perilous hours of the republic. We were no more ashamed of him when shrouded in clouds of darkness, of doubt, and defeat than when crowned with victory, honor, and glory. Our faith in him was often taxed and strained to the uttermost, but it never failed. When he tarried long in the mountain; when he strangely told us that we were the cause of the war; when he still more strangely told us to leave the land in which we were born; when he refused to employ our arms in defence of the Union; when, after accepting our services as colored soldiers, he refused to retaliate when we were murdered as colored prisoners; when he told us he would save the Union if he could with slavery; when he revoked the proclamation of emancipation of General Fremont; when he refused to remove the commander of the Army of the Potomac, who was more zealous in his efforts to protect slavery than suppress rebellion; when we saw this, and more, we were at times stunned, grieved, and greatly bewildered; but our hearts believed while they ached and bled. Nor was this, even at that time, a blind and unreasoning superstition. Despite the mist and haze that surrounded him; despite the tumult, the hurry, and confusion of the hour, we were able to take a comprehensive view of Abraham Lincoln, and to make reasonable allowance for the circumstances of his position.

We saw him, measured him, and estimated him; not by stray utterances to injudicious and tedious delegations, who often tried his patience; not by isolated facts torn from their connection; not by any partial and imperfect glimpses, caught at inopportune moments; but by a broad survey, in the light of the stern logic of great events: and, in view of "that divinity which shapes our ends, rough hew them as we will," we came to the conclusion that the hour and the man of our redemption had met in the person of Abraham Lincoln. It mattered little to us what language he might employ upon special occasions; it mattered little to us, when we fully knew him, whether he was swift or slow in his movements; it was enough for us that Abraham Lincoln was at the head of a great movement, and was in living and earnest sympathy with that movement which, in the nature of things, must go on till slavery should be utterly and forever abolished in the United States.

When, therefore, it shall be asked what we have to do with the memory of Abraham Lincoln, or what Abraham Lincoln had to do with us, the answer is ready, full, and complete. Though he loved Cæsar less than Rome, though the Union was more to him than our freedom or our future, under his wise and beneficent rule we saw ourselves gradually lifted from the depths of slavery to the heights of liberty and manhood; under his wise and beneficent rule, and by measures approved and vigorously pressed by him, we saw that the handwriting of ages, in the form of prejudice and proscription, was rapidly fading away from the face of our whole country; under his rule, and in due time,— about as soon, after all, as the country could tolerate the strange spectacle,— we saw our brave sons and brothers laying off the rags of bondage, and being clothed all over in the blue uniforms of the soldiers of the United States; under his rule we saw two hundred thousand of our dark and dusky people responding to the call of Abraham Lincoln, and, with muskets on their shoulders and eagles on their buttons, timing their high footsteps to liberty and union under the national flag; under his rule we saw the independence of the black republic of Hayti, the special object of slaveholding aversion and horror, fully recognized, and her minister, a colored gentleman, duly received here in the city of Washington; under his rule we saw the internal slave trade which so long disgraced the nation abolished, and slavery abolished in the District of Columbia; under his rule we saw for the first time the law enforced against the foreign slave trade and the first slave-trader hanged, like any other pirate or murderer; under his rule and his inspiration we saw the Confederate States, based upon the idea that our race must be slaves, and slaves forever, battered to pieces and scattered to the four winds; under his rule, and in the fulness of time, we saw Abraham Lincoln, after giving the slaveholders three months of grace in which to save their hateful slave system, penning the immortal paper which, though special in its language, was general in its principles and effect, making slavery forever impossible in the United States.

Though we waited long we saw all this and more.

Can any colored man, or any white man friendly to the freedom of all men, ever forget the night which followed the first day of January, 1863? When the world was to see if Abraham Lincoln would prove to be as good as his word? I shall never forget that memorable night, when in a distant city I waited and watched at a public meeting, with three thousand others not less anxious than myself, for the word of deliverance which we have heard read to-day. Nor shall I ever forget the outburst of joy and thanksgiving that rent the air when the lightning brought to us the emancipation. In that happy hour we forgot all delay, and forgot all tardiness, forgot that the President had bribed the rebels to lay down their arms by a promise to withhold the bolt which would smite the slave system with destruction; and we were thenceforward willing to allow the President all the latitude of time, phraseology, and every honorable device that statesmanship might require for the movement of a great and beneficent measure of liberty and progress.

Fellow citizens, there is little necessity on this occasion to speak at length and critically of this great and good man, and of his high mission in the world. That ground has been fully occupied and completely covered both here and elsewhere. The whole field of fact and fancy has been gleaned and garnered. Any man can say things that are true of Abraham Lincoln, but no man can say anything new of Abraham Lincoln. His personal traits and public acts are better known to the American people than are those of any other man of his age. He was a mystery to no man who saw and heard him. Though high in position, the humblest could approach him and feel at home in his presence. Though deep, he was transparent; though strong, he was gentle; though decided and pronounced in his convictions, he was tolerant toward those who differed from him, and patient under reproaches.

Even those who only knew him through his public utterances obtained a tolerably clear idea of his character and personality. The image of the man went out with his words, and those who read him knew him. I have said that President Lincoln was a white man, and shared the prejudices common to his countrymen toward the colored race. Looking back to his times and to the condition of the country, this unfriendly feeling on his part may safely be set down as one element of his wonderful success in organizing the loyal American people for the tremendous conflict before them, and bringing them safely through that conflict.

His great mission was to accomplish two things; first, to save his country from dismemberment and ruin, and second, to free his country from the great crime of slavery. To do one or the other, or both, he must have the earnest sympathy and the powerful co-operation of his loyal fellow countrymen. Without this primary and essential condition to success, his efforts must have been vain and utterly fruitless. Had he put the abolition of slavery before the salvation of the Union, he would have inevitably driven from him a powerful class of American people, and have rendered resistance to rebellion impossible.

Viewed from the genuine abolition ground, Mr. Lincoln seemed tardy, cold, dull, and indifferent; but measuring him by the sentiment of his country, a sentiment he was bound as a statesman to consult, he was swift, zealous, radical, and determined. Though Mr. Lincoln shared the prejudices of his white fellow countrymen against the negro, it is hardly necessary to say that in his heart of hearts he loathed and hated slavery. He was willing while the South was loyal that it should have its pound of flesh, because he thought it was so nominated in the bond, but further than this no earthly power could make him go.

Fellow citizens, whatever else in this world may be partial, unjust, and uncertain, time! time! is impartial, just, and certain in its actions. In the realm of mind, as well as in the realm of matter, it is a great worker and often works wonders. The honest and comprehensive statesman, clearly discerning the needs of his country, and earnestly endeavoring to do his whole duty, though covered and blistered with reproaches, may safely leave his course to the silent judgment of time.

Few great public men have ever been the victims of fiercer denunciation than Abraham Lincoln was during his administration. He was often wounded in the house of his friends. Reproaches came thick and fast upon him from within and without, and from opposite quarters. He was assailed by Abolitionists; he was assailed by slaveholders; he was assailed by men who were for peace at any price; he was assailed by those who were for a more vigorous prosecution of the war; he was assailed for not making the war an abolition war; and he was most bitterly assailed for making the war an abolition war.

But now behold the change; the judgment of the present hour is, that taking him for all in all, measuring the tremendous magnitude of the work before him, considering the necessary means to ends, and surveying the end from the beginning, infinite wisdom has seldom sent any man into the world better fitted for his mission than was Abraham Lincoln.

His birth, his training, and his natural endowments, both mental and physical, were strongly in his favor. Born and reared among the lowly, a stranger to wealth and luxury, compelled to grapple single-handed with the flintiest hardships from tender youth to sturdy manhood, he grew strong in the manly and heroic qualities demanded by the great mission to which he was called by the votes of his countrymen. The hard condition of his early life, which would have depressed and broken down weaker men, only gave greater life, vigor, and buoyancy to the heroic spirit of Abraham Lincoln. He was ready for any kind and quality of work. What other young men dreaded in the shape of toil, he took hold of with the utmost cheerfulness.

> " A spade, a rake, a hoe,
> A pick-axe or a bill;
> A hook to reap, a scythe to mow,
> A flail, or what you will."

All day long he could split heavy rails in the woods, and half the night long he could study his English grammar by the uncertain flare and glare of the light made by a pine knot. He was at home on the land with his axe, with his maul, with gluts and his wedges; and he was equally at home on water, with his oars, with his poles, with his planks, and with his boathooks. And whether in his flatboat on the Mississippi river, or at the fireside of his frontier cabin, he was a man of work. A son of toil himself, he was linked in brotherly sympathy with the sons of toil in every loyal part of the republic.

This very fact gave him tremendous power with the American people, and materially contributed not only to selecting him to the presidency, but in sustaining his administration of the government. Upon his inauguration as President of the United States, an office even where assumed under the most favorable conditions, it is fitted to tax and strain the largest abilities, Abraham Lincoln was met by a tremendous pressure. He was called upon not merely to administer the government, but to decide, in the face of terrible odds, the fate of the republic. A formidable rebellion rose in his path before him; the Union was already practically dissolved. His country was torn and rent asunder at the centre. Hostile enemies were already organized against the republic, armed with the munitions of war which the republic had provided for its own defence. The tremendous question for him to decide was whether his country should survive the crisis and flourish or be dismembered and perish. His predecessor in office had already decided the question in favor of national dismemberment, by denying it the right of self-defence and self-preservation.

Happily for the country, happily for you and for me, the judgment of James Buchanan, the patrician, was not the judgment of Abraham Lincoln, the plebeian. He brought his strong common sense, sharpened in the school of adversity, to bear upon the question. He did not hesitate, he did not doubt, he did not falter, but at once resolved at whatever peril, at whatever cost, the union of the States should be preserved. A patriot himself, his faith was firm and unwavering in the patriotism of his countrymen.

Timid men said before Mr. Lincoln's inauguration that we had seen the last President of the United States. A voice in influential quarters said, Let the Union slide. Some said that a Union maintained by the sword was worthless. Others said, A rebellion of 8,000,000 cannot be suppressed. But in the midst of all this tumult and timidity, and against all this, Abraham Lincoln was clear in his duty, and had an oath in heaven. He calmly and bravely heard the voice of doubt and fear all around him, but he had an oath in heaven, and there was not power enough on earth to make this honest boatman, backwoodsman, and broad-handed splitter of rails evade or violate that sacred oath. He had not been schooled in the ethics of slavery; his plain life favored his love of truth. He had not been taught that treason and perjury were the proofs of honor and honesty. His moral training was against his saying one thing when he meant another. The trust which Abraham Lincoln had of himself and in the people was surprising and grand, but it was also enlightened and well founded. He knew the American people better than they knew themselves, and his truth was based upon this knowledge.

Had Abraham Lincoln died from any of the numerous ills to which flesh is heir; had he reached that good old age to which his vigorous constitution and his temperate habits gave promise; had he been permitted to see the end of his great work; had the solemn curtain of death come down but gradually, we should still have been smitten with a heavy grief and treasured his name lovingly. But dying as he did die, by the red hand of violence; killed, assassinated, taken off without warning, not because of personal hate, for no man who knew Abraham Lincoln could hate him, but because of his fidelity to Union and liberty, he is doubly dear to us and will be precious forever.

Fellow citizens, I end as I began, with congratulations. We have done a good work for our race to-day. In doing honor to the memory of our friend and liberator we have been doing highest honor to ourselves and those who come after us. We have been fastening ourselves to a name and fame imperishable and immortal. We have also been defending ourselves from a blighting slander. When now it shall be said that a colored man is soulless; that he has no appreciation of benefits or benefactors; when the foul reproach of ingratitude is hurled at us, and it is attempted to scourge us beyond the range of human brotherhood, we may calmly point to the monument we have this day erected to the memory of Abraham Lincoln.

JAY

JOHN JAY, a distinguished American diplomatist and reformer, born in New York city, June 23, 1817, was the son of the great Abolitionist Judge William Jay. He was prepared for college at Muhlenburg's Institute and graduated at Columbia College in 1836. He was admitted to the bar three years later, and immediately became prominent in his opposition to slavery. In 1847 he became secretary of the Irish Relief Committee and was counsel for a number of fugitive slaves. He was active in the formation of the Republican party, at Syracuse, in September, 1855. In 1866 and again in 1877 he was president of the Union League. In 1869 he was appointed minister to Austria, and remained in Vienna till 1875. Two years later Secretary Sherman nominated him chairman of the so-called Jay commission to investigate the New York custom house system. In 1883 Governor Cleveland made him Republican member of the State civil service commission. He was interested in the American Geographical and Statistical Society and was for many years manager and secretary of the New York Historical Society as well as president of the Huguenot Society. Mr. Jay delivered a great number of speeches on emancipation, episcopacy, and other public questions. Many of them have been published.

AMERICA FREE—OR AMERICA SLAVE

DELIVERED AT BEDFORD, WESTCHESTER COUNTY, NEW YORK,
OCTOBER 8, 1856

FELLOW CITIZENS OF WESTCHESTER,—Whatever local incentives may be found in other parts of our country, arising from historic association, or the memory of the departed, to keep alive a spirit of patriotism and a love of freedom, no spot in America has more of such associations than this our native county of Westchester.

During the first year of our Revolutionary struggle—the memorable year of the Declaration of Independence—'76—the active operations of the war were confined to this region and the two hostile armies were constantly on the alert under their respective commanders-in-chief.

The British with a numerous army and a powerful marine in possession of New York, Washington with an inferior and badly supplied army endeavoring to keep them in check, and "the battle of White Plains on the 28th of October," says the historian, "will long be remembered, as well as the dismal prospects of that year, when the patriot fathers of America had still the courage to declare their own independence and to assert the rights of nature and of nations."

Westchester was subsequently known—as those of you remember who have read "The Spy," of Fenimore Cooper, himself a Westchester man—as "the Neutral Ground;" and its citizens were exposed to the marauding bands of "Cowboys" and of "Skinners"—their homes plundered, their fields laid waste, their enclosures burnt, their families outraged and insulted by brutal deeds, such as are to-day announced to us by telegraph as being re-enacted on the plains of Kansas.

But in the patriotism of the farmers of Westchester there was no neutrality. It breathed in the State papers of the First Congress, which compelled the admiration of the British senate—it fought and bled on the battle-field of White Plains and the other battle-fields of America—and it exhibited its incorruptibility and its "backbone" in the three captors of Major André, whose virtue—proof against all temptations—saved the country from the treachery of Arnold when that traitor's plot for the betrayal of our liberties was on the verge of completion.

The integrity of Paulding, Williams, and Van Wart—whose descendants are yet among us—is a matter of history, familiar to every school-boy from the Atlantic to the Pacific, and remembered with pride by every American wherever the story is recalled—whether he visit the familiar spots, or chances upon a volume in which it is alluded to, or treads the aisles of Westminster Abbey where the remains of André repose and a sculptured monument to his memory reminds the American traveller that in the darkest period of the Revolution his country was saved from treachery and ruin by the incorruptibility of Westchester farmers.

You are not unmindful of that memorable event, or of the other Revolutionary associations that cluster about the Hudson on our west, Long Island Sound upon our south, the Harlem River, the Bronx, the Croton, and the hills and valleys and streams that add so much of beauty to Westchester. They are memories that cannot and ought not to be forgotten. Year by year our national anniversary revives them in all their greenness; and at all times they may be invoked to quicken our love of liberty and the common law if we cherish the principles of the founders of our Republic—or to reproach us if we are unfaithful guardians of that heritage of freedom which they bequeathed to us that we might transmit it unimpaired to our children.

This guardianship of American principles—I say American principles, because, although eternal in their origin and their character, they are American in their national development, American as contra-distinguished from European theories and modes of government—this guardianship of American principles devolves upon us at every election of our rulers, legislative or executive; but never was the responsibility deeper or more solemn than at this moment, when a sectional and aristocratic oligarchy, trampling upon faith and encroaching on our rights, aspires to rule the American people, and when the federal government, converted into a military despotism, is engaged, in the language of its master-spirit, in " crushing out " Freedom from our youngest Territory.

I have not hesitated to recall to you the memories of the past, familiar as they are to all of us; for I believe we are entering upon a contest involving the same great principles as those for which our fathers fought for seven long years.

"Let it ever be remembered," was their language, "that the rights for which we have contended are the rights of human nature;" and changeable as we are said to be—immersed in active pursuits as we undoubtedly are—I believe there are comparatively few among our countrymen—not one, I trust, among those whom I address—who do not cherish a love for the land of their birth—who do not remember with emotion its Revolutionary history—who do not contemplate with pride its progress in all that contributes to a nation's greatness, or who do not sometimes recall and dwell upon the glorious mission of the Republic among the nations of the earth as foreshadowed by her founders.

I trust there are comparatively but few in our free States at least who do not hope and pray that while in the Old World we may witness, in a single generation, the rise and fall of dynasties and of empires, this federal Union may stand till the rights of human nature, proclaimed in our "Declaration of Independence," are practically acknowledged throughout our own borders and throughout the world.

At this time it will hardly be contended by any one that the federal government, whether we look to the scenes recently enacted in the Capitol, or to the outrages now being perpetrated in Kansas, is advancing in that course of wisdom and equal justice in which its first movements were directed, and in which its founders trusted it would forever continue. Some will attribute this retrograde course to a general corruption of the American people. I am unwilling so to regard it.   The address of the First Congress to the people of Great Britain, drafted by a citizen of Westchester, commenced with words so signally appropriate to the present time that they sound like a voice from the dead—the voice of the fathers to their sons.

" When a nation, led to greatness by the hand of liberty, and possessed of all the glory that heroism, munificence, and humanity can bestow, descends to the ungrateful task of forging chains for her friends and children, and instead of giving support to freedom, turns advocate for slavery and oppression, there is reason to believe that she has ceased to be virtuous or has been extremely negligent in the appointment of her rulers."

Let us not believe, despite of all the apparent evidence to the contrary in the present character and conduct of our federal government, that the virtue which raised us from feeble colonies to a mighty Republic, clasping a continent in its embrace, has ceased out of the land.   Let us accept the alternative explanation of the crimes and inconsistencies that are at this moment startling the world, that " we have been extremely negligent in the appointment of our rulers."

Dwelling peacefully in free homes—enjoying quietly the reward of labor—acting generously toward our neighbors of the South, resting trustfully on ancient compacts, our people have slumbered in a false security.   But there is at last an uprising throughout the land that shows that the slumber is broken and they find their security was a dream.

And now that another presidential election approaches compelling the nation to look its destiny in the face—an election that involves a principle and an issue more momentous than any which have been submitted to this people since we became a nation—an election that is to pronounce the solemn judgment of the people on the conduct of the Pierce administration—an election that is to shape, for weal or woe, for freedom with its boundless blessings, or slavery with its untold curses, the territories of the great west and the mighty future of this continent possibly to the end of time; we are so searchingly to consider and so advisedly to act that the picture drawn by the First Congress of the mother country shall no longer be applicable to ourselves; "that, led to greatness by the hand of liberty and possessed of all the glory that heroism, munificence, and humanity can bestow," our country shall no longer "descend to the task of forging claims for her friends and children;" that from giving support to freedom she shall no longer turn advocate for slavery and oppression. We are so to act and so to vote that neither the people of Kansas and the farther west, nor the future historian, may have occasion to declare that we had either ceased to be virtuous or had been extremely negligent in the appointment of our rulers.

But, gentlemen, admissible as the plea of negligence may be for the past it will not avail you for the future. If you indorse the conduct of the Pierce administration as the Democratic party at Cincinnati have indorsed it—or if, by the adoption of any side issue, you permit that policy to continue, then the crime of the administration will become your own and its future consequences will rest upon your heads.

From this responsibility no citizen can exempt himself. By the constitution of our country every voter is one of its sovereigns—and is charged with the sacred duty of exercising his right of suffrage. A single vote, a few years since, elected a governor of Massachusetts. Frequently a single vote in Congress has had an important bearing upon the politics of the country; and at a moment like this, when the destiny of our country—the character of the great west—our domestic policy among ourselves—our foreign policy toward other nations, all depend upon the coming election, it is the duty of every man, whatever his party ties, whatever his personal preferences, to examine for himself carefully, truthfully, and impartially, the real issues involved in the contest—the conduct of the Pierce administration—the platform of the rival parties, and the claims to confidence of the rival candidates.

I propose now not to institute the thorough searching examination which I ask you to make—for, to do this, time would fail us—but I propose to direct your attention to the great facts of the case, and then to glance at the platforms and the candidates that are offered for your support; and while I confess an interest in this great subject, that dates from my boyhood, and has strengthened with my strength, I will endeavor, as far as possible, to let my remarks be calm, careful, truthful, and impartial.

The slavery question, as now presented to us by the administration of Mr. Pierce and the platform of Mr. Buchanan, however it may hitherto have been regarded, is certainly not, at this moment, a remote theoretical abstraction, but a stern, present, practical reality.

Great as are the wrongs which slavery inflicts upon the blacks, it is not these wrongs that have aroused the country. Fearful as may be the consequence both to the soil and the people of the South of that domestic system which Jefferson declares to be an " unremitting despotism on the one part," and " degrading submission on the other," it is not with the evils of slavery in the States that the nation has now to do. What the Republican party propose, is not interference with the constitutional rights of the slaveholders, but resistance to their aggression upon our rights, and such a reform in the administration of the Federal government, that whatever policy the slave-masters may think proper to pursue on their own plantations, and within their own State limits, they shall no longer monopolize the control of the nation—no longer use the federal government to extend and support their sectional interests—no longer interfere as they are now interfering with the rights of free laborers, and with the peace, prosperity, and fair fame of the Republic.

It is admitted by all—for the fact is too plain for denial, that the quiet pervading the country when Mr. Pierce was inaugurated, and which he called heaven to witness should not be disturbed by him, was interrupted, not by any efforts of the Abolitionists, but by the repeal of the Missouri Compromise. That repeal was the head and front of all the crimes against Kansas and against freedom, which have since aroused the people of the free States to such intense and absorbing indignation; and as such, you will allow me, I trust, to recall to you the prominent features of that compact, now violated and broken.

In 1802 the Louisiana Territory, embracing an area of 899,579 square miles—larger than all the then existing States, including the State of Missouri and the Territories of Kansas and Nebraska, was purchased from France. In 1820, Missouri having applied for admission as a State, with a constitution sanctioning slavery, and having been refused admission by the House of Representatives on that account, was admitted on the 20th of March of that year, by the adoption of the Missouri Compromise. That compromise was proposed by the slave States to the free States. They said to the free States, admit Missouri with slavery and we will agree that slavery shall never go into the remainder of the territory north of 36 degrees 30 minutes. The free State representatives yielded and the compact was embodied in the act preparatory to admitting Missouri, in these words:

" Sec. 8. Be it further enacted that in all that territory ceded by France to the United States, under the name of Louisiana, which lies north of thirty-six degrees thirty minutes of north latitude, not included within the limits of the State contemplated by this act, slavery and involuntary servitude, otherwise than as the punishment of crime, shall be, and is hereby forever prohibited."

It has been said that this was simply an agreement made by one Congress, which any subsequent Congress had the right to repeal. Such was not the view taken of it by the Southern statesmen, who urged its adoption on the North. They declared it to be, in the language of Mr. Louis McLane of Delaware, " A compact which shall be binding upon all parties and all subsequent legislatures—which cannot be changed, and will not fluctuate with the diversity of feeling and of sentiment to which this empire in its march must be destined."

The character of the compromise as an honorable and irrepealable compact, as binding upon the sons as upon the fathers, was recognized by the Southern press.

" It is true," said " Niles' Register," published at Baltimore, " it is true the compromise is supported only by the letter of the law, repealable by the authority which enacted it ; but the circumstances of the case give this law a moral force equal to that of a positive provision of the constitution ; and we do not hazard anything in saying that the constitution exists in its observance."

You probably know that it has been said by the facile demagogues of the day that the compromise was unconstitutional, that Congress had no power to prohibit slavery in the Territories, and that every man who contends for such a power is a traitor to the country.

I shall not respond at length to this arrogant assumption. It has been most ably disposed of by our own Senator Seward, foremost among the statesmen of our land; by Chase, whose clear tones aroused the country to its danger, and who has animated with his brave spirit the great State over which he presides; and by Charles Sumner, at whose name your pulses quicken, and around whose couch cluster the sympathies of the Christian world, listening to a silence more eloquent than speech. Whether he shall rise from that couch, which may God soon grant, to resume the vacant chair that is now teaching the Senate and the nation so profound a lesson, or whether he shall descend to the grave in his early manhood, he will live on the page of history and in the hearts of his countrymen—among those who, in the language of Burke, are the guide-posts and landmarks of a State.

I need not repeat the elaborate exposures by these statesmen of the fallacy of " popular sovereignty " in the Territories as opposed to congressional legislation on the subject of slavery; but let me remind you that the very first Congress under the constitution, in the year 1789, recognized and affirmed this doctrine, embodied by Jefferson in the great western ordinance of 1787, which forever excluded slavery from the Territory that now embraces Ohio, Indiana, and Illinois. Remember that this doctrine was then sanctioned and approved by Washington; that in 1800 it was approved by John Adams, in the Territorial Act for Indiana; in 1805, and again in 1804 by Thomas Jefferson, in the act for Michigan and Illinois. In 1834 by Andrew Jackson, with reference to Wisconsin and Iowa. In 1836 and 1838 by Martin Van Buren, in reference to the same Territories. In 1848 by James K. Polk, as regards the whole of Oregon, and in March, 1853, by Millard Fillmore, in reference to the Territory of Washington. In all of these acts slavery was expressly prohibited by Congress.

The right of Congress to prohibit slavery in the Territories is as well settled as any doctrine can be by the contemporaneous authority of the framers of the constitution; by its unquestioned and practical recognition by successive Congresses for nearly seventy years, and by the uniform unbroken acquiescence of the American people. Whose are the dicta that are to outweigh the recorded judgment and will of the nation, of its legislatures and its presidents from Washington to Fillmore?

The Missouri Compromise, when adopted, was hailed by the South as " a great triumph," in the language of Mr. Pinckney, of South Carolina, and at the North was accepted as a defeat, and most of the free States men who voted for it were repudiated by their constituents and retired to private life. The compact however was regarded as an eternal landmark, never to be removed, and none dreamed of questioning in regard to its observance the good faith of the Southern people.

If ever men were bound in honor to abide by a bargain the people of the slave States were bound religiously by that compact. We had yielded to them an organized State, adding on the instant to their political strength; taking in return only a future and distant right to an unsettled Indian Territory, that was likely to remain unsettled for at least another generation.

Years rolled on; the generation of that day pass from the stage; their successors repeatedly approve the principle of the compromise made in the division of the Louisiana Territory. They establish the line of 36 degrees and 30 minutes as the limit to slavery in New Mexico. They even propose to us to make a similar bargain in reference to the Territory ceded by Mexico, and to extend the line to the Pacific, and having thus estopped themselves from ever questioning its constitutionality, or binding force, these very men, when the time comes for us to occupy our share of the Louisiana Territory, consecrated to freedom, repudiate the bargain; violate their compact, break their faith, and open wide the doors to slavery.

For that deed of infamy history has no precedent and language no fitting name.

Of the probability of accomplishing so immense a fraud, the chief perpetrators themselves entertained at one time the greatest doubts. The very author of the bill declared the hand " ruthless " that should attempt to disturb the Missouri Compromise. Even Atchison, the senator from Missouri and the arch leader in the scheme of perfidy, declared but the session before, on the floor of the Senate, that much as he regretted the ordinance of 1787 and the Missouri Compromise " they are both irremediable. There is no remedy for them. We must submit to them. I am prepared to do it. It is evident that the Missouri Compromise cannot be repealed. . . . I have no hope that the restriction will ever be repealed."

The attempt however was resolved to be made, and the instrument of the slave power, selected for the purpose, was Stephen Arnold Douglas, a senator from Illinois, and it was then pretended that the freemen of the North volunteered by this free State senator to surrender their rights to this mighty Territory, and that the South were guiltless of violating their compact in accepting such voluntary surrender.

As reasonable would it have been for the British spy to have claimed that the American colonist had commissioned Benedict Arnold to surrender West Point to Hessian troops, as for the slave masters to pretend that the freemen of the North had commissioned Arnold Douglas, or any other Arnolds, either in the Senate or the House, to surrender to slave labor and slave policy that noble Territory, the " West Point " of our Northern and Eastern States, and yet destined to stand, as I firmly believe, in despite of treachery and of traitors, the stronghold and citadel of American freedom.

The idle pretence was disposed of almost as soon as it was uttered. The free States, at first uttered incredulous, unable to believe in the possibility of such bad faith on the part of their Southern brethren, were soon convinced that the treachery was real, and there arose from every free State, from cities, towns and villages, from mass meetings and the public press, from the stump and from the pulpit, one indignant shout of reprobation and of warning.

But the slave power, conscious of its waning political and essential strength, and dreading the sight of free States prosperous and happy on the plains of Kansas, hazarded all upon this die. The hesitating confederates of Arnold Douglas, startled by the bursts of thunder that reverberated through the northern skies, were yet in the hands of masters accustomed to wield the lash and enforce obedience. Backed by a pliant Executive, whose inaugural promises were as chaff scattered by the wind, the rules of the House of Representatives were violated; the proper business of the nation was suspended, and at midnight on the 30th of May, 1854, the deed was done and the fact recorded on the page of history, never to be forgotten, never to be effaced, that while there may be faith among savages and honor among thieves, the slave masters of America, their tools, aiders and abettors, know not honor and keep not faith.

That day changed the relation in which the freemen of

the North and the slaveholders of the South had before stood to each other. For faith, the great ligament of society, had been broken and confidence was at an end. Freedom had before been yielding to and confiding, even more generous to the South than just to herself; ready to give and take, and ever giving more than she received, but never expecting to be swindled out of the whole. The settlement of disputes by compromise had frequently been resorted to and had been regarded with favor; but now that a time-honored and solemn compact had been ruthlessly violated and the too credulous North had been cheated out of her allotted portion, the sentiment of the free States, applauded to the echo in public assemblies, has been and will continue to be " no more compromises with slavery."

The repudiation of good faith by the slave power has been followed by the consequences that might in part have been expected by those who remembered the olden maxim, " false in one thing, false in all," or that other maxim which teaches us that " where law ends, tyranny begins." . . .

Let us see, gentlemen, what this slave power is, which, trampling upon compacts and defying the constitution, controls the federal government and employs its army and its treasury to force slavery upon an unwilling people.

It has long been believed by those who have carefully scrutinized the institutions and policy of the slave-holding States that but a small proportion of their citizens were holders of slaves; but until the publication of the last census of 1850 the statistics were wanting to confirm this belief. That census disclosed the astounding fact that the slaveholders of the South, men, women, and children, including the hirers of slaves, all told, numbered only 347,820,—about half the number of persons residing in the city of New York and its immediate vicinity; that of these, 68,820 own but a single slave, and 105,683 less than five slaves each. So that, deducting those who have only a few home servants for convenience, and are not specially interested in the perpetuation and extension of the system, there remain but about 200,000 slaveholders composing that slave power which rules as with a rod of iron not only the 6,000,000 of non-slaveholders at the South, but the 20,000,000 of the whole nation.

It has been said with truth that the privileged aristocracy of England is far less powerful, and infinitely less arrogant, than this aristocratic oligarchy of slaveholders.

The census further discloses the relative proportion between the slaveholders and non-slaveholders in each State, and shows us that there is not one slaveholding State in the Union where the slaveholders constitute one tenth of the white population, and in some of them not a thirtieth part.

The value of the slaves held by this handful of men from whose lawless ambition come all the disturbances to our peace, is estimated by Mr. Shater of Alabama at two thousand millions of dollars—a large advance on Mr. Clay's estimate a few years ago, of twelve hundred millions; but whether the amount be correctly estimated or not it constitutes an immense capital, hardly to be realized and comprehended without some mental effort; a capital which, firmly united and skilfully wielded, is now waging so fierce a war with the free labor of the northern States.

Discarding for the present all those considerations of right and justice which instinctively occur to every right-minded person when slavery is mentioned—foregoing on this occasion all expression of sympathy for the millions of beating hearts that in the arithmetic of slavery count but as units under the sign of dollars—dispensing with aught that might seem to savor of philanthropy, or, as some style it, fanaticism, and leaving the entire question of slavery in the States to the people of those States who, in the language of Mr. Faulkner of Virginia, " have a right to demand its extermination," let me direct your attention to the bearing of the question upon yourselves, to the direct, permanent, practical, and pecuniary interest which you and your children have in the rescue of Kansas from the grasp of slavery.

I need not remind you that slave labor and free labor are antagonistic. They cannot flourish, they hardly co-exist together. This fact was declared in the strongest terms by the ablest statesman of Virginia in the constitutional convention of 1830.

The hon. C. J. Faulkner said:

" Slavery is an institution which presses heavily against the best interests of the State. It banishes free white labor, it exterminates the mechanic, the artisan, the manufacturer; it deprives them of occupation, it deprives them of bread; it converts the energy of a community into indolence, its power into imbecility, its efficiency into weakness. Sir, being thus injurious, have we not a right to demand its extermination? Shall society suffer that the slaveholder may continue to gather his crop of human flesh? Must the country languish, droop, and die that the slaveholder may flourish ? "

Shall all interests be subservient to one, all right subordinate to those of the slaveholder ? Has not the mechanic, have not the middle classes their rights—rights incompatible with the interests of slavery?

The hon. T. J. Randolph:

" Slavery has the effect of lessening the free population of a country . . . Those who remain, relying upon the support of casual employment, often become more degraded in their condition than the slaves themselves."

The hon. James Marshall said:

" Wherefore, then, object to slavery? Because it is ruinous to the whites, retards improvement, roots out an industrious population, banishes the yeomanry of the country,
deprives the spinner, the weaver, the smith, the shoemaker,
the carpenter of employment and support. The evil admits
of no remedy; it is increasing, and will increase, until the
whole country will be inundated by one black wave with a
few white faces here and there floating on the surface. The
master has no capital but what is invested in human flesh;
the father, instead of being richer for his sons, is at a loss
to provide for them. There is no diversity of occupation,
no incentive to enterprise. Labor of every species is dis-
reputable, because performed by slaves. Our towns are
stationary, our villages everywhere declining and the general
aspect of the country marks the course of a wasteful, idle,
reckless population, who have no interest in the soil and care
not how much it is impoverished."

We may assume therefore that if Kansas is given up to
slavery, it will be thereby closed to the better class of free-
laborers not only of our own country, but of Europe. The
great body of emigration westward-bound from our Atlantic
States, never seeks and never will seek slave soil where not
labor but the laborers themselves are bought and sold, and
where labor is stripped of the dignity that belongs to it, and is
treated with contempt.

Now look on the map blackened by slavery and you will
see that Kansas is the key to the large territory lying to the
west of it, the boundless regions of Utah and New Mexico,
extending hundreds of miles till they meet the eastern boundary of California. Is it not clear that if we lose Kansas
we shall in all probability lose not only the Indian Territory
lying to the south of it, but those vast Territories stretching
to the westward and large enough to make more than six
States of the size of Pennsylvania? Governor Reeder, in a

speech at New York, put this grave question in the clearest light. He said:

" With Kansas a slave State—and you will remember that Kansas is 900 miles long—I will thank any one to tell me how he is going to save the second, the third, or the fourth, each one further and further out of reach—each one with more slave States intervening."

If Kansas is lost to freedom, those Territories are all lost. We are fighting the battle once for all. Now or never—now and forever.

Secure Kansas and all the blessings of freedom—free labor, free schools, free speech, a free press, enlightened legislation, humane institutions, and that priceless heritage, the common law, are secured for our children.

Lose Kansas and what will be the result? Not only will the curse of slavery fasten like a cancer upon that beautiful Territory—spreading desolation physical and moral in its extending course, but the vast emigration from abroad that is now poured into our midst and overflows westward, stopped suddenly by a line of slave States, will fall back upon our free States, giving us a surplus population that we do not want and which will necessarily interfere with the employment and the wages of our own citizens. This is a practical view of the case which every farmer, every mechanic, and every laborer in the free States should carefully consider.

Compare again the relative addition made to the commercial prosperity of the Atlantic States, and particularly of the city of New York, by Ohio and Kentucky, and then glancing forward to the future, if but for fifty or an hundred years hence, endeavor to estimate the superior benefits to accrue to the Atlantic States from these western Territories if organized as free States over those to accrue from their establish-

'ment as slave communities. Think too of the difference it will make to your children and grandchildren if they wish to emigrate to those Territories whether they are to enter a State on an equal footing with the highest citizen or as one whose condition is regarded as inferior to that of the southern slave.

Of its hatred to free society the Democratic party at the South do not pretend to make a secret. " Free society," says the " Muscogee (Ala.) Herald," a Buchanan organ—" we sicken at the name. What is it but a conglomeration of greasy mechanics, filthy operatives, small-fisted farmers, and moon-struck theorists? All the northern and especially the New England States are devoid of society fitted for well-bred gentlemen. The prevailing class one meets with is that of mechanics struggling to be genteel and small farmers who do their own drudgery, and yet who are hardly fit for association with a southern gentleman's body servant."

Contrast, gentlemen, with that sentiment, now reiterated by the Buchanan organs at the South, the sentiment expressed by the leader of the Republican party: " Free labor—the natural capital which constitutes the real wealth of this great country and creates that intelligent power in the masses alone to be relied on as the bulwark of free institutions."

You have in these rival sentiments the gist of the issue now submitted to the American people. It is a struggle between slavery and freedom—between the small oligarchy of slave masters with its capital of $2,000,000,000 invested in human flesh and the great body of free laborers who constitute the bulk of the nation for the possession of the unorganized Territories of the United States.

These Territories exceed in extent by some thirty-three thousand square miles all of the United States both free and slave States; and whose area is more than twice as large as

that of the free States now admitted to the Union. The
slave States have already secured for slavery an area of 857,-
508 square miles, while the free States embrace only 612,596
square miles, and with this immense preponderance in their
favor, with millions of acres yet unoccupied, they seek to de-
fraud us of Kansas and Nebraska Territories, doubly ours by
divine right and by human compact, and to force slavery into
every part of the continent where the flag of our Union
waves and federal authority has sway.

It is idle to talk of pacification or compromise; it is idle to
speak of the repeal of the Missouri Compromise as a thing to
be regretted but at the same time to be acquiesced in. That
repeal has not yet made Kansas a slave State, and if we are
true to ourselves it never will make Kansas a slave State. It
was but the commencement, not the end of the battle. Its
passage shows not that we have lost Kansas, but only that
slaveholders have lost their honor. It shows that henceforth
against the slave power which mocks at faith and tramples on
compacts, which glories in the brutality that struck down a
defenceless senator and insulted at one blow the sovereignty
of Massachusetts, and the right of the people and which now
holds Kansas by the throat—that against this power our only
safety is in the rescue of the government from its control,
and its absolute restriction of slavery to the States where it
now exists. With a foe that treaties cannot bind, and that
glories alike in national perfidy and social treachery, eternal
vigilance must be the price of liberty—vigilance to protect
the people from the betrayal of their dearest rights; vigilance
to shield their representatives in Congress in unsuspecting
moments from the stealthy blow of the assassin. . . .

Of Cuba, the design to annex it is intimated in the last
resolution of the Cincinnati platform, where it is declared

that " the Democratic party will expect of the next administration, that every proper effort be made to ensure our ascendency in the Gulf of Mexico." And Mr. Keitt recently declared in public that Cuba would be taken and that " the Democratic party would take it."

" The proper efforts" to this end, which are expected of Mr. Buchanan, should he be elected to the presidency, were disclosed by him in advance in the Ostend manifesto. A price is to be offered to Spain for Cuba far beyond its present value; when that has been refused, as it has been, and as in all probability it will be again, then the question is to be considered, " Does Cuba, in the possession of Spain, seriously endanger our peace and the existence of our cherished Union? " " Should this question be answered in the affirmative, then, by every law, human and divine, we shall be justified in wresting it from Spain if we have the power ! "

This is the " proper method," approved by Mr. Keitt, and which in a certain contingency he proposes to apply not only to the gem of Spain, but to the treasury of the United States,—

> — " the good old plan,
> That they shall take who have the power,
> And they shall keep who can."

It was to the credit of Mr. Marcy that this proposal was repudiated and its morality denied. But if Mr. Buchanan shall become the President of the Republic, and his piratical doctrines avowed at Ostend become, as Mr. Keitt expects, a leading principle of his administration, we may live to see our once gallant navy manned with lawless buccaneers, setting forth to seize Cuba—" if they have the power "—with the black flag of slavery and the death's head and cross-bones of the pirate flaunting defiance to the world, above the star-spangled banner of our country.

On the question of disunion, as on that of the Missouri Compromise, the fact that the candidate of the Democratic party is " no longer James Buchanan," is evident when we recall his former sentiments on the subject and compare them with that of the platform which he has now adopted as " his guide, philosopher, and friend." " Disunion," said Mr. James Buchanan, " is a word which ought not to be breathed even in a whisper. The word ought to be considered one of direful omen, and our children taught that it is sacrilege to pronounce it."

Mr. A. G. Brown, one of the committee who announced the Cincinnati nomination to Mr. Buchanan, in anticipating the possible success of the Republican party, said in a recent speech :

" If indeed it has come to this that the Union is to be used for these accursed purposes, then, sir, by the God of my fathers, I am against the Union; and, so help me heaven, I will dedicate the remainder of my life to its dissolution."

Mr. Keitt frankly avows that he " has been a disunionist since he began to think."

The " Richmond Enquirer " declares, after enumerating the preparations of Virginia for war:

" Virginia makes no boast of these preparations, but, sure as the sun shines over her beautiful fields, she will treat the election of an Abolitionist candidate as a breach of the treaty of 1789 and a release of every sovereign State in the South from all part and lot in its stipulations."

The Southern Democracy are aware, in the language of the " Nashville Banner," that if the Republican party succeeds, they " can have no more fortunate wars—no more judicious purchases of territory—no more annexing of independent States on the southern border."

They are using every effort to secure Kansas and our other Territories; with Cuba, Nicaragua, and a part or the whole of Mexico, as also Southern California, with the view of forming an independent Southern Empire. The thought of disunion to some of them is an ever-present thought. The "South Carolinian" declares that "the success of Buchanan might stave off the dissolution of the Union for a time, but that the event is inevitable."

Another South Carolina paper exultingly declares that "the southern skies are looking bright, and all the auguries foretell southern union, southern independence, and the coming greatness of a southern republic."

"Disunion," a word that Mr. Buchanan would not have spoken in a whisper, the candidate of the Democratic party hears shouted exultingly in crowds; and he has added fuel to the treasonable flames that his partisans are kindling in the South, by unjustly intimating that the people of the North are "intermeddling" with the domestic concerns of the South when they resist pro-slavery aggression upon rights secured to them by compact. . . .

The platform of the American (sometimes called the Know-Nothing) party practically ignores the one great issue now agitating the country; and, as regards the rights of Kansas on the one hand and the schemes for pro-slavery extension on the other, preserves so significant a silence and so positive a neutrality that those entertaining the most opposite opinions on these points are expected to meet in harmony and elect a President upon the ground of proposed reforms in the naturalization of aliens, with neither pledges nor principles on the one question of the day. The Northern members of the national convention at which the platform was adopted, offered a resolution to the effect "that we will nominate no candidate for President or vice-president who is not in favor of interdicting the introduction of slavery north of 36 degrees 30 minutes." The resolution was laid on the table by a vote of yeas 141 to nays 52; and Mr. Fillmore was nominated on this neutral platform, which offers no opposition whatsoever to the extension of slavery. Mr. Fillmore himself stands before the country a perfect cipher on the question of Kansas, whose wrongs have elicited from him neither sympathy nor rebuke. . . .

It is pleasant, gentlemen, to turn from these schemes for slavery extension to glance at the Republican party that has sprung into existence, like the armed Minerva, from the brain of Jove—beautiful in its proportions and terrible in its strength—with the principles of Washington and the Fathers for its chart, and " the pathfinder of empire " to bear aloft its standard.

The platform of the Republicans, as adopted at Philadelphia on the 18th of June, 1856, is at once so simple and comprehensive as to admit all Americans who are in favor of restoring the government to the principles of Washington, and putting a final stop to the extension of slavery, without compromising their individual preferences on the other political questions which naturally exist in our government, but which are, for the time, overshadowed by this paramount issue.

The Republican party holds that an adherence to the principles of the Fathers and the Declaration of Independence— which the sham democracy of the day ridicules as a tissue of glittering sounding generalities—is essential to the preservation of our republican institutions, of the federal constitution, of the rights of the people, and the union of the States. It denies the authority of Congress, or of any territorial legislature, or of any association of individuals to establish slavery in the Territories, and claims that it is the right and the duty of Congress to prohibit in the Territories those twin relics of barbarism—slavery and polygamy. It arraigns the Pierce administration before the country and the world for the crimes it has instigated and perpetrated against Kansas. It declares that Kansas should be admitted as a free State, with its present free State constitution; and, having thus declared its policy at home, it denounces the highwayman's plea, that might makes right, as declared in the Ostend circular, as unworthy of American diplomacy.

Is there a single point in that platform to which you cannot heartily subscribe? Do you find there anything that conflicts with the rights of the South, with the duties of the North, or with the proper harmony of the Union? For myself, I believe that the triumph of these principles—making it a fixed fact for all coming time, that slavery shall not be extended beyond its present limits—can alone quiet the country and secure the stability and repose of the Republic. If the struggle is not now ended it will undoubtedly continue. The election of Buchanan and the triumph of slavery would be not a settlement but only a postponement of the question.

Such are the principles of the Republicans, which they have not invented in Cincinnati nor imported from Ostend, but which they find in the writings of the Fathers of the Republic, and in the constitution that they ordained for the establishment of liberty and justice. Such is the platform,—now for the candidate. . . .

The hour for a change has come and with the hour appears the man. The country demands a change not only of policy but of rulers.

We want no longer men who have made politics a trade—

who have grown gray in party traces—who in the pursuit of office have veered from federalism to democracy, from democracy to slavery and buccaneering, and who now merge principles and ideality in the Cincinnati platform,—nor do we want one who has plunged from abolitionism into slave-catching and from slave-catching by a natural transition, I cannot call it a descent, into sectionalism and disunionism—viewing the while with cold indifference the sacrifice of freedom and the wrongs of Kansas. Our people demand one whose heart beats responsive to their own—who unites the generous enthusiasm of youth with the matured vigor and wisdom of manhood.

They need one who has given a guarantee in the past for his career in the future—one whose identity and individuality is stamped upon his life—who fears not to avow in outspoken words his manly principles and who would scorn to become the padlocked plank of a platform or the pliant puppet of a party.

The day approaches when you are to do your part toward determining the question of America free or America slave. One of the famous laws promulgated by Solon for the governance of the Athenians declared dishonored and disfranchised every citizen who in a civil sedition stood aloof and took part with neither side. Here, gentlemen, the very government is in rebellion against the constitution and the people and Kansas looks to you to free her from its tyrannic grasp. Remember the dignity of your position—ponder the importance of your vote. Upon the ballots cast in your quiet village may depend the future of the republic—the destiny of the continent.

The issue is the broad one of freedom and slavery. All other issues are for the time absorbed in this, and personal animosities and prejudices should disappear before a common danger as in the early days of the republic. Shall our constitutional liberties be preserved? Shall the mission of the country be accomplished? Shall peace and freedom shower their blessings over our western Territories? or shall club-law rule at Washington? Shall honorable murderers stalk unpunished in the capital? Shall a military despotism trample the life-blood from our Territories, and an arrogant oligarchy of slave masters rule as with the plantation-whip twenty millions of American citizens?

That is the issue. It concerns not only the North, but the South, where an immense majority of non-slaveholders are now shorn of their rights by the exacting influence of slavery.

Ours is no sectional party. It is bounded by no geographic lines. We believe with Burke that virtue does not depend on climate or degrees. We fight not against a section but a class; not against a people but a system. Our leader is one whom the South has delighted to honor, and it should not be forgotten that to South Carolina that gave birth to a Brooks, whom the House of Representatives spurned as the assassin-like assailant of Charles Sumner—to the same South Carolina belongs the credit of having reared Fremont, whom by God's blessing we hope to install as the constitutional defender of the liberties of the country.

Our opponents would have us believe that instead of "Fremont and victory," we are on the verge of a defeat. Whether victory or defeat await us duty is ours, consequences are God's, and I have long regarded the battle for freedom in America as one that we are to wage steadfastly if not hopefully while life lasts, preserving untarnished the weapons of our fathers, and bequeathing them unrusted to our sons. Stand by the principles of the Declaration of Independence, whose irresistible point and divine temper converted rebellion into revolution—contend as your fathers contended for " the rights of human nature."

Nothing, it is said, can be more uncertain than the near future of American politics. Men's judgments in such cases are naturally biased by their wishes and influenced perhaps, more or less, by the predominancy of one party or another in their own neighborhood. The " New Orleans Delta," reviewing from that far corner the whole country, declares that party leaders engaged with the loaves and fishes have culpably kept them in ignorance of the real strength of the Republican party, which it says threatens to swallow up every other in the North as the rod of Moses swallowed up those of the Egyptians. It admits that the Republican party has increased, is increasing, and is not likely to be diminished, a fact that, it remarks, has just spoken with 8,000 voices in Iowa, 15,000 in Vermont, and 20,000 in Maine with Blair, a Fremonter from a slave State, and that these, as signs of the times, possess the utmost significance. It reminds its readers that like causes produce like effects and it anticipates a similar result in all of the free States.

There are two disturbing causes that may prevent this result: one, the deception that has been practised by the Democratic leaders in some of the States in pretending to be opposed to the extension of slavery, and the belief which they have been successful in propagating, that the rights involved in the Missouri Compromise have been definitely disposed of by its repeal, whereas it is the very question in an intensified form that is now directly put by the people of Kansas to the people of the United States.

It is no longer shall slavery be permitted to pass the line

J of 36 degrees 30 minutes quietly and under the sanction of "popular sovereignty ?" but shall it be permitted to pass that line by the aid of fraudulent elections, a lawless executive, and a corrupt judiciary by the connivance of the federal government and the power of the federal arm, trampling upon the constitution of the United States, the sovereignty of Kansas, and the rights and liberties of its people?

The blood already spilt in consequence of the repeal of the Missouri compact drips from the hands of every man who aided that breach of faith. But he who now votes for either Buchanan, who indorses, or for Fillmore, who by his silence approves the encroachment of slavery upon Kansas, not only incurs, with the original repealer of the compact the ancient curse, "Cursed be he that removeth his neighbor's landmark. And all the people shall say, amen," but he assumes the responsibility of all the blood that is destined to water the plains of Kansas if the slave power is now supported in its attempt to force slavery upon that consecrated soil.

The other disturbing cause is the power of money in the hands of men whose principles allow them to approve the election frauds perpetrated in Kansas, and who may be ready to repeat the experiment nearer home. With a certain class of politicians the importation of illegal votes and other frauds upon the purity of elections seem to be regarded as venial offences, if not actually entitling them to the gratitude of their party, when in truth no act of treason can strike more directly at the sovereignty of the people and the stability of the Republic.

Looking at our future prospects it is to be remembered that the people of the slave States also are awakening to a knowledge of their strength and a remembrance of their right and truest interest. Not only Missouri but Virginia too are preparing to throw off the insolent domination of the slave power, and the manly spirit shown by Professor Hedrick of South Carolina, in avowing his principles and preference for Fremont, is an indication that the Reign of Terror which banishes booksellers, silences presses, and gags all expression of anti-slavery sentiment, will soon suffer interruption.

Tyranny and treachery though they may prosper for a while irresistibly sow the seeds of their own destruction, and if we are but true to ourselves, true to the principles of our fathers, true to the historic associations that cluster about our soil, let us trust that we shall soon restore freedom to Kansas and quiet to the Union, and let us resolve and re-resolve never to falter in our course until we have placed the federal government on the side of freedom and rein-augurated that olden policy of Washington and Jefferson by which they ordained that throughout the wide extent of our western Territories " the sun should not rise upon a master nor set upon a slave."

DAVIS

HENRY WINTER DAVIS, an American statesman, was the son of an Episcopal clergyman in Annapolis, Maryland, and was born in that city August 16, 1817. He was educated at Kenyon College, and, after studying law at the University of Virginia, began the practice of his profession in Alexandria. In 1840 he removed to Baltimore, where he soon rose to prominence socially and professionally. He entered Congress in 1855 as a Whig member and on the dissolution of the Whig party joined the American or Know-Nothing party. In 1859 he voted for Pennington, the Republican candidate for speaker of the House; and, when censured for this act by the Maryland legislature, announced to his constituents that if they were not disposed to allow him to use his private judgment regarding the best interests of his State they might send a slave to Congress if they chose, but they should not send him. After the attack upon the Massachusetts troops in Baltimore, in April, 1861, Davis declared himself an unconditional Union candidate for Congress. He was subjected to much abuse for this announcement and was defeated at the polls. He sat in Congress, nevertheless, 1863-65, and was chairman of the committee on foreign affairs. He was an ardent advocate of emancipation and strongly favored the enlistment of negro soldiers in the federal army. In 1865 he spoke in Chicago in favor of negro suffrage. His death took place in Baltimore, December 30, 1865. Davis was a man of intense convictions, with great courage in their avowal, and as an orator was both brilliant and forcible. His published works include "The War of Ormuzd and Ahriman in the Nineteenth Century" (1853); "Speeches and Addresses" (1867).

ON RECONSTRUCTION

DELIVERED IN THE HOUSE OF REPRESENTATIVES, MARCH 22, 1864

MR. SPEAKER,—The bill which I am directed by the committee on the rebellious States to report is one which provides for the restoration of civil government in States whose governments have been overthrown. It prescribes such conditions as will secure not only civil government to the people of the rebellious States, but will also secure to the people of the United States permanent peace after the suppression of the rebellion. The bill challenges the support of all who consider slavery the cause of the rebellion, and that in it the embers of rebellion will always smoulder; of those who think that freedom and permanent peace are inseparable and who are determined, so far as their constitutional authority will allow them, to secure these fruits by adequate legislation. The vote of gentlemen upon this measure will be regarded by the country with no ordinary interest. Their vote will be taken to express their opinion on the necessity of ending slavery with the rebellion and their willingness to assume the responsibility of adopting the legislative measures without which the result cannot be assured, and may wholly fail of accomplishment. . . .

What is the nature of this case with which we have to deal, the evil we must remedy, the danger we must avert? In other words, what is that monster of political wrong which is called secession? It is not, Mr. Speaker, domestic violence, within the meaning of that clause of the constitution, for the violence was the act of the people of those States through their governments, and was the offspring of their free and unforced will. It is not invasion, in the meaning of the constitution, for no State has been invaded against the will of the government of the State by any power except the United States marching to overthrow the usurpers of its territory.

It is therefore the act of the people of the States carrying with it all the consequences of such an act. And therefore it must be either a legal revolution, which makes them independent and makes of the United States a foreign country, or it is a usurpation against the authority of the United States, the erection of governments which do not recognize the constitution of the United States, which the constitution does not recognize, and therefore not republican governments of the States in rebellion. The latter is the view which all parties take of it. I do not understand that any gentleman on the other side of the House says that any rebel government which does not recognize the constitution of the United States and which is not recognized by Congress is a State government within the meaning of the constitution. Still less can it be said that there is a State government, republican or unrepublican, in the State of Tennessee, where there is no government of any kind, no civil authority, no organized form of administration except that represented by the flag of the United States, obeying the will and under the orders of the military officer in command

It is the language of the President of the United States in every proclamation of Congress, in every law on the statutebook, of both Houses in their forms of proceeding, and of the courts of the United States in their administration of the law.

It is the result of every principle of law, of every suggestion of political philosophy, that there can be no republican government within the limits of the United States that does not recognize but does repudiate the constitution and which the President and the Congress of the United States do not, on their part, recognize.

Those that are here represented are the only governments existing within the limits of the United States. Those that are not here represented are not governments of the States, republican under the constitution. And if they be not then they are military usurpations, inaugurated as the permanent governments of the States, contrary to the supreme law of the land, arrayed in arms against the government of the United States; and it is the duty, the first and highest duty, of the government, to suppress and expel them. Congress must either expel or recognize and support them. If it do not guarantee them it is bound to expel them; and they who are not ready to suppress are bound to recognize them.

We are now engaged in suppressing a military usurpation of the authority of the State governments. When that shall have been accomplished there will be no form of State authority in existence which Congress can recognize. Our success will be the overthrow of all semblance of government in the rebel States. The government of the United States is then in fact the only government existing in those States, and it is there charged to guarantee them republican governments.

What jurisdiction does the duty of guaranteeing a republican government confer under such circumstances upon Congress? What right does it give? What laws may it pass? What objects may it accomplish? What conditions may it insist upon and what judgment may it exercise in determining what it will do?

The duty of guaranteeing carries with it the right to pass all laws necessary and proper to guarantee. The duty of guaranteeing means the duty to accomplish the result. It means that the republican government shall exist. It means that every opposition to republican government shall be put down. It means that everything inconsistent with the permanent continuance of republican government shall be weeded out.

It places in the hands of Congress to say what is and what is not, with all the light of experience and all the lessons of the past, inconsistent, in its judgment, with the permanent continuance of republican government; and if in its judgment any form of policy is radically and inherently inconsistent with the permanent and enduring peace of the country, with the permanent supremacy of republican government, and it have the manliness to say so, there is no power, judicial or executive, in the United States that can even question this judgment but the people; and they can do it only by sending other representatives here to undo our work.

The very language of the constitution and the necessary logic of the case involve that consequence. The denial of the right of secession means that all the territory of the United States shall remain under the jurisdiction of the constitution. If there can be no State government which does not recognize the constitution, and which the authorities of the United States do not recognize, then there are these alternatives, and these only: The rebel States must be governed by Congress till they submit and form a State government under the constitution; or Congress must recognize State governments which do not recognize either Congress or the constitution of the United States; or there must be an entire absence of all government in the rebel States—and that is anarchy.

To recognize a government which does not recognize the constitution is absurd, for a government is not a constitution; and the recognition of a State government means the acknowledgment of men as governors and legislators and judges, actually invested with power to make laws, to judge of crimes, to convict the citizens of other States, to demand the surrender of fugitives from justice, to arm and command the militia, to require the United States to repress all opposition to its authority, and to protect it against invasion— against our own armies; whose senators and representatives are entitled to seats in Congress, and whose electoral votes must be counted in the election of the President of a government which they disown and defy. To accept the alternative of anarchy as the constitutional condition of a State is to assert the failure of the constitution and the end of republican government. Until therefore Congress recognizes a State government organized under its auspices there is no government in the rebel States except the authority of Congress. In the absence of all State government the duty is imposed on Congress to provide by law to keep the peace, to administer justice. . . .

When military opposition shall have been suppressed, not merely paralyzed, driven into a corner, pushed back, but gone, the horrid vision of civil war vanished from the South, then call upon the people to reorganize in their own way, subject to the conditions that we think essential to our permanent peace, and to prevent the revival hereafter of the rebellion—a republican government in the form that the people of the United States can agree to.

Now for that purpose there are three modes indicated. One is to remove the cause of the war by an alteration of the constitution of the United States, prohibiting slavery everywhere within its limits. That, sir, goes to the root of the matter and should consecrate the nation's triumph. But there are thirty-four States; three fourths of them would be twenty-six. I believe there are twenty-five States represented in this Congress; so that we on that basis cannot change the constitution. It is therefore a condition precedent in that view of the case that more States shall have governments organized within them. . . . But under any circumstances, even upon that basis, it will be difficult to find three fourths of the States, with New Jersey, or Kentucky, or Maryland, or Delaware, or other States that might be mentioned, opposed to it, under existing auspices, to adopt such a clause of the constitution after we shall have agreed to it. If adopted it still leaves all laws necessary to the ascertainment of the will of the people, and all restrictions on the return to power of the leaders of the rebellion wholly unprovided for. The amendment of the constitution meets my hearty approval, but it is not a remedy for the evils we must deal with.

The next plan is that inaugurated by the President of the United States in the proclamation of the 8th December (1863), called the amnesty proclamation. That proposes no guardianship of the United States over the reorganization of the governments, no law to prescribe who shall vote, no civil functionaries to see that the law is faithfully executed, no supervising authority to control and judge of the election. But if in any manner by the toleration of martial law, lately proclaimed the fundamental law, under the dictation of any military authority, or under the prescription of a provost marshal, something in the form of a government shall be presented, represented to rest on the votes of one tenth of the population, the President will recognize that, provided it does not contravene the proclamation of freedom and the laws of Congress; and to secure that an oath is exacted.

There is no guaranty of law to watch over the organization of that government. It may be recognized by the military power and not recognized by the civil power, so that it would have a doubtful existence, half civil and half military, neither a temporary government by law of Congress nor a State government, something as unknown to the constitution as the rebel government that refuses to recognize it.

The only prescription is that it shall not contravene the provisions of the proclamation. Sir, if that proclamation be valid then we are relieved from all trouble on that score. But if that proclamation be not valid, then the oath to support it is without legal sanction, for the President can ask no man to bind himself by an oath to support an unfounded proclamation or an unconstitutional law even for a moment, still less after it shall have been declared void by the supreme court of the United States.

It is the paramount right of every American citizen to judge for himself on his own responsibility of his constitutional rights, and an oath does not bind him to submit to that which is illegal. . . .

By the bill we propose to preclude the judicial question by the solution of a political question. How so? By the paramount power of Congress to reorganize governments in those States, to impose such conditions as it thinks necessary to secure the permanence of republican government, to refuse to recognize any governments there which do not prohibit slavery forever.

Ay, gentlemen, take the responsibility to say in the face of those who clamor for the speedy recognition of governments tolerating slavery, that the safety of the people of the United States is the supreme law; that their will is the supreme rule of law, and that we are authorized to pronounce their will on this subject. Take the responsibility to say that we will revise the judgments of our ancestors; that we have experience written in blood which they had not; that we find now what they darkly doubted, that slavery is really, radically inconsistent with the permanence of republican governments; and that being charged by the supreme law of the land on our conscience and judgment to guarantee, that is to continue, maintain and enforce, if it exist, to institute and restore, when overthrown, republican government throughout the broad limits of the Republic, we will weed out every element of their policy which we think incompatible with its permanence and endurance.

The purpose of the bill is to preclude the judicial question of the validity and effect of the President's proclamation by the decision of the political authority in reorganizing the State governments. It makes the rule of decision the provisions of the State constitution, which, when recognized by Congress, can be questioned in no court; and it adds to the authority of the proclamation the sanction of Congress. If gentlemen say that the constitution does not bear that construction, we will go before the people of the United States on that question, and by their judgment we will abide.

GOUGH

JOHN BARTHOLOMEW GOUGH, a famous American temperance orator, was born in Sandgate, Kent, England, August 22, 1817. His early education was scanty, and at twelve years of age he came to the United States, where he learned the bookbinder's trade. Losing his situation after a time, he grew dissipated and was fast becoming a hopeless drunkard. In 1842, however, he was induced to take the temperance pledge at Worcester, Massachusetts, and at once reformed. He had great natural gifts as a speaker and now devoted them to the temperance cause, becoming ere long the foremost advocate of temperance in the United States. He made a tour of Great Britain in 1853, lecturing in many cities, and returned there in 1857, remaining and lecturing three years, and paying a third visit in 1878. In the latter part of his career he lectured upon other topics than temperance and met with equal success. Temperance reform was nevertheless the work to which he devoted his chief energies, and, keeping entirely aloof from politics, he relied wholly upon moral influence and the pledge of abstinence to obtain results. He was intensely earnest, and mingled humor and pathos in his speeches in a way which always found favor with his audiences. His home for many years was at West Boylston, Massachusetts, where he had purchased a fine country estate. He died at Frankford, Pennsylvania, February 18, 1886. His published works include " Autobiography " (1853); " Orations " (1854); " Temperance Lectures " (1879); " Sunlight and Shadow " (1880); " Temperance Dialogues," " Platform Echoes " (1885).

TEMPERANCE ADDRESS

DELIVERED AT TREMONT TEMPLE, BOSTON, SEPTEMBER 17, 1860

I STAND before you, ladies and gentlemen, to-night, as a trophy of the temperance movement. I am the servant of this movement, and I will be, God helping me, to the day of my death. But I stand here also as a trophy of this temperance movement. Last November I had spoken in the City Hall of Glasgow to twenty-five hundred people. I was staying at the house of one of the merchant-princes of that city, and, when we came down-stairs his carriage was at the door, silver-mounted harness, coachman in livery, footman in plain clothes. You know it is seldom teetotal lecturers

(7780)

ride in such style, and it is proper therefore that we should speak of it when it does happen for the good of the cause.

As we came down the gentleman said to me: " It is so drizzly and cold you had better get into the carriage and wait until the ladies come down." I think I never had so many persons to shake hands with me.

" God bless you, Mr. Gough!" said one; " you saved my father."

" God bless you!" said another; " you saved my brother." Said a third, " God bless you! I owe everything I have in the world to you."

My hands absolutely ached as they grasped them one after another. Finally, a poor wretched creature came to the door of the carriage. I saw his bare shoulder and naked feet; his hair seemed grayer than mine. He came up and said:

" Will you shake hands with me?"

I put my hand into his hot, burning palm, and he said:

" Don't you know me?"

" Why," said I, " isn't your name Aiken?"

" Yes."

" Harry Aiken?"

" Yes."

" You worked with me in the bookbinder's shop of Andrew Hutchinson, in Worcester, Massachusetts, in 1842, didn't you?"

" Yes."

" What is the matter with you?"

" I am desperately poor."

I said, " God pity you; you look like it!"

I gave him something and obtained the services of Mr. Marr, the secretary of the Scottish League to find out about him. He picks up rags and bones in the streets of Glasgow

and resides in a kennel in one of the foulest streets of that
city. When the ladies came to the carriage and got in I
said:

" Stop! don't shut that door! Look there at that half-
starved, ragged, miserable wretch, shivering in the cold and
in the dim gaslight. Look at him !"

The ring of that audience was in my ears, my hands aching
with the grasp of friendship from scores, my surroundings
bright, my prospects pleasant, and I said:

" Ladies, look there! There am I but for the temperance
movement! That man worked with me, roomed with me,
slept with me, was a better workman than I, his prospects
brighter than mine. A kind hand was laid on my shoulder in
Worcester Street in 1842; it was the turning-point in my history. He went on. Seventeen years have passed and we
meet again with a gulf as deep as hell between us."

I am a trophy of this movement and I thank God for it.

When I was leaving England five weeks ago last Wednes-
day night, they gave me a farewell in Exeter Hall (and there
are some in this audience who saw it); and the reformed
drunkards who had signed the pledge at my meetings during
the ninety-five lectures I had delivered in that hall sub-
scribed the means to buy me a Bible. A Bible from reformed drunkards! It is one of the most precious gifts I
have ever received. I have brought it here for you to look
at. That is it. A Bible from reformed drunkards, presented to me by a judge of the court of sessions for Middlesex County! A Bible!

I had had a presentation of a Bible once before; and I
told them when they gave it to me, that I would put the
books together. A Bible! Thirty years ago nearly, when I
left England for America, I had this. Here they are! As

much "glory gilds the sacred page" in this (the small one) as that. There has been more comfort derived from this than from the other. That was my mother's Bible. When I was a boy twelve years old, and went from England to the United States to seek my fortune, she put that in my hand. Here on the cover I read,

"JANE GILBERT, born August 10, 1776.
"JOHN GOUGH, his mother's gift on leaving England.
"JANE GOUGH."

My mother had nothing to give me but that. That book was lost for years and years and years; but at last it was found in a garret in Bristol by Rev. Dr. Choules and his daughter kindly sent it to me.

I look at this Bible and I find marks all through it. They are very old; the ink is very brown; but there are marks round such passages as these: "Where the poor and needy seek water and there is none, I the Lord will hear them; I the God of Jacob will answer them. I will open fountains of water in dry places." And again: "For thy redeemer is thy husband, the Holy One of Israel." Mark after mark; and I love to look at them. That was the comfort of my mother, whose whole life was spent in battling for bread. Yet she had faith and patience and courage and love to the last. Her only child except myself, a sister, is present in this house, and, by the mercy of God, has been recently brought to receive the redeemer of her mother as her Saviour and her king. I glory in this.

I speak of these things because I have endeavored as far as I have been able (I speak now of myself) to base the whole work of reform upon this book. The Bible first, and everything else in subservience to this. And in Great Britain I have sometimes been pretty severely taxed because they sustain the drinking customs of society by the Bible. My great object (and you will allow me to speak personally just now) is to advocate a sure plan for the removal of the evil of drunkenness; and I believe that the plan we adopt, of personal abstinence, is the best.

" Believing that the use of intoxicating liquor as a beverage is not only useless, but hurtful to the social, civil, and religious interests of the community, and that while it continues to be used as a beverage it will never be done away, we do therefore agree that we will not use it."

That I consider to be the basis, the grand foundation, of our efforts—total abstinence from intoxicating beverages and a hatred and antagonism to drink wherever we find it, whether it is on the side-board of the wealthy merchant, on the table of the clergyman, or in the dram-shop. Wherever I see the drink used as a beverage I hold myself ready to battle it to the death.

Now in England we have objection brought against that principle from the Bible; and as my pastor has told you, and as you all know very well, I am not a learned man: I do not understand Hebrew or Greek. If you show me a Greek and a Hebrew word, they are both Greek to me; and if you get them mixed up I am sure I cannot separate them again. I respect learning in others, and I wish I had more of it myself; but I do not understand what you mean by " tirosh," " yain," or " oinon." But unlearned men must have a position which they can hold against the learned, and I believe that the prudent position for a man to occupy is not to advocate a question any further than he understands it. A person once came to me in England and said to me:

"Ah! Mistar Gough—ah!—why don't you give us a physicologico lecture ?"

"I suppose you mean," said I, " a physiological lecture; and the reason why I don't is because I don't understand physiology."

If I should undertake to talk about the pathology of drunkenness, and the influence of drink on the brain, the stomach, and the blood, I might talk away very learnedly and not understand a word I was saying, and when I had got through, a gentleman who is a physiologist might upset me entirely with two or three hard words which I did not comprehend. He is wrong, and I am right; but he has got the sympathy of the people because I have attempted to argue a question I don't understand and have got beyond my depth.

I wish to say here that the clergymen of the Church of England are positively doing more for the temperance movement than dissenters, and the same is true of their wives. I was invited to church with a clergyman who is now the Bishop of Carlisle, and we had a discussion for about two hours. A titled lady was present, and she helped him. I was alone and had to bear the whole brunt of the battle on the scriptural argument.

" The Bible permits the use of wine," said he.

" Very well," said I; " suppose it does."

" The Bible sanctions the use of wine."

" Very well; suppose it does."

" Our Saviour made wine."

" I know he did."

" Why, we thought you were prepared to deny this."

" I do not deny it; I can read."

" Wine is spoken of in the Bible as a blessing."

I replied, " There are two kinds of wine spoken of in the Bible."

" Now, then, you are not a learned man, prove it."

" Well," I said, " I know there is."

" Prove it."

" I know there are two kinds of wine spoken of in the Bible."

" Prove it."

" I do not know that I can, but I will tell you what it is: The wine that is spoken of as a blessing is not the same wine that is called a mocker; and the wine that is to be drunk in the kingdom of Heaven cannot be the wine of the wrath of God; so that although I cannot prove it learnedly I know it is so."

Now, there are others who go farther than I go; but you will please let me go just as far as I can understand it, and if I cannot go any farther don't find fault with me. I hold that the Bible permits total abstinence, and I would rather search the Bible for permission to give up a lawful gratification for the sake of my weaker-headed brother, who stumbles over my example into sin, than to see how far I can follow my own propensities without committing sin and bringing condemnation upon any one's soul.

Another gentleman who came to me for a long talk said: " I have a conscientious objection to teetotalism; and it is this: Our Saviour made wine at the marriage of Cana in Galilee."

" I know he did."

" He made it because they wanted it."

" So the Bible tells us."

" He made it of water."

" Yes."

" Well, he performed a miracle to make that wine."

" Yes."

" Then he honored and sanctified wine by performing a

miracle to make it. Therefore," said he, "I feel that if I should give up the use of wine I should be guilty of ingratitude and should be reproaching my Master."

"Sir," said I, "I can understand how you should feel so; but is there nothing else that you put by which our Saviour honored?"

"No, I do not know that there is."

"Do you eat barley bread?"

"No," and then he began to laugh.

"And why?"

"Because I don't like it."

"Very well, sir," I said; "our Saviour sanctified barley bread just as much as he ever did wine. He fed five thousand people with barley loaves manufactured by a miracle. You put away barley bread from the low motive of not liking it. I ask you to put away wine from the higher motive of bearing the infirmity of your weaker brother and so fulfilling the law of Christ."

I wish to say that that man signed a pledge three days afterward.

I only mention this that I may give you some idea of the manner in which we have to advocate the movement in Great Britain.

Then there is a class of persons there—and I believe there are some in this country—who say, "Ah! you teetotalers are putting temperance in the place of religion." What do you think Mr. Spurgeon said to his people? I refer to what he was reported to have said in the papers, and I believe it; for I have it from an eye-witness that he drank a whole bottle of champagne at a dinner and ridiculed teetotalism; and if he can ridicule temperance publicly we may speak of him in public.

He said, " drunkenness is the curse of Great Britain; but total abstinence, my friends, is not the cure for drunkenness!"

Why, there is not a booby in the kingdom who does not know better than that. Now, I advocate teetotalism as a cure for drunkenness: I do not advocate it as a cure for anything else. A man may be a teetotal thief, a teetotal liar, a teetotal slanderer (and we have proved that, I think, within the past three years, pretty effectually); he may be a teetotal sabbath-breaker or a teetotal infidel, but he cannot be a teetotaler and a drunkard; can he? The principle I advocate cures drunkards; it cures nothing else, and we say it is folly for a man to tell us that we are putting temperance in the place of the gospel and undertaking to do that through its instrumentality which can only be accomplished by the grace of God. As the blood in my arm circulates upward, contrary to the law of nature, by the power of life that is in me; so the grace of God, operating upon a man's heart, changes the whole nature of the man. Teetotalism does no such work as that. We look upon teetotalism as one of the greatest agents to remove one of the most terrible hindrances to the hearing of the gospel; and if we look into Great Britain we shall see it. What is the great hindrance there to men's hearing the gospel? Drunkenness stood more in the way than any other agency; and, if I advocate teetotalism, I advocate it as an agency to remove one evil and only indirectly to do other work. To give you an illustration:

I spoke in Dundee to the outcasts of that town. The Right Honorable Lord Kinnaird and his lady were instrumental in getting up that meeting. It was such a meeting, I suppose, as you cannot see in this country; at least I never saw such a one. If such an audience can be gathered together here, I should like to see it and to address it. The town missionaries had got together a large mass of men and women, and you would have looked almost in vain to find one lingering trace of human beauty left. It seemed as if the foul hoof of debauchery had dashed it out. It was a horrid sight to look at,—rags, filth, nakedness,—a festering, steaming mass of putrefying humanity.

A woman sat at my feet, and the place was so crowded that I touched her. Her nickname for years had been " Hell-Fire." The boys called her " Fire," and she was known by no other name in the vicinity of her wretched residence. Fifty-three times she had been convicted and sentenced for from six days' to four months' imprisonment.

The ex-provost of the town (George Rough) said to me: " I never sent one policeman to take her; she was never mastered by one man. She is a muscular woman, and she will hit right and left. She has been dragged before me, time after time, with the blood streaming from her face."

The Rev. Mr. Hannay and Mr. Rough said to me: " If she kicks up a row, as she probably will, you will see one of the most comical rows you ever beheld. It is dreadful; but there is a comicality about it; she has such power with her tongue that it is amazing. We have seen men who could stand any amount of common swearing run when ' Fire ' began to blaspheme."

She sat there at my feet, and as I went on she interrupted me a little. I told that audience what they had been, what they might be, and what God meant they should be. I showed them that they were thwarting God's good designs toward every one of them. I asked that mother if she did not remember sending that half-starved little child for a pennyworth of oatmeal and four pennyworth of whiskey. I asked that young man to remember what he promised when he married that girl, and to go and look at that bed of rags to which he had brought her. Some of them lifted up their naked arms and said, " Oh! that is all true."

By and by the woman at my feet looked up and said, " Where did you learn all that?" Then she looked as if she had some important communication to make to the people, and she said, " Thet man kens a' about it. Would you give the likes o' me the pledge?"

" To be sure I will," said I.

" Oh, no, no!" said some; " it won't do for her to take the pledge."

I said, " Why not?"

" She can't keep it."

" How do you know?"

" She 'll be drunk before she goes to bed to-night."

" How do you know?"

" Madam," I said to her, " here is a gentleman who says you cannot keep the pledge if you sign it."

The woman flew into a rage. Said I, " Before you fight about it, tell me, can you keep it?"

The reply was, " If I say I will, I can."

I said, " Then you say you will?"

" I will."

" Give me your hand."

" I will."

" Then," said I, " put down your name."

After she had done it I said, " Give me your hand again." She did so and said, " I will keep it."

" I know you will," I said, " and I shall come back again to see you."

" Come back when you will," said she, " and you will find I have kept it."

Some three years after, I went back. Lord Kinnaird presided over the meeting. The woman was there. After the meeting I introduced her to Lord Kinnaird, not as "Fire," but as Mrs. Archer, a very respectable Scotchwoman. She had on her white cap, and her cloak pinned across her breast. He shook hands with her. I went to her house. I wish I could tell you what she told me; I wish I could make you feel as she made me feel. She said, "I am a puir body; I dinna ken much; and what little I did ken has been knocked out o' me by the staves of the policemen; they pounded me o'er the head, sir. I dinna ken how to pray—I never went to God's house these twenty-eight years—I canna pray—but sometimes I dream" (and then her eyes filled). "I dream I am drunk, and I canna pray; but I get out of my bed, sir, and I kneel by the side of it, and I never get back to it until day-dawn; and all I can say is, 'God keep me!' I canna get drunk any more."

Her daughter said, "Ay, mon; and I have heard my mother, at the dead of night, on the bare floor, in the bitter winter-time, cry out, 'God keep me!' and I said, 'Mother, go to your bed;' and she said, 'No, no; I had a dream, and I cannot go and drink any more.'" That woman is now to be seen going every Sabbath to hear God's word preached,—she who had not entered God's house for twenty-eight years!

Teetotalism is not religion; but I thank God it has removed a hindrance to many a man and woman hearing that truth which must be believed, and must be heard before it is believed.

They are doing a grand work in England. Mrs. Bailey, the authoress of "Ragged Homes, and How to Mend Them," and Mrs. Wightman, authoress of "Haste to the Rescue," are noble women. Mrs. Bailey found poor wretched creatures in such a state of degradation that she went to work among the women first, teaching them how to make their homes more happy; but their cry was, "We can do nothing while our husbands drink." What did she do? Setting an example to the women of Boston, she invited sixteen of the worst of the men (and bad enough they were; for they used to go out into the fields near the Kensington potteries and pummel each other to a jelly for a pot of ale; their fists were used to beat out God's image),—she invited, I say, sixteen of the worst of them to come to tea. Very much embarrassed were they after tea.

"I suppose," she said, "you hardly think any one has been caring for you for a great many years past?"

"Oh, yes!" they said, "we know well the policemen have been caring for us."

She told them she had been caring for them. She began, and at last she had seventy-eight of these men teetotalers; seventy-eight of them signed the pledge. She works with religion as well as with temperance. She instituted evening readings; and I tell you, ladies and gentlemen, that to see seventy or eighty men who are covered with scars that have been received in Satan's service, with fists that have been used for fighting folded in their laps, sitting there, great men, and hearing that little woman reading—what?—"A new commandment give I unto you, that you love one another even as I have loved you;" and then to see the eyes grow dim, and the great hard hand brush away the tear, and hear the great heaving sob that shakes the strong man from head to foot as he hears for the first time these strange, sweet words,—I tell you that is a sight to stir the very soul. I say, sir, and I appeal to these ministers of the gospel, that if there is a movement based on a lawful principle that will bring men from the deep, dark depths of drunkenness, only to hear such words as these, it demands your sympathy and the sympathy of every Christian minister and man the wide world over.

I said, when I began, that I was a trophy of this movement, and therefore the principal part of my work has been (not ignoring other parts) in behalf of those who have suffered as I have suffered. You know there is a great deal said about the reckless victims of this foe being "brutes." No, they are not brutes. I have labored for eighteen years among them and I have never found a brute. I have had men swear at me; I have had a man dance around me as if possessed of a devil and spit his foam in my face; but I never found a man I would give up. It may take a long time to reach his manhood; but he is not a brute. I think it is Charles Dickens who says, "Away up a great many pair of stairs, in a very remote corner, easily passed by, there is a door, and on that door is written—'WOMAN;'" and so in the heart of the vilest outcast, away up a great many pair of stairs, in a very remote corner, easily passed by, there is a door on which is written "MAN." Here is our business,—to find that door. It may take a long time; but begin and knock. Don't get tired; but remember God's long-suffering to us and keep knocking a long time if need be. Don't get weary if there is no answer; remember him whose locks were wet with the dew. Knock on; just try it; you try it; and just so sure as you do, just so sure, by and by, will the quivering lip and starting tear tell you you have been knocking at the heart of a man and not of a brute. It is because these poor wretches are men, and not brutes, that we have hopes of them.

I once picked up a man in the market-place. They said, "He is a brute; let him alone." I took him home with me and kept the " brute " fourteen days and nights through his delirium, and he nearly frightened Mary out of her wits one night, chasing her all about the house with a boot in his hand. But she recovered her wits and he recovered his. He said to me, " You wouldn't think I had a wife and child? "

" Well, I shouldn't."

" I have; and—God bless her dear little heart!—my little Mary is as pretty a little thing as ever stepped," said the " brute."

I asked, " Where do they live? "

" They live two miles away from here."

" When did you see them last? "

" About two years ago."

Then he told me his sad story. I said, " You must go back again."

" I mustn't go back; I won't: my wife is better without me than with me. I will not go back any more. I have knocked her, and kicked her, and abused her; do you suppose I will go back again?"

I went to the house with him. I knocked at the door and his wife opened it.

" Is this Mrs. Richardson?"

" Yes, sir."

" Well, that is Mr. Richardson; and Mr. Richardson, that is Mrs. Richardson. Now come into the house."

They went in. The wife sat on one side of the room and the " brute " on the other. I waited to see who would speak first; and it was the woman. But before she spoke she fidgeted a good deal. She pulled up her apron until she got hold of the hem, and then she pulled it all down again. Then she folded it up closely and jerked it out through her fngers an inch at a time; and then she spread it all down again; and then she looked all about the room and said, "Well, William!" and the "brute" said, "Well, Mary!" He had a large handkerchief around his neck; and she said, "You had better take the handkerchief off, William, you will need it when you go out." He began to fumble about it. The knot was large enough; he could have untied it if he liked; but he said, "Will you untie it, Mary?" And she worked away at it, but her fingers were clumsy and she couldn't get it off. Their eyes met, and the love-light was not all quenched: he opened his arms gently and she fell into them. If you could have seen those white arms clasped about his neck, and he sobbing on her breast, and the child looking in wonder first at one and then at the other, you would have said, "It is not a brute: it is a man, with a great big warm heart in his breast."

I tell you it is a glorious work to get at these hearts: it is a glorious work to play upon a man; to play upon him until you make him sing,—ay, and sing sweet music, too.

A man came to me at Covent Garden, summer before last, and said, "Mr. Gough, I want you to come into my place of business."

I replied, "I am in a little hurry now."

"You must come into my place of business!"

So, when he had got me there,—into a large fruit-stall, where he was doing business to the amount of two hundred and fifty or three hundred pounds (a thousand or twelve hundred and fifty dollars) a week,—he caught hold of my hand and said,

"God bless you, sir!"

"What for?—have I ever seen you before?"

"I heard you, sir," he said, "in Exeter Hall, in 1853. I was a brute!"

"No, you were not."

"Well, I was worse."

"No, you were not."

"Well, I was as bad as ever I could be."

Then he told me some sad things and went on:

"God bless you, sir! See what a business I am doing! Look here! See that woman in the corner: it is my wife. La! how I have knocked her about! Would you go and shake hands with her?"

"I have no objection."

"Do, sir."

"I went up to her and offered my hand. She held back and said, "My fingers are so sticky with fruit, sir!"

"La!" said the husband; "Mr. Gough, you don't mind a little sticky fingers?"

"No, sir,"—and I shook hands with her. Our fingers stuck together: they were more sticky than I had expected. Again the man said to me,

"God bless you, sir! I wish I could give you something. Do you like oranges?"

"Sometimes."

He went to a shelf that was full of them and began to fill a bag with them. "That's enough, sir;" but he paid no attention to me, but filled the bag and put it into my arms. "Go along with you!" said he; "don't say a word; go along with you! God bless you!" I had positively to hire a cab to get home.

The day before Christmas I took an American lady—who is in this house to-night—to see this man, saying, "I am going to call on a gentleman whom I want you to see." I had spoken on the preceding Monday evening in Exeter Hall for the eighty-first time; and you know when a man speaks eighty-one times in one place on the same subject he gets pretty well pushed for matter: so I told this story there. The first thing he said when I entered his place of business was, "Oh! you gave somebody a terrible rub last Monday, didn't you?"

"You didn't mind it?"

"Mind it? No; I liked it. The man next to me kept a-nudging me and saying, 'That means you.' But, Mr. Gough, just look at that cellar!"

"I see the cellar."

"I want to show you this letter. I have a letter from Manchester ordering me to send them five hundred pounds of fruit. Now, do you suppose anybody would have ordered that of such a fellow as I used to be? Look at that cellar. I spent a whole Sunday in that cellar, on a heap of rotten vegetables, with a rope to hang myself by. I heard the bells chime for church, and knew when they were singing and when they were praying and when they were preaching. They little thought a poor wretch was down here fighting; for it was a steady fight all that day between that rope and me and my conscience. Now, sir, I lease that cellar and clear a hundred pounds a year. Here come my children—just from boarding-school—four of 'em. Shake hands with 'em. Oh, how I wish you lived where I do!"

Perhaps you are getting tired of these incidents; but there is one more of which I would like to speak to you, because it shows that we who work among the hardest and vilest outcasts are repaid by the fact that we are working for men. I was to speak in a certain place, and a poor fellow came with what is called a "fly,"—that is, a one-horse cab,—to take me some six miles to the railway station where I was to speak. I noticed that he was leaning forward, and then took

a handkerchief out of his pocket and tied it around his face.
I said: "Have you a cold?"

"No."

Then he tied the handkerchief up this way.

"Have you the toothache?"

"No."

He seemed to lean forward and sit so uneasily that I said
to him, "Why do you sit forward in that way?"

"Why, sir," he said, "the window of the carriage is
broken, and I am trying to keep the wind off of you, sir."

"The Lord bless you, my friend! what do you mean by that?
Are you putting your head in that hole to keep the wind
from me?"

"Yes, sir, I a .."

"And why?"

He burst into tears: "It's because I owe everything I have
in the world to you. When I first heard you I was singing
ballads in the streets with my half-starved wife following
me with a baby in her arms. Now I have a comfortable
home. God bless you, sir! I'd stick my head in any hole
under heaven for you."

The next morning I breakfasted with him at six o'clock.
I have breakfasted and dined where they have had footmen,—
with a great preponderance of calf, and top-knots, or whatever they call them, on their shoulders,—snatching your plate
away before you got half through; but I have never had such
a breakfast as that in my life. I believe that man and his
wife had been up all night to get it ready for me. There
was no floor except an earthen floor; the ceiling was of great
rafters, blackened with smoke; but such a breakfast!

These are the men we are working for; and we defend the
principle of total abstinence as a lawful principle in the

highest sense of the term; as an expedient principle; as a benevolent principle calculated to do this one work of rescuing the drunkard.

And another thing you will allow me to say, though certainly I did not intend or expect to make a long speech. I came laboring under this heavy affliction which has been referred to and I felt that it would be almost impossible for me to face an audience to-night; and therefore you must bear with me under the circumstances if I speak chiefly of these reminiscences of the past. I love this temperance movement. I ought to love it, and in that day for which all other days were made it will be seen that my love for the temperance movement has been next to my love for the blessed religion of the Lord Jesus Christ nearest to my heart. Do you suppose I can look at a scene like this and not recur to the past?

The past is ever before me; the past is to me one perpetual photograph that will never fade out; that grows more and more distinct the longer I live. The fire that scorched me in the distance seems to burn brighter, the iron that entered my flesh seems to be sharper the further I remove from it. For the love I bear the temperance movement I take no credit to myself. The temperance movement has made me what I am, if I am anything, if I am worth anything in this world; and for the temperance movement I mean to work to the day of my death. And I pray you that when I die I may die in the harness. I come back to you here. I see your young men plunged in dissipation. Oh, it is pitiful to go through the streets as I have in Boston to-day and see boldly and openly displayed the signs that tell us of the dreadful, horrible traffic that is carried on in spite of the will of the people. Who are these few men that dare to ignore the expressed will of the people? Who are they that dare to fill the lower parts of your city with the horrible stench of the accursed distillery? Who are they that dare do this when the people say they shall not? Up, up, up, men of Boston! Crush it out! You can do it! Can? Some people say it is impossible. A great many begin and end all their effort by saying it is impossible. Do you remember the incident that occurred when Mr. Webster delivered his great oration at the foot of Bunker Hill monument? The crowd was pressing up on all sides toward the platform, and the committee said "Gentlemen, stand back." "We can't," said the crowd, and they never attempted it. They continued to press up. The platform began to crack, endangering life and limb.

"Stand back."

"We can't stand back," said the people and made no effort.

Mr. Webster rose to his feet and said, "Gentlemen, you must stand back."

"Mr. Webster, it is impossible to stand back." "Impossible?" said Webster; "On Bunker Hill nothing is impossible," and down the hill they went. They felt they could and they did. Impossible! It is not our business to create results; we cannot create results, but it is our business to work for results; and the highest position a man can occupy in this world is to stand as a machine, connected with his Maker by a band of loving faith,—God the motor-power, and man the machine. That is your business,—working where he will, when he will, as he will. No matter if you don't see a dramshop closed; that is not your business; work as if the next blow was to dash to pieces the Moloch of drunkenness; and if no results are visible till you lie down to die, die in faith that others are coming up to gather a full harvest on the field that you have planted and tended and prayed over, but have not been able to reap. It is ours to work.

CAMPOAMOR

RAMON DE CAMPOAMOR Y CAMPOOSORIO, a distinguished Spanish poet and statesman, was born at Navia in the ancient province of Asturias, September 24, 1817. He entered literature and political life at almost the same time, in the former field being the earliest Spanish writer of his century to free himself from the spirit of romanticism; in the latter revealing himself a conservative with strong royalist sympathies. During the reign of Isabella he was successively governor of Alicante and Valencia, and while a member of the Cortes he engaged in a long discussion with Castelar in the columns of "El Estudio," his articles being subsequently reissued in a volume as "Polémicas con la Democracía" (1862). In the reign of Amadeo he held the position of director-general, and under Alfonso XII was counsellor of state. He is the inventor of a new species of composition frequently imitated by the younger school of Spanish writers, consisting of small, humorous, sentimental poems with a touch of morality or philosophy, called "Doloras." His principal works in verse include "Ternezas y Flores" (1840); "Ayes del Alma" (1842); "Fabulas Morales y Politicas" (1842); "Colon" (1853); "El Drama Universal" (1873); "El Amor y el Rio Piedra" (1882); "El Trén Express" (1885). Among dramas by him may be named "Dies Iræ" (1873); "Cuerdos y Locos" (1887); "El Honor" (1874). His principal philosophical writings include "Filosofía de las Leyes" (1846); "Lo Absoluto" (1865); "El Idealismo ". (1883). A collection of his verse, in three volumes, "Obras Escogidas" was made in 1885.

SPEECH AGAINST THE PRESS LAW

"Fortune gives favors
That are not written."

I SAY this because we formerly had some liberty of the press, but we had no law on the subject. We are now going to have a press law, but in exchange we shall have no liberty.

I have risen to speak against the enactment of the press law because this press law has no other object, and will have no other result, than to put the press outside of the law.

Law, gentlemen, is a compact that joins two parties in equal rights and equal duties. In this project for a press law

I see expressed the duties which he that commands imposes upon him that has to obey; but where are expressed the duties which he that has to obey has the right to impose upon him that commands? In this project for a press law I see the rights which authority reserves to itself; but where are the rights reserved to liberty? Since in this projected law I see no rights for liberty, it follows that what I said at the beginning is true, that is, that this projected press law has no other object, and will have no other result, than to put the press outside of the law. I am going to prove this assertion: at the same time I will answer the honorable Minister of Administration, who complained yesterday that the orators who opposed the press law all said that the law was bad but did not say why.

I, even though I injure the gentlemen's natural feelings of paternity, am going to say why the law is bad, and I am going to say it in the most temperate and accommodating speech that the gentleman may have heard in all the days of his life. At the same time I am going to reply to the intelligent and honorable Minister of State, who yesterday laid before us a synthetic elaboration to prove that the law was good; and I, proceeding by the opposite method, am going to prove by analysis—not arbitrary like the synthesis of the gentleman, but real and genuine—that the law is not good; thus I shall prove to the honorable Minister of State that the law is not good, and to the honorable Minister of Administration that the law is completely bad. To prove this we shall begin by laying down three or four or five propositions.

First proposition.—This law legalizes the arbitrary.

Second proposition.—This law represents the negation, the impossibility of exercising virtue.

Third proposition.—This law represents the inevitable bankruptcy of the press.

Fourth proposition.—This law represents the blockade of public opinion.

Fifth proposition.—This law represents a state of siege for human intelligence.

We have said that the first proposition was that this law legalizes the arbitrary.—Proof. All those acts that, since they may be sanctioned or legalized by the sanction of a tribunal, are left to the free volition of political authorities, essentially movable, essentially and almost from duty impassioned, are so many other arbitrary acts.

In this law there is left to the disposition and the volition of the governing authorities all the following extremes:

First.—The law begins by demanding an impossibility; it begins by demanding that a responsible editor shall pay 2,000 reales in direct taxation, and that moreover he must have paid it three years in anticipation; an exigency which, in truth, I do not even know what object it may have, notwithstanding the reasons given by the honorable Minister of State. I do not know wherefore comes this representation of an editor who does not have to be responsible, for that which is definitely responsible is the deposit.

Very well. I would like to have the honorable deputies tell me if a responsible editor who pays a direct tax of 2,000 reales is not an important personage, worthy of the most aristocratic distinction. I would like to have them tell me what object this new aristocracy may have unless the government is thinking of introducing some new reform and is proposing to establish a new category of senators in their own right. For I can assure you that immediately this law becomes a fact almost all the responsible editors may become senators, while there will be many senators who may not become responsible editors.

Second extreme.—By article 13 of this law the government reserves to itself the faculty of admitting or not admitting the editor of a periodical according to the information which it may find it convenient to request; and I would like to know what object the government has in not constituting a tribunal for deciding upon the qualities of a responsible editor. The object which the government proposes I comprehend: it is the object of the government to admit an editor or not according as it may be found convenient, according to the information which it may request. But there is yet more. By this article the government reserves to itself the faculty of examining at any time and at any hour whether the editor continues to possess the qualities that give him the aptitude for the discharge of his duties. The newspapers of the Opposition may be well assured that with this article there will be a removal of editorial bones much more frequently than may be convenient to their tranquillity.

Third extreme.—By article 4 of this law the government retains the faculty of suspending the sale and distribution of any publication. First step in which the spiritual collides with the material. And it not only retains this faculty, but with the reservation of the right to select the accuser from among the fiscal promoters nominated by the ordinary method: when, among the fiscal promoters nominated by the ordinary method, there may not be one sufficiently ductile for denunciation at the pleasure of the government, the latter has the right of nominating a special fiscal at any time and without any restriction, even though he be a fiscal who knows not Latin. . . .

Fifth extreme.—By article 5 of this law the government

reserves to itself the right of prohibiting the introduction into Spanish territory of all publications made abroad. I would like to be told what proof of intellectual eminence it is sufficient for the governing powers of Spain to give in return for the extraordinary faculty of exercising not only the particular monopoly of cutting down in its flower all indigenous intelligence, but also the universal monopoly of cutting down in its flower all exotic intelligence.

Sixth extreme.—In addition to all these reservations the government retains the right to dictate the regulations that it may find convenient for the police in regard to the sale and distribution of publications. According to the spirit of the law the Opposition newspapers must already know what facilities they will have for the sale and circulation of their editions. All these acts, when the greater part may be legitimatized by the sanction of a tribunal left to the free volition of the political authorities, essentially movable, essentially and almost by duty impassioned, constitute the most absolute legalization of the most absolutely arbitrary. Leaving out of consideration, gentlemen, that the arbitrary is a two-edged sword, and that if to-day we may wound our enemies at will without motive and without necessity, to-morrow our enemies, without necessity and without motive, will be able to assassinate us at will. Let the honorable Minister of Administration not deceive himself! All these faculties placed at the discretion of the governing authorities are no more than bread of government for to-day and hunger of justice for to-morrow.

Second proposition.—This law represents the negation, the impossibility, of exercising virtue.—Proof. It is twenty years since I have been writing for the public, and I have not learned—and I say it frankly—I have not learned what may not be committed by means of the press,—whether the more sins against God, against the king, and, as they used to say, against the mistress of our thoughts; or in other words, against religion, against the monarchy, and against good customs. The honorable Minister of Administration, who is known to be very well versed in the subject, has presented to us an interminable list of offences, and he has made me see that I have been in the greatest error, and that whether these offences are offences or are not offences, virtue by means of the press is a negation. Outside of those that are marked by ordinary laws, those that are comprehended in the following categories are indictable offences when committed by the press :

First. Everything that censures religion or any of its ministers. (Question.—Even though its ministers are of the sort that do not exercise religion with the decorum that we are all obliged to respect?)

Second. All that censures or attacks any prince whatever. (Question.—Even though that prince meddles with politics and in a controversy commits an offence against us or offends the decorum of our country?)

Third. All that tends to restrict the liberty of the authorities. (And I ask: Even though these authorities tend to restrict our own liberty?)

Fourth. All that which tends to restrict the free exercise of constituted authority. (I would like to know if this is also to be understood as applying when the constituted authorities are lacking in the duties, lacking in the obligations, lacking in the necessities of that for which they were constituted?)

Fifth. All that which offends against good customs. (And what are often intended by good customs? Do not the editors of the law know that in many parts various activities are regarded as good customs when in the eyes of reason and of morality they are evidently bad?)

Sixth. All that which publishes actions that offend the employees of the government. (Even though these actions are committed by very blameworthy employees and which belong to the domain of the public? In this law we find that every· thing is an offence, absolutely everything; only one thing is not an offence, which, with due respect to the moral intention of the authors of the law, appears to me abominable. This thing is the transgression authorized by the second paragraph of article 52, and the injury and the calumny directly authorized by the third paragraph against foreign monarchs who may be at war with Spain.)

And at the same time that this transgression and this calumny is not an offence, it is an offence, according to article 29, to suppose wrong intentions in official acts; to suppose wrong intentions, which is the positive duty of all oppositions in the world; to suppose wrong intentions in acts, in official acts, to the end that the governing powers prove by means of their official acts that their intentions are good.

Also a delinquent under this law is even the unfortunate one who, that he may not go to prison, appeals for a subscription to pay the expenses, the damages, and the costs of the case. I would like to know what the law proposes by the prohibition of this subscription, charitable or not charitable, Is it proposed to prevent public opinion from taking sides with the delinquent and giving an indirect vote of censure against the government?

If this is so, what are we doing here? Are we going to govern with public sentiment or against public sentiment?

In this law so little account is taken of the privileges of the press that under article 62 every newspaper, even though acquitted, is not permitted to publish the defence of the denounced article. That is to say that to-day, the same as twenty or thirty years ago, the level of political liberty is below the level of civil liberty. By this means anybody in authority will be able to trample in advance upon the individuals in opposition; and these, even though their article may be absolved, will not by any means whatever be able to appeal to the recourse of publication in order to obtain a moral reparation. It appears that this law has the melancholy presentiment of making its penalties an honor to the delinquents. And is it not true that a law where the obligations are converted into crimes, and duties translate themselves into acts of insubordination, is it not true, I say, that it makes totally impossible the exercise of virtue? Is it not true that in this law there are no rights except for authority, there are no duties except for liberty? Is it not true that this law might be summed up in one single article that could read: " Newspapers are authorized to write freely under penalty of death?" Is it not true that this law runs contrary in a radical manner, in an absolute manner, against all the tendencies, all the aspirations, of our epoch of publicity? From publicity, gentlemen, more than from any other origin, will always be derived the palladium of liberty, will always be derived the sword of justice, will always be derived the torch of virtue and of morals, and it was publicity—and my friend, Señor Canga Argüelles, representative of other ideas, will pardon me—that put an end to those epochs of secrecy that lay at the foundation of all tyranny, that were the safeguard of all concussions; that were the occasion, the fundamental cause—and if it were not for arousing the hilarity of the Congress, I would say that secrecy was the phosphoritic producer of all vices.

Third proposition.—This law represents the inevitable bankruptcy of the press.—Let us suppose that an individual from a royal family invades the province of the press, becomes a public writer, publishes a given manifesto, and that some controversionist says that that individual of the royal family has published a manifesto unworthy of himself, or perhaps that that manifesto is unworthy an individual of the royal family. The newspaper is denounced; the judge-instructor institutes the preliminary proceedings. Under article 38 the honorable justices of the jury abandon their jurisdictions, leave public justice orphaned, and go to the capital to constitute themselves a tribunal. This done, under the provision of article 25, which says " that it is a delinquency on the part of the press to attack or offend any individual of the royal family," there is nothing left but to condemn the newspaper. Hence proceed the following injuries: The newspaper has left off circulating; the subscribers have left off subscribing; the enterprise has suffered the losses inherent to a denunciation, and in the end has had to pay a respectable sum. This is an unhappy bankruptcy.

But let us suppose a happy bankruptcy, that of an absolution, and it will be seen that it is nevertheless an inevitable bankruptcy. A correspondent of some periodical or other writes, for example, that Señor Olózoga is a notable man. There is some fiscal of the press who takes upon himself the duty of seeing that Señor Olózoga is not to be called a notable man, but a notable statesman. Perhaps Señor Nocedal will say that these are hyperbolical exaggerations of Señor Campoamor, and that it is not possible that there would be a fiscal who would so occupy himself. But this, unbelievable as it is for many, is something that actually happened. Only a little time ago the correspondent of a newspaper wrote saying that Señor Olózoga was a notable man, and on seeing him thus characterized the fiscal of the press sent an officer of the police to see that this expression was varied as commanded, substituting that of notable statesman. And lest the honorable minister might doubt the truth of this assertion, I have here the proof written in red ink, in commemoration doubtless of that celebrated prescription of Sila. Let us suppose that the correspondent is a writer who becomes exasperated, like myself, at unjust contradictions, and that he insists upon notable man instead of notable statesman.

New denunciation, new abandonment of their judicial limitations on the part of the honorable judges. They constitute themselves a tribunal, and I do them the favor of believing that they acquit the newspaper. Now it can be said that Señor Olózoga is a notable man. Here the result has been the following injuries: The newspaper has left off circulating; the subscribers have left off subscribing; the expenses inherent in a judicial procedure have been incurred; it is true that acquittal has come; but, acquittal or no acquittal, it will be a felicitous bankruptcy; nevertheless it will be bankruptcy, and, felicitous or unfortunate, the bankruptcy, as I have said, will it be the less inevitable?

All these things were well to laugh at were it not that in the course of time, as I believe, they will cause us many tears.

Very soon, with this law edited in this manner, there may be brought about at will the most inevitable bankruptcy of the press. This law, more than a serious law, appears to have been made to sport with the destinies of the country's liberty. This law seems like an iron cage made for the imprisonment of all the tendencies, all the aspirations, all the grandeurs of the nineteenth century; and I say grandeurs of the nineteenth century with all intention to avail myself of the opportunity of expressing my astonishment that the honorable Marqués de Pidal, when I believed that he would reply to the representatives of certain doctrines in which this century constantly meets the most bitter diatribes —when I believed that he would have felt that the decorum of a society represented in the government was outraged— rather paid certain respect to those bitter diatribes and to the partisans of those doctrines that have gone by forever. Therefore I say the grandeurs of the nineteenth century, which will be the honor of history, which for posterity will be the pride of humankind. Of the nineteenth century, so great in morality that to-day the least of our convicts would be ashamed to have imputed to him some of the qualities of the virtuous Cato. Of the nineteenth century, so grandly illustrious that to-day the humblest of our lackeys would disdain to have his ignorance compared with the ignorance of those princes of letters who not long ago actually framed a case against somebody for flying and other excesses. Of the nineteenth century, which, should time need more immortality than the immortality of its being, might add to the immortality of time the immortality of glory!

Fourth proposition.—This law is the blockade of public opinion.—Proof. Suppose the case of the election of a president for this Congress! The election finds two contesting candidates, one very tolerant with the minority and hence more agreeable to public opinion; the other much less tolerant, and therefore more agreeable to the government of her Majesty.

The government seeks to procure the election of the less tolerant candidate, and consequently has to defeat the candidate of public opinion. To effect this, what does the government of her Majesty do? A very easy thing. Declare public opinion in a state of blockade. And how can public opinion be put in a state of blockade? By one of two modes at the disposition of the government. Exaggerate certain or supposed good qualities of its candidate, and impede public opinion from doing the same with its candidate! Permit to be sent to the place of residence of one candidate all the good things that may be deemed desirable; and at the same time sequestrate, under the authority given by article 4, all the newspapers that bear eulogies of the candidate of public opinion! But the honorable deputies will tell me: "The newspapers that publish the good qualities of the candidates of public opinion have the recourse of resort to the tribunals." Consequently they resort to the tribunals promptly and speedily: by the diligence of the judge-instructor all very promptly, with the promptness with which we must suppose a functionary would work who knows that he is going to do a thing unpleasant to the government of her Majesty.

Promptly and speedily, also, new journeys of the honorable judges who abandon their jurisdictional limits and assemble to constitute a tribunal, and I will suppose that they also promptly give their verdict for the press. Now the eulogies of the candidate of public opinion may be published. But, *O dolor!* the opportunity has passed; the election has taken place, and the government candidate has been victorious, and the candidate of public opinion has perished for want of help, not having received as much as one loaf from the munition of praise. Is it not true, gentlemen, that it may be said that this law is the perfect blockade of public opinion? Is it not true that this law is a half law, which has inscribed upon one page the obligations, and yet to be written upon the other the guarantees?

Or, better said, is not this law like a half-minted coin bearing on the reverse the cross of duty and lacking on the obverse the face of right? Is it not true that this law proposes the solution of a problem completely insoluble; that it seeks to make possible the metaphysically impossible; that it seeks to prove that a thing may be and not be at the same time? Is it not true that this law contains the attempt to make of representative government, which is a government essentially open, which is a government essentially talkative, a species of constitutional deaf-mute?

Fifth proposition.—This law is the perfect state of siege of human intelligence.—Example. Let us suppose there is a newspaper written with such skill and justice that the government has no means of getting it out of the way; and since justice and skill are not always agreeable to the government it is necessary for the newspaper to disappear, and the newspaper will disappear. But how will it disappear?—the honorable deputies will ask me. Very easily; putting the newspaper in a state of siege. And how can a newspaper be put in a state of siege? With this law, by the following mode:

Every newspaper, however skilful and just it may be, has to have a responsible editor who some time will have to be ill, for health does not depend upon justice and upon skill. It may also happen that in consequence of this illness the editor cannot sign the newspaper, and hence the governor has nothing more to do than to institute a reconnaissance of the editorship by the police, and if the editor is found to be ill and has not been able to sign the newspaper with hand and letter, he can impose a fine of 1,000 reales upon the printer of the newspaper, and following that familiar tale of one of the candle, of the candle two, the editor, for the same offence, is mulcted to the extent of 4,000 reales.

But let us suppose that this newspaper is published in Madrid. The mail closes at eight o'clock in the evening, and if the newspaper is to be well edited it cannot be printed until five or six and consequently must certainly be issued before the two hours are over within which a copy has to be taken to the governor of the province.

Consequence of this infraction: The governor imposes, by virtue of article 21, a fine of 4,000 reales, and since the offence is for every day we shall have a fine of 4,000 reales daily, which amounts to 120,000 reales a month, which is the same as 1,440,000 reales annually. All this without counting upon the power remaining with the governor of the province to impose a fine of 1,000 reales daily for the following:

First. When it appears to him there is a lack of decency.

Second. When according to his judgment, which may very well be lack of judgment, there is committed any offence against good customs without his being obliged to cite an example.

Third. Whenever he sees mischievous allusions, however veiled they may be,—and he will not fail to see them whenever he finds it convenient.

Fourth. Whenever the publication of a fact gives offence to families, such as the publication of a death, etc.

And now let the honorable deputies inform me if a newspaper, however just and skilful it may be, can afford to incur daily a fine of at least 1,000 reales.

It is true that against all these injustices of the governor of the province, nominated by the government, the press has the right to appeal to the government that nominated the governor. Is it not true, gentlemen, that this law is the state of siege of human intelligence? Is it not true that this law is a two-edged sword, and that if to-day we may wound our enemies at free will without motive and without necessity, to-morrow our enemies, without necessity and without motive, will be able to assassinate us at free will?

Is it not true that all this integument of prescriptions in opposition to all political equity, that all this accumulation of arbitrary principles, are no more than bread of government for to-day and hunger of justice for to-morrow? Does it appear prudent to the honorable admirers of this blazing law; does it appear just; does it appear foresighted,—that to sustain our miserable governmental existence one day we leave this terrible weapon in the hands of future governments that may be our most implacable enemies; that we leave them this atrocious weapon which makes legitimate the arbitrary, which makes virtue impossible, which ruins the press, which blockades opinion, and which is the state of siege for human intelligence? Is it possible that the Moderate party—that party which by antonomasia is called the party of supreme intelligence—cannot be aware of the full terror, the full atrocity of that weapon until it may be seen in the hands of its implacable enemies? If this is the case, gentlemen, then the Moderate party may well be addressed by that well-known apostrophe:

> "What fatal misfortune is that
> Of soliciting thine own harm?
> I lament, when thou wak'st in alarm
> It will cost thee thy life!"

I, the first of the Ministerialists; I, who am one of the most important members of the Moderate party, in which I was born politically, in which politically I shall die, who do not belong to that caste of politicians of whom Clement XIV, said "That they pass their lives in sinning and repenting;" I have some explanations to make, I have to give my reasons for washing my hands of this act that sacrifices the first of public liberties. I say sincerely that my face flushes and I feel myself involuntarily seized with a fever every time I hear our common enemies launch against us the accusation that the Liberal party is a party of a temperament so cowardly, of a rectitude so equivocal, and of an intelligence so exiguous, that it can only rule by means of a freedom of the press so restricted, intimidated, and well-nigh muzzled.

As I have had the honor to say on another occasion, I should like to issue a scientific challenge and a moral provocation against all the exaggerated schools to prove to them that the freedom of the press, in place of being their patrimony has always been the triumphant crown of conservative ideas. I should like to prove to our enemies that the Moderate party is a party with temperament so lofty, of rectitude so insuperable, and of intelligence so vast, that it has always been able, is able, and always will be able, to govern with a press, a liberty of the press, open, rationalistic, and even well-nigh unlimited.

Of all the militant political parties there is not one that has less to fear from the liberty of the press than the Moderate party. Depositary of almost the entire social force, of almost the entire public fortune, possessing the intellectual majority, the Moderate party cannot refuse discussion, cannot reject light. On the contrary the Moderate party superabounds in grand qualities of virtue, wisdom, intelligence, reason, justice, and right with which to battle with its enemies. Not in a closed passage and in darkness; no, it can seek them out in an open thoroughfare, it can fight them hand to hand in the light of day, in the light of the sun, and if it were possible, in the light of all the stars of the firmament.

There appears to be a fatal law for all human institutions that they should love that which would slay them and fly from that which should give them life. The Moderate party clings to mutism, which means its death; and loves not the liberty of the press, which is that which would give it horizon, which is that which would lend it atmosphere, which is that which would inform it with vitality.

I have always believed, I do believe, and I shall continue to believe that for the Moderate party the liberty of the press will be what it has been until now, the true battle-steed with which we are to conquer all our enemies; those who attack us on the right flank as well as those who attack us on the left flank. I have always believed, do believe, and will continue to believe, that for the Moderate party the liberty of the press as until now it has always been the ship that has saved us from all despotic wreck, will in the future be for us the sacred ark that will rescue us from every communistic deluge. I have always believed, do believe, and shall continue to believe, that for the Moderate party the liberty of the press will be hereafter as it has been until now the true firm-standing wall against which in a way most fatal, in a way inevitable, there will vainly dash on the one hand all the surges of democracy, on the other hand all the avalanches of reaction.

Gentlemen, I am going to relate the coming history of this fatal law which is to have the sad privilege of slaying its own mother before its birth. When this law is published the safety-valve of representative government will be shut down:

all the lawful passions, all the legal tendencies, all the just aspirations will not be able to satisfy their legitimate desires for growth; these repressed lawful passions will be converted into concentrated hatreds; these concentrated hatreds are going to charge the political atmosphere with electricity; this electricity is going to accumulate in the atmosphere and is going to form a sullen tempest whose mutterings will arouse the rancor of our enemies; and for our friends it will make them pass a life filled with fear and tribulation, and then by the most unforeseen of happenings this invisible tempest, on a day least looked for, will fall upon our heads in the shape of a bloody revolution.

Whatever the consideration in which you hold the prophet, forget not the prophecy!

[Specially translated by Sylvester Baxter.]

BOUTWELL

GEORGE SEWALL BOUTWELL, an American statesman, was born in Brookline, Massachusetts, January 28, 1818. His education was obtained in private schools and by prolonged private study in early manhood. He was admitted to the bar in 1846, but did not begin practice till some years later. He entered politics early as a supporter of Van Buren, and served seven terms as a Democratic member of the State legislature of Massachusetts between 1842 and 1851. He was defeated as a Congressional candidate in 1844, 1846, and 1848, and in the following years was the unsuccessful candidate of the Democrats for governor. In 1851, however, he was elected governor by a coalition of the Democrats and Free-Soilers. After the repeal of the Missouri Compromise in 1854, he helped to found the Republican party, and in 1860 was a member of the national convention which nominated Lincoln for the presidency. He organized the department of internal revenue and was its first commissioner, 1862-63. From 1863 to 1869 he was a member of the lower house of Congress, and secretary of the treasury during President Grant's first administration, 1869-73, resigning in March of the year last named in order to fill the seat in the Senate vacated by Senator Wilson, who had become Vice-President. After leaving the Senate in 1877 he was appointed to codify and edit the Statutes at Large, and he subsequently practised law in Washington for some years. His interest in politics has continued unabated since his retirement from professional labors. He has published "Thoughts on Educational Topics" (1860); "A Manual of the Direct and Excise System of the United States" (1863); "The Taxpayer's Manual" (1865); "Speeches and Papers Relating to the Rebellion" (1876); "Why I am a Republican: a History of the Republican Party" (1884); "The Lawyer, the Statesman, the Soldier" (1887); "The Constitution of the United States at the End of the First Century" (1895).

ON THE PROGRESS OF AMERICAN INDEPENDENCE

ADDRESS BEFORE N. Y. HISTORICAL SOCIETY, APRIL 2, 1889

AT the close of the French war England entered systematically upon a policy whose object was the establishment of the supremacy of Parliament over the colonies of North America. For one hundred and thirty years this supremacy had been denied whenever the claim was presented. In that time manufactures and commerce, although borne down by the weight of legislative restrictions, had so increased as to arrest the attention of the ministry and the board of trade, and excite the prejudices of the laborers upon the Thames and in the manufactories. The population of the thirteen colonies, then estimated at 2,500,000, had doubled by natural increase every twenty-five years, and it was then certain that it would be largely augmented by immigration from Europe.

This population was better fed and better clothed than the corresponding classes in England. The inhabitants of the colonies had acquired great experience in the Indian wars, the siege of Louisbourg, and the invasion of Canada. Their bravery was unquestioned. The future greatness of America had been predicted, its natural resources had in a degree been unfolded.

England was burdened with debt and she thought that America might be compelled to contribute to its payment. The first question was this: Has Parliament a right to legislate for America? An affirmative answer suggested a second; what shall be the character of the legislation? In regard to the first question it ought not to have been expected that " ex parte " opinions, whether accompanied by a show of power or not, would lead to an amicable adjustment of the controversy.

The only ground of hope was in negotiation and this appears not to have been thought of. England proceeded to legislate, and upon the question of policy she made a most fatal mistake. With sole reference to her own interests she would have exercised the power that she assumed in the least offensive way. She would have so legislated that in equity no issue could have been made with her acts. But on the contrary, guided apparently by an insensate lust of power she passed laws which would have kindled rebellion if the right of Parliament had been undisputed. For the purpose of aiding the officers in the collection of the revenue an old and obsolete law was revived under which writs, called writs of assistance, were granted.

By these writs the agents of the government were empowered to search ships, shops, houses, and stores. They were in fact general search warrants. The first application was from the collector of the port of Salem, Massachusetts. The court hesitated. The merchants employed Thatcher and James Otis to resist the application. The writ was granted, but the speech of Otis so excited the people that John Adams fifty years afterward declared that "American independence was then and there born."

In the series of offensive laws first came the Stamp Act, then a declaration that Parliament had a right to legislate for the colonies in all cases whatsoever, then the acts for shutting up the port of Boston, then the act for altering the charter and government of Massachusetts Bay, an act for the better administration of justice, an act to establish the Roman Catholic religion in the Province of Quebec, an act for quartering the army upon the people and various acts for raising a revenue.

The Stamp Act was met by marked opposition in all the colonies, and in some of them the people adopted measures of injustice and violence.

It was determined on all hands that the stamps should not be landed and that no one should hold the office of agent. Those who accepted were compelled to resign. It was in vain that these officials claimed exemption from all responsibility for the existence of the statute, or that they set forth as an excuse that if they did not perform the service other persons less acceptable would be appointed in their places. The people's ears were closed, there was no alternative but resignation.

In New York a gallows was erected in the park of the present City Hall and on it Governor Colden was hung in effigy; handbills were circulated warning those who sold or used stamped paper that their persons, houses, and effects were in peril, and the house of Major James, the commander of the king's artillery, was sacked by the mob and the colors of his regiment were carried away by the excited crowd.

Finally the stamp agent resigned and the stamps were delivered to the mayor and corporation of the city of New York, with the advice of his majesty's council unanimously given and the concurrence of the commander-in-chief of the king's forces.

In Boston the supporters of the ministry and of the Stamp Act were hung in effigy on a tree afterwards known as "Liberty tree," which stood at the corner of Essex and Washington streets. Oliver, the secretary of the Province and stamp distributor, was frightened into resignation. Jonathan Mayhew, the minister of the West Church, preached a violent sermon against the Stamp Act and its supporters, and the next day the house of the governor was broken into and its contents were destroyed.

Apparently the public sentiment condemned these violations of law and order, but the rioters though known were suffered to go unpunished.

The nature of the opposition to the Stamp Act is illustrated by the proceedings in Connecticut. Jared Ingersoll was appointed stamp master, and immediately he was required to resign. A friend, when endeavoring to conciliate the people said, "Had you not rather that these duties would be collected by your brethren than by foreigners?"

"No, vile miscreant, indeed we had not," said one, "if your father must die is there no defect in filial duty in becoming his executioner, that the hangman's part of the estate may remain in the family?" "If the ruin of your country is decreed are you free from blame in taking part in the plunder?"

"The act is so contrived," said Ingersoll, "as to make it your interest to buy the stamps. When I undertook the office I intended a service to you."

"Stop advertising your wares until they come safe at market," he was answered. "The two first letters of his name," said one, "are those of the traitor of old. It was decreed our Saviour should suffer; but was it better for Judas Iscariot to betray him, so that the price of his blood might be saved by his friends?"

After much equivocation and with the fear of death upon him Ingersoll shouted "Liberty and property," three times and then resigned his office. The mob spirit evoked by the Stamp Act soon subsided and a calm determined purpose of resistance took its place. Surrounded by these violent and exciting scenes the dejected ones said, "North American liberty is dead." "She is dead," said those of more faith, "but happily she has left one son, the child of her bosom prophetically named Independence, now the hope of all when he shall come of age."

"I am clear on this point," said Mayhew, "that no people are under a religious obligation to be slaves, if they are able to set themselves at liberty."

This was in 1765, and from that time forth the spirit and purpose of independence animated and controlled the representative men and the organs of public sentiment in every part of the country. It was during the existence of the Stamp Act and pending the measures of oppression which followed its repeal, that declarations were made and measures adopted of the greatest importance to the cause of American independence.

It was then that Patrick Henry, speaking for the Assembly of Virginia, declared " that every attempt to vest the power of taxation in any person or persons whatsoever, other than the said assembly, has a manifest tendency to destroy British as well as American freedom; that he proposed by resolution that the Colony of Virginia be immediately put into a state of defence, and that a committee should be appointed to prepare a plan for embodying, arming, and disciplining such a number of men as may be sufficient for that purpose;" that in the memorable debate on the resolution, in the language if not with the spirit of prophecy, he declared it vain to indulge the fond hope of peace and reconciliation, that an appeal to arms and to the God of Hosts was all that was left; that John Morin Scott of New York said if the mother country deny to the colonies the right of making their own laws and disposing of their own property by representatives of their own choosing then the connection between them ought to cease and sooner or later it must inevitably cease; that the Sons of Liberty of the city of New York as early as the 7th day of January, 1766, forecast the American union in the declaration that " there was safety for the colonies only in the firm union of the whole;" that the assembly of New York declared that that " colony lawfully and constitutionally has and enjoys an internal legislature of its own, in which the crown and the people of this colony are constitutionally represented, and the power and authority of the said legislature cannot lawfully or constitutionally be suspended, abridged, abrogated, or annulled by any power, authority, or prerogative whatsoever;" that the Committee of One Hundred of the city of New York, upon the receipt of the news of the massacre on Lexington Green, resolves that all the horrors of civil war would never compel America to submit to taxation by authority of Parliament; that the assembly demanded " exemption from the burdens of ungranted, involuntary taxes as the grand principle of every free State," and as " without such a right vested in the people themselves there can be no liberty, no happiness, no security;" that Mr. Jefferson said, " We want neither inducement nor power to declare and assert a separation; we are reduced to the tyranny of irritable masters or resistance by force;" that the alternative of choosing an unconditional submission to the county " of Hanover, Virginia, instructed its delegates to assent to such measures as would produce the hearty union of all their countrymen and sister colonies;" that William Hooper, of North Carolina, early in 1774, declared that " the colonies are striding fast to independency and will ere long build an empire on the ruins of Britain, will adopt its constitution purged of its impurities and, from an experience of its defects, will guard against those evils which have wasted its vigor and brought it to an untimely end;" that the same State, the 12th day of April, 1776, empowered its delegates to " declare independency;" that Joseph Hawley of Massachusetts asserted that " independence was the only way to union and harmony;" that General Greene in 1775 recommended a Declaration of Independence; that Samuel Adams said, " I am perfectly satisfied of the necessity of a public and explicit Declaration of Independence;" that the press of Philadelphia declared that " none in this day of liberty will say that duty binds us to yield obedience to any man or body of men, forming part of the British constitution when they exceed the limits prescribed by that constitution; that the Stamp Act is unconstitutional and no more obligatory than a decree of the Divan of Turkey;" that the town of Boston said,—and may their words be remembered,—" We are not afraid of poverty, but we disdain slavery;" that the county of Suffolk in 1774 resolved, " that no obedience is due from this province to either or any part of the obnoxious acts;" that Middlesex, speaking for the men of Lexington, Concord, and Bunker Hill, said, " We are sensible that he can never die too soon who lays down his life in support of the laws and liberties of his country;" that the Continental Congress of 1774 sent forth its immortal remonstrances, memorials, manifestoes, and addresses to the king, to Parliament, to the people of England, to the people of Ireland, to their brethren of Canada, and to the colonies of America; that ancient hostilities were forgotten, that local barriers were broken down, the spirit of union fostered and the colonies made one in purpose and in destiny; and finally, that the formal and authoritative Declaration of Independence introduced an era of freedom, not for this country and people only, but ultimately, for all who shall speak the English language.

Thus does it appear from this array of facts, gathered from an era of a century and a half, that the independence of the American colonies had a slow growth, but its progress was perceptible, and from the year 1764 there could have been no ground for doubt as to the ultimate result. When the Declaration came the country was prepared to give it a substantial if not a united support.

The controversy and the contest were carried on by young men and by men in the meridian period of life. Jefferson was in his thirty-fourth year. Washington was his senior by only eleven years, and it is said of the signers of the Declaration that their average age was less than forty years.

It is a remarkable but a well-authenticated phenomenon in human history that when the minds of many men are directed to one subject they often arrive at similar results and find similar modes of expression. This peculiarity has been observed in purely scientific researches, and it is more probable that it should have existed in the controversy preceding the independence of these colonies. It is not a marvel then, nor in disparagement of Mr. Jefferson or of the Congress of 1776, that the historian is compelled to admit that the Declaration of Independence is but the last and best expression of the sentiment and purposes of colonial America.

The rights and grievances of the colonies had been set forth by the Congress of 1774; the doctrine of the equality of all men, not as a theory merely, but in the substance of their natural, political rights, had been enunciated by Otis; and the citizens of Mecklenburg, North Carolina, had anticipated the Declaration of Jefferson and in some respects its exact language, and yet there is no reason to believe that the substance of the document was known to any member of Congress, and there is much evidence that neither Mr. Jefferson nor any one of his colleagues of the committee was aware of its existence.

The great merit of the Declaration of Independence is in this: That it asserted with unrivalled precision and power what the country had resolved and what it was prepared to maintain. It proclaimed the natural rights of men; it embodied the history of colonial America and it set forth the nature of the oppressions that the colonists had endured, the sacrifices they had made, the loyalty they had exhibited, their poverty and forbearance all crowned by a statement of their purposes in the future. The colonies were represented by Mr. Jefferson, of Virginia; Mr. Robert R. Livingston, of New York; John Adams, of Massachusetts; Dr. Franklin, of Pennsylvania, and Roger Sherman, of Connecticut.

The draft as prepared by Mr. Jefferson was as remarkable for what was omitted finally, upon the suggestion of Georgia and South Carolina, as for what was preserved. As prepared by Mr. Jefferson and agreed to by the committee the king of Great Britain was denounced for the crime of perpetuating the traffic in African slaves.

In the year 1774 North Carolina resolved not to import nor purchase slaves; the county of Hanover, Virginia, had pronounced the African trade in slaves " most dangerous to the virtue and welfare of the country;" the Congress of 1774 had discountenanced the trade in slaves, and James Otis with nervous eloquence had denounced the whole system of human bondage.

As we turn from the consideration of the main theme of the occasion a restatement of the leading thoughts may not be inappropriate:

When the colonists laid the foundations of their respective governments they asserted those doctrines of political and personal freedom which constituted finally the legal and moral basis of the Revolution; and although in their weakness they submitted to acts which in their view were oppressive they never recognized the authority of the British Parliament, but upon their records and during a period of nearly a century and a half they asserted and as far as practicable they maintained their independence as political organizations.

The laws which they annulled or evaded were enacted by an assembly whose authority they never acknowledged and in which they were not represented.

Our fathers were careful to maintain their loyalty to the king as the sovereign of the British Empire and to perform all their duties as members of that empire, that the injustice of others might not have root in their own errors and wrongs.

The American Union did not originate in the present constitution, nor even in the articles of confederation; but it is elementary in the history of the country, and as far as we can judge it is essential to our form of liberty.

From 1643, when the union was formed between Massachusetts, New Plymouth, Connecticut and New Haven for "their own mutual safety and welfare," with the name "The United Colonies of New England," there seems never to have been a moment when the idea of union did not exist in the public mind. Union was the necessity of their weakness, as it now is the emblem of our origin and the source of our strength.

I turn now from this array of ancient facts; in conclusion I may direct your thoughts to some of the possibilities of the future. We are now passing from the first to the second century of our national existence. In 1790 the United States had less than 4,000,000 inhabitants, and in 1890 our population will be largely in excess of 60,000,000. We rank as the third nation on the globe if we consider only the number of persons dwelling upon contiguous territory, and in less than half a century we shall stand in the second place.

Our population is at least fifteen times as great as it was a hundred years ago, but we must not assume upon the same ratio of increase for the next century. Relatively there will be a decrease in the number of immigrants, and it is quite probable that the spirit of enterprise or the love of adventure will carry away the successors of our frontier population to Africa and South America, the continents of the future. At the present rate of increase our population in the year 2000 would exceed 800,000,000, and if the ratio of increase should fall to fifteen per cent in each decennial period the course for the year 2000 will show an aggregate of about 280,000,000.

Whether so vast a population can be sustained within our present limits is a problem of the future, but for one I entertain no doubt that the sustaining force of the United States is adequate to the support of 400,000,000 inhabitants without any impairment of the enjoyments and comforts of social and domestic life. If we assume the habitable area of the United States to be 2,500,000 square miles, an average population of 300 to the square mile, the present average of the State of Massachusetts, would give an aggregate of 750,000,000 souls. And our capacity may be further measured by considering the fact that if the present inhabitants of the United States could be transferred to the State of Texas the average would not exceed 300 persons to the square mile.

And these statements even do not measure and limit the possibilities of comfortable existence on this continent. The diversification of human pursuits, due to science, art, and a wise public policy, is making constant and appreciable additions to the capacity of this globe to sustain human life. The 60,000,000 within our limits are better fed, better clothed, better housed than were the 2,500,000 who inaugurated the Revolutionary War.

Popular education enlarges the views and elevates the aspirations of the masses of men and women, and it also increases their opportunities for advancement and comfort in life.

We may also rely with much confidence upon the simplicity of our system of land titles and the facility with which the soil may be conveyed from one party to another. With the increase of population and of wealth there will be an increasing tendency to make investments in land, and consequently there will be an ever-increasing peril from agrarian controversies. These may be controlled in some degree if not averted altogether by taking security against the existence of land monopolies, and by limiting the possessions of business corporations, of educational, charitable and eleemosynary institutions, and of churches to such areas as may be necessary to the performance of the duties imposed upon them. In all countries the landless classes are the dangerous classes, and it is therefore a wise public policy to encourage the possession of land even though the holdings should be small and in value relatively insignificant. Every title deed is security for the public peace. By the fable of Antæus we are taught that whoever touches the earth becomes strong, and by experience we are taught that whoever owns the earth becomes quiet minded and patriotic.

Henceforth the attention of this country will be withdrawn from Europe by degrees and it will be directed to Canada, Mexico, Central and South America, and the continent of Asia. In the arts and in manufactures Europe is our competitor, but in these departments we are without a rival upon this continent. Our future greatness as a manufacturing and trading nation must rest chiefly upon the kindly dispositions of the Asiatic peoples, upon the development of this continent and the constant friendship of the States and communities between the two great oceans.

I am confident that we have as a nation passed the period when the maxim "in peace prepare for war" was a necessary condition of our public life. First of all we should never indulge the thought of acquiring territory by aggressive means. Not that an honorable extension of the territory of the Union would be unwise under all circumstances, but a war for the enlargement of our dominion would be an unjust war in the very nature of the case.

Our position and influence in the affairs of the world for all purposes consistent with the rights of other nations depend no longer upon the exhibition of military force either upon the sea or upon the land.

We are separated by vast oceans from the great powers of the world; our trade is so valuable that neither England, France, nor Germany can forego its advantages for a single month; and our resources in men and in money are so ample that we may rely confidently upon the forbearance of those rulers from whom we may not be able even to command respect.

In this aspect of the future of the republic I do not accept the opinion that a wise public policy requires us to enter upon the construction of a seagoing navy in competition with the great nations of Europe that exist only under the constant menace of war. Better will it be for us to employ our resources in the construction of small, fast-sailing steamships to be employed in the transportation of the mails to and from all the principal ports of Central and South America and the eastern parts of Asia, thus opening new avenues through which the enterprise and business of the country may have free course.

The time has passed when the fate or the fortunes of nations were dependent upon naval battles lost or won. For

L the future a war on the ocean is a war on commerce, and for such a war the heavily armored vessels of great navies are worthless utterly. Let science and skill furnish such protection to our sea coast cities as science and skill can command, but let us abandon the thought of constructing great navies at a cost of tens of millions on tens of millions for anticipated war on the open sea or as aids to the conquest of foreign lands. Let republican America, warned and instructed by the lesson which downtrodden Europe teaches, enter upon its second century with the purpose of demonstrating the truth that a government in which the people rule may be at once peaceful, powerful, and just.

EVARTS

WILLIAM MAXWELL EVARTS, a noted American lawyer, was born in Boston February 6, 1818, and educated at Yale University. He studied law at the Harvard law school, was admitted to the bar of New York in 1841, and began practice in New York city. He soon became known as one of the most learned men in his profession, being often consulted by other lawyers in perplexing cases, and was district attorney in New York city, 1849-53. He took an active interest in political affairs and was one of the earliest members of the Republican party. He was the chief counsel for President Johnson in the impeachment trial of the latter, and from July, 1868, to March, 1869, was attorney-general of the United States. In 1872 Evarts was counsel for the United States in the Geneva arbitration tribunal respecting the Alabama claims, and in 1875 was senior counsel for Henry Ward Beecher in the famous Tilton-Beecher suit. He appeared for the Republican party before the Electoral Commission in 1877, and served as secretary of state during the administration of President Hayes. From 1885 to 1891 he was a United States senator. He was noted as a brilliant speaker on social occasions and an eloquent orator on more formal ones. Among his most noted orations are his eulogy on Chief Justice Chase in 1873, the Centennial oration in Philadelphia (1876), and speeches on the unveiling of statues of Seward and Webster in New York city. He died February 28, 1901.

WHAT THE AGE OWES TO AMERICA

FROM CENTENNIAL ORATION DELIVERED AT PHILADELPHIA, JULY 4, 1876

FELLOW CITIZENS,—The event which to-day we commemorate supplies its own reflections and enthusiasms and brings its own plaudits. They do not at all hang on the voice of the speaker nor do they greatly depend upon the contracts and associations of the place. The Declaration of American Independence was when it occurred a capital transaction in human affairs; as such it has kept its place in history; as such it will maintain itself while human interest in human institutions shall endure. The scene and the actors for their profound impression upon the world at the time and ever since have owed nothing to dramatic effects, nothing to epical exaggerations.

To the eye there was nothing wonderful, or vast, or splendid, or pathetic in the movement or the display. Imagination or art can give no sensible grace or decoration to the persons, the place, or the performance which made up the business of that day. The worth and the force that belong to the agents and the action rest wholly on the wisdom, the courage, and the faith that formed and executed the great design, and the potency and permanence of its operation upon the affairs of the world, which, as foreseen and legitimate consequences, followed.

The dignity of the act is the deliberate, circumspect, open, and serene performance by these men in the clear light of day, and by a concurrent purpose of a civic duty, which embraced the greatest hazards to themselves and to all the people from whom they held this disputed discretion, but which to their sober judgments promised benefits to that people and their posterity from generation to generation exceeding these hazards and commensurate with its own fitness.

The question of their conduct is to be measured by the actual weight and pressure of the manifold considerations which surrounded the subject before them and by the abundant evidence that they comprehended their vastness and variety. By a voluntary and responsible choice they willed to do what was done and what without their will would not have been done.

Thus estimated, the illustrious act covers all who participated in it with its own renown and makes them forever conspicuous among men, as it is forever famous among events. And thus the signers of the Declaration of our Independence "wrote their names where all nations should behold them and all time should not efface them." It was "in the course of human events" intrusted to them to determine whether the fulness of time had come when a nation should be born in a day. They declared the independence of a new nation in the sense in which men declare emancipation or declare war; the Declaration created what was declared.

Famous always among men are the founders of States, and fortunate above all others in such fame are these, our fathers, whose combined wisdom and courage began the great structure of our national existence, and laid sure the foundations of liberty and justice on which it rests. Fortunate, first, in the clearness of their title and in the world's acceptance of their rightful claim. Fortunate, next, in the enduring magnitude of the State they founded and the beneficence of its protection of the vast interests of human life and happiness, which have here had their home. Fortunate, again, in the admiring imitation of their work, which the institutions of the most powerful and most advanced nations more and more exhibit; and, last of all, fortunate in the full demonstration of our later time, that their work is adequate to withstand the most disastrous storms of human fortunes, and survives unwrecked, unshaken, and unharmed.

This day has now been celebrated by a great people at each recurrence of its anniversary for a hundred years, with every form of ostentatious joy, with every demonstration of respect and gratitude for the ancestral virtue which gave it its glory, and with the firmest faith that growing time should neither obscure its lustre nor reduce the ardor, nor discredit the sincerity of its observance. A reverent spirit has explored the lives of the men who took part in the great transaction; has unfolded their characters and exhibited to an ad-

the execution of the single design which it is the glory of this great instrument of our national existence to have framed and announced. The recognition of our independence, first by France, and then by Great Britain, the closer union by the Articles of Confederation and the final unity by the federal constitution were all but muniments of title of that " liberty and union, one and inseparable," which were proclaimed at this place and on this day one hundred years ago, which have been our possession from that moment hitherto, and which we surely avow shall be our possession forever. . . .

What half a century ago was hopefully prophesied for our far future goes out to its fulfilment. The prophecy then uttered has become a truth—a realization.

" As the sun rises one Sabbath morning and travels westward from Newfoundland to the Oregon, he will behold the countless millions assembling, as if by a common impulse, in the temples with which every valley, mountain, and plain will be adorned. The morning psalm and the evening anthem will commence with the multitudes on the Atlantic coast, be sustained by the loud chorus of ten thousand times ten thousand in the valley of the Mississippi, and be prolonged by the thousands of thousands on the shores of the Pacific."

What remains but to search the spirit of the laws of the land as framed by, and modeled to, the popular government to which our fortunes were committed by the Declaration of Independence? I do not mean to examine the particular legislation, State or general, by which the affairs of the people have been managed, sometimes wisely and well, at others feebly and ill, nor even the fundamental arrangement of political authority, or the critical treatment of great junctures in our policy and history. The hour and the occasion concur to preclude so intimate an inquiry.

The chief concern in this regard to us and to the rest of the world, is, whether the proud trust, the profound radicalism, the wide benevolence which spoke in the Declaration, and were infused into the constitution at the first, have been in good faith adhered to by the people, and whether now these principles supply the living forces which sustain and direct government and society.

He who doubts needs but to look around to find all things full of the original spirit, and testifying to its wisdom and strength. We have taken no steps backward, nor have we needed to seek other paths in our progress than those in which our feet were planted at the beginning. Weighty and manifold have been our obligations to the great nations of the earth, to their scholars, their philosophers, their men of genius and of science, to their skill, their taste, their invention, to their wealth, their arts, their industry. But in the institutions and methods of government; in civil prudence, courage, or policy; in statesmanship, in the art of "making of a small town a great city," in the adjustment of authority to liberty; in the concurrence of reason and strength in peace, of force and obedience in war; we have found nothing to recall us from the course of our fathers, nothing to add to our safety or aid our progress in it.

So far from this all modifications of European politics accept the popular principles of our system and tend to our model. The movements toward equality of representation, enlargement of the suffrage, and public education in England; the restoration of unity in Italy; the confederation of Germany under the lead of Prussia; the actual republic in France; the unsteady throne of Spain; the new liberties of Hungary; the constant gain to the people's share in government throughout all Europe; all tend one way, the way pointed out in the Declaration of Independence.

The care and zeal with which our people cherish and invigorate the primary supports and defences of their own sovereignty have all the unswerving force and confidence of instincts. The community and publicity of education at the charge and as an institution of the State is firmly embedded in the wants and desires of the people. Common schools are rapidly extending through the only part of the country which has been shut against them, and follow close upon the footsteps of its new liberty to enlighten the enfranchised race. Freedom of conscience easily stamps out the first sparkles of persecution and snaps as green withes the first bonds of spiritual domination. The sacred oracles of their religion the people wisely hold in their own keeping as the keys of religious liberty, and refuse to be beguiled by the voice of the wisest charmer into loosing their grasp.

Freedom from military power and the maintenance of that arm of the government in the people; a trust in their own adequacy as soldiers when their duty as citizens should need to take on that form of service to the State; these have gained new force by the experience of foreign and civil war, and a standing army is a remoter possibility for this nation in its present or prospective greatness than it was in the days of its small beginnings.

But in the freedom of the press and the universality of the suffrage as maintained and exercised to-day throughout the length and breadth of the land we find the most conspicuous and decisive evidence of the unspent force of the institutions of liberty, and the jealous guard of its principal defences. These indeed are the great agencies and engines of the people's sovereignty. They hold the same relations to the vast Democracy of modern society that the persuasions of the orators and the personal voices of the assembly did in the narrow confines of the Grecian States. The laws, the customs, the impulses, and sentiments of the people have given wider and wider range and license to the legislations of the press, multiplied and more frequent occasions for the exercise of the suffrage, larger and larger communication of its franchise.

The progress of a hundred years finds these prodigious activities in the fullest play—incessant and all powerful—indispensable in the habits of the people and impregnable in their affections. The public service and their subordination to the public safety stand in their play upon one another, and in their freedom thus maintained. Neither could long exist in true vigor in our system without the other. Without the watchful, omnipresent, and indomitable energy of the press the suffrage would languish, would be subjugated by the corporate power of the legions of placemen which the administration of the affairs of a great nation imposes upon it and fall a prey to that " vast patronage which " we are told, " distracted, corrupted, and finally subverted the Roman Republic."

On the other hand, if the impressions of the press upon the opinions and passions of the people found no settled and ready mode of their working out through the frequent and peaceful suffrage, the people would be driven to satisfy their displeasure at government or their love of change to the coarse methods of barricades and batteries, by the force of arms, as it were.

We cannot then hesitate to declare that the original principles of equal society and popular government still inspire the laws, live in the habits of the people and animate their

purposes and their hopes. These principles have not lost
their spring or elasticity. They have sufficed for all the
methods of government in the past; we feel no fear for their
adequacy in the future. Released now from the tasks and
burdens of the formative period, these principles and methods
can be directed with undivided force to the everyday conduct
of government, to the staple and steady virtues of administration.

The feebleness of crowding the statute-books with unex-
ecuted laws; the danger of power outgrowing or evading
responsibility, the rashness and fickleness of temporary ex-
pedients, the constant tendency by which parties decline into
factions and end in conspiracies, all these mischiefs beset
all governments and are part of the life of each generation.
To deal with these evils, the tasks and burdens of the immediate future, the nation needs no other resources than the
principles and the examples which our past history supply.
These principles, these examples of our fathers, are the
strength and the safety of our State to-day: *Moribus an-
tiquis, stat res Romana, virisque.*

Unity, liberty, power, prosperity—these are our possessions to-day. Our territory is safe against foreign dangers;
its completeness dissuades from further ambition to extend
it, and its rounded symmetry discourages all attempts to dis-
member it. No division into greatly•unequal parts would be
tolerable to either. No imaginable union of interests or
passions large enough to include one half the country, but
must embrace much more. The madness of partition into
numerous and feeble fragments could proceed only from the
hopeless degradation of the people, and would form but
an incident in the general ruin.

The spirit of the nation is at the highest—its triumph over

the inborn, inbred perils of the constitution has chased away all fears, justified all hopes and with universal joy we greet this day. We have not proved unworthy of a great ancestry; we have had the virtue to uphold what they so wisely, so firmly established. With these proud possessions of the past, with powers matured, with principles settled, with habits formed, the nation passes as it were from preparatory growth to responsible development of character and the steady performance of duty. What labors await it, what trials shall attend it, what triumphs for human nature, what glory for itself, are prepared for this people in the coming century, we may not presume to foretell. "One generation passeth away and another generation cometh, but the earth abideth forever," and we reverently hope that these, our constituted liberties, shall be maintained to the unending line of our posterity and so long as the earth itself shall endure.

In the great procession of nations, in the great march of humanity, we hold our place. Peace is our duty, peace is our policy. In its arts, its labors, and its victories, then we find scope for all our energies, rewards for all our ambitions, renown enough for all our love and fame. In the august presence of so many nations which, by their representatives, have done us the honor to be witnesses of our commemorative joy and gratulation, and in sight of the collective evidences of the greatness of their own civilization with which they grace our celebration, we may well confess how much we fall short, how much we have to make up in the emulative competitions of the times.

Yet even in this presence and with a just deference to the age, the power, the greatness of the other nations of the earth, we do not fear to appeal to the opinion of mankind whether, as we point to our land, our people, and our laws, the contemplation should not inspire us with a lover's enthusiasm for our country.

Time makes no pauses in his march. Even while I speak, the last hour of the receding, is replaced by the first hour of the coming century, and reverence for the past gives way to the joys and hopes, the activities and the responsibilities of the future; a hundred years hence the piety of that generation will recall the ancestral glory which we celebrate to-day, and crown it with the plaudits of a vast population which no man can number.

By the mere circumstance of this periodicity, our generation will be in the minds, in the hearts, on the lips of our countrymen at the next centennial commemoration in comparison with their own character and condition and with the great founders of the nation. What shall they say of us? How shall they estimate the part we bear in the unbroken line of the nation's progress? And so on, in the long reach of time, forever and forever, our place in the secular roll of the ages must always bring us into observation and criticism; will place us under the observant gaze of all peoples.

Under this double trust, then, from the past and for the future let us take heed to our ways and while it is called to-day, resolve that the great heritage we have received shall be handed down through the long line of the advancing generations, the home of liberty, the abode of justice, the stronghold of faith among men, "which holds the moral elements of the world together," and of faith in God, which binds that world to his throne.

THE DAY WE CELEBRATE

ADDRESS AT THE BANQUET OF THE NEW ENGLAND SOCIETY,
DECEMBER 22, 1876

EVER since I have been a member of this Society, which
is ever since I have been a resident of the city of New
York, it has been the same day that is celebrated, the
same people that celebrated it, and they have celebrated it in
the same way. It must have been a great day that would bear
so much celebration. They must have been a great people
that could celebrate it even to their own satisfaction so often,
and they must have had a very good way of celebrating it
when it could have maintained its freshness so many successive years. I have taken part myself in a good many of these
celebrations and have furnished my share of the gratification
or amusement of the occasion. I have laughed with you year
after year at your favorite President Choate's efforts here.
My labors in this behalf, full of fidelity to the memory of
our Pilgrim Fathers, have earned for me, let me say here in
advance, some respect and regard for my present position,
and a little of the indulgence that I have extended to others
is all I ask for myself.

Now, there are several considerations about a New England dinner speech which relieve it from embarrassments. In
the first place our New England ancestors and their descendants for the most part have always held that it was what a
man did, and not what he said, that was of any account.
Besides it was always understood that whatever was said in
this room never went any further; and thirdly, that no man
ever was to be called into question elsewhere for what he

said. A New England dinner is favorably known, no doubt, in the luxury of your accustomed celebrations, regarded only as a dinner of courses; but it is as a dinner of discourses that it has its greatest fame. All opinions, provided they concur in praising ourselves and our ancestors; all criticism upon others, provided they do not disparage our own superiority; all homage to the rest of the country, and in fact, to the rest of the world, if it only be compatible with the supremacy of the little corner of it from which we come— this classification, New England first and the rest of the world next, we consider a sufficient honor to them: we only wish we could do better justice to ourselves. And now we have a great deal to admire in what we see before us here and that is an emotion which all can equally share. It needs no mirrors for the display, for each New Englander, looking upon each other New Englander, sees the reflection of the noblest specimens of humanity. Now, it is not at all surprising to us who have studied the subject, that we have these opinions, but it is surprising that the rest of the world is ready to take us at our own words, and that perhaps is the reason we don't think so much of the rest of the world.

New England, I observe, while it retains all its sterling qualities is nevertheless moving forward in the direction of conciliation and peace. I remember, when I was a boy, I travelled 240 miles by stage coach from Boston to New Haven to avoid going to Harvard University, which was across the bridge. It was because of the religious animosities which pervaded the community and I suppose animated my youthful breast; and now here I come to a New England Society and sit between the two presidents of those renowned universities, who have apparently come here for the purpose of enjoying themselves, and of exhibiting that proximity is no longer dangerous to the peace of those universities. No doubt there is a considerable warfare going on between them as to the methods of instruction, but to us who have looked on, we have seen no more obtrusive manifestation of it than that the president on my left, of Yale, in dealing with the subjects that have successively been placed before him, has pursued the method of that university, its comprehensive method, that takes in the whole curriculum; while on my right, the eclectic principle is exercised by my friend, President Eliot, and he has confined himself to the dainty morsels of the repast. I speak of this to show that although an amelioration of climate or an obliteration of virtues is not to be expected in New England, or in New England men, yet there may be an advancement of the sunshine of the heart and that an incorporation of our narrow territory in a great nation, and a transfusion of our opinions, our ideas, our purposes, into the veins of a nation of 40,000,000 of people, may enlarge and liberalize even the views, the plans, and the action of New England.

The quest upon which emigrants from the Old World sought the New, the motives which led their migration, were, as we all know, for the most part to find an abode where they could secure abundant wealth with little labor. But the New Englanders, either by choice or guided by Providence, found a new home which offered them nothing but abundant labor with no wealth at all. And what has come of that? and who possess as much of the wealth, the power, the glory, and the strength of this world as the descendants of the New Englanders who courted labor without wealth? This narrow and barren and weak territory could say to the newcomers only this, " Silver and gold have I none, but such as I have give I thee;" and out of that possession, out of the power of labor, out of the frugality, out of the self-denial, out of the rigorous virtues they bred, they have gone out and possessed and ransacked its wealth.

Now, if there be one trait in the New England character more valuable than another, more admirable and more constant, it is this: That the New Englanders are ready to meet the duties of their time, when those duties are to be performed, and at the sacrifice and the cost that the present discharge of those duties requires. It is easy for philosophers and for scholars, for poets and for people, to warm with the patriotism of ancient Greece and to glow with the enthusiasm of future generations. The New Englanders thought at the time of the first plantation and have thought ever since that this retrospective and prospective enthusiasm and energy were of very little account in the affairs of this world. They have courted always the duties of the present hour; they have not disguised their difficulty; they have not retreated before their danger; they have had but one purpose —to take their share of every conflict and honestly to bear their share of the common result. Now, if these springheads of New England virtue, that never will be removed from her soil, can be maintained and defended, the streams of life and prosperity to the rest of the country will never fail. Let us, then, with honest enthusiasm, without form and without ceremony, feel that it is a great thing in our continuing life that we do celebrate that day, and love to celebrate it as the greatest day in our history.

New England in itself to-day, within its own boundaries, is the richest, the best cultivated, the most instructed, and the most energetic portion of the land. In the country of which it forms a part it finds a nation of prodigious energies and of magnificent proportions; and that nation, take it through and through, with all defects, with all shortcomings, with all difficulties, and all dangers, even a New England judgment, censorious though it is apt to be, could but pronounce a land of which the sternest of our New England ancestors would have been proud to-day. If, then, we look at this nation in its relations to the rest of the world, these few outcasts of fortune, cast upon the New England shore in a December night, being the beginnings and the foundations of the nation, this nation, it is not too much to say, finds every other nation ready to respect its power and confess its justice; so much so that in the preservation of the peace of the world this nation has the readiest and the safest part that ever a nation had. Nobody that is powerful desires to quarrel with it and nobody that is powerless is it possible for us to quarrel with.

Thus all our energies, all our duties, all our labors, dangers, and difficulties are within our own borders; and the New England of to-day, placing itself in present relations to things as they are, must determine what line of duty, what path of honor, what purposes, and what results it proposes to follow in the current questions of the day. Its duty, its temper, are not necessarily the same as they have been heretofore. The same principles are to guide, but the action may be different. We have finished a struggle that has made permanent and general in the constitution, in the laws, in the arrangements of society, a complete admission of the equality of man, of the safety of citizenship, and of the duty of mutual love. Now, after a great civil war, greater than any nation has ever endured separately without disintegration or injury to its integrity, there are duties that do not belong to the condition either preparatory to the strife or when the strife was in progress. We have found out what

bayonets mean in this country; and you remember what
Hosea Biglow says on that subject:

> " Lord! didn't I feel streaked,
> The first time I found out why bayonets were peaked."

And you will observe that their utility is of a somewhat
demonstrative character. But I think it is Bismarck who
is credited with the *mot* that bayonets are not an institution
to sit down on. And so the American people, as averse as
any people could be to the use or the administration of bayonets, is the last nation of the world that would wish to sit
down on that institution.

When, therefore, we have come to a time when, having
secured every purpose of war; when, having enlisted the law
and the institutions of society in furtherance of New England virtues, that justice and duty and right should prevail
throughout this land, let us accept at once what we shall
be recreant and faithless to our inheritance if we do not accept,—that New England opinions, New England ideas, and
New England results are to make their way in this country
by moral and intellectual methods. And when we talk of
reactionary influences and tendencies let us understand that
if we are not willing to be patient and faithful laborers in
building up the wastes of this land, if we are impatient to
precipitate, that we are those that will be the leaders in reaction from the moral and intellectual processes to the finished
methods of force. Whenever those methods shall become
necessary, whenever justice and right shall require that defence, New England will resume her arms. But New England will not resort to animosities or jealousies in order to
reach the ruder and grosser methods of hostility when moral
suasion cannot prevail. I say, then, that New England will
practise in patience and in faith these methods; and if they

be slow it is because the moral position of the country, the pervasion of the whole community by character, sentiments, the diffusion of manners, of habits, of systems, is a gradual and a slow process; and the moral government and the moral forces of this world are not to be changed even in honor of our New England ancestry.

Now, there are three questions before the people of the country to-day and they are all public, all unselfish, all patriotic, all elevated, and all ennobling as subjects of contemplation and of action. They are the public peace in this large and general sense that I have indicated. They are the public faith, without which there is no such thing as honorable national life; and the public service, which unless pure and strong and noble makes all the pæans of free government but doggerel in our ears.

Now, in regard to the public faith, the same principles which I have indicated as showing that we have passed the stage of antagonism, of hostility, and must reach the stage of co-operation, of sympathy, and of succor, apply to all these great questions of the public debt and of the nation's burdens. They are great burdens; they do impose great difficulties; they do include perhaps great dangers. We need no hostilities between North and South, none between East and West, none between debtor and creditor; we need all our resources, all our wealth, all our gold, all our silver, all our industry, and all our thrift. Bear, then, with such differences of opinion as grow out of differences of situation; make the most of brotherhood and the least of dissension; see that great and common burdens rest unequally and are to be borne unequally; see to it that there shall be no failures in that perfect disposition on the part of the wealthy and powerful States of New England and their wealthy distribu-

tive share of the country in bearing the burdens that rest
more heavily upon others than upon ourselves. Let us remember that generous and wise maxim of Mr. Webster, who
in the bitterest of the strifes of his declining years used no
words of harshness against disputants, and was ready to say
of them, as he did say, " They are not bad men, but bad
reasoners."

And now about the public service. Well, on that subject it may be said that one good example teaches more than
many precepts, and perhaps in an after-dinner speech the
least said is the soonest mended. But nevertheless there
should be no step backward in magistrates, in statesmen, in preachers, in teachers, in editors, in the people. We
must go on. We do understand as a people the difficulties
that we are in; we do understand as a people the methods
by which we have reached them; and we do understand, I
think, the way out of them. It may be hedged with difficulties and opposed with dangers. It touches the very life
of free government; it touches the very sincerity of the public methods of the nation. For such is human nature that,
as Mr. Burke has said (and I hope I do not too much mis-
quote his words), " By whatever paths the great places in a
State are to be reached by its public men that path will be
trod; and if the path be devious, and slimy, and wicked, and
horrid with calumnies and jealousies, nevertheless, if that be
the only path upward, the statesman will take it." It is for
you to say—you as a people to say—whether or no the paths
of your public life shall be clean and bright and noble and ever
tending upward. I believe there is great good fortune in
this people that, to start with, you have a president who has
never pursued any devious paths and does not propose to encourage their pursuit by others.

FROUDE

JAMES ANTHONY FROUDE, a distinguished English historian, was born at Dartington, Devonshire, April 23, 1818, and was educated at Westminster and at Oriel College, Oxford. In 1842 he was elected to a fellowship at Exeter, and two years later received deacon's orders; but having to a certain extent changed his views he wrote the "Nemesis of Faith," which was regarded as so heretical that he lost his fellowship and a prospective appointment in Tasmania. In 1856 he published the first two volumes of his "History of England from the Fall of Wolsey to the Defeat of the Spanish Armada," which was completed in twelve volumes in 1869, and met with the highest praise for its literary style, and the severest criticism for its historical accuracy, especially for its paradoxical estimate of King Henry VIII as a hero. In 1869 he was appointed rector of St. Andrew's University, and received the degree of LL.D. In 1874, and again in 1875, he was sent on a governmental mission to South Africa and published his impressions in "Two Lectures" (1880); and in "Oceana" (1886). He was Carlyle's literary executor and edited several volumes of letters and reminiscences and finally his "Life" (1882-84). In 1892 he succeeded E. A. Freeman as professor of modern history. He died October 20, 1894, at Salcombe, Devonshire. Among his other works are four volumes of "Short Studies on Great Subjects" (1867-82); "The English in Ireland in the Eighteenth Century" (1871-74); "Cæsar: a Sketch" (1879); "The English in the West Indies" (1888); "The Two Chiefs of Dunboy," an Irish historical romance (1889); "The Divorce of Katherine of Aragon" (1891); "Life and Letters of Erasmus" (1894).

INFLUENCE OF THE REFORMATION ON SCOTTISH CHARACTER

DELIVERED AT EDINBURGH, NOVEMBER, 1865

I HAVE undertaken to speak this evening on the effects of the Reformation in Scotland, and I consider myself a very bold person to have come here on any such undertaking. In the first place, the subject is one with which it is presumptuous for a stranger to meddle. Great national movements can only be understood properly by the people whose disposition they represent. We say ourselves about our own history that only Englishmen can properly comprehend it. The late Chevalier Bunsen once said to me of our

own Reformation in England that for his part he could not
conceive how we had managed to come by such a thing. We
seemed to him to be an obdurate, impenetrable, stupid people,
hide-bound by tradition and precedent, and too self-satisfied
to be either willing or able to take in new ideas upon any
theoretic subject whatever, especially German ideas. That
is to say, he could not get inside the English mind. He did
not know that some people go farthest and go faster when
they look one way and row the other. It is the same with
every considerable nation. They work out their own political and spiritual lives through tempers, humors, and passions
peculiar to themselves; and the same disposition which pro-
duces the result is required to interpret it afterwards. This
is one reason why I should feel diffident about what I have
undertaken. Another is that I do not conceal from myself
that the subject is an exceedingly delicate one. The blazing
passions of those stormy sixteenth and seventeenth centuries
are no longer, happily, at their old temperature. The story
of those times can now be told or listened to with something
like impartiality. Yet, if people no longer hate each other
for such matters, the traditions of the struggle survive in
strong opinions and sentiments, which it is easy to wound
without intending it.

My own conviction with respect to all great social and
religious convulsions is the extremely commonplace one that
much is to be said on both sides. I believe that nowhere and
at no time any such struggles can take place on a large scale
unless each party is contending for something which has a
great deal of truth in it. Where the right is plain, honest,
wise, and noble-minded men are all on one side and only
rogues and fools are on the other. Where the wise and good
are divided the truth is generally found to be divided also.

But this is precisely what cannot be admitted as long as the conflict continues. Men begin to fight about things when reason and argument fail to convince them. They make up in passion what is wanting in logic. Each side believes that all the right is theirs—that their enemies have all the bad qualities which their language contains names for; and even now, on the subject on which I have to talk to-night, one has but to take up any magazine, review, newspaper, or party organ of any kind which touches on it, to see that opinion is still Whig or Tory, Cavalier or Roundhead, Protestant or Catholic, as the case may be. The unfortunate person who is neither wholly one nor wholly the other is in the position of Hamlet's " baser nature," " between the incensed points of mighty opposites." He is the Laodicean, neither cold nor hot, whom decent people consider bad company. He pleases no one and hurts the sensitiveness of all.

Here, then, are good reasons why I should have either not come here at all, or else should have chosen some other matter to talk about. In excuse for persisting I can but say that the subject is one about which I have been led by circumstances to read and think considerably; and though undoubtedly each of us knows more about himself and his own affairs than any one else can possibly know, yet a stranger's eye will sometimes see things which escape those more immediately interested, and I allow myself to hope that I may have something to say not altogether undeserving your attention. I shall touch as little as possible on questions of opinion; and if I tread by accident on any sensitive point I must trust to your kindness to excuse my awkwardness.

Well, then, if we look back on Scotland as it stood in the first quarter of the sixteenth century we see a country in which the old feudal organization continued, so far as it generally affected the people, more vigorous than in any other part of civilized Europe.   Elsewhere the growth of trade and of large towns had created a middle class, with an organization of their own, independent of the lords.   In Scotland the towns were still scanty and poor; such as they were, they were for the most part under the control of the great nobleman who happened to live nearest to them, and a people, as in any sense independent of lords, knights, abbots, or prelates, under whose rule they were born, had as yet no existence.   The tillers of the soil (and the soil was very miserably tilled) lived under the shadow of the castle or the monastery.   They followed their lord's fortunes, fought his battles, believed in his politics, and supported him loyally in his sins or his good deeds, as the case might be.   There was much moral beauty in the life of those times.   The loyal attachment of man to man—of liege servant to liege lord—of all forms under which human beings can live and work together has most of grace and humanity about it.   It cannot go on without mutual confidence and affection—mutual benefits given and received.   The length of time which the system lasted, proves that in the main there must have been a fine fidelity in the people—truth, justice, generosity in their leaders. History brings down many bad stories to us out of those times; just as in these islands nowadays you may find bad instances of the abuses of rights of property.   You may find stories—to many also—of husbands ill-using their wives and so on.   Yet we do not therefore lay the blame on marriage, or suppose that the institution of property, on the whole, does more harm than good.   I do not doubt that down in that feudal system somewhere lie the roots of some of the finest qualities in the European peoples.

So much for the temporal side of the matter; and the spirit-

ual was not very unlike it. As no one lived independently, in
our modern sense of the word, so no one thought independently. The minds of men were looked after by a church,
which, for a long time, also did, I suppose, very largely fulfil
the purpose for which it was intended. It kept alive and
active the belief that the world was created and governed by
a just Being, who hated sins and crimes and steadily punished such things. It taught men that they had immortal
souls and that this little bit of life was an entirely insignificant portion of their real existence. It taught these truths
indeed along with a great deal which we now consider to
have been a mistake—a great many theories of earthly things
which have since passed away, and special opinions clothed in
outward forms and ritual observances which we here, most of
us at least, do not think essential for our soul's safety. But
mistakes like these are hurtful only when persisted in in the
face of fuller truth after truth has been discovered. Only a
very foolish man would now uphold the Ptolemaic astronomy.
But the Ptolemaic astronomy, when first invented, was based
on real if incomplete observations and formed a groundwork
without which further progress in that science would have
been probably impossible. The theories and ceremonials of
the Catholic Church suited well with an age in which little
was known and much was imagined; when superstition was
active and science was not yet born. When I am told here or
anywhere that the Middle Ages were times of mere spiritual
darkness and priestly oppression, with the other usual formulas, I say, as I said before, if the Catholic Church, for those
many centuries that it reigned supreme over all men's con-
sciences was no better than the thing which we see in the
generation which immediately preceded the Reformation it
could not have existed at all. You might as well argue that

the old fading tree could never have been green and young. Institutions do not live on lies. They either live by the truth and usefulness which there is in them or they do not live at all.

So things went on for several hundred years. There were scandals enough, and crimes enough, and feuds, and murders, and civil wars. Systems, however good, cannot prevent evil. They can but compress it within moderate and tolerable limits. I should conclude, however, that, measuring by the average happiness of the masses of the people the mediæval institutions were very well suited for the inhabitants of these countries as they then were. Adam Smith and Bentham themselves could hardly have mended them if they had tried.

But times change and good things as well as bad grow old and have to die. The heart of the matter which the Catholic Church had taught was the fear of God; but the language of it and the formulas of it were made up of human ideas and notions about things which the mere increase of human knowledge gradually made incredible. To trace the reason of this would lead us a long way. It is intelligible enough but it would take us into subjects better avoided here. It is enough to say that, while the essence of religion remains the same, the mode in which it is expressed changes and has changed—changes as living languages change and become dead, as institutions change, as forms of government change, as opinions on all things in heaven and earth change, as half the theories held at this time among ourselves will probably change—that is, the outward and mortal parts of them. Thus the Catholic formulas, instead of living symbols, became dead and powerless cabalistic signs. The religion lost its hold on the conscience and the intellect, and the effect, singularly enough, appeared in the shepherds before it made itself felt among the flocks. From the See of St. Peter to the far monasteries in the Hebrides or the Isle of Arran, the laity were shocked and scandalized at the outrageous doings of high cardinals, prelates, priests, and monks. It was clear enough that these great personages themselves did not believe what they taught; so why should the people believe it? And serious men, to whom the fear of God was a living reality, began to look into the matter for themselves. The first steps everywhere were taken with extreme reluctance; and had the popes and cardinals been wise they would have taken the lead in the inquiry, cleared their teaching of its lumber, and taken out a new lease of life both for it and for themselves. An infallible pope and an infallible council might have done something in this way if good sense had been among the attributes of their omniscience. What they did do was something very different. It was as if, when the new astronomy began to be taught, the professors of that science in all the universities of Europe had met together and decided that Ptolemy's cycles and epicycles were eternal verities; that the theory of the rotation of the earth was and must be a damnable heresy; and had invited the civil authorities to help them in putting down by force all doctrines but their own. This, or something like it, was the position taken up in theology by the Council of Trent. The bishops assembled there did not reason. They decided by vote that certain things were true and were to be believed; and the only arguments which they condescended to use were fire and fagot and so on. How it fared with them and with this experiment of theirs we all know tolerably well.

The effect was very different in different countries. Here in Scotland the failure was most marked and complete, but the way in which it came about was in many ways peculiar. In Germany Luther was supported by princes and nobles. In

England the Reformation rapidly mixed itself up with politics and questions of rival jurisdiction. Both in England and Germany the Revolution, wherever it established itself, was accepted early by the crown or government and by them legally recognized. Here it was far otherwise; the Protestantism of Scotland was the creation of the commons, as in turn the commons may be said to have been created by Protestantism. There were many young, high-spirited men, belonging to the noblest families in the country, who were among the earliest to rally round the reforming preachers; but authority, both in Church and State, set the other way. The congregations who gathered in the fields around Wishart and John Knox were for the most part, farmers, laborers, artisans, tradesmen, or the smaller gentry; and thus, for the first time in Scotland, there was created an organization of men detached from the lords and from the Church—brave, noble, resolute, daring people, bound together by a sacred cause, unrecognized by the leaders whom they had followed hitherto with undoubting allegiance. That spirit which grew in time to be the ruling power of Scotland—that which formed eventually its laws and its creed, and determined its afterfortunes as a nation—had its first germ in these half-outlawed, wandering, congregations. In this it was that the Reformation in Scotland differed from the Reformation in any other part of Europe. Elsewhere is found a middle class existing—created already by trade or by other causes. It raised and elevated them but it did not materially affect their political condition. In Scotland the commons, as an organized body, were simply created by religion. Before the Reformation they had no political existence; and therefore it has been that the print of their origin has gone deeply into their social constitution. On them, and them only, the burden of the work of the Reformation was eventually thrown; and when they triumphed at last, it was inevitable that both they and it should react upon the other.

How this came about I must endeavor to describe, although I can give but a brief sketch of an exceedingly complicated matter. Everybody knows the part played by the aristocracy of Scotland in the outward revolution, when the Reformation first became the law of the land. It would seem at first sight as if it had been the work of the whole nation—as if it had been a thing on which high and low were heartily united. Yet on the first glance below the surface you see that the greater part of the noble lords concerned in that business cared nothing about the Reformation at all; or, if they cared, they rather disliked it than otherwise. How, then, did they come to act as they did? or how came they to permit a change of such magnitude when they had so little sympathy with it? I must make a slight circuit to look for the explanation.

The one essentially noble feature in the great families of Scotland was their patriotism. They loved Scotland and Scotland's freedom with a passion proportioned to the difficulty with which they had defended their liberties; and yet the wisest of them had long seen that, sooner or later, union with England was inevitable; and the question was, how that union was to be brought about—how they were to make sure that, when it came, they should take their place at England's side as equals and not as a dependency. It had been arranged that the little Mary Stuart should marry our English Edward VI, and the difficulty was to be settled so. They would have been contented, they said, if Scotland had had the "lad" and England the "lass." As it stood they broke their bargain and married the little queen away into France to prevent the

M Protector, Somerset, from getting hold of her. Then however appeared an opposite danger; the queen would become a Frenchwoman; her French mother governed Scotland with French troops and French ministers; the country would become a French province and lose its freedom equally. Thus an English party began again; and as England was then in the middle of her great anti-Church revolution, so the Scottish nobles began to be anti-Church. It was not for doctrines. Neither they nor their brothers in England cared much about doctrines; but in both countries the Church was rich—much richer than there seemed any occasion for it to be. Henry VIII had been sharing among the laity the spoils of the English monastries—the Scotch lords saw in a similar process the probability of a welcome addition to their scanty incomes. Mary of Guise and the French stood by the Church, and the Church stood by them; and so it came about that the great families—even those who, like the Hamiltons, were more closely connected with France—were tempted over by the bait to the other side. They did not want reformed doctrines but they wanted the Church lands; and so they came to patronize, or endure, the Reformers because the Church hated them and because they weakened the Church; and thus for a time, and especially as long as Mary Stuart was Queen of France, all classes in Scotland, high and low, seemed to fraternize in favor of the revolution.

And it seemed as if the union of the realms could be effected at last, at the same juncture, and in connection with the same movement. Next in succession to the Scotch crown, after Mary Stuart, was the house of Hamilton. Elizabeth, who had just come to the English throne was supposed to be in want of a husband. The heir of the Hamiltons was of her own age and in years past had been thought of for her by her father. What could be more fit than to make a match between those two? Send a Scot south to be King of England, find or make some pretext to shake off Mary Stuart, who had forsaken her native country, and so join the crowns, the "lass" and the "lad" being now in the right relative position. Scotland would thus annex her old oppressor and give her a new dynasty.

I seem to be straying from the point; but these political schemes had so much to do with the actions of the leading men at that time that the story of the Reformation cannot be understood without them. It was thus, and with these incongruous objects, that the combination was formed which overturned the old Church of Scotland in 1559-60, confiscated its possessions, destroyed its religious houses, and changed its creed. The French were driven away from Leith by Elizabeth's troops; the Reformers took possession of the churches; and the Parliament of 1560 met with a clear stage to determine for themselves the future fate of the country. Now I think it certain that if the Scotch nobility, having once accepted the Reformation, had continued loyal to it—especially if Elizabeth had met their wishes in the important point of the marriage,—the form of the Scotch Kirk would have been something extremely different from what it in fact became. The people were perfectly well inclined to follow their natural leaders if the matters on which their hearts were set had received tolerable consideration from them, and the democratic form of the ecclesiastical constitution would have been inevitably modified. One of the conditions of the proposed compact with England was the introduction of the English Liturgy and the English Church constitution. This too, at the outset, and with fair dealing, would not have been found impossible. But it soon became clear that the religious interests of Scotland were the very last thing which would receive consideration from any of the high political personages concerned. John Knox had dreamt of a constitution like that which he had seen working under Calvin at Geneva—a constitution in which the clergy as ministers of God should rule all things; rule politically at the council board, and rule in private at the fireside. It was soon made plain to Knox that Scotland was not Geneva. " Eh, mon," said the younger Maitland to him, " then we may all bear the barrow now to build the House of the Lord." Not exactly. The churches were left to the ministers; the worldly good things and worldly power remained with the laity; and as to religion, circumstances would decide what they would do about that. Again, I am not speaking of all the great men of those times. Glencairn, Ruthven, young Argyll—above all the Earl of Moray—really did in some degree interest themselves in the Kirk. But what most of them felt was perhaps rather broadly expressed by Maitland when he called religion " a bogle of the nursery." That was the expression which a Scotch statesman of those days actually ventured to use. Had Elizabeth been conformable, no doubt they would in some sense or other have remained on the side of the Reformation. But here too there was a serious hitch. Elizabeth would not marry Arran. Elizabeth would be no party to their intrigues. She detested Knox. She detested Protestantism entirely in all shapes in which Knox approved of it. She affronted the nobles on one side, she affronted the people on another; and all idea of uniting the two crowns after the fashion proposed by the Scottish Parliament she utterly and entirely repudiated. She was right enough perhaps so far as this was concerned; but she left the ruling families extremely perplexed as to the course which they would follow. They had allowed the country to be revolutionized in the teeth of their own sovereign, and what to do next they did not very well know.

It was at this crisis that circumstances came in to their help. Francis II died. Mary Stuart was left a childless widow. Her connection with the crown of France was at an end and all danger on that side to the liberties of Scotland at an end also. The Arran scheme having failed, she would be a second card as good as the first to play for the English crown; as good as he, or better, for she would have the English Catholics on her side. So, careless how it would affect religion, and making no conditions at all about that, the same men who a year before were ready to whistle Mary Stuart down the wind, now invited her back to Scotland; the same men who had been the loudest friends of Elizabeth now encouraged Mary Stuart to persist in the pretension to the crown of England, which had led to all the past trouble. While in France she had assumed the title of Queen of England. She had promised to abandon it, but, finding her own people ready to support her in withdrawing her promise, she stood out, insisting that at all events the English Parliament should declare her next in the succession; and it was well known that as soon as the succession was made sure in her favor some rascal would be found to put a knife or a bullet into Elizabeth. The object of the Scotch nobles was political, national, patriotic. For religion it was no great matter either way; and as they had before acted with the Protestants so now they were ready to turn about and openly or tacitly act with the Catholics. Mary Stuart's friends in England and on the Continent were Catholics and therefore it would not do to offend them. First, she was allowed to have mass at Holyrood; then there was a move for a broader toleration. That one mass, Knox said, was more terrible to him than ten thousand armed men landed in the country, and he had perfectly good reason for saying so. He thoroughly understood that it was the first step toward a counter-revolution which in time would cover all Scotland and England and carry them back to Popery. Yet he preached to deaf ears. Even Murray was so bewitched with the notion of the English succession that for a year and a half he ceased to speak to Knox; and as it was with Murray so it was far more with all the rest, their zeal for religion was gone no one knew where. Of course Elizabeth would not give way. She might as well, she said, herself prepare her shroud; and then conspiracies came and underground intrigues with the Romanist English noblemen. France and Spain were to invade England; Scotland was to open its ports to their fleets, and its soil to their armies, giving them a safe base from which to act and a dry road over the marches to London. And if Scotland had remained unchanged from what it had been,—had the direction of its fortunes remained with the prince and with the nobles, sooner or later it would have come to this. But suddenly it appeared that there was a new power in this country which no one suspected till it was felt.

The commons of Scotland had hitherto been the creatures of the nobles. They had neither will nor opinion of their own. They thought and acted in the spirit of their immediate allegiance. No one seemed to have dreamt that there would be any difficulty in dealing with them if once the great families agreed upon a common course. Yet it appeared, when the pressure came, that religion, which was the plaything of the nobles, was to the people a clear matter of life and death. They might love their country; they

might be proud of anything which would add lustre to its
crown; but if it was to bring back the Pope and Popery,
—if it threatened to bring them back,—if it looked that way
they would have nothing to do with it; nor would they allow
it to be done. Allegiance was well enough; but there was a
higher allegiance suddenly discovered which superseded all
earthly considerations. I know nothing finer in Scottisn
history than the way in which the commons of the Lowlands
took their places by the side of Knox in the great convulsions which followed. If all others forsook him they at
least would never forsake him while tongue remained to
speak and hand remained to strike. Broken they might have
been, trampled out as the Hugenots at last were trampled
out in France, had Mary Stuart been less than the most im-
prudent or the most unlucky of sovereigns. But providence,
or the folly of those with whom they had to deal, fought
for them. I need not follow the wild story of the crimes and
catastrophies in which Mary Stuart's short reign in Scotland
closed. Neither is her own share, be it great or small, or
none at all, in those crimes, of any moment to us here. It
is enough that both before that strange business and after
it, when at Holyrood or across the border, in Sheffield or
Tutbury, her ever-favorite dream was still the English
throne. Her road toward it was through a Catholic revolution and the murder of Elizabeth. It is enough that, both
before and after, the aristocracy of Scotland, even those
among them who had seemed most zealous for the Reformation, were eager to support her. John Knox alone, and the
commons, whom Knox had raised into a political power, remained true.

Much indeed is to be said for the Scotch nobles. In the
first shock of the business at Kirk-o'-Field they forgot their

politics in a sense of national disgrace. They sent the queen to Loch Leven. They intended to bring her to trial, and if she was proved guilty, to expose and perhaps punish her. All parties for a time agreed in this, even the Hamiltons themselves; and had they been left alone they would have done it. But they had a perverse neighbor in England, to whom crowned heads were sacred. Elizabeth, it might have been thought, would have had no particular objection; but Elizabeth had aims of her own which baffled calculation. Elizabeth, the representative of revolution, yet detested revolutionists. The Reformers in Scotland, the Huguenots in France, the insurgents in the United Provinces, were the only friends she had in Europe. For her own safety she was obliged to encourage them; yet she hated them all and would at any moment have abandoned them all if in any other way she could have secured herself. She might have conquered her personal objection to Knox; she could not conquer her aversion to a Church which rose out of revolt against authority, which was democratic in constitution and republican in politics. When driven into alliance with the Scotch Protestants she angrily and passionately disclaimed any community of creed with them; and for subjects to sit in judgment on their prince was a precedent which she would not tolerate. Thus she flung her mantle over Mary Stuart. She told the Scotch Council here in Edinburgh that if they hurt a hair of her head she would harry their country and hang them all on trees round the town, if she could find any trees there for that purpose. She tempted the queen to England with her fair promises after the battle of Langside and then to her astonishment imprisoned her. Yet she still shielded her reputation, still fostered her party in Scotland, still incessantly threatened and incessantly endeavored to restore her. She kept her safe because in her lucid intervals her ministers showed her the madness of acting otherwise. Yet for three years she kept her own people in a fever of apprehension. She made a settled government in Scotland impossible; till, distracted and perplexed, the Scottish statesmen went back to their first schemes. They assured themselves that in one way or other the Queen of Scots would sooner or later come again among them. They, and others besides them, believed that Elizabeth was cutting her own throat, and that the best that they could do was to recover their own queen's favor and make the most of her and her titles; and so they lent themselves again to the English Catholic conspiracies.

The Earl of Moray—the one supremely noble man then living in the country—was put out of the way by an assassin. French and Spanish money poured in and French and Spanish armies were to be again invited over to Scotland. This is the form in which the drama unfolds itself in the correspondence of the time. Maitland, the soul and spirit of it all, said in scorn that "he would make the queen of England sit upon her tail and whine like a whipped dog." The only powerful noblemen who remained on the Protestant side were Lennox, Morton, and Mar. Lord Lennox was a poor creature and was soon dispatched; Mar was old and weak; and Morton was an unprincipled scoundrel who used the Reformation only as a stalking horse to cover the spoils which he had clutched in the confusion and was ready to desert the cause at any moment if the balance of advantage shifted. Even the ministers of the Kirk were fooled and flattered over. Maitland told Mary Stuart that he had gained them all except one.

John Knox alone defied both his threats and his persuasions. Good reason has Scotland to be proud of Knox. He only, in this wild crisis, saved the Kirk which he had founded, and saved with it Scottish and English freedom. But for Knox and what he was able still to do it is almost certain that the Duke of Alva's army would have been landed on the eastern coast. The conditions were drawn out and agreed upon for the reception, the support, and the stay of the Spanish troops. Two thirds of the English peerage had bound themselves to rise against Elizabeth and Alva waited only till Scotland itself was quiet. Only that quiet would not be. Instead of quiet came three dreadful years of civil war. Scotland was split into factions to which the mother and son gave names. The queen's lords, as they were called, with unlimited money from France and Flanders held Edinburgh and Glasgow, all the border line was theirs, and all the north and west. Elizabeth's council, wiser than their mistress, barely squeezed out of her reluctant parsimony enough to keep Mar and Morton from making terms with the rest; but there her assistance ended. She would still say nothing, promise nothing, bind herself to nothing, and so far as she was concerned the war would have been soon enough brought to a close. But away at St. Andrews, John Knox, broken in body and scarcely able to stagger up the pulpit stairs still thundered in the parish church; and his voice, it was said, was like ten thousand trumpets braying in the ear of Scottish Protestantism. All the Lowlands answered to his call. Our English Cromwell found in the man of religion a match for the man of honor. Before Cromwell, all over the Lothians, and across from St. Andrews to Stirling and Glasgow,—through farm, and town, and village,—the words of Knox had struck the inmost chords of the Scottish commons' hearts. Passing over knight and noble he had touched the farmer, the peasant, the petty tradesman, and the artisan, and turned the men of clay into men of steel. The village preacher when he left his pulpit doffed cap and cassock and donned morion and steel-coat. The Lothian yeoman's household became for the nonce a band of troopers who would cross swords with the night riders of Buccleuch. It was a terrible time, a time rather of anarchy than of defined war, for it was without form or shape. Yet the horror of it was everywhere. Houses and villages were burned and women and children tossed on pike-points into the flames. Strings of poor men were dangled day after day from the walls of Edinburgh Castle. A word any way from Elizabeth would have ended it, but that word Elizabeth would never speak; and maddened with suffering the people half believed that she was feeding the fire for her own bad purposes, when it was only that she would not make up her mind to allow a crowned princess to be dethroned. No earthly influence could have held men true in such a trial. The noble lords—the Earl of Morton and such like—would have made their own conditions and gone with the rest; but the vital force of the Scotch nation, showing itself where it was least looked for would not have it so.

A very remarkable account of the state of the Scotch commons at this time is to be found in a letter of an English emissary who had been sent by Lord Burleigh to see how things were going there. It was not merely a new creed that they had got; it was a new vital power. "You would be astonished to see how men are changed here," this writer said. "There is little of that submission to those above them which there used to be. The poor think and act for themselves. They are growing strong, confident, independent. The farms are better cultivated; the farmers are growing rich. The merchants at Leith are thriving, and notwithstanding the pirates they are increasing their ships and opening a brisk trade with France."

All this while civil war was raging and the flag of Queen Mary was still floating over Edinburgh Castle. It surprised the English; still more it surprised the politicians. It was the one thing which disconcerted, baffled, and finally ruined the schemes and the dreams of Maitland. When he had gained the aristocracy he thought that he had gained everybody, and as it turned out he had all his work still to do. The Spaniards did not come. The prudent Alva would not risk invasion till Scotland at least was assured. As time passed on the English conspiracies were discovered and broken up. The Duke of Norfolk lost his head; the Queen of Scots was found to have been mixed up with the plots to murder Elizabeth; and Elizabeth at last took courage and recognized James. Supplies of money ceased to come from abroad and gradually the tide turned. The Protestant cause once more grew toward the ascendant. The great families one by one came round again; and as the backward movement began the massacre of St. Bartholomew gave it a fresh and tremendous impulse. Even the avowed Catholics—the Hamiltons, the Gordons, the Scotts, the Kers, the Maxwells—quailed before the wail of rage and sorrow which at that great horror rose over their country. The Queen's party dwindled away to a handful of desperate politicians who still clung to Edinburgh Castle. But Elizabeth's " peacemakers," as the big English cannon was called, came round at the Regent's request from Berwick; David's Tower, as Knox had long ago foretold, " ran down over the cliff like a sandy brae;" and the cause of Mary Stuart in Scotland was extinguished forever. Poor Grange, who deserved a better end, was hanged at the Market Cross. Secretary Maitland, the cause of all the mischief,—the cleverest man as far as intellect went in all Britain,—died (so later rumor said) by his own hand. A nobler version of his end is probably a truer one: He had been long ill,—so ill that when the castle cannon were fired he had been carried into the cellars as unable to bear the sound. The breaking down of his hopes finished him. " The secretary," wrote some one from the spot to Cecil, " is dead of grief, being unable to endure the great hatred which all this people bears toward him." It would be well if some competent man would write a life of Maitland, or at least edit his papers. They contain by far the clearest account of the inward movements of the time; and he himself is one of the most tragically interesting characters in the cycle of Reformation history.

With the fall of the castle then, but not till then, it became clear to all men that the Reformation would hold its ground. It was the final trampling out of the fire which for five years threatened both England and Scotland with flames and ruin. For five years, as late certainly as the massacre of St. Bartholomew, those who understood best the true state of things felt the keenest misgivings how the event would turn. That things ended as they did was due to the spirit of the Scotch commons. There was a moment when, if they had given way, all would have gone, perhaps even to Elizabeth's throne. They had passed for nothing; they had proved to be everything; had proved—the ultimate test in human things—to be the power which could hit the hardest blows, and they took rank accordingly. The creed began now in good earnest to make its way into hall and castle; but it kept the form which it assumed in the first hours of its danger and trial and never after lost it. Had the aristocracy dealt sincerely with things in the earlier stages of the business again, I say the democratic element in the Kirk might have been softened or modified. But the Protestants had been trifled with by their own natural leaders. Used and abused by Elizabeth, despised by the worldly intelligence and power of the times, they triumphed after all, and as a natural consequence they set their own mark and stamp upon the fruits of the victory.

The question now is, what has the Kirk so established done for Scotland? Has it justified its own existence? Briefly, we might say, it has continued its first function as the guardian of Scottish freedom. But that is a vague phrase, and there are special accusations against the Kirk and its doctrines which imply that it has cared for other things than freedom. Narrow, fanatical, dictatorial, intrusive, superstitious, a spiritual despotism, the old priesthood over again with a new face—these and other such epithets and expressions we have heard often enough applied to it at more than one stage of its history. Well, I suppose that neither the Kirk nor anything else of man's making is altogether perfect. But let us look at the work which lay before it when it had got over its first perils. Scotch patriotism succeeded at last in the object it had so passionately set its heart upon. It sent a king at last of the Scotch blood to England, and a new dynasty; and it never knew peace or quiet after. The Kirk had stood between James Stuart and his kingcraft. He hated it as heartily as did his mother; and when he got to England he found people there who told him it would be easy to destroy it, and he found the strength of a fresh empire to back him in trying to do it. To have forced prelacy upon Scotland would have been to destroy the life out of Scotland. Thrust upon them by force, it would have been no more endurable than Popery. They would as soon, perhaps sooner, have had what the Irish call the "rale thing" back again. The political freedom of the country was now wrapped up in the Kirk; and the Stuarts were perfectly well aware of that, and for that very reason began their crusade against it.

And now, suppose the Kirk had been the broad, liberal, philosophical, intellectual thing which some people think it ought to have been, how would it have fared in that crusade; how altogether would it have encountered those surplices of Archbishop Laud or those dragoons of Claverhouse? It is hard to lose one's life for a "perhaps;" and philosophical belief at the bottom means a "perhaps" and nothing more. For more than half the seventeenth century the battle had to be fought out in Scotland, which in reality was the battle between liberty and despotism; and where, except in an intense, burning conviction that they were maintaining God's cause against the devil, could the poor Scotch people have found the strength for the unequal struggle which was forced upon them? Toleration is a good thing in its place, but you cannot tolerate what will not tolerate you and is trying to cut your throat. Enlightenment you cannot have enough of; but it must be true enlightenment, which sees a thing in all its bearings. In these matters the vital questions are not always those which appear on the surface; and in the passion and resolution of brave and noble men there is often an inarticulate intelligence deeper than what can be expressed in words. Actions will sometimes hit the mark when the spoken word either misses it or is but half the truth. On such subjects, and with common men, latitude of mind means weakness of mind. There is but a certain quantity of spiritual force in any man. Spread it over a broad surface, the stream is shallow and languid; narrow the channel and it becomes a driving force. Each may be well at its own time.   The mill-race which drives the water-wheel is dispersed in rivulets over the meadow at its foot. The Covenanters fought the fight and won the victory, and then, and not till then, came the David Humes with their essays on miracles, and the Adam Smiths with their political economies, and steam-engines, and railroads, and philosophical institutions, and all the other blessed or unblessed fruits of liberty.

But we may go further.   Institutions exist for men, not men for institutions; and the ultimate test of any system of politics, or body of opinions, or form of belief, is the effect produced on the conduct and condition of the people who live and die under them.   Now, I am not here to speak of Scotland of the present day.   That happily is no business of mine.   We have to do here with Scotland before the march of intellect; with Scotland of the last two centuries; with the three or four hundred thousand families who for half a score of generations believed simply and firmly in the principles of the Reformation and walked in the ways of it.

Looked at broadly, one would say they had been an eminently pious people.   It is part of the complaint of modern philosophers about them, that religion, or superstition, or whatever they please to call it, had too much to do with their daily lives.   So far as one can look into that commonplace round of things, which historians never tell us about, there have rarely been seen in this world a set of people who have thought more about right and wrong and the judgment of the upper powers.   Longheaded, thrifty industry—a sound hatred of waste, imprudence, idleness, extravagance—the feet planted firmly upon the earth, a conscientious sense that the worldly virtues are nevertheless very necessary virtues, that without these honesty for one thing is not possible, and that without honesty no other excellence, religious or moral, is worth anything at all,—this is the stuff of which Scotch life was made, and very good stuff it is. It has been called gloomy, austere, harsh, and such other epithets. A gifted modern writer has favored us lately with long strings of extracts from the sermons of Scotch divines of the last century, taking hard views of human short-comings and their probable consequences and passing hard censures upon the world and its amusements. Well, no doubt amusement is a very good thing; but I should rather infer from the vehemence and frequency of these denunciations that the people had not been in the habit of denying themselves too immoderately; and after all it is no very hard charge against those teachers that they thought more of duty than of pleasure. Sermons always exaggerate the theoretic side of things; and the most austere preacher, when he is out of the pulpit, and you meet him at the dinner-table, becomes singularly like other people. We may take courage, I think: we may believe safely that in those minister-ridden days men were not altogether so miserable; we may hope that no large body of human beings have for any length of time been too dangerously afraid of enjoyment. Among other good qualities the Scots have been distinguished for humor—not for venomous wit but for kindly, genial humor, which half loves what it laughs at—and this alone shows clearly enough that those to whom it belongs have not looked too exclusively on the gloomy side of the world. I should rather say that the Scots have been an unusually happy people. Intelligent industry, the honest doing of daily work, with a sense that it must be done well, under penalties; the necessaries of life moderately provided for, and a sensible content with the situation of life in which men are born—this through the week, and at the end of it the "Cotter's Saturday Night"—the homely family gathered reverently and peacefully together and irradiated with a sacred presence. Happiness! such happiness as we creatures are likely to know upon this world will be found there if anywhere.

The author of the "History of Civilization" makes a naïve remark in connection with this subject. Speaking of the other country, which he censures equally with Scotland for its slavery to superstition, he says of the Spaniards that they are a well-natured, truthful, industrious, temperate, pious people, innocent in their habits, affectionate in their families, full of humor, vivacity, and shrewdness, yet that all this "has availed them nothing"—"has availed them nothing," that is his expression—because they are loyal, because they are credulous, because they are contented, because they have not apprehended the first commandment of the new covenant: "Thou shalt get on and make money and better thy condition in life;" because therefore they have added nothing to the scientific knowledge, the wealth, and the progress of mankind. Without these it seems the old-fashioned virtues avail nothing. They avail a great deal to human happiness. Applied science, and steam, and railroads, and machinery, enable an ever-increasing number of people to live upon the earth, but the happiness of those people remains, so far as I know, dependent very much on the old conditions. I should be glad to believe that the new view of things will produce effects upon the character in the long run half so beautiful.

There is much more to say on this subject were there time to say it, but I will not trespass so far upon your patience; and I would gladly have ended here had not the mention of Spain suggested one other topic which I should not leave unnoticed. The Spain of Cervantes and Don Quixote was the Spain of the inquisition. The Scotland of Knox and Melville was the Scotland of the witch trials and the witch burnings. The belief in witches was common to all the world. The prosecution and punishment of the poor creatures was more conspicuous in Scotland when the Kirk was most powerful; in England and New England when Puritan principles were also dominant there. It is easy to understand the reasons. Evil of all kinds was supposed to be the work of a personal devil; and in the general horror of evil this particular form of it, in which the devil was thought especially active, excited the most passionate detestation. Thus, even the best men lent themselves unconsciously to the most detestable cruelty. Knox himself is not free from reproach. A poor woman was burned when he was living there and when a word from him would have saved her. It remains a lesson to all time, that goodness, though the indispensable adjunct to knowledge, is no substitute for it; and when conscience undertakes to dictate beyond its province the result is only the more monstrous.

It is well that we should look this matter in the face; and as particular stories leave more impression than general statements, I will mention one, perfectly well authenticated, which I take from the official report of the proceedings: Toward the end of 1593 there was trouble in the family of the Earl of Orkney. His brother laid a plot to murder him and was said to have sought the help of a " notorious witch " called Alison Balfour. When Alison Balfour's life was looked into no evidence could be found connecting her either with the particular offence or with witchcraft in general; but it was enough in these matters to be accused. She swore she was innocent; but her guilt was only held to be aggravated by perjury. She was tortured again and again. Her legs were put in the caschilaws,—an iron frame which was gradually heated till it burned into the flesh,—but no confession could be wrung from her. The caschilaws failed utterly and something else had to be tried. She had a husband, a son, and a daughter, a child seven years old. As her own sufferings did not work upon her she might be touched perhaps by the sufferings of those who were dear to her. They were brought into court and placed at her side; and the husband first was placed in the " lang irons " —some accursed instrument; I know not what. Still the devil did not yield. She bore this; and her son was next operated on. The boy's legs were set in " the boot,"—the iron boot you may have heard of. The wedges were driven in, which, when forced home, crushed the very bone and marrow. Fifty-seven mallet strokes were delivered upon the wedges. Yet this too failed. There was no confession yet. So last of all the little daughter was taken. There was a machine called the piniwinkies—a kind of thumb-screw which brought blood from under the finger-nails, with a pain successfully terrible. These things were applied to the poor child's hands and the mother's constancy broke down and she said she would admit anything they wished. She confessed her witchcraft,—so tried, she would have confessed to the seven deadly sins,—and then she was burned, recalling her confession and with her last breath protesting her innocence.

It is due to the intelligence of the time to admit that after this her guilt was doubted, and such vicarious means of extorting confession do not seem to have been tried again.

Yet the men who inflicted these tortures would have borne them all themselves sooner than have done any act which they consciously knew to be wrong. They did not know that the instincts of humanity were more sacred than the logic of theology, and in fighting against the devil they were themselves doing the devil's work. We should not attempt to apologize for these things, still less to forget them. No martyrs ever suffered to instill into mankind a more wholesome lesson—more wholesome or one more hard to learn. The more conscientious men are the more difficult it is for them to understand that in their most cherished convictions when they pass beyond the limits where the wise and good of all sorts agree they may be the victims of mere delusion. Yet after all and happily, such cases were but few and affected but lightly the general condition of the people.

The student running over the records of other times finds certain salient things standing out in frightful prominence. He concludes that the substance of those times was made up of the matters most dwelt on by the annalist. He forgets that the things most noticed are not those of everyday experiences but the abnormal, the extraordinary, the monstrous. The exceptions are noted down, the common and usual are passed over in silence. The philosophic historian studying hereafter this present age, in which we are ourselves living, may say that it was a time of unexampled prosperity, luxury, and wealth; but, catching at certain horrible murders which have lately disgraced our civilization, may call us a nation of assassins. It is to invert the pyramid and stand it on its point. The same system of belief which produced the tragedy which I have described, in its proper province as the guide of ordinary life, has been the immediate cause of all that is best and greatest in Scottish character.

TILLEY

SIR SAMUEL LEONARD TILLEY, a Canadian statesman, was born at Gagetown, New Brunswick, May 8, 1818. He attended for a few years the grammar school in his native town, but at the age of twelve was apprenticed to an apothecary, and subsequently set up in business for himself. At seventeen he joined a debating society and was early a warm advocate of temperance, remaining a total abstainer all his life. In 1850 he entered the New Brunswick legislature as member for St. John, and for the remainder of his career was almost never out of public life. From 1857 to 1865 he was premier of the province of New Brunswick, and after the union of the British provinces in the Dominion of Canada he was made the first minister of customs in the Dominion cabinet. He subsequently held the posts of minister of public works and minister of finance, and was lieutenant-governor of New Brunswick, 1873-78. During the administration of Sir John Macdonald he was again minister of finance, 1878-85, and in 1879 received the honor of knighthood from the Marquis of Lorne. On account of ill health he retired from the cabinet in the summer of 1885, but in the following November was persuaded to accept the post of lieutenant-governor of New Brunswick for the second time, holding office until 1893. His death took place at St. John, New Brunswick, June 25, 1896. Sir Leonard Tilley during his long public career instituted many public measures of importance, the chief of which was the act relating to the readjustment and reorganization of the customs tariff. See Rose's "Canadian Biography."

ON NATIONAL POLICY

DELIVERED MARCH 14, 1879

MR. CHAIRMAN,—It is only recently that I have quite realized the great changes that have taken place throughout the Dominion of Canada since I last had the honor of a seat in Parliament. To-day I fully realize them, and the increased difficulties devolving upon me as finance minister, compared with the position of affairs when I submitted my financial statement in 1873. Then my work was a very easy one indeed. Honorable ministers on the opposite benches were pleased on that occasion to compliment me on that statement, but I felt that I had earned no compliment, that if that speech was acceptable to the House it was because of the satisfactory statements I was able to make with reference to the condition of the Dominion and also of the finances of the Dominion.

Then, sir, I was able to point to steady and increasing surpluses and revenue, and that too in the face of a steady reduction of taxation. Then I was able to point with some degree of confidence to the prospective expenditures of the Dominion, extending oven ten years. To-day I cannot speak of it with the same confidence. Then the construction of the Pacific railway was under regulations that confined and limited the liabilities of the Dominion to $30,000,000. To-day I am not in a position to say what expenditure or responsibilities we may incur with reference to that great undertaking. There has been a change in the policy.

But it will become the duty of the government and of Parliament to consider, while we have not the limit to our liabilities that we had, whether we cannot by some means construct that great work largely out of the 200,000,000 acres of land lying within the wheat area of that magnificent country.

Then, sir, I could point with pride and with satisfaction to the increased capital of our banks and the large dividend they paid. To-day I regret to say that we must point to depreciated values and to small dividends. Then I could point to the general prosperity of the country. To-day we must all admit that it is greatly depressed. Then I could point with satisfaction to the various manufacturing industries that were in operation throughout the length and breadth of the Dominion remunerative to the men who had invested their capital in them and giving employment to tens of thousands.

To-day many of the furnaces are cold, the machinery in many cases is idle, and those establishments that are in operation are only employed half time and are scarcely paying the interest on the money invested.

Then, sir, we could point to the agricultural interest as most prosperous, with a satisfactory home market and satisfactory prices abroad. To-day they have a limited market with low prices and anything but a satisfactory market abroad. Then, sir, we could point to a very valuable and extensive West India trade; to-day it does not exist. Then, sir, we could point to a profitable and direct tea trade that has been demoralized and destroyed. Then everything appeared to be prosperous; to-day, though it looks gloomy, I hope there is a silver lining to the cloud, that we may yet see illuminating the whole of the Dominion and changing our present position to one of happiness and prosperity.

Mr. Chairman, there has been, and very naturally so, a good deal of interest and anxiety manifested on the part of the friends of the National Policy, as it is called, in regard to its early introduction. I can quite understand that, because, believing as they do, and as a majority of this House do, that that policy is calculated to bring prosperity to the country, it was but natural that they should be anxious for its introduction and that not a day should be lost.

And it is satisfactory to know that, great and difficult as is the responsibility which rests upon me here, I may trust that the proposition I am about to submit will be sustained, not only by a majority of this House but by an overwhelming majority in the country.

It was natural therefore, Mr. Chairman, that the friends of this policy should be anxious for its introduction, and it was pleasing and satisfactory to see that even the opposition

vied with the friends of the government in that anxiety. It
is most encouraging to me, because of course all oppositions
are patriotic, and certainly a patriotic opposition anxious for
the introduction of this measure could not have desired that
a bad measure and one not calculated to benefit the country
should be forced hastily upon it. Therefore, I take it for
granted that in addition to the support from the gentlemen
behind me we shall have the support of the gentlemen opposite to our policy and the propositions we are about to submit.

But perhaps it will not be out of place for me to offer
a few remarks in justification of the apparent delay that has
taken place. It will be remembered that the government
was only formed on October 19th. Some delay took place
in awaiting the arrival in Canada of an honorable member
who, I am satisfied, is one whom, whatever the political opinions of gentlemen of this House may be, all would have been
anxious to see consulted before the government was formed—
I mean the minister of militia. The government therefore
was not completed till October 19th. The members of the
government had to return for re-election, and those elections,
though they were hastened with all possible rapidity, because
we felt there was a great deal of work to be done, were not
over until the early part of November when we returned to
the city of Ottawa.

And what did we find? As minister of finance, I cannot
say I found the finances in the most satisfactory condition
I found, sir, that we had maturing in London between the
early part of November and January 1st, an indebtedness of
$15,500,000, with nothing to meet it but the prospective pay-
ment of the fishery award. On this side of the Atlantic we
had in the various banks of the Dominion something like

$5,000,000, and between that date and January 1st, with the subsidy of the provinces, and payments to contractors who were constructing public works, something like $3,000,000 had to be paid; and then, considering the position the banks were in all over the Dominion, the uncertainty as to what might transpire, it was just possible that a reduction in the reserves might take place, and that meant a demand on the Dominion treasury. Every dollar we found it necessary to take from the banks at the time was embarrassing and was reluctantly withdrawn. But it was inevitable that the finance minister should proceed to London with the least possible delay that arrangements might be made to sustain the credit and the honor of the Dominion. Well, sir, in order to avoid that, feeling the importance of every member of the government being at his post in order to prepare measures for the meeting of Parliament, a cable message was sent to our agents on the other side to ask if the journey of the finance minister to London could not be avoided. The answer was " No ; his presence here is absolutely necessary." Under these circumstances I proceeded to London, and I placed a loan of £3,000,000 sterling upon the market there.

Then, sir, after my return to Canada it became necessary that we should consider the whole question of the tariff. It is not a question that can be settled in a day. It is not a question that can be settled intelligently in weeks, indeed it would have been well if we could have had more time to consider it than we have had, considering the magnitude and importance of the work. I can appeal to other finance ministers, and especially to my immediate predecessor, who in 1874 made several changes in the tariff of that day, to speak of the difficulties there are in making even as few changes as were then made.

But if we undertake, as the present government have undertaken, to readjust and reorganize, and, I may say, make an entirely new tariff having for its object not only the realization of $2,000,000 more revenue than will be collected this year, but in addition to providing for that deficiency, to adjust the tariff with a view of giving effect to what has been and is to-day declared to be the policy of the majority of this House—I mean the protection of the industries of the country—the magnitude of the undertaking will be the better appreciated.

Sir, we have invited gentlemen from all parts of the Dominion and representing all interests in the Dominion to assist us in the re-adjustment of the tariff, because we did not feel—though perhaps we possess an average intelligence in ordinary government matters—we did not feel that we knew everything. We did not feel that we were prepared, without advice and assistance from men of experience with reference to these matters, to readjust and make a judicious tariff.

We therefore invited those who were interested in the general interests of the country or interested in any special interests. Gentlemen who took an opposite view met us and discussed these questions, and I may say that down to as late a period as yesterday, though the propositions are submitted to-day, we were favored with the co-operation and opinion of gentlemen who represent their particular or general views with reference to the great questions we have under consideration.

We have labored zealously and arduously, and I trust it will be found successfully; and we are now about to submit our views for the consideration of this House. I think we may appeal with some degree of confidence to gentlemen in opposition, in approval of the early period at which this tariff is being introduced, when I call to the mind of these honorable gentlemen that their government was formed on November 7, 1873; ours on October 19th; that my predecessor did not submit his tariff and budget speech until April 14th, this being March 14th.

When we submit to this House the result of our deliberations you will all understand the nature and extent of the consideration that must necessarily have been given to them. I trust that this House and the country will feel that we have presented our views at as early a period as possible, taking all these facts into consideration.

Let me refer to some circumstances that led to the present depression in the revenue. During and after the war in the United States it is well understood that that country lost a large portion of its export trade, and its manufacturing industries were to a certain extent paralyzed; and it was only about 1872 or 1873 that they really commenced to restore their manufacturing industries and endeavored to find an extended market elsewhere for the manufactures of their country.

Lying as we do alongside that great country we were looked upon as a desirable market for their surplus products, and our American neighbors, always competent to judge of their own interests and act wisely in regard to them, put forth every effort to obtain access to our market. It is well known by the term slaughter-market what they have been doing for the last four or five years in Canada; that in order to find an outlet for their surplus manufactures they have been willing to send them into this country at any price that would be a little below that of the Canadian manufacturer.

It is well known also that they had their agents in every part of the Dominion seeking purchasers for their surplus, and that those agents have been enabled under our existing laws to enter those goods at a price much lower than they ought to have paid, which was their value in the place of purchase. It is well known moreover that the United States government, in order to encourage special interests in that country, granted a bounty upon certain manufactures and so gave to them the exclusive market of the Dominion, and under those circumstances we have lost a very important trade, possessed previous to 1873. In addition to the loss of the West India trade by the repeal of the ten per cent on tea we lost the direct tea trade and all the advantages resulting from it, by its transfer from the Dominion to New York and Boston.

Under all those circumstances and with the high duty imposed by the United States on the agricultural products of the Dominion, by which we are to a great extent excluded from them while the manufactures of that country are forced into our market, we could not expect prosperity or success in the Dominion so long as that state of things continued. These are some of the difficulties which have led to our present state of affairs.

Now, after having made these few remarks on that head, I desire to call the attention of the House to the remedy. I know this is a difficult question—that it is the opinion of some honorable members that no matter what proposition you may make or what legislation you introduce it cannot improve or increase the prosperity of the country. The government entertain a different opinion. I may say at the outset it would have been much more agreeable if we could have met the House without the necessity of increased taxation. But in the imposition of the duties we are now about to ask the House to impose, it may be said we shall receive from the imports from foreign countries a larger portion of the $2,000,000 we require than we shall receive from the mother country.

I believe such will be the effect, but I think that in making such a statement to this House, belonging as we do to and forming a part of that great country—a country that receives our natural products without any taxation, everything we have to send to her—apart from our national feelings, I think this House will not object if, in the propositions before me, they touch more heavily the imports from foreign countries than from our fatherland.

I have this to say to our American friends: In 1865 they abrogated the reciprocity treaty, and from that day to the present a large portion of the imports from that country into the Dominion have been admitted free. We have hoped and hoped in vain that by the adoption of that policy we would lead our American friends to treat us in a more liberal spirit with regard to the same articles. Well, after having waited twelve years for the consideration of this subject, the government, requiring more revenue, have determined to ask this House to impose upon the products of the United States that have been free such a duty as may seem consistent with our position.

But the government couple with the proposal, in order to show that we approach this question with no unfriendly spirit, a resolution that will be laid on the table containing a proposition to this effect: That as to articles named, which are the natural products of the country, including lumber, if the United States take off the duties in part or in whole, we are prepared to meet them with equal concessions. The government believe in a reciprocity tariff, yet may discuss free trade or protection, but the question of to-day is: Shall we have a reciprocity tariff or a one-sided tariff?

We found, as I stated before, that it was important to encourage the exportation of our manufactures to foreign countries, and we are prepared now to say that the policy of the government is to give every manufacturer in the Dominion of Canada a drawback on the duties they may pay upon goods used in the manufactures of the Dominion exported. We found also, sir, as I have already pointed out, that under the bounty system of some foreign countries our sugar-refining trade and other interests were materially affected.

Well, sir, the government have decided to ask this House to impose countervailing duties under such circumstances. I trust that this proposition will receive the support of both sides of the House, because some six months since when the deputation of sugar refiners in London waited upon Mr. Gladstone and Sir Stafford Northcote, both of them being gentlemen representing free-trade views, they declared in the most emphatic terms that when a government came in and thus interfered with the legitimate trade of the country they were prepared to impose countervailing duties.

To make this matter plain, and place it beyond dispute, the government propose to ask the House for authority to collect on all such articles an ad valorem duty on their value, irrespective of drawbacks. My colleagues say explain it. For instance, a cent and a quarter drawback per pound is granted on cut nails exported to the Dominion of Canada; the duty will be calculated on the value of the nails irrespective of that drawback. Now, a bounty is given on sugar in excess of the duty which is paid by the sugar refiners;

the government will exact an ad valorem duty on the value of that sugar irrespective of the drawback.

I may also state, Mr. Chairman, that another reason why I think our American neighbors should not object to the imposition of the duties we propose is this: It is a fact, though not generally known, that the average percentage of revenue that is imposed on all imports into the Dominion of Canada at the present time, taking the returns for last year as our criterion, is 13 3-4 per cent. The amount of duty collected on the imports from Great Britain is a fraction under 17 1-2 per cent; while the amount of duty collected on the imports from the United States is a fraction under 10 per cent.

[After dealing minutely with the changes which would be effected by the new tariff, Mr. Tilley concluded as follows:]

It appears to me, Mr. Chairman, and I think the House will agree with me, that the government have endeavored, whether successfully or not, to carry out the policy that we were pledged to inaugurate. We have endeavored to meet every possible interest—the mining, the manufacturing, and the agricultural interests. We have endeavored to assist our shipping and ship-building interest, which is in a very depressed condition.

We have endeavored not to injure the lumber interest, because they now have a very important article used by their people at about the same rate of duty they had it before—I refer to pork. They have tea at a cheaper price than before; they have molasses cheaper. These articles enter largely into consumption with them. They have, as have every other class of exporters in the Dominion, many advantages under the propositions that we are about to submit that they did not have before. In the interest of lumbermen and of commerce generally, the present government, as well as our predecessors, have expended large sums of money for the improvement of the navigation of our rivers and of our coast by the erection of lighthouses and in their maintenance. This of course is an advantage to the shipping interests as well.

A proposition is also to be sumitted to the House which you will find in the estimates, to extend a telegraph down the St. Lawrence. This proposition was submitted to the people of the Dominion by an able and experienced gentleman, a member of the House. I need not name him because the interest he has taken is well known. This proposition is in the interest of commerce, and of our shipping, and of humanity. It is the interest of every industry that exports any article from this country to the Old World, because an expenditure of this kind will reduce the rate of charges in the shape of insurance and other charges on the shipping, and that is more absolutely in the interest of the exporter than in the interest of the owner of the ship.

In our policy, as just propounded, we have dealt with the agricultural interest, the mining interest, the shipping interest, indirectly with the lumbering interest, and with very many other interests, and it does appear to me that we have now arrived at a time when it becomes necessary for this country, for this Parliament, to decide whether we are to remain in the position we now occupy, with a certainty that within two years, with the existing laws upon our statute-book, almost every manufacturing industry in the country will be closed up and the money invested in it lost. The time has arrived, I think, when it becomes our duty to decide whether the thousands of men throughout the length and breadth of this country who are unemployed shall seek employment in another country or shall find it in this Dominion;

N the time has arrived when we are to decide whether we will
be simply hewers of wood and drawers of water; whether we
will be simply agriculturists raising wheat, and lumbermen
producing more lumber than we can use or Great Britain and
the United States will take from us at remunerative prices;
whether we will confine our attention to the fisheries and
certain other small industries, and cease to be what we have
been, and not rise to be what I believe we are destined to
be under wise and judicious legislation,—or whether we will
inaugurate a policy that will by its provisions say to the industries of the country, we will give you sufficient protection;
we will give you a market for what you can produce; we will
say that while our neighbors build up a Chinese wall we
will impose a reasonable duty on their products coming into
this country; at all events we will maintain for agricultural
and other productions largely the market of our own
Dominion.

The time has certainly arrived when we must consider
whether we will allow matters to remain as they are, with
the result of being an unimportant and uninteresting portion
of her Majesty's dominions, or will rise to the position which
I believe Providence has destined us to occupy, by means
which, I believe, though I may be over-sanguine; which my
colleagues believe, though they may be over-sanguine; which
the country believes, are calculated to bring prosperity and
happiness to the people, to give employment to the thousands
who are unemployed, and to make this a great and prosperous
country, as we all desire and hope it will be.

BUTLER

BENJAMIN FRANKLIN BUTLER, a noted American lawyer, statesman, and soldier, was born in Deerfield, New Hampshire, November 5, 1818, and received his education at Waterville College, now Colby University. After studying law he was admitted to the bar in 1841, and beginning practice in Lowell, Massachusetts, soon built up a large and lucrative practice and acquired at the same time a high reputation as a lawyer, especially in his conduct of criminal cases. He was active in political affairs, entering the lower house of the State legislature as a Democratic member in 1853, and the State senate in 1859. At the opening of the Civil War he was a brigadier-general of the State militia and when the call for troops was received on April 15, 1861, he at once gave orders for the mustering of his brigade. On April 18th he went to Annapolis, Maryland, at the head of the Eighth Massachusetts Regiment, and on May 16th was commissioned major-general and placed in command at Fortress Monroe. While there he declined to return fugitive slaves to their owners, declaring them "property contraband of war," a phrase original with himself. In February, 1862, he was assigned to the command of the land forces of the New Orleans expedition, and after Admiral Farragut had passed the forts below the city, Butler took possession of New Orleans, remaining in command there until the 16th of the following December. During the remainder of the war he was active in various commands of importance. In 1866 he entered Congress as a Republican representative, continuing there, except for the term of 1875-77, until 1879. He was a conspicuous figure in twenty-one important congressional debates and was especially prominent in the impeachment of President Johnson. In 1871 he was defeated as a Republican candidate for governor of Massachusetts and suffered defeat also in 1878 and 1879 as the candidate of the Independent Greenback party. In 1882, however, he was elected governor by the Democrats, but was defeated in the year following. In 1884 he was the candidate of the Greenback party for the Presidency. He died in Washington, January 11, 1893. Butler was an exceedingly able lawyer and military commander, and a ready debater. He published his "Autobiography and Personal Reminiscences" in 1892.

CHARACTER AND RESULTS OF THE WAR

DELIVERED APRIL 2, 1863

MR. MAYOR,—With the profoundest gratitude for the too flattering commendation of my administration of the various trusts committed to me by the government, which, in behalf of your associates, you have been pleased to tender, I ask you to receive my most heart-felt thanks. To the citizens of New York here assembled, graced by the fairest and loveliest, in kind appreciation of my services supposed to have been rendered to the country, I tender the deepest acknowledgments. I accept it all, not for myself, but for my brave comrades of the Army of the Gulf. I receive it as an earnest of your devotion to the country—an evidence of your loyalty to the constitution under which you live and under which you hope to die.

In order that the acts of the Army of the Gulf may be understood, perhaps it would be well, at a little length, with your permission, that some details should be given of the thesis upon which we fulfilled our duties. The first question, then, to be ascertained is, what is this contest in which the country is engaged? At the risk of being a little tedious, at the risk, even, of calling your attention to what might seem otherwise too elementary, I propose to run down through the history of the contest to see what it is that agitates the whole country at this day and this hour.

That we are in the midst of a civil commotion, all know. But what is that commotion? Is it a riot? Is it an insurrection? Is it a rebellion? Or is it a revolution? And pray, sir, although it may seem still more elementary, what is a riot? A riot, if I understand it, is simply an outburst of the passions of a number of men for the moment, in breach of the law, by force of numbers, to be put down and subdued by the civil authorities; if it goes further to be dealt with by the military authorities. But you say, sir, "Why treat us to a definition of a riot upon this occasion? Why, of all things, should you undertake to instruct a New York audience in what a riot is?"

To that I answer, because the administration of Mr.

Buchanan dealt with this great change of affairs as if it were a riot; because his government officer gave the opinion that in Charleston it was but a riot; and that, as there was no civil authority there to call out the military, therefore Sumter must be given over to the rioters, and such was the beginning of this struggle. Let us see how it grew up. I deal not now with causes but with effects—facts.

Directly after the guns of the rebels had turned upon Sumter, the several States of the South, in convention assembled, inaugurated a series of movements which took out from the Union divers States, and as each was attempted to be taken out, the riots, if such existed, were no longer found in them, but they became insurrectionary, and the administration, upon the 15th of April, 1861, dealt with this state of affairs as an insurrection and called out the militia of the United States to suppress an insurrection. I was called at that time into the service to administer the laws in putting down an insurrection.

I found a riot at Baltimore. The rioters had burned bridges; but the riot had hardly arisen to the dignity of an insurrection, because the State had not moved as an organized community. A few men were rioting at Baltimore; and as I marched into the State at the head of the United States troops, the question came up, what have I before me? You will remember that I offered then to put down all kinds of insurrections so long as the State of Maryland remained loyal to the United States. Transferred from thence to a wider sphere at Fortress Monroe, I found that the State of Virginia through its organization had taken itself out of the Union and was endeavoring to erect for itself an independent government, and I dealt with that State as being in rebellion and thought the property of the rebels of whatever name or nature should be deemed rebellious property and contraband of war, subject to the laws of war.

I have been thus careful in stating these various steps, because, although through your kindness replying to eulogy, I am here answering every charge of inconsistency and wrong of intention for my acts done before the country. Wrong in judgment I may have been, but I insist wrong in intention or inconsistent with my former opinions never. Upon the same theory by which I felt myself bound to put down insurrection in Maryland, while it remained loyal, whether that insurrection was the work of blacks or whites— by the same loyalty to the constitution and laws I felt bound to confiscate slave property in the rebellious State of Virginia. Pardon me, sir, if right here I say that I am a little sensitive upon this topic.

I am an old-fashioned Andrew Jackson Democrat of twenty years' standing. And so far as I know I have never swerved, so help me God, from one of his teachings. Up to the time that disunion took place, I went as far as the farthest in sustaining the constitutional rights of the States. However bitter or distasteful to me were the obligations my fathers had made for me in the compromise of the constitution, it was not for me to pick out the sweet from the bitter, and, fellow Democrats, I took them all because they were constitutional obligations, and sustaining them all I stood by the South and by Southern rights under the constitution until I advanced so far as to look into the very pit of disunion into which they plunged, and then not liking the prospect I quietly withdrew.

And from that hour we went apart, how far apart you can judge when I tell you that on the 28th of December, 1860, I shook hands on terms of personal friendship with Jefferson

Davis, and on the 28th of December, 1862, you had the pleasure of reading his proclamation that I was to be hanged at sight.

And now, my friends, if you will allow me to pause for a moment in this line of thought, as we come up to the point of time when these men laid down their constitutional obligations, let me ask, what then were my rights and what were theirs? At that hour they repudiated the constitution of the United States by vote in solemn convention, and not only that, but they took arms in their hands and undertook by force to rend from the government what seemed to them the fairest portion of the heritage which my fathers had given to you and me as a rich legacy for our children. When they did that they abrogated, abnegated, and forfeited every constitutional right, and released me from every constitutional obligation so far as they were concerned.

Therefore when I was thus called upon to say what should be my action thereafter with regard to slavery, I was left to the natural instincts of my heart as prompted by a Christian education in New England, and I dealt with it accordingly. The same sense of duty to my constitutional obligations, and to the rights of the several States that required me, so long as those States remained under the constitution, to protect the system of slavery,—that same sense of duty after they had gone out from under the constitution, caused me to follow the dictates of my own untrammelled conscience.

So you see—and I speak now to my old Democratic friends that, however misjudging I may have been, we went along together, step by step, up to the point of disunion, and I claim that we ought still to go on in the same manner. We acknowledged the right of those men to hold slaves, because it was guaranteed to them by the compromise of our fathers in the constitution, but if their State rights were to be respected, because of our allegiance to the constitution and our respect for State rights, when that sacred obligation was taken away by their own traitorous acts, and we, as well as the negroes, were disenthralled, why should not we follow the dictates of God's law and humanity?

By the exigencies of the public service removed once more to another sphere of action, at New Orleans, I found this problem coming up in another form, and that led me to examine and see how far had progressed this civil commotion now carried on by force of arms.

I believe, under our complex system of States, each having an independent government, with the United States covering all, that there can be treason to a State and not to the United States; revolution in a State and not as regards the United States; loyalty to a State and disloyalty to the Union; and loyalty to the Union and disloyalty to the organized government of a State. As an illustration, take the troubles which lately arose in the State of Rhode Island, where there was an attempt to rebel against the State government and to change the form of that government, but no rebellion against the United States. All of you are familiar with the movements of Mr. Dorr; in that matter there was no intent of disloyalty against the United States, but a great deal against the State government.

I therefore, in Louisiana, found a State government that had entirely changed its form and had revolutionized itself so far as it could; had created courts and imposed taxes, and put in motion all kinds of governmental machinery; and so far as her State government was concerned, Louisiana was no longer in and of itself one of the United States of America. It had, so far as depended on its own action, changed its State government and by solemn act forever seceded from the United States of America and attempted to join a new national government,—hostile to us, as one of the so-called Confederate States.

I found, I respectfully submit, a revolutionized State. There had been a revolution, by force; beyond a riot, which is an infraction of the law; beyond an insurrection, which is an abnegation of the law; beyond a rebellion, which is an attempt to override the law by force of numbers; a new State government formed that was being supported by force of arms.

Now, I asked myself, upon what thesis shall I deal with this people? Organized into a community under forms of law, they had seized a portion of the territory of the United States and were holding it by force of arms; and I respectfully submit I had to deal with them as alien enemies. They had forever passed the boundary of "wayward sisters" or "erring brothers," unless indeed they erred toward us as Cain did against his brother Abel. They had passed beyond brotherhood by treason added to murder. Aye, and Louisiana had done this in the strongest possible way, for she had seized on territory which the government of the United States had bought and paid for, and to which her people could advance no shadow of claim save as citizens of the United States. Therefore I dealt with them as alien enemies.

And what rights have alien enemies captured in war? They have the right, so long as they behave themselves and are noncombatants, to be free from personal violence; they have no other rights; and therefore it was my duty to see to it (and I believe the record will show I did see to it) that order was preserved and that every man who behaved well and did not aid the Confederate States was not molested in his person. I held, by the laws of war, that everything else they had was at the mercy of the conqueror. They have claims to mercy and clemency; but no rights. Permit me to state the method in which their rights were defined by one gentleman of my staff. He very coolly paraphrased the Dred Scott decision and said they had no rights which a negro was bound to respect. But, dealing with them in this way, I took care to protect all men in personal safety.

Now, I hear a friend behind me say: " But how does your theory affect loyal men ? " The difficulty in answering that proposition is this: In governmental action the government in making peace and carrying on war cannot deal with individuals, but with organized communities, whether organized wrongly or rightly; and all I could do, so far as my judgment taught me, for the individual loyal citizen, was to see to it that no exaction should be made of him and no property taken away from him that was not absolutely necessary for the success of military operations.

I know nothing else that I could do. I could not alter the carrying on of the war because loyal citizens were, unfortunately, like Dog Tray, found in bad company; to their persons, and to their property even, all possible protection I caused to be afforded. But let me repeat—for it is quite necessary to keep this in mind, and I am afraid that for want of so doing some of my old Democratic friends have got lost in going with one portion of the country rather than the other in their thoughts and feelings—let me repeat that, in making war or making peace, carrying on governmental operations of any sort, governments and their representatives, so far as I am instructed, can deal only with organized communities, and men must fall or rise with the communities in which they are situated.

You in New York must follow the government as expressed by the will of the majority of your State until you can revolutionize that government and change it; and those loyal at the South must, until this contest comes into process of settlement, also follow the action of the organized majorities in which their lot has been cast, and no man, no set of men, can see the possible solution of this or any other governmental problem as affecting States, except upon this basis.

Now, then, to pass from the particular to the general, to leave the detail in Louisiana, of which I have run down the account, rather as illustrating my meaning than otherwise, I come back to the question: What is now the nature of the contest with all the States that are banded together in the so-called Confederate States? Into what form has it come? It started in insurrection: it grew up a rebellion; it has become a revolution, and carries with it all the rights and incidents of a revolution.

Our government has dealt with it upon that ground. When the government blockaded Southern ports they dealt with it as a revolution; when they sent out cartels of exchange of prisoners they dealt with these people no longer as simple insurrectionists and traitors, but as organized revolutionists who had set up a government for themselves upon the territory of the United States.

Sir, let no man say to me, " Why then you acknowledge the right of revolution in these men! " I beg your pardon, sir; I only acknowledge the fact of revolution—that which has actually happened. I look these things in the face and I do not dodge them because they are unpleasant; I find this a revolution and these men are no longer, I repeat, our erring brethren, but they are our alien enemies, foreigners carrying on war against us, attempting to make alliances against us, attempting surreptitiously to get into the family of nations. I agree that it is not a successful revolution and a revolution never to be successful,—pardon me, I was speaking theoretically, as a matter of law,—never to be successful until acknowledged by the parent State. Now, then, I am willing to unite with you in your cheers when you say a revolution, the rightfulness or success of which we, the parent State, never will acknowledge.

Why, sir, have I been so careful in bringing down with great particularity these distinctions? Because in my judgment there are certain logical consequences following from them as necessarily as various corollaries from a problem in Euclid. If we are at war, as I think, with a foreign country, to all intents and purposes, how can a man here stand up and say that he is on the side of that foreign country and not be an enemy to his country?

A man must be either for his country or against his country. He cannot, upon this theory, be throwing impediments all the time in the way of the progress of his government, under pretence that he is helping some other portion of his country. If any local man thinks that he must do something to bring back his erring brethren (if he likes that form of phrase) at the South, let him take his musket and go down and try it in that way. If he is still of a different opinion and thinks that is not the best way to bring them back, but he can do it by persuasion and talk, let him go down with me to Louisiana and I will set him over to Mississippi and if the rebels do not feel for his heart-strings, but not in love, I will bring him back. Let us say to him: "Choose ye this day whom ye will serve. If the Lord thy God be God, serve him; if Baal be God, serve ye him. But no man can serve two masters, God and Mammon."

Again, there are other logical consequences to flow from the view which I have ventured to take of this subject, and one is as regards to our relations from past political action. If they are now alien enemies I am bound to them by no ties of party fealty or political affinity. They have passed out of that, and I think we ought to go back only to examine and see if all ties of party allegiance and party fealty as regards them are not broken, and satisfy ourselves that it is your duty and mine to look simply to our country and to its service, and leave them to look to the country they are attempting to erect, and to its service; and then let us try the conclusion with them, as we are doing by arms and the stern arbitrament of war.

Mark, by this I give up no territory of the United States. Every foot that was ever circumscribed on the map by the lines around the United States belongs to us. None the less because bad men have attempted to organize worse government upon various portions of it. It is to be drawn in under our laws and our government as soon as the power of the United States can be exerted for that purpose, and therefore, my friends, you see that next one of the logical consequences that proceed from our theory: that we have no occasion to carry on the fight for the constitution as it is.

Who is interfering with the constitution as it is? Who makes any attacks upon the constitution? We are fighting with those who have gone out and repudiated the constitution, and made another constitution for themselves. And now, my friends, I do not know but I shall speak some heresy, but as a Democrat, and as an Andrew Jackson Democrat, I am not for the Union as it was. I say, as a Democrat, as an Andrew Jackson Democrat, I am not for the Union to be again as it was. Understand me, I was for the Union because I saw or thought I saw the troubles in the future which have burst upon us, but having undergone those troubles, having spent all this blood and this treasure I do not mean to go back again and be cheek by jowl with South Carolina as I was before, if I can help it.

Mark me, let no man misunderstand me, and I repeat, lest I may be misunderstood—there are none so slow to understand as those who do not want to—mark me, I say I do not mean to give up a single inch of the soil of South Carolina. If I had been in public life at that time and had had the position, the will, and the ability, I would have dealt with South Carolina as Jackson did and kept her in the Union at all hazards, but now she has gone out, and I will take care that when she comes in again she comes in better behaved, that she shall no longer be the firebrand of the Union—aye, and that she shall enjoy what her people never yet have enjoyed—the blessings of a republican form of government.

Therefore in that view I am not for the reconstruction of the Union as it was. I have spent treasure and blood enough upon it, in conjunction with my fellow citizens, to make it a little better. I think we can have a better Union the next time. It was good enough if it had been let alone. The old house was good enough for me, but as they have pulled down all the L-part, I propose, when we build it up, to build it up with all the modern improvements.

Another of the logical sequences, it seems to me, that follow in inexorable and not-to-be-shunned sequence upon this proposition, that we are dealing with alien enemies, is with regard to our duties as to the confiscation of rebel property, and that question would seem to me to be easy of settlement under the constitution and without any discussion, if my first proposition is right. Has it not been held from the beginning of the world down to this day, from the time the Israelites took possession of the land of Canaan, which they got from alien enemies—and is it not the well-settled law of war to-day, that the whole property of alien enemies belonged to the conqueror, and that it is at his mercy and his clemency what should be done with it?

For one I would take it and give the loyal man who was loyal in his heart, at the South, enough to make him as well as he was before, and I would take the balance of it and distribute it among the volunteer soldiers who have gone—[The remainder of the sentence was drowned in a tremendous burst of applause]. And so far as I know them, if we should settle South Carolina with them, in the course of a few years I would be quite willing to receive her back into the Union.

This theory shows us how to deal with another proposition: What shall be done with the slaves? Here again the laws of war have long settled, with clearness and exactness, that it is for the conqueror, for the government which has maintained or extended its jurisdiction over conquered territory, to deal with slaves as it pleases, to free them or not as it chooses. It is not for the conquered to make terms, or to send their friends into the conquering country to make terms for them. Another corollary follows from the proposition that we are fighting with alien enemies, which relieves us from a difficulty which seems to trouble some of my old Democratic friends, and that is in relation to the question of arming the negro slaves.

If the seceded States are alien enemies, is there any objection that you know of, and if so, state it, to our arming one portion of the foreign country against the other while they are fighting us? Suppose that we were at war with England.

Who would get up here in New York and say that we must not arm the Irish, lest they should hurt some of the English? And yet at one time, not very far gone, all those Englishmen were our grandfathers' brothers. Either they or we erred, but we are now separate nations. There can be no objection, for another reason, because there is no law of war or of nations,—no rule of governmental action that I know of, which prevents a country from arming any portion of its citizens; and if the slaves do not take part in the rebellion, they become simply our citizens residing in our territory which is at present usurped by our enemies to be used in its defence as other citizens are. At this waning hour I do not propose to discuss but merely a hint at these various subjects.

There is one question I am frequently asked, and most frequently by my old Democratic friends: " General Butler, what is your experience? Will the negroes fight?"

To that I answer, I have no personal experience, because I left the Department of the Gulf before they were fairly brought into action. But they did fight under Jackson at Chalmette. More than that; let Napoleon III answer, who has hired them to do what the veterans of the Crimea cannot do—to whip the Mexicans. Let the veterans of Napoleon I, under Le Clerc, who were whipped by them out of San Domingo, say whether they will fight or not.

What has been the demoralizing effect upon them as a race by their contact with white men I know not, but I cannot forget that their fathers would not have been slaves, but that they were captives of war in their own country in hand-to-hand fights among the several chiefs. They would fight at some time, and if you want to know any more than that I can only advise you to try them.

Passing to another logical deduction from the principle that we are carrying on war against alien enemies (for I pray you to remember that I am only carrying out the same idea upon which the government acted when it instituted the blockade), I meet the question whether we thereby give foreign nations any greater rights than if we considered them as a rebellious portion of our country. We have heretofore seemed to consider that if we acknowledged that this was a revolution, and the rebels were alien enemies in this fight, that therefore we should give to foreign nations greater apparent right to interfere in our affairs than they would have if the insurgents were considered and held by us as rebels only, in a rebellious part of our own country.

The first answer to that is this: that so far as the rebels are concerned, they are estopped to deny that they are exactly what they claim themselves to be, alien enemies; and so far as foreign nations are concerned, while the rebels are alien to us yet they are upon our territory, and until we acknowledge them there is no better settled rule of the law of nations than that the recognition of them as an independent nation is an act of war. They have no right to recognize them, because we say to them, " We will deal with you as belligerent alien enemies," than they would have to treat with them if we hold them simply as rebels; and no country is more sternly and strongly bound by that view than is England, because she claimed the recognition by France of our independence to be an act of war and declared war accordingly.

Therefore I do not see why we lose any rights. We do not admit that this is a rightful rebellion—we do not recognize it as such—we do not act toward it except in the best way we can to put it down and to re-revolutionize the country.

What is the duty then of neutrals if these are alien enemies? We thus find them a people with whom no neutral nation has any treaty of amity or alliance: they are strangers to every neutral nation. For example let us take the English. The English nation have no treaty with the rebels—have no relations with the rebels—open relations I mean, none that are recognized by the laws of nations. They have a treaty of amity, friendship, and commerce with us, and now what is their duty in the contest between us and our enemies to whom they are strangers? They claim it to be neutrality, only such neutrality as they should maintain between two friendly nations with each of whom they have treaties of amity. Let me illustrate: I have two friends that have got into a quarrel—into a fight if you please; I am on equally good terms with both and I do not choose to take a part with either. I treat them as belligerents and hold myself neutral. That is the position of a nation where two equally friendly nations are fighting.

But again I have a friend who is fighting with a stranger, with whom I have nothing to do, of whom I know nothing that is good, of whom I have seen nothing except that he would fight—what is my duty to my friend in that case? To stand perfectly neutral? It is not the part of a friend so to do between men and it is not the part of a friendly nation as between nations. And yet from some strange misconception our English friends profess to do no more than to stand perfectly neutral while they have treaties of amity and commerce with us and no treaty which they acknowledge with the South.

And therefore I say there is a much higher duty on the part of foreign nations toward us when we are in contest with a people with which they have no treaty of amity than there possibly can be toward them. To illustrate how this fact bears upon this question: the English say, "Oh! we are going to be neutral; we will not sell you any arms, because to be neutral strictly we should have to sell the same to the Confederates."

To that I answer: You have treaties of amity and commerce with us by which you have agreed to trade with us. You have no treaty of amity and commerce with them by which you agree to trade with them. Why not then trade with us? Why not give us that rightful preference except for reasons of hostility to us that I will state hereafter? I have been thus particular upon this, because in stating my proposition to gentlemen in whose judgment I have great confidence they have said to me, "I agree with your theory, Mr. Butler, but I am afraid you will involve us with other nations by the view that you take of that matter."

But I insist, and I can only state the proposition for want of time—your own minds will carry it out particularly—I insist that there is a higher and closer duty to us—treating the rebels as a strange nation not yet admitted into the family of nations—that there is a higher duty from our old friendship on her part, from our old relations toward Great Britain, than there is to this rebellious, pushing, attempting-to-get-into-place member of the family of nations.

There is still another logical sequence which in my judgment follows from this view of the case. The great question put to me by my friends and the great question which is now agitating this country is, How are we to get these men back? How are we to get this territory back? How are we to reconstruct the nation? I think it is much better answered upon this hypothesis than any other. There are but two ways in which this contest can be ended; one is by re-revolutionizing a portion of this seceding territory and have the people ask to be admitted into the Union; another is, to bring it all back so that if they do not come back in the first way they shall come back bound to our triumphal car of victory. Now when any portion of the South becomes loyal to the North and to the Union, or to express it with more care when any portion of the inhabitants of the South wish to become again a part of the nation and will throw off the government of Jefferson Davis, erect themselves into a State, and come and ask us to take them back with such a State constitution as they ought to be admitted under, there is no difficulty in its being done. There is no witchery about this. This precise thing has been done in the case of Western Virginia. She went out—stayed out for a while.

By the aid of our armies and by the efforts of her citizens she re-revolutionized, threw off the government of the rest of the State of Virginia; threw off the Confederate yoke; erected herself into a State with a constitution such as I believe is quite satisfactory to all of us, especially the amendment. She has asked to come back and has been received back and is the first entering wedge of that series of States who will come back that way.

But suppose they will not come back?

We are bound to subjugate them. What then do they become? Territories of the United States—acquired by force of arms—precisely as we acquired California, precisely as we acquired Nevada, precisely as we acquired—not exactly though—as we acquired Texas—and then is there any difficulty in treating with these men? Was there any difficulty in dealing with the State of California when our men went there and settled in sufficient numbers so as to give that State the benefits of the blessings of a republican form of government? Was there any difficulty in obtaining her beyond our transactions with Mexico?

None whatever. Will there be any difficulty in taking to ourselves the new State of Nevada when she is ready to come and ripe to come? Was there any difficulty in taking into the Union any portion of the Louisiana purchase when we bought it first? Will there be any difficulty when her people get ready to come back to the United States of our taking her back again more than perhaps to carry out the parallel a little further, to pay a large sum of money besides, as we did in the case of California after we conquered it from Mexico? These States having gone out without cause, without our right, without grievance, and having formed themselves into new States and taken upon themselves new alliances, I am not for having them come back without readmission.

I feel, perhaps, if the ladies will pardon the illustration, like a husband whose wife has run away with another man, and has divorced herself from him; he will not take her to his arms until they have come before the priest and been remarried. I have, I say, the same feeling in the case of these people that have gone out; when they repent and ask to come back I am ready to receive them, and I am not ready until then.

And now, having gone by far too discursively over many of these points which I desired to bring to your attention, let us return to what has been done in the Department of the Gulf, to which you have so flatteringly alluded, and to which I will answer. While I am very much gratified at the kind expression of your regard, whether that expression is justified can be told in a single word. When I left the Department of the Gulf, I sat down and deliberately put in the form of an address to the people of that Department, the exact acts I had done while in their Department; I said to them, "I have done these things." I have now waited more than three months, and I have yet to hear a denial from that Department that the things therein stated were done.

And to that alone, sir, I can point as a justification of your too flattering eulogy, and to that I point forever as my answer to every slander and every calumny. The ladies of New Orleans knew whether they were safe; has any one of them ever said she was not? The men of New Orleans knew whether life and property were safe; has any man ever said they were not? The poor of New Orleans knew whether the money which was taken from the rich rebels was applied to the alleviation of their wants; has any man denied that it was? To that record I point—and it will be the only answer that I shall ever make; and I only do it now because I desire that you shall have neither doubt nor feeling upon this subject—it is the only answer I can ever make to the thousand calumnies that have been poured upon me and mine, and upon the officers who worked with me for the good of our country.

I desire now to say a single word upon the question, what are the prospects of this war? My simple opinion would be no better than that of another man; but let me show you the reason for the faith that is in me that this war is progressing steadily to a successful termination. Compare the state of the country on January 1, 1863, with the state of the country on January 1, 1862, and tell me whether there has not been progress. At that time the Union armies held no considerable portion of Missouri, of Kentucky, or of Tennessee; none of Virginia, except Fortress Monroe and Arlington Heights; none of North Carolina save Hatteras, and none of South Carolina save Port Royal. All the rest was ground of struggle at least, and all the rest furnishing supplies to the rebels.

Now they hold none of Missouri, none of Kentucky, none of Tennessee, for any valuable purpose of supplies, because the western portion is in our hands, and the eastern portion has been so run over by the contending armies that the supplies are gone. They hold no portion of Virginia valuable for supplies, for that is eaten out by their armies. We hold one third of Virginia and half of North Carolina. We hold our own in South Carolina, and I hope that before the eleventh of this month we shall hold a little more. We hold two thirds of Louisiana in wealth and population. We hold all Arkansas and all Texas so far as supplies are concerned, so long as Farragut is between Port Hudson and Vicksburg. And I believe the colored troops held Florida at the last accounts.

Now, then, let us see to what the rebellion is reduced. It is reduced to the remainder of Virginia, part of North and South Carolina, all of Georgia, Alabama, and Mississippi, and a small portion of Louisiana and Tennessee; Texas and Arkansas, as I said before, being cut off. Why I draw strong hopes from this is, that their supplies come either from Kentucky, Tennessee, Missouri, Arkansas, or Texas, and these are now completely beyond their reach. To this fact I look largely for the suppression of this rebellion and the overthrow of this revolution.

They have got to the end of their conscription; we have not begun ours. They have got to the end of their national credit; we have not put ours in any market in the world. And why should any man be desponding? Why should any man say that this great work has gone on too slowly? Why, should men feel impatient? The war of the Revolution was seven years. Why should men be so anxious that nations should march faster than they are prepared to march—faster than the tread of nations has ever been in the Providence of God? Nations in war have ever moved slowly. We are too impatient—we never learn anything, it would seem to me, from reading history—I speak of myself as well as you—I have shared in that impatience myself. I have shared in your various matters of disappointment.

I was saying but the other day to a friend of mine, "It seems strange to me that our navy cannot catch that steamer 'Alabama,' there must be something wrong in the Navy Department, I am afraid," and I got quite impatient. I had hardly got over the wound inflicted by the capture of the "Jacob Bell," when came the piracies of the "Golden Eagle," and the "Olive Jane," and as one was from Boston, it touched me keenly.

He replied: "Don't be impatient; remember that Paul Jones, with a sailing-ship on the coast of England, put the whole British navy at defiance for many months, and wandered up and down that coast, and worked his will upon it, and England had no naval power to contend with, and had not twenty-five hundred miles of sea coast to blockade as we have."

I remember that in the French war, Lord Cochrane, with one vessel, and that was by no means a steamship, held the whole French coast in terror against the French navy. And so it has been done by other nations. Let us have a little patience, and possess our souls with a little patriotism and less politics, and we shall have no difficulty.

But there is one circumstance of this war, I am bound to say in all frankness to you, that I do not like the appearance of, and that is because we cannot exactly reach it. I refer to the war made upon our commerce, which is not the fault of the navy, nor of any department of the government, but is the fault of our allies. Pardon me a moment, for I am speaking now in the commercial city of New York, where I think it is of interest to you, and of a matter to which I have given some reflection—pardon me a moment, while we examine and see what England has done. She agreed to be neutral—I have tried to demonstrate to you that she ought to have been a little more than neutral—but has she been even that? ["No, no, no."] Let us see the evidences of that "No."

In the first place there has been nothing of the Union cause that her orators and her statesmen have not maligned; there has been nothing of sympathy or encouragement which she has not afforded our enemies; there has been nothing which she could do under the cover of neutrality which she has not done to aid them. Nassau has been a naval arsenal for pirate rebel boats to refit in. Kingston has been their coal depot, and Barbadoes has been the dancing hall to fête pirate chieftains in.

What cause, my friends; what cause, my countrymen, has England so to deal with us? What is the reason she does so deal with us? Is it because we have never shown sympathy toward her or love to her people? And mark me here, that I make a distinction between the English people as a mass and the English government. I think the heart of her people beats responsive to ours—but I know her government and aristocracy hate us with a hate which passeth all understanding. I say, let us see if we have given any cause for this. I know, I think, what the cause is; but let us see what we have done.

You remember that when the famine overtook the Irish in 1847, the " Macedonian " frigate carried out the bread from this country to feed the poor that England was starving. When afterward the heir to her throne arrived here, aye, in this very house, our people assembled to do him welcome in such numbers that the very floor would not uphold them, and to testify our appreciation of the high qualities of his mother and sovereign, and our love of the English people—we gave him such a reception as Northern gentlemen give to their friends, and his present admirers at Richmond gave him such a reception as Southern gentlemen give to their friends. What further has been done by us? No, I have no right to claim any portion of it. What has been done by the merchants of New York? The " George Griswold " goes out to feed the starving poor of Lancashire, to which yourselves all contributed, and it was only God's blessing on that charity that prevented that vessel being overhauled and burned by the " Alabama," fitted out from an English port.

And to-day at Birkenhead the " Sumter " is being fitted out—at Barbadoes the captain of the " Florida " is being fêted—and somewhere the " 290," the cabalistic number of the British merchants who contributed to her construction, is preying upon our commerce, while we hear that at Glasgow a steamer is being built for the Emperor of China, and at Liverpool another is about to be launched for the Emperor of China. Pardon me, I don't believe the Emperor of China will buy many ships of Great Britain until they bring back the silk gowns they stole out of his palace at Pekin. And even now, I say that our commerce is being preyed upon by ships in the hands of the rebels built by English builders. And I ask the merchants of the city of New York whether it has not already reached the point where our commerce, to be safe, has to be carried in British bottoms.

Now I learn from the late correspondence of Earl Russell with the rebel commissioner Mason, that the British have put two articles of the treaty of Paris in compact with the rebels: First, that enemies' goods shall be covered by neutral flags, and there shall be free trade at the ports and open trade with neutrals. Why didn't Great Britain put the other part of the treaty in compact; namely, that there should be no more privateering, if she was honest and earnest, and did not mean our commerce should be crippled by rebel piracy?

Again, when we took from her deck our two senators and rebel ambassadors, Slidell and Mason, and took them, in my judgment, according to the laws of nations, what did she do but threaten us with war? I agree that it was wisely done, perhaps, not to provoke war at that time—we were not quite in a condition for it—but I thank God, and that always, that we are fast getting in a condition to remember that threat always and every day! Why is it all this has been done? Because we alone can be the commercial rivals of Great Britain! and because the South has no commercial marine.

There has been in my judgment a deliberate attempt on the part of Great Britain, under the plea of neutrality, to allow our commerce to be ruined for her own benefit, if human actions indicate human thoughts. It is idle to tell me Great Britain does not know these vessels are fitted out in her ports. It is idle and insulting to tell me that she put the "Alabama" under $20,000 bonds not to go into the service of the Confederate States. The "Jacob Bell" alone would pay the amount of the bond over and over again.

We did not so deal with her when she was at war with Russia. On the suggestion of the British minister our government stopped, with the rapidity of lightning, the sailing of a steamer supposed to be for Russia, until the minister himself was convinced of her good faith and willing to let her go. We must take some means to put a stop to these piracies and to the fitting out of pirate vessels in English ports. They are always telling us about the inefficiency of a republican government, but as they are acting now, we could stop two pirates to their one. We must in some way put a stop to the construction and fitting out of these pirate vessels in English ports to prey upon our commerce or else consent to keep our ships idle at home. We must stop them —we must act upon the people of England if we cannot secure a stoppage in any other way.

I have seen it stated that the loss to our commerce already amounts to $9,000,000—enough to have paid the expense of keeping a large number of vessels at home and out of the way of these cruisers.

What shall we do in the matter? Why, when our government takes a step toward putting a stop to it (and I believe it is taking that step now, but it is not in my province to speak of it) we must aid it in so doing. We, the people, are the government in this matter, and when our government gets ready to take a step we must get ready to sustain it.

England told us what to do when we took Mason and Slidell, and she thought there was a likelihood to be war. She stopped exportation of those articles which she thought we wanted, and which she had allowed to be exported before. Let us do the same thing.

Let us proclaim non-intercourse, so that no ounce of American food shall ever by any accident get into an Englishman's mouth until these piracies cease. [A voice: " Say that again! "] I never say anything, my friends, that I am afraid to say again. I repeat—let us proclaim non-intercourse, so that no ounce of American food shall by any accident get into an Englishman's mouth until these piracies are stopped. That we have a right to do; and when we ever do do it, my word for it, the English government will find out where these vessels are going to, and they will write to the Emperor of China upon the subject. But I hear some objectors say, " If you proclaim non-intercourse England may go to war."

Now I am not to be frightened twice running. I got frightened a little better than a year ago, but I have gotten over it. Further, this is a necessity; for we must keep our ships at home in some form to save them from these piracies when a dozen of these privateers get loose upon the seas. It will become a war measure which any nation, under any law, under any construction, would warrant our right to enforce.

And this course should be adopted toward the English nation alone, for I have never heard of any blockade runners under the French flag, nor under the Russian flag, nor under the Austrian flag, nor under the Greek flag. No! not even the Turks will do it. Therefore I have ventured to suggest the adoption of this course for your consideration as a possible,—aye, not only possible, but, unless this state of things has a remedy, a probable event; for we must see to it that we protect ourselves and take a manly place among the nations of the earth. But I hear some friend of mine say, " I am afraid your scheme would bring down our provisions; and if we do not export them to England we shall find our Western markets still more depressed." Allow me, with great deference to your judgment, gentlemen, to suggest a remedy for that at the same time.

I would suggest that the exportation of gold be prohibited and then there would be nothing to forward to meet the bills of exchange and pay for the goods we have bought, except our provisions. And, taking a hint from one of your best and most successful merchants, we could pay for our silks and satins in butter, and lard, and corn, and beef, and pork, and bring up the prices in the West, so that they could afford to pay the increased tariff in bringing them forward, now rendered necessary, I suppose, upon your railroads. And if our fair sisters and daughters will dress in silks, and satins, and laces, they will not feel any more troubled that a portion of the price goes to the Western farmer to enhance his gains instead of going into the coffers of a Jew banker in Wall street.

You will observe, my friends, that in the list of grievances with which I charge England, I have not charged her with tampering with our leading politicians. So far as any evidence I have, I don't know that she is guilty; but what shall we say of our leading politicians that have tampered with her? I have read of it in the letters of Lord Lyons with much surprise—with more surprise than has been excited in me by any other fact of this war—I had, somehow, got an inkling of the various things that came up in previous instances, so I was not very much surprised at them; but when I so read a statement, deliberately put forward, that here in New York leading politicians had consulted with the British minister as to how these United States could be separated and broken up, every drop of blood in my veins boiled; and I would have liked to have met that leading politician. I do not know that Lord Lyons is to blame. I suppose, sir, if a man comes to one of your clerks and offers to go into partnership with him to rob your neighbor's bank, and he reports him to you, you do not blame the clerk; but what do you do with the man who makes the offer?

I think we had better take a lesson from the action of Washington's administration—when the French minister, M. Genet, undertook even to address the people of the United States by letter, complaint was made to his government and he was recalled, and a law was passed preventing for all future time any interference by foreign diplomatists with the people of the United States.

I want to be understood,—I have no evidence of any interference on the part of Lord Lyons; but he says in his letter to Earl Russell that, both before and after a certain event, leading politicians came to him and desired that he would do what—(I am giving the substance and not words)—desired that he would request his government not to interfere between the North and South. Why? Because it would aid the country not to interfere? No! Because, if England did interfere the country would spurn the interference and be stronger than ever to crush the rebellion.

Mark again the insidious way in which the point was put. They knew how we felt because of the action of England; they knew that the heart of this people beat true to the constitution and that it could not brook any interference on the part of England. What, then, did these politicians do? They asked the British minister to use the influence of British diplomacy to induce other nations to interfere, but to take care that Great Britain should keep out of sight, lest we should see the cat under the meal. This is precisely the proposition that they made. You observe that in speaking of these men I have up to this moment used the word politicians. What kind of politicians? They cannot be Democratic politicians.

How I should like to hear Andrew Jackson say a few words upon such politicians who call themselves Democrats! ["He would hang them."] No, I don't think he would have an opportunity to do so; he never would be able to catch them. I have felt it my duty here in the city of New York, because of the interest I have in public affairs, to call attention to this most extraordinary fact—that there are men in the community so lost to patriotism, so bound up in the traditions of party, so selfish, as to be willing to tamper with Great Britain in order to bring about the separation of this country.

It is the most alarming fact that I have yet seen. I had rather see a hundred thousand men set in the field on the rebel side—aye, I had rather see Great Britain armed against us openly, as she is covertly—than to be forced to believe that there are amongst us such men as these, lineal descendants of Judas Iscariot, intermarried with the race of Benedict Arnold.

It has shown me a great danger with which we are threatened, and I call upon all true men to sustain the government —to be loyal to the government. As you, sir, were pleased to say, the present government was not the government of my choice, I did not vote for it or for any part of it; but it is the government of my country, it is the only organ by which I can exert the force of the country to protect its integrity; and so long as I believe that government to be honestly administered I will throw a mantle over any mistakes that I may think it has made and support it heartily, with hand and purse, so help me God!

I have no loyalty to any man or men; my loyalty is to the government; and it makes no difference to me who the people have chosen to administer the government as long as the choice has been constitutionally made and the persons so chosen hold their places and powers. I am a traitor and a false man if I falter in my support. This is what I understand to be loyalty to a government; and I was sorry to learn, as I did the other day, that there was a man in New York who professed not to know the meaning of the word loyalty. I desire to say here that it is the duty of every man to be loyal to the government, to sustain it, to pardon its errors and help to rectify them, and to do all he can to aid it in carrying the country on in the course of glory and grandeur in which it was started by our fathers.

Let me say to you, my friends—to you, young men, that no man who opposed his country in time of war ever prospered. The Tory of the Revolution, the Hartford Conventionist of 1812, the immortal seven who voted against the supplies for the Mexican War—all history is against these men. Let no politician of our day put himself in the way of the march of this country to glory and greatness, for whoever does so will surely be crushed. The course of our nation is onward and let him who opposes it beware.

> " The mower mows on—though the adder may writhe,
> Or the copperhead coil round the blade of his scythe."

It only remains, sir, for me to repeat the expression of my gratitude to you and the citizens of New York here assembled for the kindness with which you and they have received me and listened to me, for which please again accept my thanks.